American Government and Politics Today

BRIEF EDITION 2001–2002

Steffen W. Schmidt
Iowa State University

Mack C. Shelley
Iowa State University

D0222491

Barbara A. Bardes
University of Cincinnati

WADSWORTH

THOMSON LEARNING

Australia   Canada   Mexico   Singapore   Spain   United Kingdom   United States

WADSWORTH
THOMSON LEARNING

American Government and Politics Today: 2001–2002 Brief Edition
by Steffen W. Schmidt, Mack C. Shelley, and Barbara A. Bardes

Publisher: Clark Baxter
Senior Development Editor: Sharon Adams Poore
Assistant Editor: Cherie Hackelberg
Editorial Assistant: Jennifer Ellis
Marketing Manager: Diane McOscar
Marketing Assistant: Kristin Anderson
Print Buyer: Barbara Britton
Permissions Editor: Joohee Lee

Production and Illustrations: Bill Stryker
Text Design: Bill Stryker
Cover Design: Doug Abbott
Photo research: Megan Ryan and Bill Stryker
Copy Editor: Patricia Lewis
Compositor: Parkwood Composition Services
Printer: Courier
Photo Credits appear following the index

For permission to use material from this text, contact us:
Web: www.thomsonrights.com
Fax: 1-800-730-2215
Phone: 1-800-730-2214

Library of Congress Cataloging-in-Publication Data
Schmidt, Steffen W.
    American government and politics today: brief
    edition / Steffen W. Schmidt, Mack C. Shelley II,
    Barbara A. Bardes.–2001–2002 ed.
        p. cm.
    Includes bibliographical references and index.
    ISBN: 0–534–57099–2
    1. United States—Politics and government.
I. Shelley, Mack C. 1950–   II. Bardes, Barbara A.
III. Title
JK274.S425.2000
320.473–dc21   00-034957

For more information about our products, contact us:
Thomson Learning Academic Resource Center
1–800–423–0563
http://www.wadsworth.com

International Headquarters
Thomson Learning
290 Harbor Drive, 2nd Floor
Stamford, CT 06902-7477
USA

UK/Europe/Middle East
Thomson Learning
Berkshire House
168-173 High Holborn
London WC1V 7AA
United Kingdom

Asia
Thomson Learning
60 Albert Street #15-01
Albert Complex
Singapore 189969

Canada
Nelson/Thomson Learning
1120 Birchmount Road
Scarborough, Ontario M1K 5G4
Canada

Contents in Brief

Contents

Preface

As this Brief Edition of *American Government and Politics Today* goes to press, the first elections of the new century are about to occur. Voters will decide which party will win the presidency and which party will control Congress. Through their choices, the voters will set the direction for the government and for politics for at least the next four years.

Campaigns and elections for positions at all levels of government are an essential component of our democracy. The elected officeholders run the government and, in the twenty-first century, will need to address a number of pressing questions: How should the federal budget surplus be spent? How can campaign-financing reform be effected? How can demands to solve the present and future problems related to Social Security, Medicare, Medicaid, and health care in general best be met? Legislators in statehouses across the country will face other problems, such as the need for educational reform. This Brief Edition of *American Government and Politics Today* will provide the necessary background for your students to understand and critically evaluate these and other issues facing Americans today.

This edition is basically a condensed and updated version of the larger editions of *American Government and Politics Today*. This Brief Edition has been created specifically for those of you who desire, for reasons of course length or design, a text that presents the fundamental components of the American political system while retaining the quality and readability of the larger edition. You will find that this edition is up to date in every respect. The text, figures and tables, and all pedagogical features are current so that your students have the latest available data. We have also included coverage of all recently issued laws, regulations, and court decisions that have—or will have—a significant impact on American society and our political system.

THE WEB CONNECTION

While this edition may be physically brief, its scope is enlarged by numerous resources that are available on the World Wide Web. As with the larger editions of *American Government and Politics Today*, the Brief Edition is integrated with Web-based resources that students can access to gain a fuller understanding of the political issues dominating today's political arena.

A Full-Service Web Site

The Wadsworth Political Science Resource Center at

http://politicalscience.wadsworth.com

gives you and your students access to news groups, a career center, surfing lessons, links to general political sites, Election Central 2000, and an instantaneous forum for airing and discussing issues and ideas for teaching political science. The *America at Odds* section of the site corresponds to the interactive CD-ROM, which will be described shortly. We have also included a text-specific site for this Brief Edition of *American Government and Politics Today*. The text-specific site offers self-quizzes, chapter links to other related Web sites, discussion topics, and much more.

InfoTrac College Edition

InfoTrac College Edition allows your students to access a wealth of Web-based resources related to American government and politics. Updated daily and spanning four years, this world-class virtual library gives students access to full-length articles (not abstracts) from hundreds of popular and scholarly publications, including *U.S. News & World Report, National Review, Washington Monthly*, and many important political science journals. In the chapters of *American Government and Politics Today*, Brief Edition, you will find special icons in the margin indicating that InfoTrac will provide information and links relating to the particular topics being discussed in the text. Free access to InfoTrac College Edition is provided to instructors and students for a period of four months.

Internet Activities

Each chapter in the Brief Edition of *American Government and Politics Today* concludes with a *Logging on* section that lists and briefly describes important Web sites relating to topics covered in the chapter. Just following this list is a section entitled *Using the Internet for Political Analysis*, which takes the student through a specific Internet exercise. These end-of-chapter exercises are designed to help students learn how to find and analyze Web-based resources for a better understanding of American government. Further Internet exercises are included in *American Government Internet Activities*, Third Edition, which will be described in the supplements section of this Preface.

SPECIAL PEDAGOGICAL AIDS AND FEATURES

The Brief Edition of *American Government and Politics Today* retains some of the fundamental pedagogical aids and features of the larger versions, including the following:

■ *Key Terms.* Each important term is boldfaced and defined in the text when it is first used. At the end of each chapter, these boldfaced terms are included in the *Key Terms* section, along with the numbers of the pages in the chapter on which they first appeared.

■ *Chapter Summary.* A point-by-point summary of the chapter text is presented at the end of each chapter.

■ *Selected Print and Electronic Resources.* For each chapter, we include suggested readings as well as media resources.

■ *Logging on.* As already mentioned, this section contains a list and a brief description of relevant and important Web sites.

■ *Using the Internet for Political Analysis.* This contains a specific Internet exercise, as described earlier.

Additionally, for this edition we have added a special feature to each chapter entitled *At Issue.* Each of these features focuses on a controversial topic and concludes with a question *For Critical Analysis* that encourages students to think critically about a specific aspect of the issue under discussion. Topics treated in the *At Issue* features include the following:

■ Do We Really Have a Democracy? (Chapter 1).
■ How "Sovereign" Should the States Be? (Chapter 3).
■ Should the Internet Be Censored? (Chapter 4).
■ Marriage Rights for Gays and Lesbians? (Chapter 5).
■ Who Benefits from "Environmental Justice"? (Chapter 11).
■ Social Security—How Long Will It Last? (Chapter 13).

APPENDICES

The Brief Edition of *American Government and Politics Today* includes, as appendices, both the Declaration of Independence (Appendix A) and the U.S Constitution (Appendix B). The text of the Constitution has been annotated to help students understand the meaning and significance of the various provisions in this important document.

A COMPLETE SUPPLEMENTS PACKAGE

Complementing the text of the Brief Edition are the supplements listed and described below. The text and the supplements together constitute a total learning/teaching package for you and your students.

For Instructors

■ *Instructor's Manual with Test Bank.* Comprehensive in scope and detailed in coverage, this invaluable resource includes learning objectives, outlines, teaching suggestions, examples, presentation suggestions, and a wealth of ideas for supplementing your lectures. It also expands its references to all of the components of the ancillary package, including references to the InfoTrac articles and correlations to CNN video clips and to the acetate package. The Test Bank provides a mix of multiple choice, short-answer, and essay questions.

■ *ExamView.* You can create, deliver, and customize tests and study guides (both print and online) in minutes with this easy-to-use assessment and tutorial system.

ExamView offers both a Quick Test Wizard and an Online Test Wizard to guide you step by step through the process of creating tests, while its unique "WSI-WYG" capability allows you to see the test you are creating on the screen exactly as it will print or display online. You can create tests of up to 250 questions using up to twelve different question types. Using ExamView's complete word-processing capabilities, you can enter an unlimited number of new questions or edit existing questions.

■ *American Government Transparency Acetate Package.* This package contains more than seventy full-color acetates featuring diagrams, charts, tables, and figures from the text and additional sources. This is an excellent way to clarify concepts for students quickly and vividly.

■ *Political ScienceLink.* If you would rather display text images electronically, you can do so with this powerful set, which includes images from the transparency package above and more, on multiplatform CD-ROM. The set is available for Windows and Macintosh.

■ *Political Science Video Library.* You can use this exciting collection of videos to enrich your lectures and extend discussions of text material. Selections include The Presidency: Hail to the Chief?, Lawmaking, Welfare Reform: Social Responsibility, and more.

■ *CNN Today: American Government Today, Volume I.* You can launch a lecture or spark a discussion with footage from CNN, the world's leading twenty-four-hour global news television network. You will receive forty-five minutes of short, high-interest video clips on topics such as *Medical Marijuana, Young Republicans, and Political Webheads.*

■ *CNN Today: American Government Today, Volume II.* These four-to-six-minute video clips (sixty minutes in all) feature point-counterpoint debates on current and controversial issues. Topics include *The Internet and Free Speech, Negative Campaign Ads, Gun Control, Executive Privilege,* and *The Death Penalty in the United States.* Each issue concludes with a poll for classroom use.

For Students

■ *America at Odds CD-ROM.* This interactive CD-ROM was developed specifically for American government courses. It uses a topical, provocative, and interactive format to engage students and involve them in researching and discussing ideas, formulating their own opinions, and interpreting data. Students get the chance to work through twenty interactive modules that cover enduring and multidimensional issues in American politics. All issues are presented in a rich mix of digital video and audio, photos, graphics, text, and Internet technology.

■ *American Government Internet Activities, Third Edition.* This booklet takes students to numerous Web sites, each of which is related to a specific major topic in American government. Students are directed to specific sites and asked to find answers to thought-provoking questions.

■ *American Government: An Introduction Using MicroCase ExplorIt, Sixth Edition.* This award-winning workbook includes sixteen computer-based assignments, *Student ExplorIt* software, and seven real, up-to-the-minute data sets, all for a very low price. Your students can analyze data to discover and interpret trends in American politics and government. They can map electoral and popular votes for presidential elections dating back to the 1860s or analyze national surveys to discover public opinion on such issues as taxes, entitlements, abortion, civil rights, and civil liberties. They can examine dozens of national trends, including changes in federal employment, the decline of public confidence in government officials, and the fluctuations in defense spending over the last century. *ExplorIt* makes it easy for students to analyze real data using a point-and-click interface, with results presented in colorful graphics.

■ *Study Guide.* Enrich your students' experience with this superb study guide that provides learning objectives, a topical outline, a list of terms and concepts, a variety of self-study questions, and an essay on how students can improve their study skills.

■ *Readings in American Government, Third Edition.* Compiled by Steffen W. Schmidt and Mack C. Shelley, this reader has been updated to include the latest issues in American political debate. You will find numerous readings that deal with controversial issues, legal conflicts, and ethical challenges that are directly related to academia and students. The readings, of which there are two to four per chapter, deal with such topics as diversity, politicians' use of the Web, campaign reform, and cyber warfare.

■ *American Government: Readings and Responses.* Monica Bauer, of Metropolitan State College of Denver, has assembled an impressive selection of up-to-date readings to illustrate the main issues confronting Americans and their political leaders. The readings, authored by major writers across the political spectrum, cover both positions in debates concerning specific issues. In a feature unique to this text, the author includes an edited dialogue between students of varying political orientations to make the readings more real and accessible to those struggling with the material. This anthology also includes Web-site selections, press releases, congressional testimony, and student-led interviews with major political figures to give readers a real-world political orientation.

■ *An Introduction to Critical Thinking and Writing in American Politics.* This booklet is filled with rules, guidelines, and techniques to show your students how to think critically about the political process and how to write a successful research paper.

■ *Thinking Globally, Acting Locally.* This workbook is designed to help students become active citizens and get involved in politics. The author includes tips for writing letters to the editor, volunteering, registering to vote, and getting laws changed.

■ *Handbook of Selected Court Cases.* This handbook includes summaries and excerpts from more than thirty Supreme Court cases relating to important issues in American politics and government.

■ *Handbook of Selected Legislation and Other Documents.* Included in this handbook are excerpts from twelve laws passed by the U.S. Congress that have had a significant impact on American politics.

ACKNOWLEDGMENTS

Since we started this project a number of years ago, a sizable cadre of individuals has helped us in various phases of the undertaking. The following academic reviewers offered numerous constructive criticisms, comments, and suggestions during the preparation of all previous editions:

Danny M. Adkison
Oklahoma State University

Sharon Z. Alter
William Rainey Harper College, Illinois

William Arp III
Louisiana State University

Kevin Bailey
North Harris Community College, Texas

Dr. Charles T. Barber
University of Southern Indiana, Evansville,

Clyde W. Barrow
Texas A&M University

David C. Benford, Jr.
Tarrant County Junior College, Texas

John A. Braithwaite
Coastline Community College, California

Lynn R. Brink
North Lake College, Irving, Texas

Barbara L. Brown
Southern Illinois University at Carbondale

Kenyon D. Bunch
Fort Lewis College, Durango, Colorado

Ralph Bunch
Portland State University, Oregon

Carol Cassell
University of Alabama

Frank J. Coppa
Union County College, Cranford, New Jersey

Robert E. Craig
University of New Hampshire

Doris Daniels
Nassau Community College, New York

Carolyn Grafton Davis
North Harris County College, Texas

Marshall L. DeRosa
Louisiana State University, Baton Rouge

Michael Dinneen
Tulsa Junior College, Oklahoma

Gavan Duffy
University of Texas at Austin

George C. Edwards III
Texas A&M University

Mark C. Ellickson
Southwestern Missouri State University, Springfield

Larry Elowitz
Georgia College and State University

John W. Epperson
Simpson College, Indianola, Indiana

Daniel W. Fleitas
University of North Carolina at Charlotte

Elizabeth N. Flores
Del Mar College, Texas

Joel L. Franke
Blinn College, Brenham, Texas

Barry D. Friedman
North Georgia College

Robert S. Getz
SUNY–Brockport, New York

Kristina Gilbert
Riverside Community College, California

William A. Giles
Mississippi State University

Donald Gregory
Stephen F. Austin State University

Forest Grieves
University of Montana

Dale Grimnitz
Normandale Community College, Bloomington, Minnesota

Stefan D. Haag
Austin Community College, Texas

Jean Wahl Harris
University of Scranton, Pennsylvania

David N. Hartman
Rancho Santiago College, Santa Ana, California

Robert M. Herman
Moorpark College, California

Richard J. Herzog
Stephen F. Austin State University, Nacogdoches, Texas

Paul Holder
McClennan Community College, Waco, Texas

Michael Hoover
Seminole Community College, Sanford, Florida

J. C. Horton
San Antonio College, Texas

Robert Jackson
Washington State University

Willoughby Jarrell
Kennesaw College, Georgia

Loch K. Johnson
University of Georgia

Donald L. Jordan
United States Air Force Academy, Colorado

John D. Kay
Santa Barbara City College, California

Charles W. Kegley
University of South Carolina

Bruce L. Kessler
Shippensburg University, Pennsylvania

Nancy B. Kral
Tomball College, Texas

Dale Krane
Mississippi State University

Samuel Krislov
University of Minnesota

William W. Lamkin
Glendale Community College

Harry D. Lawrence
Southwest Texas Junior College, Uvaide, Texas

Ray Leal
Southwest Texas State University, San Marcos

Sue Lee
Center for Telecommunications, Dallas County
Community College District

Carl Lieberman
University of Akron, Ohio

Orma Linford
Kansas State University

Eileen Lynch
Brookhaven College, Texas

James D. McElyea
Tulsa Junior College, Oklahoma

Thomas J. McGaghie
Kellogg Community College, Michigan

William P. McLauchlan
Purdue University, Indiana

William W. Maddox
University of Florida

S. J. Makielski, Jr.
Loyola University, New Orleans

Jarol B. Manheim
George Washington University

J. David Martin
Midwestern State University, Texas

Bruce B. Mason
Arizona State University

Steve J. Mazurana
University of Northern Colorado

Stanley Melnick
Valencia Community College, Florida

Robert Mittrick
Luzurne County Community College, Pennsylvania

Helen Molanphy
Richland College, Texas

Keith Nicholls
University of Alabama

Stephen Osofsky
Nassau Community College, New York

John P. Pelissero
Loyola University of Chicago

Neil A. Pinney
Western Michigan University

George E. Pippin
Jones County Community College, Mississippi

Walter V. Powell
Slippery Rock University, Pennsylvania

Michael A. Preda
Midwestern State University, Texas

Charles Prysby
University of North Carolina

Donald R. Ranish
Antelope Valley College, California

John D. Rausch
Fairmont State University, West Virginia

Curt Reichel
University of Wisconsin

Russell D. Renka
Southeast Missouri State University

Paul Rozycki
Charles Stewart Mott Community College, Flint,
Michigan

Eleanor A. Schwab
South Dakota State University

Len Shipman
Mount San Antonio College, California

Scott Shrewsbury
Mankato State University, Minnesota

Michael W. Sonnlietner
Portland Community College, Oregon

Gilbert K. St. Clair
University of New Mexico

Carol Stix
Pace University, Pleasantville,
New York

Gerald S. Strom
University of Illinois at Chicago

John R. Todd
North Texas State University

Ron Velton
Grayson County College, Texas

Benjamin Walter
Vanderbilt University, Tennessee

B. Oliver Walter
University of Wyoming

Mark J. Wattier
Murray State University, Kentucky

Thomas L. Wells
Old Dominion University, Virginia

Jean B. White
Weber State College, Utah

Lance Widman
El Camino College, California

Allan Wiese
Mankato State University, Minnesota

J. David Woodard
Clemson University, South Carolina

Robert D. Wrinkle
Pan American University, Texas

The 2000–2001 Edition of *American Government and Politics Today*, on which this Brief Edition is based, was the result of our working closely with reviewers who each offered us penetrating criticisms, comments, and suggestions for how to improve the text. Although we haven't been able to take account of all requests, each of the reviewers listed below will see many of his or her suggestions taken to heart.

Evelyn Ballard
Houston Community College

David S. Bell
Eastern Washington University

Richard G. Buckner
Santa Fe Community College

Frank J. Coppa
Union County College, Cranford, New Jersey

Paul B. Davis
Truckee Meadows Community College, Nevada

Richard D. Davis
Brigham Young University

Ron Deaton
Prince George's Community College, Maryland

Jason F. Kirksey
Oklahoma State University

James J. Lopach
University of Montana

Thomas Louis Masterson
Butte College, California

James Morrow
Tulsa Community College

Mark E. Priewe
University of Texas at San Antonio

Bhim Sandhu
West Chester University, Pennsylvania

Pauline Schloesser
Texas Southern University

In preparing this Brief Edition of *American Government and Politics Today*, we continue to remain indebted to these reviewers for their helpful comments, suggestions, and insights. In addition, we especially wish to thank the dedicated team of publishers and editors that made this edition possible, including Susan Badger, the president of Wadsworth; Clark Baxter, our publisher; and Sharon Adams Poore, our senior developmental editor. We are also grateful to Bill Stryker for his design and for making it possible to get the text out on time. We have also benefited from the efforts of all of those who worked on the various supplements offered with this text, especially Assistant Editor Cherie Hackelberg. Finally, we thank those individuals who helped the authors coordinate and manage the project, including Lavina Leed Miller, Roxie Lee, and Sue Jasin of K&M Consulting.

Any errors, of course, remain our own. We welcome comments from instructors and students alike on how this Brief Edition of *American Government and Politics Today* can be improved and best be adapted to the changing needs of instructors and students.

Steffen Schmidt
Mack Shelley
Barbara Bardes

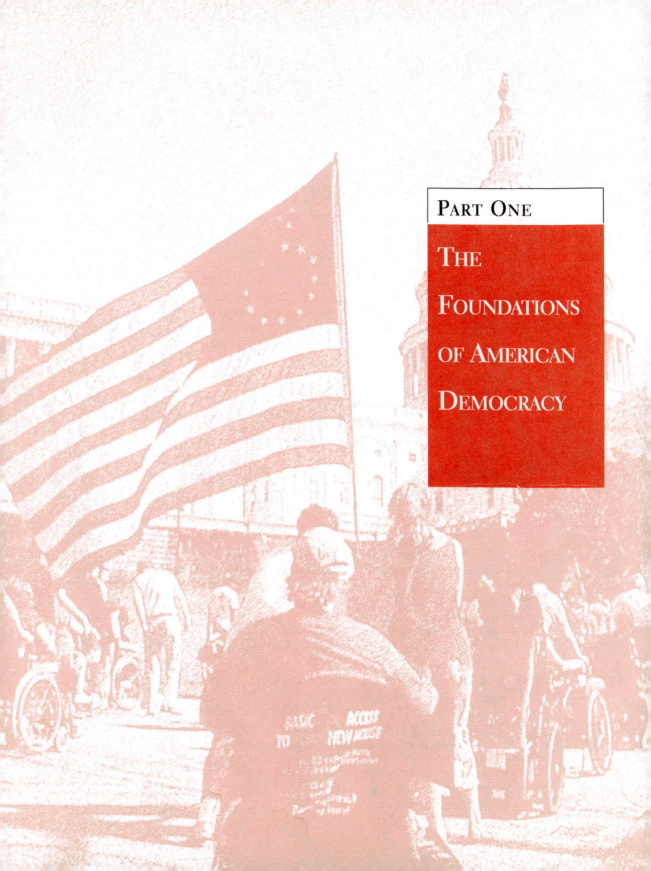

PART ONE

THE

FOUNDATIONS

OF AMERICAN

DEMOCRACY

CHAPTER 1

The Foundations of American Government

olitics is about change—changes in policies and laws to enable a society to cope with internal or external forces that affect people's lives. Politics is about the debates and struggles within a community to meet the demands of the people and further the interests of society. People may seek changes—in the law, in the structure of government, or in the officials who lead the government—as a result of external forces, such as war or worldwide economic shifts. People may seek such changes as a result of technological advances, such as the Internet, or as a result of internal forces, such as the growing belief that the traditional welfare system was not working.

Politics is also about stability. Stability in law, in economic relationships, and in social customs must exist so that individuals and groups can plan for the future and manage their affairs. The United States as a democratic society is constantly balancing the need for change to meet new conditions in the world with the need for stability in the nation and the lives of its people.

In this chapter, we will discuss some of the questions and principles that are fundamental to the construction of any political system. Part of the excitement of the American political system is that these issues and principles continue to be debated in the United States as we attempt to balance the forces of stability with the forces of change. The willingness of Americans to debate new initiatives and to demand changes in the way the government works is at the core of our democratic nation. Change—even revolutionary change—is a tribute to the success of a political system. As Abraham Lincoln put it, "This country with all its institutions, belongs to the people who inhabit it. Whenever they shall grow weary of the existing government, they can exercise their Constitutional right of amending it, or the revolutionary right to dismember or overthrow it."[1]

In the chapters that follow, we will look more closely at the **institutions**—longstanding structures—of our government and how they have changed over the decades. We will examine how the political processes of the nation work to accomplish those changes. To begin, we will look at why political institutions and processes are necessary in any society and what purposes they serve.

[1]First Inaugural Address, March 4, 1861.

WHAT IS POLITICS?

Why do nations and people struggle so hard to establish a form of government and continue to expend so much effort in politics to keep that government functioning? Politics and forms of government are probably as old as human society. There are many definitions of politics, but all try to explain how human beings regulate conflict within their society. As soon as humans began to live in groups, particularly groups that were larger than their immediate families, they found that they needed to establish rules about behavior, property, the privileges of individuals and groups, and how people would survive together. **Politics** can best be understood as the process of, as Harold Lasswell put it, "who gets what, when, and how."[2] To another social scientist, David Easton, politics should be defined as the "authoritative allocation of values."[3] Politics, then, is the struggle or process engaged in by human beings to decide which members of society get benefits or privileges and which are excluded from certain benefits or privileges.

In the early versions of human society, the tribe or village, politics was relatively informal. Tribal elders or hereditary chiefs were probably vested with the power to decide who married whom, who could build a hut on the best piece of land, and which young people succeeded them in the positions of leadership. Other societies were "democratic" from the very beginning, giving their members some form of choice of leadership and rules. Early human societies rarely had the concept of property, so few rules were needed to decide who owned which piece of property or who inherited that piece. The concepts of property and inheritance are much more modern. As society became more complex and humans became settled farmers rather than hunters and gatherers, the problems associated with property, inheritance, sales and exchanges, kinship, and rules of behavior became important to resolve. Politics developed into the process by which some of these questions were answered.

Inevitably, conflicts arise in society, because members of a group are distinct individuals with unique needs, values, and perspectives. At least three different kinds of conflicts that may require the need for political processes arise in a society:

1. People may differ over their beliefs, either religious or personal, or over basic issues of right and wrong. The kind of debate that has arisen in recent years on abortion is an example of this kind of conflict.
2. People within a society may differ greatly in their perception of what the society's goals should be. For example, Americans disagree over whether the national government should set national standards for education or whether the direction for schools should come primarily from local school boards and communities.
3. People compete for scarce resources; government benefits, and property are examples. The question of who will pay for Medicare benefits, for instance, is really

---

[2]Harold Lasswell, *Politics: Who Gets What, When and How* (New York: McGraw-Hill, 1936).
[3]David Easton, *The Political System* (New York: Knopf, 1953).

a discussion of whether younger people will pay for the health care of the older persons in the society or whether retirees must pay more for this health insurance.

THE NEED FOR GOVERNMENT

If *politics* refers to conflict and conflict resolution, **government** refers to the structures, or institutions, within which the decisions are made that resolve conflicts or allocate values. In early human societies, such as families and small tribes, there was no need for formal structures of government. Decisions were made by acknowledged leaders in those societies. In families, all members may meet together to decide values and priorities. Where there is a community that makes decisions and allocates values through informal rules, politics exists—but not government. Within most contemporary societies, these activities continue in many forms. For example, when a church decides to build a new building or hire a new minister, that decision may be made politically, but there is in fact no government. Politics can be found in schools, social groups, and any other organized group. When a society, however, reaches a certain level of complexity, it becomes necessary to establish a permanent or semipermanent group of individuals to act for the whole, to become the government.

One way to understand why governments are necessary is to examine some of the functions that they perform. We have already mentioned one important function—providing structures, or institutions, through which conflicts can be resolved. For example, at the national level members of Congress resolve conflicts in our society by debating issues and putting them to a vote. Another important government function is providing **public services**—important services that individuals cannot or would not provide for themselves, such as creating and maintaining roads, public schools, and national parks and providing for national defense. By defending the nation against foreign attacks, a government also performs another basic function—preserving the nation's culture, including its customs, beliefs, values, and language. Governments also establish and implement **public policies**—policies, such as those protecting the environment, that are designed to improve the lives and general welfare of citizens.

Governments range in size from the volunteer city council and one or two employees of a small town to the massive and complex structures of the U.S. government or those of any other large, modern nation. Generally, governments not only make the rules but also implement them through the use of police, judges, and other government officials.

WHO GOVERNS?

One of the most fundamental questions of politics has to do with which person or groups of people control society through the government. Who possesses the power to make decisions about who gets what and how the benefits of the society are distributed among the people?

Sources of Political Power

At one extreme is a society governed by a **totalitarian regime.** In such a political system, a small group of leaders or a single individual—a dictator—makes all political decisions for the society. Every aspect of political, social, and economic life is controlled by the government. The power of the ruler is total (thus, the term *totalitarianism*).

"Putin's Plutocrat Problem"

Many of our terms for describing the distribution of political power are derived from the ancient Greeks, who were the first Western people to study politics systematically. A society in which political decisions were controlled by a small group was called an **oligarchy,** meaning rule by a few members of the **elite,** who generally benefited themselves. Another form of rule by the few was known as **aristocracy,** meaning rule by the most virtuous, most talented, or the best suited to the position. Later, in European history, aristocracy meant rule by the titled or the upper classes. In contrast to such a top-down form of control was the form known as **anarchy,** or the condition of no government. Anarchy exists when each individual makes his or her own rules for behavior, and there are no laws and no government.

The Greek term for rule by the people was **democracy.** Although most Greek philosophers were not convinced that democracy was the best form of government, they understood and debated the possibility of such a political system. Within the limits of their culture, some of the Greek city-states operated as democracies.

Direct Democracy as a Model

From the ancient Greek city-states comes a model for governance that has framed the modern debate over whether the people can make decisions about their own government and laws. Athenian system of government is usually considered the model for **direct democracy** because the citizens of that community debated and voted directly on all laws, even those put forward by the ruling council of the city. The most important feature of Athenian democracy was that the **legislature** was composed of all of the citizens. Women, foreigners, and slaves, however, were excluded because they were not citizens. The outstanding feature of this early form of government was that it required a high level of participation from every citizen; that participation was seen as benefiting the individual and the city-state. The Athenians recognized that although a high level of participation might lead to instability in government, citizens, if informed about the issues, could be trusted to make decisions about the laws governing their community.

Direct democracy also has been practiced in some Swiss cantons and, in the United States, in New England town meetings and in some midwestern township meetings. At New England town meetings, which can include all of the voters who live in the town, important decisions are made for the community—such as levying taxes, hiring city officials, and deciding local ordinances—by majority vote. Some states provide a modern adaptation of direct democracy for their citizens; in most states, representative democracy is supplemented by the **initiative** or the **referendum**—processes by which the people may vote directly on laws or constitutional amendments. The **recall** process, which is available in over one-third of the states, allows the people to vote to remove an official from state office.

This town meeting in New Hampshire allows every citizen of the town to vote directly and in person for elected officials, for proposed policies, and, in some cases, for the town budget. To be effective, such a form of direct democracy requires that the citizens stay informed about local politics, attend town meetings, and devote time to discussion and decision making.

The Dangers of Direct Democracy

Although they were aware of the Athenian model, the framers of the U.S. Constitution—for the most part—were opposed to such a system. For many centuries preceding this country's establishment, any form of democracy was considered to be dangerous and to lead to instability. But in the eighteenth and nineteenth centuries, the idea of government based on the **consent of the people**—the idea that governments and laws derive their legitimacy from the consent of the governed— gained increasing popularity. Such a government was the main aspiration of the American Revolution, the French Revolution, and many subsequent ones. The masses, however, were considered to be too uneducated to govern themselves, too prone to the influence of demagogues (political leaders who manipulate popular prejudices), and too likely to abrogate minority rights.

James Madison defended the new scheme of government set forth in the U.S. Constitution, while warning of the problems inherent in a "pure democracy":

A common passion or interest will, in almost every case, be felt by a majority of the whole . . . and there is nothing to check the inducements to sacrifice the weaker party or an obnoxious individual. Hence it is that such democracies have ever been spectacles of turbulence and contention, and have ever been found incompatible with personal security or the rights of property; and have in general been as short in their lives as they have been violent in their deaths.[4]

Like many other politicians of his time, Madison feared that pure, or direct, democracy would deteriorate into mob rule. What would keep the majority of the people, if given direct decision-making power, from abusing the rights of minority groups?

Representative Democracy

The framers of the U.S. Constitution chose to create a **republic,** meaning a government in which the power rests with the people, who elect representatives to govern them and to make the laws and policies. To eighteenth-century Americans, the idea of a republic also meant a government based on common beliefs and virtues that would be fostered within small communities. The rulers were to be amateurs—good citizens—who would take turns representing their fellow citizens, in a way similar to the Greek model.[5]

To allow for change while ensuring a measure of stability, the U.S. Constitution creates a form of republican government known as a **representative democracy.** The people hold the ultimate power over the government through the election process, but policy decisions are all made by elected officials. Even this distance between the people and the government was not sufficient. Other provisions in the Constitution made sure that the Senate and the president would be selected by political elites rather than by the people, although later changes to the Constitution allowed the voters to elect members of the Senate directly. This modified form of democratic government came to be widely accepted throughout the Western world as a compromise between the desire for democratic control and the needs of the modern state.

Principles of Democratic Government. All representative democracies rest on the rule of the people as expressed through the election of government officials. In the 1790s, only free white males were able to vote, and in some states they had to be property owners as well. Women did not receive the right to vote in national elections in the United States until 1920, and the right to vote was not really secured by African Americans until the 1960s. Today, the rule is **universal suffrage;** in other words, all adults have the right to vote for their representatives.

Granting every person the right to participate in the election of officials recognizes the equal voting power of each citizen. This emphasis on the equality of every individual before the law is central to the American system. Because everyone's vote counts equally, the only way to make fair decisions is by some form of **majority rule**—a basic principle of democracy asserting that the greatest number of citizens in any political unit should select officials and determine policies. But to ensure that

---

[4]James Madison, in Alexander Hamilton, James Madison, and John Jay, *The Federalist Papers,* No. 10 (New York: Mentor Books, 1964), p. 81.
[5]See Chapter 2 for a further discussion of the founders' ideas.

majority rule does not become oppressive, modern democracies also provide guarantees of minority rights. If certain democratic principles did not protect minorities, the majority might violate the fundamental rights of members of certain groups, especially groups that are unpopular or dissimilar to the majority population. In the past, the majority has imposed such limitations on African Americans, Native Americans, and Japanese Americans, to name only a few.

One way to guarantee the continued existence of a representative democracy is to hold free, competitive elections. Thus, the minority always has the opportunity to win elective office. For such elections to be totally open, freedom of the press and speech must be preserved so that opposition candidates may present their criticisms of the government.

Constitutional Democracy. Another key feature of Western representative democracy is that it is based on the principle of **limited government.** Not only is the government dependent on **popular sovereignty,** the concept that ultimate political authority rests with the people, but the powers of the government are also clearly limited, either through a written document or through widely shared beliefs. The U.S. Constitution sets forth the fundamental structure of the government and the limits to its activities. Such limits are intended to prevent political decisions based on the whims or ambitions of individuals in government rather than on constitutional principles.

Volunteers register voters in the Spanish Harlem section of New York City. By setting up a table in the neighborhood, the election officials make registration more convenient for voters as well as less threatening. Both political parties often conduct voter registration drives in the months before general elections.

Elites may have far more power and influence on the political system than do voters from the lower and middle classes. Because they share an educational background from selective schools, a higher income level, and common lifestyles with government policymakers, they are more likely to see government policymakers on a social basis and to form friendships with elected officials.

THEORIES OF AMERICAN DEMOCRACY

The sheer size and complexity of American society seem to make it unsuitable for direct democracy on a national scale. Some scholars suggest that even representative democracy is difficult to achieve in any modern state. They point to the low level of turnout for presidential elections and the even lower turnout for local ones. Polling data have shown that many Americans are neither particularly interested in politics nor well informed. Few are able to name the persons running for Congress in their districts, and even fewer can discuss the candidates' positions. Members of Congress claim to represent their constituents, but few constituents follow the issues, much less communicate their views to their representatives. For the average citizen, the national government seems too remote, too powerful, and too bureaucratic to be influenced by one vote.

Elite Theory

If ordinary citizens are not really making policy decisions with their votes, who is? One answer suggests that elites really govern the United States. Proponents of **elite theory** see society much as Alexander Hamilton did, who said,

All communities divide themselves into the few and the many. The first are the rich and the wellborn, the other the mass of the people. . . . The people are turbulent and changing; they seldom judge or determine right. Give therefore to the first class a distinct, permanent share in the government. They will check the unsteadiness of the second, and as they cannot receive any advantage by a change, they therefore will ever maintain good government.

Elite theory describes an American mass population that is uninterested in politics and that is willing to let leaders make the decisions. Some versions of elite theory posit a small, cohesive elite class that makes almost all the important decisions regarding the nation,[6] whereas others suggest that voters choose among competing elites. New members of the elite are recruited through the educational system so that the brightest children of the masses allegedly have the opportunity to join the elite stratum.

In such a political system, the primary goal of the government is stability, because elites do not want any change in their status. Major social and economic change takes place only if elites see their resources threatened. This selfish interest of the elites does not mean, however, that they are necessarily undemocratic or always antiprogressive. Whereas some policies, such as favorable tax-avoidance laws, may be perceived as elitist in nature, other policies benefit many members of the public. Political scientists Thomas Dye and Harmon Ziegler propose that American elites are more devoted to democratic principles and rights than are most members of the mass public.[7]

Pluralist Theory

INFOTRAC®

"Deliberative Democracy Agonistic Pluralism"

A different school of thought looks at the characteristics of the American electorate and finds that our form of democracy is based on group interests. Even if the average citizen cannot keep up with political issues or cast a deciding vote in any election, the individual's interests will be protected by groups that represent him or her.

Theorists who subscribe to **pluralism** as a way of understanding American politics believe that people are naturally social and inclined to form associations. In the pluralists' view, politics is the struggle among interest groups to gain benefits for their members. Given the structures of the American political system, group conflicts tend to be settled by compromise and accommodation so that each interest is satisfied to some extent.[8]

Pluralists see public policy as resulting from group interactions carried out within Congress and the executive branch. Because there are a multitude of interests, no one group can dominate the political process. Furthermore, because most individuals have more than one interest, conflict among groups does not divide the nation into hostile camps.

---

[6]Michael Parenti, *Democracy for the Few*, 7th ed. (New York: St.Martin's Press, 1995).
[7]Thomas Dye and Harmon Ziegler, *The Irony of Democracy*, 11th ed. (Orlando, Fla.: Harcourt Brace, 1999).
[8]David Truman, *The Governmental Process* (New York: Knopf, 1951); and Robert Dahl, *Who Governs?* (New Haven, Conn.: Yale University Press, 1961).

There are a number of flaws in some of the basic assumptions of this theory. Among these are the relatively low number of people who formally join interest groups, the real disadvantages of pluralism for the poorer citizens, and the belief that group decision making always reflects the best interests of the nation.

With these flaws in mind, critics see a danger that groups may become so power-ful that all policies become compromises crafted to satisfy the interests of the largest groups. The interests of the public as a whole, then, cannot be considered. Critics of pluralism have suggested that a democratic system can be virtually paralyzed by the struggle between interest groups. This struggle results in a condition sometimes called **hyperpluralism,** meaning that groups and their needs control the government and decision making rather than the government's acting for the good of the nation.

Both pluralism and elite theory attempt to explain the real workings of American democracy. Neither approach is complete, nor can either be proved. Viewing the United States as run by elites reminds us that the founders themselves were not great defenders of the mass public. In contrast, the pluralist view underscores both the advantages and the disadvantages of Americans' inclination to join, to organize, and to pursue benefits for themselves. It points out all of the places within the American political system in which interest groups find it comfortable to work. With this knowledge, the system can be adjusted to keep interest groups within the limits of the public good. (For a further discussion of these theories of American democracy, see this chapter's feature entitled *At Issue: Do We Really Have a Democracy?*)

POLITICAL VALUES AND IDEOLOGY

The writers of the American constitution believed that the structures they had cre-ated would provide for both democracy and a stable political system. They also believed that the nation would be sustained by its **political culture**—a concept defined as a patterned set of ideas, values, and ways of thinking about government and politics.

There is considerable consensus among American citizens about certain concepts basic to the U.S. political system. Given that the vast majority of Americans are descendants of immigrants having diverse cultural and political backgrounds, how can we account for this consensus? Primarily, it is the result of **political socialization**—the process by which such beliefs and values are transmitted to new immigrants and to our children. The nation depends on several different agents to transmit to children and newcomers to our nation the precepts of our national culture.

As you will read in Chapter 6, an important agent of political socialization is the family. Parents teach their children about the value of participating in the political system through their example and through their approval. One of the primary func-tions of the public education system in the United States is to teach the values of the political culture to students through history courses, through discussions of political issues, and through the rituals of pledging allegiance to the flag and celebrating national holidays. Traditionally, political parties also have played a role in political socialization as a way to bring new voters to their ranks.

As you will read in Chapter 7, interest groups lobby, or promote their causes, at all levels of American government. Interest groups are able to exert substantial pressure on legislatures, including the U.S. Congress, by mobilizing their members to support certain issue positions, by campaign contributions, and by other means. The significant role played by interest groups in shaping national policy has caused many to question whether we really have a democracy at all.

One concern is that interest groups tend to reflect only certain segments of society, and not society as a whole. Certainly, most interest groups have a middle-class or upper-class bias. Members of interest groups can afford to pay the membership fees, are generally well educated, and normally participate in the political process to a greater extent than the "average" American. Furthermore, leaders of interest groups tend to constitute an "elite within an elite" in the sense that they usually are from a higher social class than their members. The most powerful interest groups—those with the most resources and political influence—are primarily busi-

ness, trade, or professional groups. In contrast, public-interest groups or civil rights groups make up only a small percentage of the interest groups lobbying Congress.

As discussed elsewhere in this chapter, the elite theory of politics presumes that most Americans are uninterested in politics and are willing to let a small, elite group of citizens make decisions for them. Pluralist theory, in contrast, views politics as a struggle among various interest groups to gain benefits for their members. The pluralist approach views compromise among various competing interests as the essence of political decision making. In reality, neither theory describes American politics very accurately. If interest groups led by elite, upper-class individuals are the dominant voices in Congress, then what we see is a conflict among elite groups—which would support the elitist theory, not a pluralist approach.

Many observers contend that economic and social developments in the last several years have strengthened the perception that America is indeed governed by an elite, privileged group. These observers believe that "the rich get

richer and the poor get poorer" in this country and that, as a consequence, more and more Americans are becoming alienated from the political process. There is now an underclass of Americans that has little say in government and has little hope of being able to in the future—because the possibility of joining the elite stratum is so remote. Wealthier citizens have educational opportunities that poorer individuals believe they cannot afford. Moreover, as you will read in Chapter 8, political campaigns are expensive, and campaign costs have increased steadily each year. Today, candidates for political office, unless they can raise campaign funds from wealthy supporters or interest groups, have to drop out of the race—or not enter it in the first place. Some predict that if present trends continue, we may have a democracy, but it will be a "democracy for the few," not for all Americans.

FOR CRITICAL ANALYSIS

Can you think of any changes to the American political system that would promote "democracy for the many"?

Before we discuss some of the most fundamental concepts of the American political culture, it is important to note that these values can be considered those of the dominant culture. The **dominant culture** in any society consists of the values, customs, language, and ideals established by the group or groups in the society that traditionally have controlled politics and government institutions. The dominant

Certain groups within the United States insist on maintaining their own cultural beliefs and practices. The Amish, pictured here, are descended from German religious sects and live in close communities in Pennsylvania, Ohio, Indiana, and Illinois, as well as in other states. The more conservative Amish groups do not use modern conveniences, such as automobiles or electricity, and have resisted immunizations and mandatory schooling for their children.

culture in the United States has its roots in Western European civilization. From that civilization, American politics has inherited a bias toward individualism, private property, Judeo-Christian ethics, and, to some extent, the male domination of societal decisions. As the descendants of more recent immigrant groups, especially those from Asian and Islamic nations, become part of the American mainstream, there will be more challenges to the dominant culture. Other cultural heritages honor community or family over individualism and sometimes place far less emphasis on materialism. Additionally, changes in our own society have brought about the breakdown of some values, such as the sanctity of the family structure, and the acceptance of others, such as women pursuing careers in the workplace.

The Fundamental Values

Some nations are very homogeneous, with most of their citizens having the same ethnic and religious background and sharing a common history. Achieving consensus on the basic values of the political culture is fairly easy in these nations. Because the United States is a nation of immigrants, socializing people into the political culture is an important function of the society. Over the two hundred years of its history, however, the people of the United States have formed a deep commitment to certain values and ideas. Among these are liberty, equality, and property.

Liberty. The term **liberty** can be defined as the greatest freedom of individuals that is consistent with the freedom of other individuals in the society. In the United States, our civil liberties include religious freedom—both the right to practice whatever religion one chooses and freedom from any state-imposed religion. Our civil liberties also include freedom of speech—the right to express our opinions freely on matters, including government actions. Freedom of speech is perhaps one of our most prized liberties, because a democracy could not endure without it. These and other basic guarantees of liberty are not found in the body of the U.S. Constitution but in the Bill of Rights, the first ten amendments to the Constitution.

The process of ensuring liberty for all Americans did not end with the adoption of the Bill of Rights but has continued throughout our history. Political issues often turn on how a particular liberty should be interpreted or the extent to which it should be limited in the interests of society as a whole. Some of the most emotionally charged issues today, for example, have to do with whether our civil liberties include the liberty to have an abortion or (for terminally ill persons) to commit assisted suicide.

Equality. The Declaration of Independence states, "All men are created equal." Today, that statement has been amended by the political culture to include groups other than white males—women, African Americans, Native Americans, Asian Americans, and others. The definition of **equality,** however, has been disputed by Americans since the Revolution.[9] Does equality mean simply political equality—the right to register to vote, to cast a ballot, and to run for political office? Does equality mean equal opportunity for individuals to develop their talents and skills? If the latter is the meaning of equality, what should the United States do to ensure equal opportunities for the poor or the disabled? As you will read in later chapters of this book, much of America's politics has concerned just such questions. Although most Americans believe strongly that all persons should have the opportunity to fulfill their potential, many disagree about whether it is the government's responsibility to eliminate economic and social differences.

Property. Many Americans probably remember that the "unalienable rights" asserted in the Declaration of Independence are the rights to "life, liberty, and the pursuit of happiness." The inspiration for that phrase, however, came from the writings of an English philosopher, John Locke (1632–1704), who stated that people's rights were to life, liberty, and **property.** In American political culture, the pursuit of happiness and property—defined as anything that is or may be subject to ownership—are considered to be closely related. Americans place great value on owning land, on acquiring material possessions, and on the monetary value of jobs. Property can be seen as giving its owner political power and the liberty to do whatever she or he wants. At the same time, the ownership of property immediately creates inequality in society. The desire to own property, however, is so widespread among all classes of Americans that socialist movements, which advocate the redistribution of wealth and property, have had a difficult time securing a wide following here.

---

[9]Richard J. Ellis, "Rival Visions of Equality in American Political Culture," *Review of Politics*, Vol. 54 (Spring 1992), p. 254.

Each year thousands of immigrants are sworn in as new U.S. citizens. The U.S. Constitution in Article II, Section 8, declares that Congress shall have the power to "establish a uniform Rule of Naturalization." Naturalization is the process by which individuals who are not yet citizens become U.S. citizens. Such individuals are called naturalized citizens as opposed to native-born citizens. There are myriad requirements to become a naturalized citizen. Because it is often difficult to do so, many immigrants remain in this country without proper documentation.

Democracy, liberty, equality, and property—these concepts lie at the core of American political culture. Other issues—such as majority rule and popular sovereignty—are closely related to them. These fundamental principles are so deeply ingrained in U.S. culture that most Americans rarely question them.

Political Ideology

An **ideology** is a closely linked set of beliefs about the goal of politics and the most desirable political order. Political ideologies offer their adherents well-organized theories that propose goals for the society and the political means by which those goals can be achieved. At the core of every political ideology is a set of values that guides its theory of governmental power. If we compare political ideologies on the basis of how much power the government should have within a society, we can array them on a continuum from left to right, as shown in the upper level in Table 1.1 on page 16. For each of these ideological positions, the amount of power granted to the government is intended to achieve a certain set of goals within the society, and the perfect society would completely achieve these values. The values are arrayed in the lower level in Table 1.1.

INFOTRAC®

"Law Schools vs. Dissenting Views"

Each of the ideological positions in Table 1.1 has adherents in the United States. Given the widely shared cultural values, however, only two of these belief systems consistently have played a central part in American political debates: **liberalism** and **conservatism.**

Liberalism is a set of beliefs that includes the advocacy of positive government action to improve the welfare of individuals, support for civil rights, and tolerance for political and social change. American liberals believe that government should take strong positive action to solve the nation's economic and social problems. They believe that it is the obligation of the government to enhance opportunities for the economic and social equality of all individuals. Liberals tend to support programs to reduce poverty, to endorse progressive taxation to redistribute income from wealthier classes to the poorer, and to rely on government regulation to guide the activities of business and the economy.

Conservatism is a set of beliefs that includes a limited role for the national government in helping individuals, support for traditional values and lifestyles, and a cautious response to change. Conservatives believe that the private sector probably can outperform the government in almost any activity. Believing that the individual is primarily responsible for his or her own well-being, conservatives are less supportive of government initiatives to redistribute income or to craft programs that will change the status of individuals.

In the moral sphere, conservatives tend to support more government regulation of social values and moral decisions than do liberals. Thus, conservatives tend to oppose gay rights legislation and propose stronger curbs on pornography. Liberals usually show greater tolerance for different life choices and oppose government attempts to regulate personal behavior and morals.

INFOTRAC®

"Dilemmas Conservatism"

Individuals in the society may not accept the full range of either liberal or conservative views. It is not unusual for Americans to be quite liberal on economic issues and supportive of considerable government intervention in the economy while holding conservative views on moral and social issues. Such a mixture of views

TABLE 1.1

How Much Power Should the Government Have?

MARXISM-LENINISM	SOCIALISM	LIBERALISM	CONSERVATISM	LIBERTARIANISM
Central control of economy and political system.	Active government control of major economic sectors.	Positive government action in economy and to achieve social goals.	Positive government action to support capitalism; action to uphold certain values.	Government action only for defense; almost no regulation of economy or individual behavior.

What Values Should the Government Pursue?

MARXISM-LENINISM	SOCIALISM	LIBERALISM	CONSERVATISM	LIBERTARIANISM
Total equality and security; unity and solidarity.	Economic equality; community.	Political liberty; economic security; equal opportunity.	Political liberty; economic liberty; order.	Total political and economic liberty for individuals.

makes it difficult for American political parties to identify themselves solely with either a conservative or a liberal viewpoint, because such a position may cost them votes on specific issues.

There are also smaller groups of Americans who consider themselves to be communists, socialists, or libertarians, but these groups play a minor role in the national political arena. The limited role played by these and other alternative political perspectives is reinforced by the fact that they receive little positive exposure in classrooms, the media, or public discourse

Key Terms

anarchy 5	ideology 15	politics 3
aristocracy 5	initiative 6	popular sovereignty 8
consent of the people 6	institution 2	property 14
conservatism 16	legislature 6	public policy 4
democracy 5	liberalism 16	public services 4
direct democracy 6	liberty 14	recall 6
dominant culture 12	limited government 8	referendum 6
elite 5	majority rule 7	representative democracy 7
elite theory 9	oligarchy 5	republic 7
equality 14	pluralism 10	totalitarian regime 5
government 4	political culture 11	universal suffrage 7
hyperpluralism 11	political socialization 11	

Chapter Summary

1 The willingness of Americans to debate new initiatives and to demand changes in the way the government works is at the core of our democratic nation. Americans worked hard to establish this form of government and continue to expend effort in politics to keep it functioning.

2 *Politics* was defined by Harold Lasswell as the process of "who gets what, when, and how" in a society. David Easton defined it as the "authoritative allocation of values" in a society. Government consists of the structures, or institutions, within which conflicts are resolved or values are allocated.

Governments provide public services—services that individuals cannot or would not provide themselves, such as public roads and schools and national defense.

3 Sources of political power include direct democracy, a system of government in which political decisions are made by the people directly. Fearing the problems of a direct democracy, the framers of the Constitution set up a representative, or indirect, democracy. The people control the government through the election of representatives.

Decisions are made by majority rule, although the rights of minorities are protected.

4 Some scholars believe that most of the power in our society is held by elite leaders who actively influence political decisions, while the masses are apathetic. The pluralist viewpoint, in contrast, suggests that groups that represent the different interests of the people struggle for political power. In pluralist theory, the political process is characterized by bargaining and compromise between groups.

5 The American political system is characterized by a set of cultural beliefs that includes liberty, equality, and property. These beliefs are passed on to each generation of Americans through the process of political socialization.

6 Americans' ideas about how government should act in their lives vary widely. These views may be included in liberal, conservative, or other ideological positions.

SELECTED PRINT AND ELECTRONIC RESOURCES

Suggested Readings

Brinkley, Alan. *Liberalism and Its Discontents.* Cambridge, Mass.: Harvard University Press, 1998. The author explores how cultural changes and alternative political traditions have undermined the liberal tradition.

Lasswell, Harold. *Politics: Who Gets What, When and How.* New York: McGraw-Hill, 1936. This classic work defines the nature of politics.

Tocqueville, Alexis de. *Democracy in America.* Edited by Phillips Bradley. New York: Vintage Books, 1945. Life in the United States was described by a French writer who traveled through the nation in the 1820s.

Will, George F. *The Woven Figure: Conservatism and America's Fabric, 1994–1997.* New York: Scribner, 1997. In a series of essays, this well-known conservative political columnist offers an honest analysis of both the strong points and the flaws of American conservatism.

Wolfe, Alan. *One Nation, After All: What the Middle Class Really Thinks about God, Country, and Family.* New York: Viking Press, 1998. Based on the results of a survey he conducted, sociologist Alan Wolfe concludes that middle-class Americans are far less polarized politically, far less judgmental, and much more tolerant and willing to compromise than is often thought.

Media Resources

All Things Considered—A daily broadcast of National Public Radio that provides extensive coverage of political, economic, and social news stories.

Mr. Smith Goes to Washington—A classic movie, produced in 1939, starring Jimmy Stewart as the honest citizen who goes to Congress trying to represent his fellow citizens. The movie dramatizes the clash between representing principles and representing corrupt interests.

LOGGING ON

The World Wide Web is becoming a virtual library, a telephone directory, a contact source, and a vehicle to improve your learning and understanding of issues. It therefore is important that you become familiar with Web resources. To help you do this, we have included Logging On sections at the end of each chapter in this book. Each of these sections contains a list of Internet addresses, or uniform resource locators (URLs), followed by an Internet exercise. The URLs will help you find information on topics covered within the chapters, as well as on related topics that you might find interesting. We hope this feature will lead you to some of the most interesting and productive Web locations.

The Internet should be approached with care. You should be very careful in giving out information about yourself. You also need to use good judgment because the reliability or intent of any given Web site is often unknown. Some sites are more concerned with accuracy than others, and some sites are updated to include current information, while others are not. Also, realize that sites come and go continually, so some of the Web sites that we include in these Logging On features may not exist by the time you read this book.

We also have a powerful and interesting Web site for the textbook, which you can find at

http://wadsworth.com/politics/schmidtbr/index.html

This site has many features directly related to the textbook, including the site's most popular item—the test-review questions.

You will also want to check out the Wadsworth Political Science Resource Center for additional information and learning opportunities. The URL for this site is

http://politicalscience.wadsworth.com

Finally, you may want to visit the home page of Dr. Politics—offered by Steffen Schmidt, one of the authors of this book—for some interesting ideas and activities relating to American government and politics. Go to

http://www.public.iastate.edu/~sws/homepage.html

For discussion of current public-policy issues that are facing the American political system, try the resources at the Institute for Philosophy and Public Policy at

http://www.puaf.umd.edu/ippp

Information about the rules and requirements for immigration and citizenship can be found at the Web site of the U.S. Immigration and Naturalization Service:

http://www.ins.usdoj.gov

For a basic "front door" to almost all U.S. government Web sites, click onto the very useful site maintained by the University of Michigan:

http://www.lib.umich.edu/libhome/Documents.center/govweb.html

The Pew Research Center for the People and the Press offers survey data online on a number of topics relating to American politics and government. Go to

http://www.people-press.org

Yale University Library has an excellent collection of sources relating to American history and politics at

http://www.library.yale.edu/socsci

You can access many of the laws, including court decisions, discussed in this text at the FindLaw Web site, which is probably the most comprehensive source of free legal information on the Internet. Go to

http://www.findlaw.com

The Legal Information Institute (LII) at Cornell Law School also offers extensive information and resources relating to U.S. law and government. The URL for this site is

http://www.law.cornell.edu

The Library of Congress offers extensive links to state and federal government resources at

http://www.loc.gov

Villanova University's Center for Information Law and Policy provides access to numerous resources, including opinions from the federal appellate courts. Go to

http://www.law.vill.edu

USING THE INTERNET FOR POLITICAL ANALYSIS

The Internet is an excellent place for political organizations and interest groups to advertise their positions and to try to increase the number of Americans who support their causes. Take a look at the Web sites of two of the most prominent political "think tanks" and then try to identify the differences between their positions on one or two critical issues. The two Web sites to visit are the following:

The Heritage Foundation, at http://www.heritage.org

People for the American Way, at http://www.pfaw.org

Take note of the policies that are discussed at each site and try to figure out the "liberal" and "conservative" points of view on at least two topics.

CHAPTER 2

Forging a New Government: The Constitution

We the People of the United States, in Order to form a more perfect Union, establish Justice, insure domestic Tranquillity, provide for the common defence, promote the general Welfare, and secure the Blessings of Liberty to ourselves and our Posterity, do ordain and establish this Constitution for the United States of America.

Every schoolchild in America has at one time or another been exposed to these famous words from the Preamble to the U.S. Constitution. The document itself is remarkable. The U.S. Constitution, compared with others in the states and in the world, is relatively short. Because amending it is difficult (as you will see later in this chapter), it also has relatively few amendments. Perhaps even more remarkable is the fact that it has remained largely intact for over two hundred years. In large part, this is because the principles set forth in the Constitution are sufficiently broad that they can be adapted to meet the needs of a changing society.

How and why this Constitution was created is a story that has been told and retold. It is worth repeating, because the historical and political context in which this country's governmental machinery was formed is essential to understanding American government and politics today. The Constitution was not the result of completely creative thinking. Many of its provisions were grounded in contemporary political philosophy. The delegates to the Constitutional Convention in 1787 brought with them two important sets of influences: their political culture and their political experience. In the years between the first settlements in the New World and the writing of the Constitution, Americans had developed a political philosophy about how people should be governed and had tried out numerous forms of government. These experiences gave the founders the tools with which they constructed the Constitution.

THE COLONIAL BACKGROUND

The first British outpost in North America, known as the Roanoke Island Colony, was set up by Sir Walter Raleigh in the 1580s for the purpose of harassing the Spanish treasure fleets. After a three-year absence to resupply the colony, Raleigh's captain, John White, returned in 1590 to find signs that the colony's residents apparently had moved north to Chesapeake Bay. No evidence of the fate of the "lost colony" has ever been found, but some scholars have concluded that the area experienced an extreme drought lasting three years at the time of the attempted settlement on Roanoke Island.[1]

---

[1]D. W. Stahle et al., "The Lost Colony and Jamestown Droughts," *Science*, April 24, 1998.

In 1607, the British government sent over a group of farmers to establish a trading post, Jamestown, in what is now Virginia. The Virginia Company of London was the first to establish successfully a permanent British colony in the Americas. The king of England gave the backers of this colony a charter granting them "full power and authority" to make laws "for the good and welfare" of the settlement. The colonists at Jamestown instituted a **representative assembly**—a legislature composed of individuals who represent the population—setting a precedent in government that was to be observed in later colonial adventures.

Separatists, the *Mayflower*, and the Compact

The first New England colony was established in 1620. A group of mostly extreme Separatists, who wished to break with the Church of England, came over on the ship *Mayflower* to the New World, landing at Plymouth (Massachusetts). Before going on shore, the adult males—women were not considered to have any political status—drew up the Mayflower Compact, which was signed by forty-one of the forty-four men aboard the ship on November 21, 1620. The reason for the compact was obvious. This group was outside the jurisdiction of the Virginia Company of London, which had chartered their settlement in Virginia, not Massachusetts. The Separatist leaders feared that some of the *Mayflower* passengers might conclude that they were

The signing of the compact aboard the Mayflower. *In 1620, the Mayflower Compact was signed by almost all of the men aboard the ship* Mayflower, *just before disembarking at Plymouth, Massachusetts. It stated, "We . . . covenant and combine ourselves togeather into a civil body politick . . . ; and by vertue hearof to enacte, constitute, and frame such just and equal laws . . . as shall be thought [necessary] for the generall good of the Colonie."*

no longer under any obligations of civil obedience. Therefore, some form of public authority was imperative. As William Bradford (a printer and editor in Philadelphia) recalled in his accounts, there were "discontented and mutinous speeches that some of the strangers amongst them had let fall from them in the ship; That when they came a shore they would use their owne libertie; for none had power to command them."[2]

The compact was not a constitution. It was a political statement in which the signers agreed to create and submit to the authority of a government, pending the receipt of a royal charter. The Mayflower Compact's historical and political significance is twofold: it depended on the consent of the affected individuals, and it served as a prototype for similar compacts in American history. According to Samuel Eliot Morison, the compact proved the determination of the English immigrants to live under the rule of law, based on the *consent of the people*.[3]

More Colonies, More Government

Another outpost in New England was set up by the Massachusetts Bay Colony in 1630. Then followed Rhode Island, Connecticut, New Hampshire, and others. By 1732, the last of the thirteen colonies, Georgia, was established.

During the colonial period, Americans developed a concept of limited government, which followed from the establishment of the first colonies under Crown charters. Theoretically, London governed the colonies. In practice, owing partly to the colonies' distance from London, the colonists exercised a large measure of self-government. The colonists were able to make their own laws, as in the Fundamental Orders of Connecticut in 1639. The Massachusetts Body of Liberties in 1641 supported the protection of individual rights and was made a part of colonial law. In 1682, the Pennsylvania Frame of Government was passed. Along with the Pennsylvania Charter of Privileges of 1701, it established the rationale for our modern Constitution and Bill of Rights.

All of this legislation enabled the colonists to acquire crucial political experience. After independence was declared in 1776, the states quickly set up their own constitutions.

THE ROAD TO INDEPENDENCE

The conflict between Britain and the American colonies, which ultimately led to the Revolutionary War, began in the 1760s when the British government decided to raise revenues by imposing taxes on the American colonies. Policy advisers to Britain's young King George III, who ascended the throne in 1760, decided that it was only logical to require the American colonists to help pay the costs of Britain's defending

---

[2]John Camp, *Out of the Wilderness: The Emergence of an American Identity in Colonial New England* (Middleton, Conn.: Wesleyan University Press, 1990).
[3]See Morison's "The Mayflower Compact" in Daniel J. Boorstin, ed., *An American Primer* (Chicago: University of Chicago Press, 1966), p. 18.

King George III (1738–1820) was king of Great Britain and Ireland from 1760 until his death on January 29, 1820. Under George III, the first attempt to tax the American colonies was made. Ultimately, the American colonies, exasperated at renewed attempts at taxation, proclaimed their independence on July 4, 1776.

them during the French and Indian War (1756–1763). The colonists, who had grown accustomed to a large degree of self-government and independence from the British Crown, viewed the matter differently.

In 1764, the Sugar Act was passed. Many colonists were unwilling to pay the required tax. Further regulatory legislation was to come. In 1765, the British Parliament passed the Stamp Act, providing for internal taxation, or, as the colonists' Stamp Act Congress assembled in 1765 called it, "taxation without representation." The colonists boycotted the Stamp Act. The success of the boycott (the Stamp Act was repealed a year later) generated a feeling of unity within the colonies. The British, however, continued to try to raise revenues in the colonies. When duties on glass, lead, paint, and other items were passed in 1767, the colonists boycotted the purchase of English commodities in return. The colonists' fury over taxation climaxed in the Boston Tea Party: colonists dressed as Mohawk Indians dumped almost 350 chests of British tea into Boston Harbor as a gesture of tax protest. In retaliation, the British Parliament passed the Coercive Acts (the "Intolerable Acts") in 1774, which closed Boston Harbor and placed the government of Boston under direct British control. The colonists were outraged—and they responded.

The Continental Congresses

New York, Pennsylvania, and Rhode Island proposed the convening of a colonial congress. The Massachusetts House of Representatives requested that all colonies hold conventions to select delegates to be sent to Philadelphia for such a congress. The **First Continental Congress** was held at Carpenter's Hall on September 5, 1774. It was a gathering of delegates from twelve of the thirteen colonies (Georgia did not attend until 1775). At that meeting, there was little talk of independence. The Congress passed a resolution requesting that the colonies send a petition to King George III expressing their grievances. Resolutions were also passed requiring that the colonies raise their own troops and boycott British trade. The British government condemned the Congress's actions, treating them as open acts of rebellion.

By the time the **Second Continental Congress** met in May 1775 (this time all of the colonies were represented), fighting already had broken out between the British and the colonists. One of the main actions of the Second Congress was to establish an army. It did this by declaring the militia that had gathered around Boston an army and naming George Washington as commander in chief. The participants in that Congress still attempted to reach a peaceful settlement with the British Parliament. One declaration of the Congress stated explicitly that "we have not raised armies with ambitious designs of separating from Great Britain, and establishing independent states." But by the beginning of 1776, military encounters had become increasingly frequent.

Public debate was acrimonious. Then Thomas Paine's *Common Sense* appeared in Philadelphia bookstores. The pamphlet was a colonial best seller. (To do relatively as well today, a book would have to sell between eight and ten million copies in its first year of publication.) Many agreed that Paine did make common sense when he argued that

> a government of our own is our natural right: and when a man seriously reflects on the pre-cariousness [instability, unpredictability] of human affairs, he will become convinced, that it is infinitely wiser and safer, to form a constitution of our own in a cool and deliberate manner, while we have it in our power, than to trust such an interesting event to time and chance.[4]

Students of Paine's pamphlet point out that his arguments were not new—they were common in tavern debates throughout the land. Rather, it was the near poetry of his words—which were at the same time as plain as the alphabet—that struck his readers.

Declaring Independence

On April 6, 1776, the Second Continental Congress voted for free trade at all American ports for all countries except Great Britain. This act could be interpreted as an implicit declaration of independence. The next month, the Congress suggested that each of the colonies establish state governments unconnected to Britain. Finally, on July 2, the Resolution of Independence was adopted by the Second Continental Congress:

> RESOLVED, That these United Colonies are, and of right ought to be free and inde-pendent States, that they are absolved from allegiance to the British Crown, and that all political connection between them and the state of Great Britain is, and ought to be, totally dissolved.

The actual Resolution of Independence was not legally significant. On the one hand, it was not judicially enforceable, for it established no legal rights or duties. On the other hand, the colonies were already, in their own judgment, self-governing and independent of Britain. Rather, the Resolution of Independence and the subsequent Declaration of Independence were necessary to establish the legitimacy of the new nation in the eyes of foreign governments, as well as in the eyes of the colonists them-selves. What the new nation needed most were supplies for its armies and a com-mitment of foreign military aid. Unless it appeared in the eyes of the world as a political entity separate and independent from Britain, no foreign government would enter into a contract with its leaders.

On adoption of the Resolution of Independence, Thomas Jefferson had argued that a declaration clearly putting forth the causes that compelled the colonies to sep-arate from Britain was necessary. The Second Congress assigned the task of writing it to him. The declaration, which enumerated the colonists' major grievances against Britain was passed on July 4, 1776. On July 19, the modified draft became "the

---

[4]*The Political Writings of Thomas Paine*, Vol. 1 (Boston: J. P. Mendum Investigator Office, 1870), p. 46.

unanimous declaration of the thirteen United States of America." On August 2, it was signed by the members of the Second Continental Congress.

A revolutionary concept of the Declaration was the assumption, inspired by the ideas of the English political philosopher John Locke (1632–1704), that people have **natural rights** ("unalienable Rights"), including the rights to "life, liberty, and the pursuit of happiness." Governments are established to secure these rights, and governments derive their power "from the consent of the governed."[5] The Declaration claimed that whenever government "becomes destructive to these ends, it is the Right of the People to alter or to abolish it, and to institute a new government." (See Appendix A for the text of the Declaration of Independence.) Subsequently, all of the states adopted written constitutions. Eleven of the constitutions were completely new. Two of them—those of Connecticut and Rhode Island—were old royal charters with minor modifications.

---

[5]Not all scholars believe that Jefferson was truly influenced by Locke. For example, Jay Fliegelman states that "Jefferson's fascination with Homer, Ossian, Patrick Henry, and the violin is of greater significance than his indebtedness to Locke." Jay Fliegelman, *Declaring Independence: Jefferson, Natural Language, and the Culture of Performance* (Stanford, Calif.: Stanford University Press, 1993).

Members of the Second Continental Congress adopted the Declaration of Independence on July 4, 1776. Minor changes were made in the document in the following two weeks. On July 19, the modified draft became the "unanimous declaration of the thirteen United States of America." On August 2, the members of the Second Continental Congress signed it. The first official printed version carried only the signatures of the Congress's president, John Hancock, and its secretary, Charles Thompson.

The Articles of Confederation: Our First Form of Government

Although the colonists had formally declared independence from Britain, the fight to gain actual independence continued for five more years—until the British General Cornwallis surrendered at Yorktown in 1781. In 1783, after Britain formally recognized the independent status of the United States in the Treaty of Paris, Washington disbanded the army. During these years of military struggles, the states faced the additional challenge of creating a system of self-government for an independent United States.

Anti-Royalists in New England and Virginia, who called themselves Republicans, were against a strong central government. They opposed monarchy, executive authority, and virtually any form of restraint on the power of local groups. These so-called Republicans were a major political force from 1776 to 1780. Indeed, they almost prevented victory over the British by their unwillingness to cooperate with any central authority. In the state constitutions, Republican sentiment led to increased power for the legislatures. In Pennsylvania and Georgia, **unicameral** (one-body) **legislatures** were unchecked by executive or judicial authority. Basically, the Republicans attempted to maintain the politics of 1776. In almost all states, the legislature was predominant.

In June 1776, the Second Continental Congress began the process of drafting what would become the Articles of Confederation and Perpetual Union. The Articles were adopted on November 15, 1777. The fear of a powerful central government was reflected in the Articles of Confederation. The term **confederation** is important; it means a voluntary association of *independent* **states,** in which the member states agree to only limited restraints on their freedom of action. As a result, confederations seldom have an effective executive authority.

The Structure of the Confederal Government

Under the Articles, the thirteen original colonies, now states, established on March 1, 1781, a government of the states—the Congress of the Confederation. The Congress was a unicameral assembly of so-called ambassadors from each state, with each state possessing a single vote. Each year, the Congress would choose one of its members as its president, but the Articles did not provide for a president of the United States. The Congress was authorized in Article X to appoint an executive committee of the states "to execute in the recess of Congress, such of the powers of Congress as the United States, in Congress assembled, by the consent of nine [of the thirteen] states, shall from time to time think expedient to vest with them."

The Congress was also allowed to appoint other committees and civil officers necessary for managing the general affairs of the United States. In addition, the Congress could regulate foreign affairs and establish coinage and weights and measures. But it lacked an independent source of revenue and the necessary executive machinery to enforce its decisions throughout the land. Article II of the Articles of Confederation guaranteed that each state would retain its sovereignty. Figure 2.1 on page 28

FIGURE 2.1

**The Structure of the Confederal Government
under the Articles of Confederation**

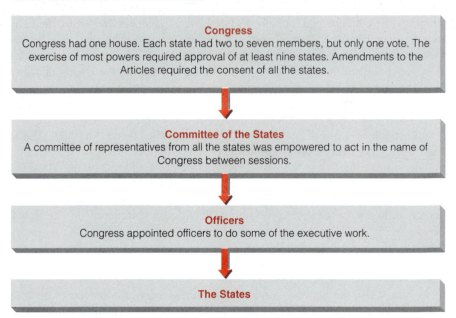

illustrates the structure of the government under the Articles of Confederation; Table 2.1 summarizes the powers—and the lack of powers—of Congress under that system.

Accomplishments under the Articles

Although the Articles of Confederation had many defects, some accomplishments were achieved during the eight years of their existence. Certain states' claims to western lands were settled. Maryland had objected to the claims of Massachusetts, New York, Connecticut, Virginia, the Carolinas, and Georgia. It was only after these states consented to give up their land claims to the United States as a whole that Maryland signed the Articles of Confederation. Another accomplishment under the Articles was the passage of the Northwest Ordinance of 1787, which established a basic pattern of government for new territories north of the Ohio River.

Weaknesses of the Articles

Although Congress had the legal right to declare war and to conduct foreign policy, it did not have the right to demand revenues from the states. It could only *ask* for them. Additionally, the actions of Congress required the consent of nine states. Any amendments to the Articles required the unanimous consent of the Congress and confirmation by every state legislature. Furthermore, the Articles did not create a

TABLE 2.1

Powers of the Congress of the Confederation

■ Declare war and make peace.	■ Provide for effective treaty-making power and control foreign relations; it could not compel states to respect treaties.
■ Enter into treaties and alliances.	
■ Establish and control armed forces.	
■ Requisition men and money from states.	■ Compel states to meet military quotas; it could not draft soldiers.
■ Regulate coinage.	
■ Borrow money and issue bills of credit.	■ Regulate interstate and foreign commerce; it left each state free to set up its own tariff system.
■ Fix uniform standards of weight and measurement.	
■ Create admiralty courts.	■ Collect taxes directly from the people; it had to rely on states to collect and forward taxes.
■ Create a postal system.	
■ Regulate Indian affairs.	
■ Guarantee citizens of each state the rights and privileges of citizens in the several states when in another state.	■ Compel states to pay their share of government costs.
	■ Provide and maintain a sound monetary system or issue paper money; this was left up to the states, and monies in circulation differed tremendously in value.
■ Adjudicate disputes between states upon state petition.	

national system of courts. Basically, the functioning of the government under the Articles depended on the goodwill of the states. Article III of the Articles simply established a "league of friendship" among the states—no national government was intended.

Probably the most fundamental weakness of the Articles, and the most basic cause of their eventual replacement by the Constitution, concerned the lack of power to raise money for the militia. The Articles lacked any language giving Congress coercive power to raise money (by levying taxes) to provide adequate support for the military forces controlled by Congress. Due to a lack of resources, the Continental Congress was forced to disband the army, even in the face of serious Spanish and British military threats.

Because of the weaknesses of the Articles of Confederation, the central government could do little to maintain peace and order in the new nation. The states bickered among themselves and increasingly taxed each other's goods. At times they prevented trade altogether. By 1784, the country faced a serious economic depression. Banks were calling in old loans and refusing to give new ones. People who could not pay their debts were often thrown into prison. By 1786, in Concord, Massachusetts, the scene of one of the first battles of the Revolution, there were three times as many people in prison for debt as there were for all other crimes combined. In Worcester County, Massachusetts, the ratio was even higher—twenty to one. Most of the prisoners were small farmers who could not pay their debts owing to the disorganized state of the economy.

In August 1786, mobs of musket-bearing farmers led by former revolutionary captain Daniel Shays seized county courthouses and disrupted the trials of debtors in Springfield, Massachusetts. Shays and his men then launched an attack on the federal arsenal at Springfield, but they were repulsed. Shays's Rebellion demonstrated that the central government could not protect the citizenry from armed rebellion or provide adequately for the public welfare. The rebellion spurred the nation's political leaders to action.

DRAFTING THE CONSTITUTION

The Virginia legislature called for a meeting of all the states to be held at Annapolis, Maryland, on September 11, 1786. Among the important problems to be solved were the relationship between the states and the central government, the powers of the national legislature, the need for executive leadership, and the establishment of policies for economic stability. At this Annapolis meeting, a call was issued to all of the states for a general convention to meet in Philadelphia in May 1787 "to consider the exigencies of the union."

The Philadelphia convention, which later became known as the Constitutional Convention, was formally opened in the East Room of the Pennsylvania State House on May 25, 1787.[6] Fifty-five of the seventy-four delegates chosen for the convention actually attended. Rhode Island was the only state that refused to send delegates.

Factions among the Delegates

We know much about the proceedings at the convention because James Madison kept a daily, detailed personal journal. A majority of the delegates were strong nationalists—they wanted a central government with real power, unlike the central government under the Articles of Confederation. George Washington and Benjamin Franklin preferred limited national authority based on a separation of powers. Among the nationalists were several monarchists, including Alexander Hamilton. Another important group of nationalists were of a more democratic stripe. Led by James Madison of Virginia and James Wilson of Pennsylvania, these democratic nationalists wanted a central government founded on popular support.

Among the other factions was a group of delegates who were totally against a national authority. Two of the three delegates from New York quit the convention when they saw the nationalist direction of its proceedings.

Politicking and Compromises

The debates at the convention started on the first day. James Madison had spent months reviewing European political theory. When his Virginia delegation arrived ahead of most of the others, it got to work immediately. By the time George Washington opened the convention, Governor Edmund Randolph of Virginia was immediately able to present fifteen resolutions.

---

[6]The State House was later named Independence Hall. This was the same room in which the Declaration of Independence had been signed eleven years earlier.

George Washington presided over the Constitutional Convention of 1787. Although the convention was supposed to have started on May 14, 1787, few of the delegates had actually arrived in Philadelphia by that date. It formally opened in the East Room of the Pennsylvania State House (later named Independence Hall) on May 25. Only Rhode Island did not send any delegates.

The Virginia Plan. Randolph's fifteen resolutions proposed an entirely new national government under a constitution. It was, however, a plan that favored the large states, including Virginia. Basically, it called for the following:

1. A **bicameral** (two-house) **legislature,** with the lower house chosen by the people and the smaller upper house chosen by the lower house from nominees selected by state legislatures. The number of representatives would be proportional to a state's population, thus favoring the large states. The legislature could void any state laws.
2. The creation of an unspecified national executive, elected by the legislature.
3. The creation of a national judiciary appointed by the legislature.

It did not take long for the smaller states to realize they would fare poorly under the Virginia plan, which would enable Virginia, Massachusetts, and Pennsylvania to form a majority in the national legislature. The debate on the plan dragged on for a number of weeks. It was time for the small states to come up with their own plan.

The New Jersey Plan. On June 15, lawyer William Paterson of New Jersey offered an alternative plan. After all, argued Paterson, under the Articles of Confederation all states had equality; therefore, the convention had no power to change this arrangement. He proposed the following:

1. The fundamental principle of the Articles of Confederation—one state, one vote—would be retained.
2. Congress would be able to regulate trade and impose taxes.

3. All acts of Congress would be the supreme law of the land.
4. Several people would be elected by Congress to form an executive office.
5. The executive office would appoint a Supreme Court.

Basically, the New Jersey plan was simply an amendment of the Articles of Confederation. Its only notable feature was its reference to the **supremacy doctrine,** which asserts the superiority of national law over state laws and was later included in the Constitution.

The "Great Compromise." The delegates were at an impasse. Most wanted a strong national government and were unwilling even to consider the New Jersey plan. But when the Virginia plan was brought up again, the small states threatened to leave. It was not until July 16 that the **Great Compromise** was achieved. Roger Sherman of Connecticut proposed the following:

1. A bicameral legislature in which the House of Representatives would be apportioned according to the number of free inhabitants in each state, plus three-fifths of the slaves.
2. An upper house, the Senate, which would have two members from each state elected by the state legislatures.

This plan, also called the Connecticut Compromise because of the role of the Connecticut delegates in the proposal, broke the deadlock. It did exact a political price, however, because it permitted each state to have equal representation in the Senate. Having two senators represent each state in effect diluted the voting power of citizens living in more heavily populated states and gave the smaller states disproportionate political powers. But the Connecticut Compromise resolved the large-state/small-state controversy. In addition, the Senate acted as part of a checks-and-balances system against the House, which many feared would be dominated by, and responsive to, the masses.

The Three-Fifths Compromise. The Great Compromise also settled another major issue—how to deal with slaves in the representational scheme. Slavery was legal everywhere except in Massachusetts, but it was concentrated in the South. The South wanted slaves to be counted equally in determining representation in Congress. Delegates from the northern states objected. Sherman's three-fifths compromise solved the issue, satisfying those northerners who felt that slaves should not be counted at all and those southerners who wanted them to be counted as free whites. Actually, Sherman's Connecticut plan spoke of three-fifths of "all other persons" (and that is the language in the Constitution itself). It is not hard to figure out, though, who those other persons were.

The slavery issue was not completely eliminated by the three-fifths compromise. Many delegates were opposed to slavery and wanted it banned entirely in the United States. Charles Pinckney of South Carolina led strong southern opposition to the idea of a ban on slavery. Finally, the delegates agreed that Congress could limit the importation of slaves after 1808. The compromise meant that the issue of slavery itself was never addressed. The South won twenty years of unrestricted slave trade and a requirement that escaped slaves in free states be returned to their owners in slave states.

Other Issues. The agrarian South and the mercantile North were in conflict. The South was worried that the northern majority in Congress would pass legislation unfavorable to its economic interests. Because the South depended on exports of its agricultural products, it feared the imposition of export taxes. In return for acceding to the northern demand that Congress be given the power to regulate commerce among the states and with other nations, the South obtained a promise that export taxes would not be imposed. Even today, such taxes are prohibited. The United States is one of the countries that does not tax its exports.

There were other disagreements. The delegates could not decide whether to establish only a Supreme Court or to create lower courts as well. They deferred the issue by mandating a Supreme Court and allowing Congress to establish lower courts. They also disagreed over whether the president or the Senate would choose the Supreme Court justices. A compromise was reached with the agreement that the president would nominate the justices and the Senate would confirm the nominations.

These compromises, as well as others, resulted from the recognition that if one group of states refused to ratify the Constitution, it was doomed.

An American slave market as depicted in a painting from the nineteenth century. The writers of the Constitution did not ban slavery in the United States but did agree to limit the importation of new slaves after 1808. Nowhere are the words slavery *or* slaves *used in the Constitution. Instead, the Constitution uses such language as "no person held in service" and "all other persons."*

Working toward Final Agreement

The Connecticut Compromise was reached by mid-July. The makeup of the executive branch and the judiciary, however, was left unsettled. The remaining work of the convention was turned over to a five-member Committee of Detail, which presented a rough draft of the Constitution on August 6. It made the executive and judicial branches subordinate to the legislative branch.

Separation of Powers. The major issue of **separation of powers** had not yet been resolved. The delegates were concerned with structuring the government to prevent the imposition of tyranny—either by the majority or by a minority. It was Madison who proposed a governmental scheme—sometimes called the **Madisonian model**—to achieve this: the executive, legislative, and judicial powers of government were to be separated so that no one branch had enough power to dominate the others. The separation of powers was by function, as well as by personnel, with Congress passing laws, the president enforcing and administering laws, and the courts interpreting laws in individual circumstances.

Each of the three branches of government would be independent of the others, but they would have to cooperate to govern. According to Madison, in *Federalist Paper No. 51,* "the great security against a gradual concentration of the several powers in the same department consists in giving to those who administer each department the necessary constitutional means and personal motives to resist encroachments of the others."

"Don't Make Harder Govern"

The "constitutional means" Madison referred to is a system of **checks and balances** through which each branch of the government can check the actions of the other branches. For example, Congress can enact laws, but the president has veto power over congressional acts. The Supreme Court has the power to declare acts of Congress and of the executive branch unconstitutional, but the president appoints the justices of the Supreme Court, with the advice and consent of the Senate. (The Supreme Court's power to declare acts unconstitutional was not mentioned in the Constitution, although arguably the framers assumed that the Court would have this power—see the discussion of judicial review later in this chapter.) Figure 2.2 outlines these checks and balances.

The Executive. Some delegates favored a plural executive made up of representatives from the various regions. This was abandoned in favor of a single chief executive. Some argued that Congress should choose the executive. To make the presidency completely independent of the proposed Congress, however, an **electoral college** was adopted. Composed of electors selected by the voters in each state and Washington, D.C., the electoral college officially elects the president and vice president. Each state has as many electors as it has representatives in both houses of Congress. To be sure, the electoral college created a cumbersome presidential election process (see Chapter 8). It could even result in a candidate who came in second in the popular vote becoming president by being the top vote getter in the electoral college. The electoral college insulated the president, however, from direct popular control. The seven-year single term that some of the delegates had proposed was replaced by a four-year term and the possibility of reelection.

FIGURE 2.2

Checks and Balances

The major checks and balances among the three branches are illustrated here. Some of these checks are not mentioned in the Constitution, such as judicial review — the power of the courts to declare federal or state acts unconstitutional — or the president's ability to refuse to enforce judicial decisions or congressional legislation. Checks and balances can be thought of as a confrontation of powers or responsibilities. Each branch checks the action of another; two branches in conflict have powers that can result in balances or stalemates, requiring one branch to give in or both to reach a compromise.

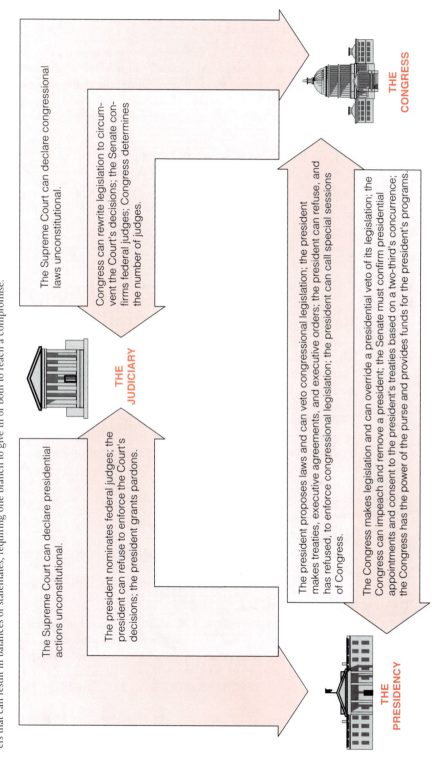

The Supreme Court can declare congressional laws unconstitutional.

Congress can rewrite legislation to circumvent the Court's decisions; the Senate confirms federal judges; Congress determines the number of judges.

The Supreme Court can declare presidential actions unconstitutional.

The president nominates federal judges; the president can refuse to enforce the Court's decisions; the president grants pardons.

The president proposes laws and can veto congressional legislation; the president makes treaties, executive agreements, and executive orders; the president can refuse, and has refused, to enforce congressional legislation; the president can call special sessions of Congress.

The Congress makes legislation and can override a presidential veto of its legislation; the Congress can impeach and remove a president; the Senate must confirm presidential appointments and consent to the president's treaties based on a two-third's concurrence; the Congress has the power of the purse and provides funds for the president's programs.

THE CONGRESS

THE JUDICIARY

THE PRESIDENCY

The Final Document

On September 17, 1787, the Constitution was approved by thirty-nine delegates. Of the fifty-five who had attended originally, only forty-two remained. Only three delegates refused to sign the Constitution. Others disapproved of at least parts of it but signed anyway to begin the ratification debate.

The Constitution that was to be ratified established the following fundamental principles:

1. Popular sovereignty, or control by the people.
2. A republican government in which the people choose representatives to make decisions for them.
3. Limited government with written laws, in contrast to the powerful monarchical British government against which the colonists had rebelled.
4. Separation of powers, with checks and balances among branches to prevent any one branch from gaining too much power.
5. Constitution is discussed in detail in Chapter 3).

RATIFICATION AND THE BILL OF RIGHTS

The founders knew that **ratification** (formal approval) of the Constitution was far from certain. Indeed, because it was almost guaranteed that many state legislatures would not ratify it, the delegates agreed that each state should hold a special convention. Elected delegates to these conventions would discuss and vote on the Constitution. Further departing from the Articles of Confederation, the delegates agreed that as soon as nine states (rather than all thirteen) approved the Constitution, it would take effect, and Congress could begin to organize the new government.

Federalists versus Anti-Federalists

The two opposing forces in the battle over ratification were the Federalists and the Anti-Federalists. The **Federalists** were those in favor of a strong central government and the new Constitution. The **Anti-Federalists** wanted to prevent the Constitution as drafted from being ratified.[7]

The Federalist Papers. In New York, opponents of the Constitution were quick to attack it. Alexander Hamilton answered their attacks in newspaper columns over the signature "Caesar." When the Caesar letters had little effect, Hamilton switched to the pseudonym Publius and secured two collaborators—John Jay and James Madison. In a very short time, those three political figures wrote a series of eighty-five essays in defense of the Constitution and of a republican form of government.

---

[7]There is some irony here. At the Constitutional Convention, those opposed to a strong central government pushed for a federal system because such a system would allow the states to retain some of their sovereign rights (see Chapter 3). The label *Anti-Federalists* thus contradicted their essential views.

These widely read essays appeared in New York newspapers from October 1787 to August 1788 and were reprinted in the newspapers of other states. Although we do not know for certain who wrote every one, it is apparent that Hamilton was responsible for about two-thirds of the essays. These included the most important ones interpreting the Constitution, explaining the various powers of the three branches, and presenting a theory of judicial review. Madison's *Federalist Paper* No. 10, however, is considered a classic in political theory; it deals with the nature of groups—or factions, as he called them. In spite of the rapidity with which *The Federalist Papers* were written, they are considered by many to be perhaps the best example of political theorizing ever produced in the United States.[8]

The Anti-Federalist Response. The Anti-Federalists used such pseudonyms as Montezuma and Philadelphiensis in their replies. Many of their attacks against the Constitution were also brilliant. They claimed that it was a document written by aristocrats and would lead to aristocratic tyranny. More important, the Anti-Federalists believed that the Constitution would create an overbearing and overburdening central government hostile to personal liberty. (The Constitution said nothing about freedom of the press, freedom of religion, or any other individual liberty.) They wanted to include a list of guaranteed liberties, or a bill of rights. Finally, the Anti-Federalists decried the weakened power of the states.

The Anti-Federalists cannot be dismissed as a bunch of unpatriotic extremists. They included such patriots as Patrick Henry and Samuel Adams. They were arguing what had been the most prevalent view of the time. This view derived from the French political philosopher Montesquieu (1689–1755), who believed that liberty was safe only in relatively small societies governed by direct democracy or by a large legislature with small districts. The Madisonian view favoring a large republic, particularly expressed in *Federalist Papers* No. 10 and No. 51, was actually the more *un*popular view of the time. Indeed, some researchers believe it was mainly the bitter experiences with the Articles of Confederation, rather than Madison's arguments, that created the setting for the ratification of the Constitution.[9]

The March to the Finish

The struggle for ratification continued. Strong majorities were procured in Delaware, Pennsylvania, New Jersey, Georgia, and Connecticut. After a bitter struggle, Massachusetts ratified the Constitution by a narrow margin on February 6, 1788. By the spring, Maryland and South Carolina had ratified by sizable majorities. Then, on

---

[8]Some scholars believe that *The Federalist Papers* played only a minor role in securing ratification of the Constitution. Even if this is true, they still have lasting value as an authoritative explanation of the Constitution.

[9]Of particular interest is the view of the Anti-Federalist position contained in Herbert J. Storing, *What the Anti-Federalists Were For* (Chicago: University of Chicago Press, 1981). Storing also edited seven volumes of the Anti-Federalist writings, *The Complete Anti-Federalist* (Chicago: University of Chicago Press, 1981). See also Josephine F. Pacheco, *Antifederalism: The Legacy of George Mason* (Fairfax, Va.: George Mason University Press, 1992).

June 21 of that year, New Hampshire became the ninth state to ratify the Constitution. Although the Constitution was formally in effect, this meant little without Virginia and New York; the latter did not ratify for yet another month. (Although the Constitution won ratification, it may not have had the support of most Americans—see this chapter's feature entitled *At Issue: Was the Constitution Truly Favored by the Majority?*)

The Bill of Rights

The U.S. Constitution would not have been ratified in several important states if the Federalists had not assured the states that amendments to the Constitution would be passed to protect individual liberties against incursions by the national government. Many of the recommendations of the state ratifying conventions included specific rights that were considered later by James Madison as he labored to draft what became the Bill of Rights.

Madison had to cull through more than two hundred state recommendations. It was no small task, and in retrospect he chose remarkably well. One of the rights appropriate for constitutional protection that he left out was equal protection under the laws—but that was not commonly regarded as a basic right at that time. It wasn't until 1868 that an amendment guaranteeing that no state shall deny equal protection to any person was ratified. (The Supreme Court has applied this guarantee to certain actions of the federal government as well.)

The final number of amendments that Madison and a specially appointed committee came up with was seventeen. Congress tightened the language somewhat and eliminated five of the amendments. Of the remaining twelve, two—dealing with the apportionment of representatives and the compensation of the members of Congress—were not ratified immediately by the states. Eventually, Supreme Court decisions led to legislative reforms relating to apportionment. The amendment relating to compensation of members of Congress was ratified 203 years later—in 1992!

On December 15, 1791, the national Bill of Rights was adopted and became part of the Constitution when Virginia agreed to ratify the ten amendments. The basic structure of American government had already been established. Now the fundamental rights and liberties of individuals were protected, at least in theory, at the national level. The proposed amendment that Madison characterized as "the most valuable amendment in the whole lot"—which would have prohibited the *states* from infringing on the freedoms of conscience, press, and jury trial—had been eliminated by the Senate. Thus, the Bill of Rights as adopted did not limit state power, and individual citizens had to rely on the guarantees contained in the particular state constitution or state bill of rights. The country had to wait until the violence of the Civil War before significant limitations on state power in the form of the Fourteenth Amendment became part of the national Constitution.

CHANGING THE CONSTITUTION

The U.S. Constitution consists of 7,000 words. It is shorter than every state constitution except that of Vermont, which has 6,880 words. One of the reasons the federal

Was the Constitution Truly Favored by the Majority?

In 1913, historian Charles Beard published *An Economic Interpretation of the Constitution of the United States,* charging that the Constitution had been produced primarily by wealthy property owners who desired a stronger government able to protect their property rights.* Beard also claimed that the Constitution had been imposed by undemocratic methods to prevent democratic majorities from exercising real power. He pointed out that there was never any popular vote on whether to hold a constitutional convention in the first place.

Furthermore, even if such a vote had been taken, state laws generally restricted voting rights to property-owning white males, meaning that most people in the country (white males without property, women, Native Americans,

and slaves) were not eligible to vote. Indeed, the delegates at the various state ratifying conventions had been selected by only 150,000 of the approximately 4 million citizens of that time. That does not seem very democratic—at least not by today's standards. Even Federalist John Marshall believed that in some of the adopting states a majority of the people opposed the Constitution.[†] Indeed, some historians have suggested that if a Gallup poll could have been taken at that time, the Anti-Federalists would probably have outnumbered the Federalists.[‡]

Beard's thesis gave rise to a long-standing debate over the purpose of the Constitution. Was it designed to protect all of the people against the power of government and their own excesses? Or was it written to serve the interests

of the people and groups that wielded economic power in the United States after the Revolution? Certainly, the fifty-five delegates to the Constitutional Convention did not represent a cross section of eighteenth-century American society. Indeed, most were members of the upper class. Recall from Chapter 1 that the *elite theory* of American government assumes that our democracy is in essence an oligarchy in which decisions are made by an elite group—or competing elite groups—of wealthy and powerful individuals. Beard's thesis accords with this view.

For Critical Analysis

Does it matter whether the Constitution was or was not favored by a majority of Americans when it was ratified?

[†]Beard, *An Economic Interpretation of the Constitution,* p. 299.
[‡]Jim Powell, "James Madison— Checks and Balances to Limit Government Power," *The Freeman,* March 1996,

[*]Charles A. Beard, *An Economic Interpretation of the Constitution of the United States* (New York: Macmillan, 1913; New York: Free Press, 1986).

Constitution is short is that the founders intended it to be only a framework for governing, to be interpreted by succeeding generations. One of the reasons it has remained short is that the formal amending procedure does not allow for changes to be made easily.

The Formal Amendment Process

Article V of the Constitution outlines the ways in which amendments may be proposed and ratified (see Figure 2.3). Two formal methods of proposing an amend-

"Restraint Key Word in
Constitutional
Amendments"

ment to the Constitution are available: (1) a two-thirds vote in each house of Congress or (2) a national convention that is called by Congress at the request of two-thirds of the state legislatures (the second method has never been used).

Ratification can occur by one of two methods: (1) by a positive vote in three-fourths of the legislatures of the various states or (2) by special conventions called in the states for the specific purpose of ratifying the proposed amendment and a positive vote in three-fourths of them. The second method has been used only once, to repeal Prohibition. That situation was exceptional because it involved an amendment (the Twenty-first) to repeal an amendment (the Eighteenth, which had created Prohibition). State conventions were necessary for repeal of the Eighteenth Amendment because the "pro-dry" legislatures in the more conservative states would never have passed the repeal. (Note that Congress determines the method of ratification to be used by all states for each proposed constitutional amendment.)

Congress has considered more than eleven thousand amendments to the Constitution. Only thirty-three have been submitted to the states after having been approved by the required two-thirds vote in each chamber of Congress, and only twenty-seven have been ratified (see Table 2.2). It should be clear that the process is much more difficult than a graphic depiction such as Figure 2.3 can indicate. Because of competing social and economic interests, the requirement that two-thirds of both the House and Senate approve the amendments is difficult to achieve. After approval by Congress, the process becomes even more arduous. Three-fourths of the state legislatures must approve the amendment. Only those amendments that have wide popular support across parties and in all regions of the country are likely to be approved.

FIGURE 2.3

The Formal Constitutional Amending Procedure

There are two ways of proposing amendments to the U.S. Constitution and two ways of ratifying proposed amendments. Among the four possibilities, the usual route has been proposal by Congress and ratification by state legislatures.

PROPOSING AMENDMENTS

EITHER...By a two-thirds vote in both houses of Congress...

OR...By a national convention called by Congress at the request of two-thirds of the states.

EITHER...By the legislatures of three-fourths of the states...

OR...By conventions in three-fourths of the states.

RATIFYING AMENDMENTS

→ Typical (used for all except one amendment)

→ Used only once (Twenty-first Amendment)

→ Never used

Table 2.2

Amendments to the Constitution

Amendments	Subject	Year Adopted	Time Required for Ratification
1st–10th	The Bill of Rights	1791	2 years, 2 months, 20 days
11th	Immunity of states from certain suits	1795	11 months, 3 days
12th	Changes in electoral college procedure	1804	6 months, 3 days
13th	Prohibition of slavery	1865	10 months, 3 days
14th	Citizenship, due process, and equal protection	1868	2 years, 26 days
15th	No denial of vote because of race, color, or previous condition of servitude	1870	11 months, 8 days
16th	Power of Congress to tax income	1913	3 years, 6 months, 22 days
17th	Direct election of U.S. senators	1913	10 months, 26 days
18th	National (liquor) prohibition	1919	1 year, 29 days
19th	Women's right to vote	1920	1 year, 2 months, 14 days
20th	Change of dates for congressional and presidential terms	1933	10 months, 21 days
21st	Repeal of the Eighteenth Amendment	1933	9 months, 15 days
22d	Limit on presidential tenure	1951	3 years, 11 months, 3 days
23d	District of Columbia electoral vote	1961	9 months, 13 days
24th	Prohibition of tax payment as a qualification to vote in federal elections	1964	1 year, 4 months, 9 days
25th	Procedures for determining presidential disability, presidential succession, and filling a vice presidential vacancy	1967	1 year, 7 months, 4 days
26th	Prohibition of setting minimum voting age above eighteen in any election	1971	3 months, 7 days
27th	Prohibition of Congress's voting itself a raise that takes effect before the next election	1992	203 years

Why was the amendment process made so difficult? The framers feared that a simple amendment process could lead to a tyranny of the majority, which could pass amendments to oppress disfavored individuals and groups. The cumbersome amendment process does not seem to stem the number of amendments that are proposed each year in Congress, however, particularly in recent years.

INFOTRAC®

"First Steps New Strategy Pro-Lifers"

Informal Methods of Constitutional Change

Formal amendments are one way of changing our Constitution, and, as is obvious by their small number, they have not been resorted to very frequently. If we discount the first ten amendments (the Bill of Rights), which passed soon after the ratification of the Constitution, there have been only seventeen formal alterations of the Constitution in the more than two hundred years of its existence.

But looking at the sparse number of formal constitutional changes gives us an incomplete view. The brevity and ambiguity of the original document have permitted great changes in the Constitution by way of changing interpretations over time. As the United States grew, both in population and territory, new social and political realities emerged. The courts, Congress, and presidents found it necessary to interpret the Constitution's provisions in light of these new realities. The Constitution has proved to be a remarkably flexible document, adapting itself time and again to new events and concerns.

Judicial Review

One informal way of changing the Constitution—or of making it more flexible—is through the power of judicial review. **Judicial review** refers to the power of U.S. courts to invalidate actions undertaken by the legislative and executive branches of government. A state court, for example, may rule that a statute enacted by the state legislature is unconstitutional. Federal courts (and ultimately, the United States Supreme Court) may rule unconstitutional not only acts of Congress and decisions of the national executive branch but also state statutes, state executive actions, and even provisions of state constitutions.

The Constitution does not specifically mention the power of judicial review, and whether the power can be justified constitutionally is a question we explore in Chapter 12, in the context of the role of the judiciary. For now, suffice it to say that in 1803, the Supreme Court claimed this power for itself in *Marbury v. Madison*,[10] in which the Supreme Court ruled that a particular provision of an act of Congress was unconstitutional.

Through the process of judicial review, the Supreme Court adapts the Constitution to modern situations. Electronic technology, for example, did not exist when the Constitution was ratified. Nonetheless, in the twentieth century the Supreme Court used the Fourth Amendment guarantees against unreasonable searches and seizures to place limits on wiretapping and other electronic eavesdropping methods by government officials. Additionally, the Supreme Court has changed its interpretation of the Constitution in accordance with changing times. It ruled in 1896 that "separate-but-equal" public facilities for African Americans were constitutional; but by 1954 the times had changed, and the Supreme Court reversed that decision.[11] Woodrow Wilson summarized the Supreme Court's work when he described it as "a constitutional convention in continuous session." Basically, the law is what the Supreme Court says it is at any point in time.

Interpretation, Custom, and Usage

The Constitution has also been changed through its interpretation by both Congress and the president. For example, Article I, Section 8, of the Constitution gives Congress the power to regulate foreign and interstate commerce. Although there is no clear definition of foreign commerce or interstate commerce in the Constitution, Congress has cited the *commerce clause* as the basis for passing thousands of laws that have defined the meaning of foreign and interstate commerce.

Originally, the president had a staff consisting of personal secretaries and a few others. Today, because Congress delegates specific tasks to the president and the

[10]5 U.S. 137 (1803).
[11]*Brown v. Board of Education of Topeka*, 347 U.S. 483 (1954).

chief executive assumes political leadership, the executive office staff alone has increased to several thousand persons. The executive branch provides legislative leadership far beyond the intentions of the Constitution. Presidents have also relied on their Article II authority as commander in chief of the nation's armed forces to send American troops abroad into combat, although the Constitution provides that Congress has the power to declare war. Presidents have also conducted foreign affairs by the use of **executive agreements,** which are legally binding documents made between the president and a foreign head of state. The Constitution does not mention such agreements.

"Frail Precedents
Three-Judge Panels"

Changes in the ways of doing political business have also altered the Constitution. The Constitution does not mention political parties, yet these informal, "extraconstitutional" organizations make the nominations for offices, run the campaigns, organize the members of Congress, and in fact change the election system from time to time. The emergence and evolution of the party system, for example, have changed the way of electing the president. The Constitution calls for the electoral college to choose the president. Today, the people vote for electors who are pledged to the candidate of their party, effectively choosing the president themselves. Perhaps most strikingly, the Constitution has been adapted from serving the needs of a small, rural republic with no international prestige to providing a framework of government for an industrial giant with vast geographic, natural, and human resources.

KEY TERMS

Anti-Federalist 36	First Continental Congress 24	Second Continental Congress 24
bicameral legislature 31	Great Compromise 32	
checks and balances 34	judicial review 42	separation of powers 34
confederation 27	Madisonian model 34	state 27
electoral college 34	natural rights 26	supremacy doctrine 32
executive agreement 43	ratification 36	unicameral legislature 27
Federalist 36	representative assembly 22	

CHAPTER SUMMARY

1 An early effort by England to establish North American colonies was unsuccessful. The first English colonies were established at Jamestown in 1607 and Plymouth in 1620. The Mayflower Compact created the first formal government. By the mid-1700s, other British colonies had been established along the Atlantic seaboard from Georgia to Maine.

2 In 1763, the British tried to reassert control over their increasingly independent-minded colonies through a series of taxes and legislative acts. The colonists responded with boycotts of British products and protests. Representatives of the colonies formed the First Continental Congress in 1774. The delegates sent a petition to the king of England expressing their grievances. The Second Continental Congress established an army in 1775 to defend colonists against any attacks by British soldiers.

3 On July 4, 1776, the Second Continental Congress approved the Declaration of Independence. Perhaps the most revolutionary aspects of the Declaration were its assumptions that people have natural rights to life, liberty, and the pursuit of happiness; that governments derive their power from the consent of the governed; and that people have a right to overthrow oppressive governments. All of the colonies subsequently adopted written constitutions that severely curtailed the power of executives, thus giving their legislatures predominant powers.

4 The Articles of Confederation created a weak central government with few powers. The Articles proved to be unworkable because the national government had no way to assure compliance by the states with such measures as securing tax revenues.

5 General dissatisfaction with the Articles of Confederation prompted delegates to call the Philadelphia convention in 1787. The discussions soon focused on creating a constitution for a new form of government. The Virginia plan and the New Jersey plan were offered but did not garner widespread support. A compromise offered by the state of Connecticut helped to break the large-state/small-state disputes dividing the delegates. The final version of the Constitution provided for the separation of powers and for checks and balances.

6 Fears of a strong central government prompted the addition of the Bill of Rights to the Constitution. The Bill of Rights secured a wide variety of freedoms for Americans, including the freedoms of religion, speech, and assembly. It was initially applied only to the federal government, but amendments to the Constitution following the Civil War made it clear that the Bill of Rights also applied to the states.

7 An amendment to the Constitution may be proposed by either a two-thirds vote in each house of Congress or by a national convention called by Congress at the request of two-thirds of the state legislatures. Ratification can occur by either a positive vote in three-fourths of the legislatures of the various states or a positive vote in three-fourths of special conventions called in the states for the specific purpose of ratifying the proposed amendment. Informal methods of constitutional change include judicial review and changing interpretations of the Constitution, as well as actions by Congress and the executive branch.

SELECTED PRINT AND ELECTRONIC RESOURCES

Suggested Readings

Casper, Gerhard. *Separating Power: Essays on the Founding Period.* Cambridge, Mass.: Harvard University Press, 1997. The author argues that the founders had not fully worked through their principles of constitutional government. Therefore, when scholars and judges try to interpret the Constitution by looking at the intentions of the framers, they run into difficulty.

Hamilton, Alexander, James Madison, and John Jay. *The Federalist Papers.* Cambridge, Mass.: Harvard University Press, 1961. The complete set of columns from the *New York Packet* defending the new Constitution is presented.

Holder, Angela Roddey, and John T. Roddey Holder. *The Meaning of the Constitution.* 3d ed. Hauppauge, N.Y.: Barron's Educational Series, Inc., 1997. This slim book brings the Constitution to life by giving examples of how each article and amendment apply to the world of everyday life and politics. An excellent resource for understanding the key role that the Constitution plays in the American political system.

Maier, Pauline. *American Scripture: Making the Declaration of Independence*. New York: Knopf, 1997. Maier offers an analysis of the Declaration of Independence, the context in which it was written, and its significance in American political life as "American Scripture." Her book has been acclaimed as the most scholarly and insightful work on this topic to appear in the last seventy-five years.

Media Resources

In the Beginning—A Bill Moyers program that features discussions with three prominent historians about the roots of the Constitution and its impact on our society.

John Locke—A video exploring the character and principal views of John Locke.

Where America Began—A video tour of American colonial history, including Jamestown, Williamsburg, and Yorktown.

LOGGING ON

For U.S. founding documents, including the Declaration of Independence, the U.S. Constitution, scanned originals of the U.S. Constitution, and *The Federalist Papers*, go to Emory University School of Law's Web site at

http://www.law.emory.edu/FEDERAL

The University of Oklahoma Law Center has a number of U.S. historical documents online, including many of those discussed in this chapter. Go to

www.law.ou.edu/hist

The National Constitution Center provides information on the Constitution—including its history, current debates over constitutional provisions, and news articles—at the following site:

http://www.constitutioncenter.org

A study aid for the U.S. Constitution is available at the following Web site, which has links to many different views for each segment of the Constitution:

http://members.aol.com/tcnbp/index.htm

If you want to look at state constitutions, state codes of law, state court opinions, or state executive decisions, go to

http://www.findlaw.com/casecode/state.html

To find constitutions for other countries, go to

http://www.uni-wuerzburg.de/law

USING THE INTERNET FOR POLITICAL ANALYSIS

As noted in this chapter, the U.S. Constitution is one of the most concise in the world. It clearly reflects the basic values of the framers in its emphasis on republican government, liberty, and limited government. Take a look at some modern constitutions at the following site, which is maintained by Washburn University School of Law:

http://www.washlaw.edu/forint

Choose at least two constitutions from non-Western nations—that is, from Africa, Asia, or the

Middle East. Compare these constitutions to that of the United States in terms of guarantees of the people's rights and liberties, the power of the central government, and the relationship between religion and the government.

CHAPTER 3

Federalism

There are many separate governments in this country. One national government and fifty state governments, plus local governments, create a grand total of more than 80,000 governments in all!

Visitors from France or Spain are often awestruck by the complexity of our system of government. Consider that a criminal action can be defined by state law, by national law, or by both. Thus, a criminal suspect can be prosecuted in the state court system or in the federal court system (or both). Often, economic regulation over exactly the same matter exists at the local level, the state level, and the national level—generating multiple forms to be completed, multiple procedures to be followed, and multiple laws to be obeyed. Numerous programs are funded by the national government but administered by state and local governments.

There are various ways of ordering relations between central governments and local units. *Federalism* is one of these ways. Understanding federalism and how it differs from other forms of government is important in understanding the American political system. Indeed, many political issues today would not arise if we did not have a federal form of government in which governmental authority is divided between the central government and various subunits.

THREE SYSTEMS OF GOVERNMENT

There are basically three ways of ordering relations between central governments and local units: (1) a unitary system, (2) a confederal system, and (3) a federal system. The most popular, both historically and today, is the unitary system.

A Unitary System

A **unitary system** of government can be defined as a centralized governmental system in which local or subdivisional governments exercise only those powers given to them by the central government. In other words, in a unitary system ultimate governmental authority rests in the hands of the national, or central, government. Consider a typical unitary system—France. There are departments and municipalities in France. Within the departments and the municipalities are separate government entities with elected and appointed officials. So far, the French system appears to be very similar to the U.S. system, but the similarity is only superficial. Under the unitary French system, the decisions of the governments of the departments and municipalities can be overruled by the national government. The national government also can cut off the funding of many departmental and municipal government activities. Moreover, in a unitary system such as that in France, all questions related to education, police, the use of land, and welfare are handled by the national government.[1] Great Britain, Sweden, Israel, Egypt, Ghana, and the Philippines also have unitary systems of government, as do most countries today.

A Confederal System

You were introduced to the elements of a **confederal system** of government in Chapter 2, when we examined the Articles of Confederation. A confederation is the opposite of a unitary governing system. It is a league of independent states in which a central government or administration handles only those matters of common concern expressly delegated to it by the member states. The central governmental unit has no ability to make laws directly applicable to individuals unless the member states explicitly support such laws. The United States under the Articles of Confederation and the Confederate States during the American Civil War were confederations.

There are few, if any, confederations in the world today that resemble those that existed in the United States. Switzerland is a confederation of twenty-three sovereign cantons, and several republics of the former Soviet Union formed the Commonwealth of Independent States.

A Federal System

The **federal system** lies between the unitary and confederal forms of government. In a federal system, authority is divided, usually by a written constitution, between a central government and regional, or subdivisional, governments (often called constituent governments). The central government and the constituent governments both act directly on the people through laws and through the actions of elected and appointed governmental officials. Within each government's sphere of authority, each is supreme, in theory. Contrast a federal system with a unitary one in which the central government is supreme and the constituent governments derive their authority from it. Australia, Canada, Mexico, India, Brazil, and Germany are examples of nations with federal systems. See Figure 3.1 for a comparison of the three systems.

WHY FEDERALISM?

Why did the United States develop in a federal direction? We look here at that question as well as at some of the arguments for and against a federal form of government.

---

[1]In the past decade, legislation has altered somewhat the unitary character of the French political system.

FIGURE 3.1

The Flow of Power in Three Systems of Government

In a unitary system, the flow of power is from the central government to the local and state governments. In a confederal system, the flow of power is in the opposite direction—from the state and local governments to the central government. In a federal system, the flow of power, in principle, goes both ways.

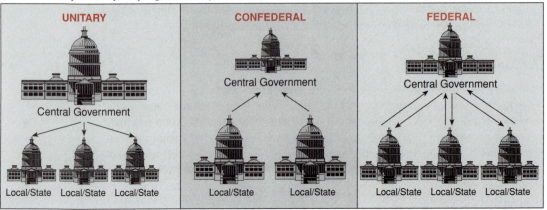

A Practical Solution

As you saw in Chapter 2, the historical basis of the federal system was laid down in Philadelphia at the Constitutional Convention, where strong national government advocates opposed equally strong states' rights advocates. This dichotomy continued through to the ratifying conventions in the several states. The resulting federal system was a compromise. The supporters of the new constitution were political pragmatists—they realized that without a federal arrangement, the new Constitution would not be ratified. The appeal of federalism was that it retained state traditions and local power while establishing a strong national government capable of handling common problems.

Even if the colonial leaders had agreed on the desirability of a unitary system, the problems of size and regional isolation would have made such a system difficult operationally. At the time of the Philadelphia convention, the thirteen colonies taken together were larger geographically than England or France. Slow travel and communication, combined with geographic spread, contributed to the isolation of many regions within the colonies. For example, it could take up to several weeks for all of the colonies to be informed about one particular political decision.

Other Arguments for Federalism

The arguments for federalism in the United States and elsewhere involve a complex set of factors, some of which we already have noted. First, for big countries, such as the United States, India, and Canada, federalism allows many functions to be "farmed out" by the central government to the states or provinces. The lower levels of government, accepting these responsibilities, thereby can become the focus of political dissatisfaction rather than the national authorities. Second, even with modern transportation and communications systems, the sheer geographic or population size of some nations makes it impractical to locate all political authority in one place. Finally, federalism brings government closer to the people. It allows more direct access to, and influence on, government agencies and policies, rather than leaving the population restive and dissatisfied with a remote, faceless, all-powerful central authority.

In the United States, federalism historically has yielded many benefits. State governments long have been a training ground for future national leaders. Presidents Ronald Reagan and Bill Clinton made their political mark as state governors. The states themselves have been testing grounds for new government initiatives. As United States Supreme Court justice Louis Brandeis once observed:

> It is one of the happy incidents of the federal system that a single courageous state may, if its citizens choose, serve as a laboratory and try novel social and economic experiments without risk to the rest of the country.[2]

Examples of programs pioneered at the state level include unemployment compensation, which began in Wisconsin, and air-pollution control, which was initiated in California. Currently, states are experimenting with policies ranging from educational reforms to the medical use of marijuana. Since the passage of the 1996 Welfare Reform Act, which gave more control over welfare programs to state governments, states are also experimenting with different methods of delivering welfare assistance.

Additionally, the American way of life always has been characterized by a number of political subcultures, which divide along the lines of race and ethnic origin, wealth, education, and, more recently, age, degree of religious fundamentalism, and sexual preference. The existence of diverse political subcultures would appear to be at odds with a political authority concentrated solely in a central government. Had the United States developed into a unitary system, the various political subcultures certainly would have been less able to influence government behavior (relative to their own regions and interests) than they have been, and continue to be, in our federal system.

Arguments against Federalism

Not everyone thinks federalism is such a good idea. Some see it as a way for powerful state and local interests to block progress and impede national plans. Others see dangers in the expansion of national powers at the expense of the states. President Ronald Reagan said, "The Founding Fathers saw the federalist system as constructed something like a masonry wall. The States are the bricks, the national government is the mortar. . . . Unfortunately, over the years, many people have increasingly come to believe that Washington is the whole wall."[3]

---

[2]*New State Ice Co. v. Liebmann*, 285 U.S. 262 (1932).

[3]Text of the address by the president to the National Conference of State Legislatures, Atlanta, Georgia (Washington, D.C.: The White House, Office of the Press Secretary, July 30, 1981), as quoted in Edward Millican, *One United People: The Federalist Papers and the National Idea* (Lexington, Ky.: The University Press of Kentucky, 1990).

Smaller political units are more likely to be dominated by a single political group, and the dominant groups in some cities and states have resisted implementing equal rights for all minority groups. (This was essentially the argument that James Madison put forth in *Federalist Paper* No. 10.) Others point out, however, that the dominant factions in other states have been more progressive than the national government in many areas, such as the environment.

THE CONSTITUTIONAL BASIS FOR AMERICAN FEDERALISM

No mention of the designation "federal system" can be found in the U.S. Constitution. Nor is it possible to find a systematic division of governmental authority between the national and state governments in that document. Rather, the Constitution sets out different types of powers (see Figure 3.2). These powers can be classified as (1) the powers of the national government, (2) the powers of the states, and (3) prohibited powers. The Constitution also makes it clear that if a state or local law conflicts with a national law, the national law will prevail.

Powers of the National Government

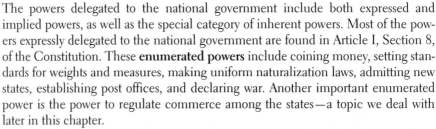

INFOTRAC®

"Congressional
Inconsistencies"

The powers delegated to the national government include both expressed and implied powers, as well as the special category of inherent powers. Most of the powers expressly delegated to the national government are found in Article I, Section 8, of the Constitution. These **enumerated powers** include coining money, setting standards for weights and measures, making uniform naturalization laws, admitting new states, establishing post offices, and declaring war. Another important enumerated power is the power to regulate commerce among the states—a topic we deal with later in this chapter.

The implied powers of the national government are also based on Article I, Section 8, which states that the Congress shall have the power

> [t]o make all laws which shall be necessary and proper for carrying into Execution the foregoing Powers, and all other Powers vested by this Constitution in the Government of the United States, or in any Department or Officer thereof.

This clause is sometimes called the **elastic clause,** or the **necessary and proper clause,** because it provides flexibility to our constitutional system. It gives Congress all of those powers that can be reasonably inferred but that are not expressly stated in the brief wording of the Constitution. The clause was first used in the Supreme Court decision of *McCulloch v. Maryland*[4] (discussed later in this chapter) to develop the concept of implied powers. Through this concept, the national government has succeeded in strengthening the scope of its authority to meet the numerous problems that the framers of the Constitution did not, and could not, anticipate.

A special category of national powers that is not implied by the necessary and proper clause consists of what have been labeled the inherent powers of the national

---

[4] 4 Wheaton 316 (1819).

FIGURE 3.2

The American Federal System—The Division of Powers between the National Government and the State Governments

Here we look at the constitutional powers of both the national government and the state governments together. Then we look at the powers denied by the Constitution to each level of government.

SELECTED CONSTITUTIONAL POWERS

National Government	National and State Governments	State Governments
EXPRESSED	CONCURRENT	RESERVED TO THE STATES
• To coin money	• To levy and collect taxes	• To regulate intrastate commerce
• To conduct foreign relations	• To borrow money	• To conduct elections
• To regulate interstate commerce	• To make and enforce laws	• To provide for public health, safety, and morals
• To levy and collect taxes	• To establish courts	• To establish local governments
• To declare war	• To provide for the general welfare	• To ratify amendments to the federal constitution
• To raise and support the military	• To charter banks and corporations	• To establish a state militia
• To establish post offices		
• To establish courts inferior to the Supreme Court		
• To admit new states		

IMPLIED
"To make all Laws which shall be necessary and proper for carrying into Execution the foregoing Powers, and all other Powers vested by this Constitution in the Government of the United States, or in any Department or Officer thereof."
(Article 1, Section 8, Clause 18)

SELECTED POWERS DENIED BY THE CONSTITUTION

National Government	National and State Governments	State Governments
• To tax articles exported from any state	• To grant titles of nobility	• To tax imports or exports
• To violate the Bill of Rights	• To permit slavery	• To coin money
• To change state boundaries	• To deny citizens the right to vote because of race, color, or previous servitude	• To enter into treaties
• To suspend the right of *habeas corpus*	• To deny citizens the right to vote because of gender	• To impair obligations of contracts
• To make ex post facto laws		• To abridge the privileges or immunities of citizens or deny due process and equal protection of the laws
• To subject officeholders to a religious test		

government. These powers derive from the fact that the United States is a sovereign power among nations, and as such, its national government must be the only government that deals with other nations. Under international law, it is assumed that all nation-states, regardless of their size or power, have an *inherent* right to ensure their own survival. To do this, each nation must have the ability to act in its own interest among and with the community of nations—by, for instance, making treaties, waging war, seeking trade, and acquiring territory. The national government has these powers whether or not they have been enumerated in the Constitution. Some constitutional scholars categorize inherent powers as a third type of power, completely distinct from the delegated powers (both expressed and implied) of the national government.

Powers of the State Governments

The Tenth Amendment states that the powers not delegated to the United States by the Constitution, nor prohibited by it to the states, are reserved to the states, or to the people. These are the reserved powers that the national government cannot deny to the states. Because these powers are not expressly listed—and because they are not limited to powers that are expressly listed—there is sometimes a question as to whether a certain power is delegated to the national government or reserved to the states. State powers have been held to include each state's right to regulate commerce within its borders and to provide for a state militia. States also have the reserved power to make laws on all matters not prohibited to the states by the national or state constitutions and not expressly, or by implication, delegated to the national government. The states also have **police power**—the authority to legislate for the protection of the health, morals, safety, and welfare of the people. Their police power enables states to pass laws governing such activities as crimes, marriage, contracts, education, traffic laws, and land use.

The police power of the states includes the power to create and enforce traffic laws and to regulate commerce within their borders.

The ambiguity of the Tenth Amendment has allowed the reserved powers of the states to be defined differently at different times in our history. When there is widespread support for increased regulation by the national government, the Tenth Amendment tends to recede into the background. When the tide turns the other way, as it has in recent years (see the discussion of the new federalism later in this chapter), the Tenth Amendment is resurrected to justify arguments supporting increased states' rights.

Concurrent Powers

In certain areas, the states share **concurrent powers** with the national government. Most concurrent powers are not specifically stated in the Constitution; they are only implied. An example of a concurrent power is the power to tax. The types of taxation are divided between the levels of government. States may not levy a tariff (a set of taxes on imported goods); the federal government may not tax real estate; and neither may tax the facilities of the other. If the state governments did not have the power to tax, they would not be able to function other than on a ceremonial basis. Other concurrent powers include the power to borrow money, to establish courts, and to charter banks and corporations. Concurrent powers are normally limited to the geographic area of the state and to those functions not delegated by the Constitution exclusively to the national government—such as the coinage of money and the negotiation of treaties.

Prohibited Powers

The Constitution prohibits or denies a number of powers to the national government. For example, the national government has expressly been denied the power to impose taxes on goods sold to other countries (exports). Moreover, any power not delegated expressly or implicitly to the federal government by the Constitution is prohibited to it. For example, the national government cannot create a national public school system. The states are also denied certain powers. For example, no state is allowed to enter into a treaty on its own with another country.

The Supremacy Clause

The supremacy of the national constitution over subnational laws and actions can be found in the **supremacy clause** of the Constitution. The supremacy clause (Article VI, Clause 2) states the following:

> This Constitution and the Laws of the United States which shall be made in Pursuance thereof; and all Treaties made . . . under the Authority of the United States, shall be the supreme Law of the Land; and the Judges in every State shall be bound thereby, any Thing in the Constitution or Laws of any State to the Contrary notwithstanding.

In other words, states cannot use their reserved or concurrent powers to thwart national policies. All national and state officers, as well as judges, must be bound by oath to support the Constitution. Hence, any legitimate exercise of national governmental power supersedes any conflicting state action.[5] Of course, deciding whether a conflict actually exists is a judicial matter, as you will soon read about in the case of *McCulloch v. Maryland.*

National government legislation in a concurrent area is said to *preempt* (take precedence over) conflicting state or local laws or regulations in that area. One of the ways in which the national government has extended its powers, particularly during the twentieth century, is through the preemption of state and local laws by national legislation. Consider that in the first decade of the twentieth century, fewer than 20 national laws preempted laws and regulations issued by state and local governments. By the end of the century, this number had risen to nearly 120.

Some political scientists believe that national supremacy is critical for the longevity and smooth functioning of a federal system. Nonetheless, the application of this principle has been a continuous source of conflict. Indeed, as you will see, the most extreme result of this conflict was the Civil War.

THE GROWTH OF THE NATIONAL GOVERNMENT

Recall from Chapter 2 that constitutional language, to be effective and to endure, must have some degree of ambiguity. Certainly, the powers delegated to the national government and the powers reserved to the states contain elements of ambiguity, thus leaving the door open for different interpretations of federalism. Disputes over the boundaries of national versus state powers have characterized this nation from the beginning.

Defining Constitutional Powers—The Early Years

In the early 1800s, the most significant disputes arose over differing interpretations of the implied powers of the national government under the necessary and proper clause and the respective powers of the national government and the states in regard to commerce.

Although political bodies at all levels of government play important roles in the process of settling such disputes, ultimately it is the Supreme Court that casts the final vote. As might be expected, the character of the referee will have an impact on the ultimate outcome of any boundary dispute. From 1801 to 1835, the Supreme Court was headed by Chief Justice John Marshall, a Federalist who advocated a strong central government. We look here at two cases decided by the Marshall Court: *McCulloch v. Maryland*[6] and *Gibbons v. Ogden.*[7] Both cases are considered milestones in the movement toward national government supremacy.

---

[5]An excellent example of this is President Dwight Eisenhower's disciplining of Arkansas governor Orval Faubus by federalizing the National Guard to enforce the court-ordered desegregation of Little Rock High School.

[6]4 Wheaton 316 (1819).

[7]9 Wheaton 1 (1824).

John Marshall (1755–1835) was the fourth chief justice of the Supreme Court. When Marshall took over, the Court had little power and almost no influence over the other two branches of government. Some scholars have declared that Marshall is the true architect of the American constitutional system, because he single-handedly gave new power to the Constitution. Early in his career, he was an attorney and was elected to the first of four terms in the Virginia Assembly. He was instrumental in the fight to ratify the Constitution in Virginia. Prior to being named to the Supreme Court, he won a seat in Congress in 1799 and in 1800 became secretary of state to John Adams.

McCulloch v. Maryland (1819). The U.S. Constitution says nothing about establishing a national bank. Nonetheless, at different times Congress chartered two banks—the First and Second Banks of the United States—and provided part of their initial capital; they were thus national banks. The government of Maryland imposed a tax on the Second Bank's Baltimore branch in an attempt to put that branch out of business. The branch's cashier, James William McCulloch, refused to pay the Maryland tax. When Maryland took McCulloch to its state court, the state of Maryland won. The national government appealed the case to the Supreme Court.

One of the issues before the Court was whether the national government had the implied power, under the necessary and proper clause, to charter a bank and contribute capital to it. The other important question before the Court was the following: If the bank was constitutional, could a state tax it? In other words, was a state action that conflicted with a national government action invalid under the supremacy clause?

Chief Justice John Marshall held that if establishing such a national bank aided the national government in the exercise of its designated powers, then the authority to set up such a bank could be implied. To Marshall, the necessary and proper clause embraced "all means which are appropriate" to carry out "the legitimate ends" of the Constitution. Only when such actions are forbidden by the letter and spirit of the Constitution are they thereby unconstitutional. Having established this doctrine of implied powers, Marshall then answered the other important question before the Court and established the doctrine of national supremacy. Marshall stated that no state could use its taxing power to tax an arm of the national government. If it could, "the declaration that the Constitution . . . shall be the supreme law of the land, is empty and unmeaning declamation."

Marshall's decision enabled the national government to grow and to meet problems that the Constitution's framers were unable to foresee. Today, practically every expressed power of the national government has been expanded in one way or another by use of the necessary and proper clause.

Gibbons v. Ogden (1824). One of the more important parts of the Constitution included in Article I, Section 8, is the so-called **commerce clause,** in which Congress is given the power "[t]o regulate Commerce with foreign Nations, and among the several States, and with the Indian Tribes." The meaning of this clause was at issue in *Gibbons v. Ogden*.

The background to the case was as follows. Robert Fulton and Robert Livingston secured a monopoly on steam navigation on the waters in New York State from the New York legislature in 1803. They licensed Aaron Ogden to operate steam-powered ferryboats between New York and New Jersey. Thomas Gibbons, who had obtained a license from the U.S. government to operate boats in interstate waters, decided to compete with Ogden, but he did so without New York's permission. Ogden sued Gibbons. The New York state courts prohibited Gibbons from operating in New York waters. Gibbons appealed to the Supreme Court.

There were actually several issues before the Court in this case. The first issue had to do with how the term *commerce* should be defined. New York's highest court had defined the term narrowly to mean only the shipment of goods, or the interchange of commodities, *not* navigation or the transport of people. The second issue was whether the national government's power to regulate interstate commerce extended to commerce within a state (*intra*state commerce) or was limited strictly to commerce among the states (*inter*state commerce). The third issue was whether the power to regulate interstate commerce was a concurrent power (as the New York court had concluded) or an exclusive national power.

Marshall defined *commerce* as *all* commercial intercourse—all business dealings—including navigation and the transport of people. Marshall also held that the commerce power of the national government could be exercised in state jurisdictions, even though it cannot reach *solely* intrastate commerce. Finally, Marshall emphasized that the power to regulate interstate commerce was an *exclusive* national power. Marshall held that because Gibbons was duly authorized by the national government to navigate in interstate waters, he could not be prohibited from doing so by a state court.

Marshall's expansive interpretation of the commerce clause in *Gibbons v. Ogden* allowed the national government to exercise increasing authority over all areas of economic affairs throughout the land. Congress did not immediately exploit this broad grant of power. In the 1930s and subsequent decades, however, the commerce clause became the primary constitutional basis for national government regulation—as you will read later in this chapter.

States' Rights and the Civil War

We usually think of the Civil War simply as the fight to free the slaves, but that issue was closely intertwined with another one. At the heart of the controversy that led to the Civil War was the issue of national government supremacy versus the rights of the separate states. Essentially, the Civil War brought to an ultimate and violent climax the ideological debate that had been outlined by the Federalist and Anti-Federalist parties even before the Constitution was ratified.

The Shift Back to States' Rights. As we have seen, while John Marshall was chief justice of the Supreme Court, he did much to increase the power of the national government and to reduce that of the states. During the Jacksonian era (1829–1837), however, a shift back to states' rights began. The question of the regulation of commerce became one of the major issues in federal-state relations. The business community preferred state regulation (or, better yet, no regulation) of commerce.

When Congress passed a tariff in 1828, the state of South Carolina attempted to nullify the tariff (render it void), claiming that in cases of conflict between a state and the national government, the state should have the ultimate authority over its citizens. The concept of **nullification** eventually was used by others to justify the **secession**—or formal withdrawal—of the southern states from the Union.

War and the Growth of the National Government. The ultimate defeat of the South permanently ended any idea that a state within the Union can successfully claim the right to secede. Ironically, the Civil War—brought about in large part because of the South's desire for increased states' rights—resulted in the opposite: an increase in the political power of the national government.

Thousands of new employees were hired to run the Union war effort and to deal with the social and economic problems that had to be handled in the aftermath of war. A billion-dollar ($1.3 billion, which is over $11 billion in today's dollars)

"States' Rights Foreign Policy"

The Civil War was not fought over just the question of slavery. Rather, the supremacy of the national government was at issue. Had the South won, presumably any state or states would have the right to secede from the Union.

national government budget was passed for the first time in 1865 to cover the increased government expenditures. The first (temporary) income tax was imposed on citizens to help pay for the war. Both the increased national government spending and the nationally imposed income tax were precursors to the expanded role of the national government in the American federal system.[8] Civil liberties were curtailed in the Union and in the Confederacy in the name of the wartime emergency. The distribution of pensions and widow's benefits also boosted the national government's social role. The North's victory set the nation on the path to a modern industrial economy and society.

THE CONTINUING DISPUTE OVER THE DIVISION OF POWER

Although the outcome of the Civil War firmly established the supremacy of the national government and put to rest the idea that a state could secede from the

---

[8]The future of the national government's powerful role was cemented with the passage of the Sixteenth Amendment (ratified in 1913), which authorized the federal income tax.

In the 1800s, very young children worked in coal mines. Today, child-labor laws prohibit employers from hiring such young workers. Some argue that even in the absence of child-labor laws, few, if any, children would still be working in the mines, because the United States is a much richer country than it was a hundred years ago. Presumably, today's parents, no longer at subsistence income levels, would opt to have their children go to school.

Union, the war by no means ended the debate over the division of powers between the national government and the states. The debate can be viewed as progressing through at least three stages since the Civil War: dual federalism, cooperative federalism, and the new federalism.

Dual Federalism

During the decades following the Civil War, the prevailing doctrine was that of **dual federalism**—a doctrine that emphasizes a distinction between federal and state spheres of government authority and the supremacy of each government within its own sphere. Various images have been used to describe different configurations of federalism over time. Dual federalism is commonly depicted as a layer cake, because the state governments and the national government are viewed as separate entities, like separate layers in a cake.

Generally, in the decades following the Civil War the states exercised their police powers to regulate affairs within their borders, such as intrastate commerce, and the national government stayed out of purely local affairs. The courts tended to support the states' rights to exercise their police powers and concurrent powers in regard to the regulation of intrastate activities. For example, in 1918, the Supreme Court ruled that a 1916 federal law banning child labor was unconstitutional because it attempted to regulate a local problem.[9] In the 1930s, however, the doctrine of dual federalism receded into the background as the nation attempted to deal with the Great Depression.

Cooperative Federalism

Franklin D. Roosevelt was inaugurated on March 4, 1933, as the thirty-second president of the United States. In the previous year, nearly 1,500 banks had failed (and 4,000 more would fail in 1933). Thirty-two thousand businesses closed down, and one-fourth of the labor force was unemployed. The national government had been expected to do something about the disastrous state of the economy. But for the first three years of the Great Depression, the national government did very little. That changed with the new Democratic administration's energetic intervention in the economy. FDR's "New Deal" included numerous government spending and welfare programs, in addition to voluminous regulations relating to economic activity.

Some political scientists view the era since 1937 as characterized by **cooperative federalism,** in which the states and the national government cooperate in solving complex common problems. The New Deal programs of Franklin Roosevelt, for example, often involved joint action between the national government and the states. Federal grants (discussed later) were given to the states to help pay for public works projects, housing assistance, Aid to Families with Dependent Children, unemployment compensation, and other programs. The states, in turn, were required to implement the programs and pay for at least some of the costs involved. The pattern

---

[9]*Hammer v. Dagenhart*, 247 U.S. 251 (1918). This decision was overruled in *United States v. Darby*, 312 U.S. 100 (1940).

of national-state relationships during these years gave rise to a new metaphor for federalism—that of a marble cake.

Others see the 1930s as the beginning of an era of national supremacy, in which the power of the states has been consistently diminished. Certainly, the 1960s and 1970s saw an even greater expansion of the national government's role in domestic policy. The "Great Society" program of Lyndon Johnson's administration (1963–1969) created the Job Corps, Operation Head Start, Volunteers in Service to America (VISTA), Medicaid, and Medicare. The Civil Rights Act of 1964 prohibited discrimination in public accommodations, employment, and other areas on the basis of race, color, national origin, religion, or gender. The economy was regulated further in the 1970s by national laws protecting consumers, employees, and the environment. Today, few activities are beyond the reach of the regulatory arm of the national government.

The evolving pattern of national-state-local government relationships during the 1960s gave rise to yet another metaphor—**picket-fence federalism,** a concept devised by political scientist Terry Sanford. The horizontal boards in the fence represent the different levels of government (national, state, and local), while the vertical pickets represent the various programs and policies in which each level of government is involved. Officials at each level of government work together to promote and develop the policy represented by each picket.

Federal Grants-in-Aid. As part of the system of cooperative federalism, the national government gives back to the states (and local governments) a significant amount of the tax dollars it collects—an estimated $262 billion in fiscal year 2001. Federal grants typically have taken the form of **categorical grants-in-aid,** which are grants to state and local governments designed for very specific programs or projects. For some of the categorical grant programs, the state and local governments must put up a share of the money, usually called **matching funds.** For other types of programs, the funds are awarded according to a formula that takes into account the relative wealth of the state, a process known as **equalization.**

Grants-in-aid in the form of land grants were given to the states even before the ratification of the Constitution. Cash grants-in-aid started in 1808, when Congress gave money to the states to pay for the state militias. It was not until the twentieth century, however, that the federal grants-in-aid program became significant. Grants-in-aid and the restrictions and regulations that accompany them started to mushroom during Roosevelt's administration. The major growth began in the 1960s, however, when the dollar amount of grants-in-aid quadrupled to help pay for the Great Society programs of the Johnson administration. Grants became available in numerous areas, including the fields of education, pollution control, conservation, recreation, and highway construction and maintenance.

Nowhere can the shift toward a greater role for the central government in the United States be seen better than in the shift toward increased central government spending as a percentage of total government spending. In 1929, on the eve of the Great Depression, local governments accounted for 60 percent of all government outlays, whereas the federal government accounted for only 17 percent. After Roosevelt's New Deal had been in place for several years during the Great Depression, local governments gave up half their share of the government spending pie, dropping to 30 percent, and the federal government increased its share to 47 percent. Today, the federal government accounts for about two-thirds of all government spending.

By attaching conditions to federal grants, the national government has been able to exercise substantial control over matters that traditionally have fallen under the purview of state governments. If a state does not comply with a particular require-ment, the national government may withhold federal funds for other programs. A classic example of the power of the federal government to sanction the states for lack of compliance occurred during the administration of Ronald Reagan (1981–1989). Reagan threatened to withhold federal highway funds unless the states raised the minimum drinking age to twenty-one years.

Cooperative Federalism and the Supreme Court. The full effect of Chief Justice John Marshall's broad interpretation of the commerce clause was only realized in the twentieth century. In particular, the commerce clause was used to justify national reg-ulation of virtually any activity, even what would appear to be a purely local activity. For example, in 1942, the Supreme Court held that wheat production by an individ-ual farmer intended wholly for consumption on his own farm was subject to federal regulation—because the home consumption of wheat reduced the demand for wheat and thus could have a substantial effect on interstate commerce.[10]

The commerce clause was also used to validate congressional legislation even in what would seem to be social and moral matters—concerns traditionally regulated by the states. For example, in 1964 a small hotel in Georgia challenged the consti-tutionality of the Civil Rights Act of that year, claiming that Congress had exceeded its authority under the commerce clause by regulating local, intrastate affairs. The Supreme Court held that the 1964 act was constitutional, concluding that "[i]f it is interstate commerce that feels the pinch, it does not matter how local the operation that applies the squeeze."[11] By 1980, the Supreme Court acknowledged that the commerce clause had "long been interpreted to extend beyond activities actually in interstate commerce to reach other activities, while wholly local in nature, which nevertheless substantially affect interstate commerce."[12]

The New Federalism

The third phase of federalism was labeled the **new federalism** by President Richard Nixon (1969–1974). Its goal is to restore to the states some of the powers that have been exercised by the national government since the 1930s. The word *devolution*— which means the transfer of powers to political subunits—is often used in connec-tion with this approach to federalism.

INFOTRAC®

"HBCU Projects Win Federal Funds"

Tools of the New Federalism—Block Grants. One of the major tools of the new federalism is the block grant. **Block grants** place fewer restrictions on grants-in-aid given to state and local governments by grouping a number of categorical grants under one broad purpose. Governors and mayors generally prefer block grants because they give the states more flexibility in how the money is spent.

[10]*Wickard v. Filburn*, 317 U.S. 111 (1942).
[11]*Heart of Atlanta Motel v. United States*, 379 U.S. 241 (1964).
[12]*McLain v. Real Estate Board of New Orleans, Inc.*, 444 U.S. 232 (1980).

Out of the numerous block grants that were proposed from 1966 until the election of Ronald Reagan in 1980, only five were actually legislated. At the Reagan administration's urging, Congress increased the number to nine. By the beginning of the 1990s, such block grants accounted for slightly over 10 percent of all federal aid programs. With the Republican sweep of Congress in the 1994 elections, block grants again became the focus of attention. Republicans proposed reforming welfare and a number of other federal programs by transforming the categorical grants-in-aid to block grants and transferring more of the policymaking authority to the states. Congress succeeded, in part, in achieving these goals when it passed the welfare reform bill of 1996 (discussed in Chapter 13).

Although state governments desire block grants, Congress generally prefers categorical grants so that the expenditures are targeted according to congressional priorities. These priorities include programs, such as those for disadvantaged groups and individuals, that significantly benefit many voters. As you can see in Figure 3.3, federal grants-in-aid grew rapidly during the Nixon and Ford administrations, as well as during the Carter administration. The rate of growth slowed considerably during the Reagan administration, only to speed up again under Presidents Bush and Clinton.

Federal Mandates. A major obstacle faced by those who favor returning power to the states concerns **federal mandates**—requirements in federal legislation that force states and municipalities to comply with certain rules. Examples of recent federal mandates are minimum water purity requirements for specific localities and requirements for access by persons with physical disabilities to public buildings, sidewalks, and other areas. As mentioned earlier, under the supremacy clause of the Constitution, federal laws preempt conflicting state and local laws.

FIGURE 3.3

Federal Grants-in-Aid

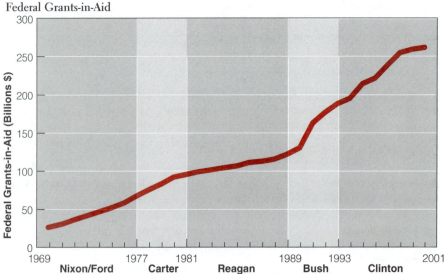

SOURCES: U.S. Department of Commerce, *Statistical Abstract of the United States* (Washington D.C.: U.S. Government Printing Office, 1999). Data for 2000 and beyond are projected.

No accurate analysis exists of the overall costs state and local governments have incurred as a result of federal mandates. Certain mandates, however, clearly are very costly. For example, one mandate involves eligibility for Medicaid. Medicaid is the federally subsidized, state-run health-care program for low-income Americans. The estimated cost of the programs for the states was $82 billion per year by the early 2000s.

The Supreme Court and the New Federalism. To an extent, the federal courts have furthered the ideals of the new federalism by placing limits on the constitutional powers of the national government. In 1992, for example, the United States Supreme Court held that requirements imposed on the state of New York under a federal law regulating low-level radioactive waste were unconstitutional. According to the Court, the act's "take title" provision, which required states to accept ownership of waste or regulate waste according to Congress's instructions, exceeded the enumerated powers of Congress. Although Congress can regulate the handling of such waste, "it may not conscript state governments as its agents" in an attempt to enforce a program of federal regulation.[13]

In 1997, in *Printz v. United States,*[14] the Court struck down the provisions of the federal Brady Handgun Violence Prevention Act of 1993 that required state employees to check the backgrounds of prospective handgun purchasers. Said the Court:

> [T]he federal government may neither issue directives requiring the States to address particular problems, nor command the States' officers, or those of their political subdivisions, to administer or enforce a federal regulatory program.

The Court held that the provisions violated "the very principle of separate state sovereignty," which was "one of the Constitution's structural protections of liberty."

The Supreme Court has also been reining in the powers of the national government under the commerce clause. In a widely publicized 1995 case, *United States v. Lopez,*[15] the Supreme Court held that Congress had exceeded its constitutional authority under the commerce clause when it passed the Gun-Free School Zones Act in 1990. The Court stated that the act, which banned the possession of guns within one thousand feet of any school, was unconstitutional because it attempted to regulate an area that had "nothing to do with commerce, or any sort of economic enterprise." This marked the first time in sixty years that the Supreme Court had placed a limit on the national government's authority under the commerce clause.

These and several other cases curbing national government authority[16] would seem to indicate that the federal courts are reversing their position in regard to the constitutional powers of the national government. For a further discussion of the Supreme Court's role in redefining the boundaries between the sovereign powers of the national and state governments, see the feature entitled *At Issue: How "Sovereign" Should the States Be?* on the next page.

INFOTRAC®

"States immune suit Individuals Disabilities Education Act"

---

[13]*New York v. United States,* 505 U.S. 144 (1992).

[14]521 U.S. 898 (1997).

[15]514 U.S. 549 (1995).

[16]See, for example, *Seminole Tribe of Florida v. Florida,* 517 U.S. 44 (1996); *City of Boerne v. Flores,* 521 U.S. 507 (1997); and *Washington v. Glucksberg,* 521 U.S. 702 (1997).

How "Sovereign" Should the States Be?

One of the rallying cries of the new federalism, particularly during the 1990s, was that the national government had been exercising powers that were reserved to the states under the Constitution. A number of federal courts, including the United States Supreme Court, seemed to agree with this conclusion. As mentioned elsewhere in this chapter, a series of court decisions during the 1990s placed curbs on the national government's authority to regulate state activities.

State Sovereign Immunity

This trend was further evidenced in a series of Supreme Court decisions enhancing state sovereignty in the late 1990s and early 2000s. For example, in a 1999 case the Court held that Maine public employees could not bring a suit against the state of Maine for violations of a federal law regulating overtime pay. The Court stated that state sovereign immunity precluded private lawsuits against state employers for violations of rights set forth in federal laws. According to the Court, such immunity is a "fundamental aspect of the sovereignty which [the states] enjoyed before the ratification of the Constitution, and which they retain today."[*]

[*]Alden v. Maine, 527 U.S. 706 (1999).

The Court returned to the issue of state sovereign immunity in *Kimel v. Florida Board of Regents,*[†] a decision issued in 2000. The decision applied to two separate cases, which were combined for review by the Supreme Court. The cases involved professors and librarians who sued their employers—two Florida state universities—for violating the federal Age Discrimination in Employment Act (ADEA) of 1967 (see Chapter 5) by denying them salary increases and other benefits because they were getting old and their successors could be hired at lower cost. The universities claimed that as agencies of a sovereign state, they could not be sued without the state's consent. The Supreme Court held that the sovereign immunity granted the states by the Eleventh Amendment precluded suits against them by private parties alleging violations of federal laws. According to the Court, Congress had exceeded its constitutional authority when it included in the ADEA a provision stating that "all employers," including state employers, were subject to the act.

Has the Supreme Court Gone Too Far?

Understandably, the *Kimel* decision has been controversial, and it

[†]120 S.Ct. 631 (2000).

may become even more so as state employees face the consequences of this decision. The Court itself was strongly divided on the issue (the vote was five to four). Shortly after rendering its decision in *Kimel,* the Court agreed to decide another question with serious implications for state employees—whether a state employer can be sued for disability discrimination under the Americans with Disabilities Act of 1990.

Clearly, the Supreme Court is redefining the boundary line that divides state and national powers under the Constitution. While some observers contend that the Court is going too far in the direction of supporting state powers, others believe that the Court is merely reminding us of our "constitutional framework of dual sovereignty."[‡]

FOR CRITICAL ANALYSIS

In your opinion, should states be immune from lawsuits brought to enforce rights guaranteed by federal laws? Why or why not?

[‡]See, for example, Marcia Coyle, "Is Rehnquist Tinkering with Revolution?" *The National Law Journal,* August 16, 1999, p. B7.

KEY TERMS

block grants 61	elastic clause 50	new federalism 61
categorical grants-in-aid 60	enumerated powers 50	nullification 57
commerce clause 56	equalization 60	picket-fence federalism 60
concurrent powers 53	federal mandate 62	police power 52
confederal system 47	federal system 47	secession 57
cooperative federalism 59	matching funds 60	supremacy clause 53
dual federalism 59	necessary and proper clause 50	unitary system 46

CHAPTER SUMMARY

1 There are three basic models for ordering relations between central governments and local units: (a) a unitary system (in which ultimate power is held by the national government), (b) a confederal system (in which ultimate power is retained by the states), and (c) a federal system (in which governmental powers are divided between the national government and the states). A major reason for the creation of a federal system in the United States is that it reflected a compromise between the views of the Federalists (who wanted a strong national government) and those of the Anti-Federalists (who wanted the states to retain their sovereignty), thus making ratification of the Constitution possible.

2 The Constitution expressly delegated certain powers to the national government in Article I, Section 8. In addition to these expressed powers, the national government has implied and inherent powers. Implied powers are those that are reasonably necessary to carry out the powers expressly delegated to the national government. Inherent powers are those held by the national government by virtue of its being a sovereign state with the right to preserve itself.

3 The Tenth Amendment to the Constitution states that powers not delegated to the United States by the Constitution, nor prohibited by it to the states, are reserved to the states, or to the people. In certain areas, the Constitution provides for concurrent powers, such as the power to tax, which are powers that are held jointly by the national and state governments. The Constitution also denies certain powers to both the national government and the states.

4 The supremacy clause of the Constitution states that the Constitution, congressional laws, and national treaties are the supreme law of the land. States cannot use their reserved or concurrent powers to override national policies. Vertical checks and balances allow the states to influence the national government and vice versa.

5 Two landmark Supreme Court cases expanded the constitutional powers of the national government. Chief Justice John Marshall's expansive interpretation of the "necessary and proper" clause of the Constitution in *McCulloch v. Maryland* (1819) enhanced the implied power of the national government. Marshall's broad interpretation of the commerce clause in *Gibbons v. Ogden* (1824) further extended the constitutional regulatory powers of the national government.

6 At the heart of the controversy that led to the Civil War was the issue of national government supremacy versus the rights of the separate states. The notion of nullification eventually led to the secession of the Confederate states from the Union. But the effect of the South's desire for increased states' rights and the subsequent Civil War was an increase in the political power of the national government.

7 Since the Civil War, federalism has evolved through at least three phases: dual federalism, cooperative federalism, and the new federalism. In dual federalism, each of the states and the federal government remain supreme within their own spheres. The era since the Great Depression has sometimes been labeled one of cooperative federalism, in which states and the national government cooperate in solving complex common problems. Others view it as the beginning of an era of national supremacy, because from the era of Franklin Roosevelt to the present, the national government continually has expanded its regulatory powers and activities.

8 The goal of the *new federalism*, labeled as such by President Nixon, is to decentralize federal programs and return more decision-making authority to the states. A major tool of the new federalism is the block grant, which groups various categorical grants together and gives more authority to the states in respect to the use of federal funds. Curbing unfunded federal mandates is seen as yet another step on the road to a new federalism.

SELECTED PRINT AND ELECTRONIC RESOURCES

Suggested Readings

Brinkley, Alan, et al. *The New Federalist Papers: Essays in Defense of the Constitution.* New York: W. W. Norton and Co., 1997. The authors of these essays argue that many of the current efforts to transfer national governmental powers to state and local governments are contrary to the Constitution and the intentions of the founders.

Donahue, John D. *Disunited States.* New York: Basic Books, 1997. The author analyzes current "devolutionary" politics and concludes that devolution may not be in the nation's best interests.

Hamilton, Alexander, James Madison, and John Jay. *The Federalist Papers.* Cambridge, Mass.: Harvard University Press, 1961. These essays remain an authoritative exposition of the founders' views of federalism.

Walker, David B. *The Rebirth of Federalism: Slouching toward Washington.* Chatham, N.J.: Chatham House, 1995. This history of American federalism offers an excellent analysis of federalism's current "feeble" condition. The book links the failure of true federalism to the decline of trust in the national government during the 1990s.

Media Resources

Can the States Do It Better?—A film in which various experts explore the debate over how much power the national government should have and use documentary film footage and other resources to illustrate historical instances of this debate.

LOGGING ON

To learn the founders' views on federalism, you can access *The Federalist Papers* online at

http://www.law.emory.edu/
FEDERAL

The following site has links to U.S. state constitutions, *The Federalist Papers*, and international federations, such as the European Union:

http://www.constitution.org/cs_feder.htm

Project Vote Smart's Web site on current issues in American government offers a number of articles on federalism/states' rights. Go to

http://www.vote-smart.org/issues/
FEDERALISM_STATES_RIGHTS

The following Web site of the Council of State Governments is a good source for information on state responses to federalism issues:

http://www.statesnews.org

The Brookings Institution's policy analyses and recommendations on a variety of issues, including federalism, can be accessed at

http://www.brook.edu

For a libertarian approach to issues relating to federalism, go to the Cato Institute's Web page at

http://www.cato.org

USING THE INTERNET FOR POLITICAL ANALYSIS

Almost all state governments have made some part of their organizations and laws available electronically. Use the Internet to compare state issues and policies by pointing your browser to the site maintained by NASIRE, the National Association of State Information Resource Executives:

http://www.nasire.org

Click on StateSearch, and then go to the pages for the Department of Parks or Environmental Resources (the name depends on the state). Compare the hot topics or "What's New" issues of at least two states from different regions of the country. What are the hot issues at the state level? How are those issues unique to that state? Can the state solve the problems alone, or is the issue national in scope? To what extent do you find evidence of national legislation in these state pages?

CHAPTER 4

Civil Liberties

Remember from Chapter 2 that to obtain ratification of the Constitution by the necessary nine states, the Federalists had to deal with the colonists' fears of a too-powerful national government. The Bill of Rights was the result. These first ten amendments to the U.S. Constitution were passed by Congress on September 25, 1789, and ratified by three-fourths of the states by December 15, 1791. Linked directly to the strong prerevolutionary sentiment for natural rights was the notion that a right was first and foremost a *limitation* on any government's ruling power. Thus, when we speak of **civil liberties** in the United States, we are referring mostly to the specific limitations on government outlined in the Bill of Rights.

As you read through these chapters, bear in mind that the Bill of Rights, like the rest of the Constitution, is relatively brief. The framers set forth broad guidelines, leaving it up to the courts to interpret these constitutional mandates and apply them to specific situations. Thus, judicial interpretations shape the true nature of the civil liberties and rights that we possess. Because judicial interpretations change over time, so do our liberties and rights. As you will read in the following pages, there have been numerous conflicts over the meaning of such simple phrases as *freedom of religion* and *freedom of the press*. To understand what freedoms we actually have, we need to examine how the courts—and particularly the Supreme Court—have resolved some of those conflicts. One important conflict has to do with whether the national Bill of Rights limited state governments as well as the national government.

EXTENDING THE BILL OF RIGHTS TO STATE GOVERNMENTS

Most citizens do not realize that, as originally intended, the Bill of Rights limited only the powers of the national government. The Bill of Rights begins with the words, "Congress shall make no law . . . ." It says nothing about *states* making laws that might abridge citizens' civil liberties. It was not until after the Fourteenth Amendment was ratified in 1868 that civil liberties guaranteed by the national Constitution began to be applied to the states. Section 1 of that amendment provides, in part, as follows:

No State shall . . . deprive any person of life, liberty, or property, without due process of law.

There was no question that the Fourteenth Amendment applied to state governments. For decades, however, the courts were reluctant to define the liberties spelled out in the national Bill of Rights as constituting "due process of law," which was protected under the Fourteenth Amendment. It was not until 1925, in *Gitlow v. New York*,[1] that the United States Supreme Court held that the Fourteenth Amendment protected the freedom of speech guaranteed by the First Amendment to the Constitution.

Only gradually, and never completely, did the Supreme Court accept the **incorporation theory**—the view that most of the protections of the Bill of Rights are incorporated into the Fourteenth Amendment's protection against state government. Table 4.1 shows the rights that the Court has incorporated into the Fourteenth Amendment and the case in which it first applied each protection. These Supreme Court decisions have bound the fifty states to accept for their respective citizens most of the rights and freedoms that are set forth in the U.S. Bill of Rights. We now look at some of those rights and freedoms, beginning with the freedom of religion.

FREEDOM OF RELIGION

In the United States, freedom of religion consists of two principal precepts as they are presented in the First Amendment. The first has to do with the separation of church and state, and the second guarantees the free exercise of religion.

---

[1]268 U.S. 652 (1925).

TABLE 4.1
_____

Incorporating the Bill of Rights into the Fourteenth Amendment

YEAR	ISSUE	AMENDMENT INVOLVED	COURT CASE
1925	Freedom of speech	I	*Gitlow v. New York*, 268 U.S. 652.
1931	Freedom of the press	I	*Near v. Minnesota*, 283 U.S. 697.
1932	Right to a lawyer in capital punishment cases	VI	*Powell v. Alabama*, 287 U.S. 45.
1937	Freedom of assembly and right to petition	I	*De Jonge v. Oregon*, 299 U.S. 353.
1940	Freedom of religion	I	*Cantwell v. Connecticut*, 310 U.S. 296.
1947	Separation of state and church	I	*Everson v. Board of Education*, 330 U.S. 1.
1948	Right to a public trial	VI	*In re Oliver*, 333 U.S. 257.
1949	No unreasonable searches and seizures	IV	*Wolf v. Colorado*, 338 U.S. 25.
1961	Exclusionary rule	IV	*Mapp v. Ohio*, 367 U.S. 643.
1962	No cruel and unusual punishment	VIII	*Robinson v. California*, 370 U.S. 660.
1963	Right to a lawyer in all criminal felony cases	VI	*Gideon v. Wainwright*, 372 U.S. 335.
1964	No compulsory self-incrimination	V	*Malloy v. Hogan*, 378 U.S. 1.
1965	Right to privacy	I	*Griswold v. Connecticut*, 381 U.S. 479.
1966	Right to an impartial jury	VI	*Parker v. Gladden*, 385 U.S. 363.
1967	Right to a speedy trial	VI	*Klopfer v. North Carolina*, 386 U.S. 213.
1969	No double jeopardy	V	*Benton v. Maryland*, 395 U.S. 784.

The Separation of Church and State

The First Amendment to the Constitution states, in part, that "Congress shall make no law respecting an establishment of religion." In the words of President Jefferson, this part of the First Amendment, called the **establishment clause,** was designed to create a "wall of separation of Church and State." Perhaps Jefferson was thinking about the religious intolerance that characterized the first colonies. Although many of the American colonies were founded by groups in pursuit of religious freedom, nonetheless they were quite intolerant of religious beliefs that did not conform to those held by the majority of citizens within their own communities. Jefferson undoubtedly was also aware that state religions were the rule; among the original thirteen American colonies, nine of them had official religions.

As interpreted by the Supreme Court, the establishment clause in the First Amendment means at least the following:

> Neither a state nor the federal government can set up a church. Neither can pass laws which aid one religion, aid all religions, or prefer one religion over another. Neither can force nor influence a person to go to or to remain away from church against his will or force him to profess a belief or disbelief in any religion. No person can be punished for entertaining or professing religious beliefs or disbeliefs, for church attendance or nonattendance. No tax in any amount, large or small, can be levied to support any religious activities or institutions, whatever they may be called, or whatever form they may adopt to teach or practice religion. Neither a state nor the federal government can, openly or secretly, participate in the affairs of any religious organizations or groups and vice versa.[2]

The establishment clause covers all conflicts about such matters as the legality of state and local government aid to religious organizations and schools, allowing or requiring school prayers, and the teaching of evolution versus fundamentalist theories of creation.

Aid to Church-Related Schools. Throughout the United States, all property owners except religious, educational, fraternal, literary, scientific, and similar nonprofit institutions must pay property taxes. A large part of the proceeds of such taxes goes to support public schools. But not all school-age children attend public schools. Fully 12 percent attend private schools, of which 85 percent have religious affiliations. In numerous cases, the Supreme Court has tried to draw a fine line between permissible public aid to students in church-related schools and impermissible public aid to religion.

These issues have arisen most often at the elementary and secondary levels. In a series of cases, the Supreme Court has allowed states to use tax funds for lunches, textbooks, diagnostic services for speech and hearing problems, standardized tests, and transportation for students attending church-operated elementary and secondary schools. In a number of cases, however, the Supreme Court has held state programs helping church-related schools to be unconstitutional. The Court has also denied state reimbursements to religious schools for field trips and for developing achievement tests.

---

[2]*Everson v. Board of Education,* 330 U.S. 1 (1947).

Fundamentalists Vicki Frost and her husband challenged certain textbooks as being too secular and violating their freedom of religion. Other people have argued that public schools cannot teach about religion because that would be a violation of the establishment clause.

In 1971, in *Lemon v. Kurtzman,*[3] the Court ruled that direct state aid could not be used to subsidize religious instruction. The Court in the *Lemon* case gave its most general statement on the constitutionality of government aid to religious schools, stating that the aid had to be secular in aim, that it could not have the primary effect of advancing or inhibiting religion, and that the government must avoid "an excessive government entanglement with religion." All laws under the establishment clause are now subject to the three-part *Lemon* test. How the test is applied, however, has varied over the years.

The Issue of School Prayer. Do the states have the right to promote religion in general, without making any attempt to establish a particular religion? That is the question in the issue of school prayer and was the precise question presented in 1962 in *Engel v. Vitale,*[4] the so-called Regents' Prayer case in New York. The State Board of Regents of New York had suggested that a prayer be spoken aloud in the public schools at the beginning of each day. The recommended prayer was as follows:

> Almighty God, we acknowledge our dependence upon Thee,
> And we beg Thy blessings upon us, our parents, our teachers, and our Country.

Such a prayer was implemented in many New York public schools.

The parents of a number of students challenged the action of the regents, maintaining that it violated the establishment clause of the First Amendment. At trial, the parents lost. The Supreme Court, however, ruled that the regents' action was

---

[3]403 U.S. 602 (1971).
[4]370 U.S. 421 (1962).

unconstitutional because "the constitutional prohibition against laws respecting an establishment of a religion must mean at least that in this country it is no part of the business of government to compose official prayers for any group of the American people to recite as part of a religious program carried on by any government." The Court's conclusion was based in part on the "historical fact that governmentally established religions and religious persecutions go hand in hand." In *Abington School District v. Schempp*[5] (1963), the Supreme Court outlawed daily readings of the Bible and recitation of the Lord's Prayer in public schools.

Although the Supreme Court has ruled repeatedly against officially sponsored prayer and Bible-reading sessions in public schools, other means for bringing some form of religious expression into public education have been attempted. In 1983, the Tennessee legislature passed a bill requiring public school classes to begin each day with a minute of silence. Alabama also had a similar law. In *Wallace v. Jaffree*[6] (1985), the Supreme Court struck down as unconstitutional the Alabama law authorizing one minute of silence in all public schools for prayer or meditation. Applying the three-part *Lemon* test, the Court concluded that the law violated the establishment clause because it was "an endorsement of religion lacking any clearly secular purpose." Since then, the lower courts have interpreted the Supreme Court's decision to mean that states can require a moment of silence in the schools as long as they make it clear that the purpose of the law is secular, not religious.

The courts have also dealt with cases involving prayer in public schools outside the classroom, particularly prayer during graduation ceremonies. In 1992, in *Lee v. Weisman*,[7] the Supreme Court held that it was unconstitutional for a school to invite a rabbi to deliver a nonsectarian prayer at graduation. The Court said nothing about *students* organizing and leading prayers at graduation ceremonies, however, and since then the lower courts have disagreed on this issue.

INFOTRAC®

"Teaching Evolution Kansas High Schools"

Forbidding the Teaching of Evolution. Since the early twentieth century, certain religious groups, particularly in the southern states, have opposed the teaching of evolution in the schools. To these groups, evolutionary theory directly counters their religious belief that human beings did not evolve but were created fully formed, as described in the biblical story of the creation. State and local attempts to forbid the teaching of evolution, however, have not passed constitutional muster in the eyes of the United States Supreme Court. For example, in 1968, the Supreme Court held, in *Epperson v. Arkansas*,[8] that an Arkansas law prohibiting the teaching of evolution violated the establishment clause, because it imposed religious beliefs on students. The Louisiana legislature passed a law requiring the teaching of the biblical story of the creation alongside the teaching of evolution. In 1987, in *Edwards v. Aguillard*,[9] the Supreme Court declared that this law was unconstitutional, in part because it had as its primary purpose the promotion of a particular religious belief.

---

[5]374 U.S. 203 (1963).
[6]472 U.S. 38 (1985).
[7]505 U.S. 577 (1992).
[8]393 U.S. 97 (1968).
[9]482 U.S. 578 (1987)

Here, a group of Hare Krishna adherents are crossing a street singing and playing drums and cymbals. This unfettered expression of their religious belief, and even the proselytization of their faith, is protected by the Constitution. Airport authorities, however, have been allowed to place physical restrictions on Hare Krishna groups to prevent them from approaching travelers. Often, they must stay behind a counter or other structure and not initiate contact with travelers unless invited to do so.

State and local groups in the so-called Bible Belt continue their efforts against the teaching of evolution. The Tennessee legislature recently considered a bill that would allow a school to fire any teacher who presents evolution as fact. A proposed amendment to the bill would also protect teachers who want to teach the biblical theories of the creation along with evolution. Alabama has approved a disclaimer to be inserted in biology textbooks, indicating that evolution is "a controversial theory some scientists present as a scientific explanation for the origin of living things." A school district in Georgia adopted a policy that creationism could be taught along with evolution. In 1999, the state board of education in Kansas decided to prohibit any mention of evolutionary theory on statewide tests. No doubt, these laws and policies will be challenged on constitutional grounds.

The Free Exercise of Religious Beliefs

The First Amendment's **free exercise clause** constrains Congress from prohibiting the free exercise of religion. Does this clause mean that no type of religious practice can be prohibited or restricted by government? Certainly, a person can hold any religious belief that he or she wants; or a person can have no religious belief. When, however, religious *practices* work against public policy and the public welfare, the government can act. For example, regardless of a child's or parent's religious beliefs, the government can require certain types of vaccinations. Similarly, although children of Jehovah's Witnesses are not required to say the Pledge of Allegiance at school, their parents cannot prevent them from accepting medical treatment (such as blood transfusions) if in fact their lives are in danger. Additionally, public school students can be required to study from textbooks chosen by school authorities.

The extent to which government can regulate religious practices always has been subject to controversy. Certainly, it has been since the early 1990s. For example, in 1990, in *Oregon v. Smith*,[10] the Supreme Court ruled that the state of Oregon could deny unemployment benefits to two drug counselors who had been fired for using peyote, an illegal drug, in their religious services. The counselors had argued that using peyote was part of the practice of a Native American religion. Many criticized the decision as going too far in the direction of regulating religious practices.

In 1993, Congress responded to the public's criticism by passing the Religious Freedom Restoration Act (RFRA). One of the specific purposes of the act was to overturn the Supreme Court's decision in *Oregon v. Smith*. The act required national, state, and local governments to "accommodate religious conduct" unless the government could show that there was a *compelling* reason not to do so. Moreover, if the government did regulate a religious practice, it had to use the least restrictive means possible.

Many people felt that the RFRA went too far in the other direction—it accommodated practices that were contrary to the public policies of state governments. Proponents of states' rights complained that the act intruded into an area traditionally governed by state laws, not the national government. In 1997, in *City of Boerne v. Flores*,[11] the Supreme Court agreed and held that the RFRA was unconstitutional because Congress had exceeded its constitutional authority. According to the Court, the act's "sweeping coverage ensures its intrusion at every level of government, displacing laws and prohibiting official actions of almost every description and regardless of subject matter."

FREEDOM OF EXPRESSION

Perhaps the most frequently invoked freedom that Americans have is the right to free speech and a free press without government interference. Each of us has the right to have our say, and all of us have the right to hear what others say. For the most part, Americans can criticize public officials and their actions without fear of reprisal or imprisonment by any branch of our government.

Permitted Restrictions on Expression

At various times, restrictions on expression have been permitted. A description of several such restrictions follows.

---

[10]494 U.S. 872 (1990).
[11]521 U.S. 507 (1997).

Clear and Present Danger. When a person's remarks present a clear and present danger to the peace or public order, they can be curtailed constitutionally.[12] According to the **clear and present danger test,** expression may be restricted if evidence exists that such expression would cause a condition, actual or imminent, that Congress has the power to prevent.

The Supreme Court modified the clear and present danger test in a 1951 case, *Dennis v. United States.*[13] At the time, there was considerable tension between the United States and the Soviet Union, whose government was run by the Communist Party. Twelve members of the American Communist Party were convicted of violating a statute that made it a crime to conspire to teach, advocate, or organize the violent overthrow of any government in the United States. The Supreme Court affirmed the convictions, significantly modifying the clear and present danger test in the process. The Court applied a "grave and probable danger rule." Under this rule, "the gravity of the 'evil' discounted by its improbability justifies such invasion of free speech as is necessary to avoid the danger." This rule gave much less protection to free speech than did the clear and present danger test. (Concerns over national security have led the U.S. government not only to restrain free speech but also to curb other civil liberties as well.)

The Bad-Tendency Rule. According to the **bad-tendency rule,** speech or other First Amendment freedoms may be curtailed if there is a possibility that such expression might lead to some "evil." In *Gitlow v. New York,*[14] a member of a left-wing group was convicted of violating New York state's criminal anarchy statute when he published and distributed a pamphlet urging the violent overthrow of the U.S. government. In its majority opinion, the Supreme Court held that although the First Amendment afforded protection against state incursions on freedom of expression, Gitlow could be punished legally in this particular instance because his expression would tend to bring about evils that the state had a right to prevent.

No Prior Restraint. Restraining an activity before that activity has actually occurred is referred to as **prior restraint.** It involves censorship, as opposed to subsequent punishment. Prior restraint of expression would require, for example, a permit before a speech could be made, a newspaper published, or a movie or TV show exhibited. Most, if not all, Supreme Court justices have been especially critical of any governmental action that imposes prior restraint on expression.[15]

One of the most famous cases concerning prior restraint was *New York Times v. United States*[16] (1971), the so-called Pentagon Papers case. The *Times* and the *Washington Post* were about to publish the Pentagon Papers, an elaborate secret history of the U.S. government's involvement in the Vietnam War (1964–1975). The

---

[12]*Schenck v. United States*, 249 U.S. 47 (1919).

[13]341 U.S. 494 (1951).

[14]268 U.S. 652 (1925).

[15]See, for example, *Nebraska Press Association v. Stuart*, 427 U.S. 539 (1976). See also *Near v. Minnesota*, 283 U.S. 697 (1931).

[16]403 U.S. 713 (1971).

secret documents had been obtained illegally by a disillusioned former Pentagon official. The government wanted a court order to bar publication of the documents, arguing that national security was being threatened and that the documents had been stolen. The newspapers argued that the public had a right to know the information contained in the papers and that the press had the right to inform the public. The Supreme Court ruled six to three in favor of the newspapers' right to publish the information. This case affirmed the no prior restraint doctrine.

The Protection of Symbolic Speech

Not all expression is in words or in writing. Gestures, movements, articles of clothing, and other forms of expressive conduct are considered **symbolic speech.** Such speech is given substantial protection today by our courts. For example, in 1989, in *Texas v. Johnson,*[17] the Supreme Court ruled that state laws that prohibited the burn-

---

[17]488 U.S. 884 (1989).

These individuals are burning an American flag as a symbolic expression of their opposition to government policy. Would a constitutional amendment to prohibit such desecration of the American flag place unacceptable limitations on symbolic speech?

ing of the American flag as part of a peaceful protest also violated the freedom of expression protected by the First Amendment. Congress responded by passing the Flag Protection Act of 1989, which was ruled unconstitutional by the Supreme Court in June 1990.[18] Congress and President Bush immediately pledged to work for a constitutional amendment to "protect our flag"—an effort that has yet to be successful.

In *R.A.V. v. City of St. Paul, Minnesota*[19] (1992), the Supreme Court ruled that a city statute banning bias-motivated disorderly conduct (in this case, the placing of a burning cross in another's front yard as a gesture of hate) was an unconstitutional restriction of speech. Freedom of speech can also apply to group-sponsored events. In 1995, the Supreme Court held that forcing the organizers of Boston's St. Patrick's Day parade to include gays and lesbians violated the organizers' freedom of speech.[20]

The Protection of Commercial Speech

Commercial speech is usually defined as advertising statements. Until the 1970s, the Supreme Court held that such speech was not protected at all by the First Amendment. By the mid-1970s, however, more and more commercial speech was brought under First Amendment protection. According to Justice Harry A. Blackmun, "Advertising, however tasteless and excessive it sometimes may seem, is nonetheless dissemination of information as to who is producing and selling what product for what reason and at what price."[21] Generally, the Supreme Court will consider a restriction on commercial speech valid as long as it (1) seeks to implement a substantial government interest, (2) directly advances that interest, and (3) goes no further than necessary to accomplish its objective.

Unprotected Speech: Obscenity

Numerous state and federal statutes make it a crime to disseminate obscene materials. Generally, the courts have not been willing to extend constitutional protections of free speech to what they consider obscene materials. But what is obscenity? Justice Potter Stewart once stated, in *Jacobellis v. Ohio,*[22] a 1964 case, that even though he could not define obscenity, "I know it when I see it." In 1973, however, in *Miller v. California,*[23] Chief Justice Warren Burger created a formal list of requirements that currently must be met for material to be legally obscene. Material is obscene if (1) the average person finds that it violates contemporary community standards; (2) the work taken as a whole appeals to a prurient interest in sex; (3) the work shows patently offensive sexual conduct; and (4) the work lacks serious redeeming literary,

---

[18]*United States v. Eichman,* 496 U.S. 310 (1990).

[19]505 U.S. 377 (1992).

[20]*Hurley v. Irish-American Gay, Lesbian and Bisexual Group of Boston,* 515 U.S. 557 (1995).

[21]*Virginia State Board of Pharmacy v. Virginia Citizens Consumer Council, Inc.,* 425 U.S. 748 (1976).

[22]378 U.S. 184 (1964).

[23]413 U.S. 5 (1973).

artistic, political, or scientific merit. The Court went on to state that the definition of prurient interest would be determined by the community's standards.

The problem, of course, is that one person's prurient interest is another person's medical interest or artistic pleasure. The Court thus left this determination to local and state authorities. Consequently, the *Miller* case has had widely inconsistent applications.

Obscenity remains a constitutionally unsettled area. Many women's rights activists, often in alliance with religious fundamentalists, have pushed for antipornography laws on the basis that pornography violates women's rights. In regard to child pornography, the Supreme Court has upheld state laws making it illegal to sell materials showing sexual performances by minors. In 1990, in *Osborne v. Ohio*,[24] the Court ruled that states can outlaw the possession of child pornography in the home. The Court reasoned that the ban on private possession is justified because owning the material perpetuates commercial demand for it and for the exploitation of the children involved.

A major public concern today has to do with access to pornographic materials via the Internet. For a further discussion of this issue, see this chapter's feature entitled *At Issue: Should the Internet Be Censored?*

INFOTRAC®

"Net Endangers Basic American Liberty"

Unprotected Speech: Slander, Fighting Words, and Hecklers' Veto

Can you say anything you want about someone else? Not really. Individuals are protected from **defamation of character,** which is defined as wrongfully hurting a person's good reputation. The law has imposed a general duty on all persons to refrain from making false, defamatory statements about others. Breaching this duty orally involves the wrongdoing called **slander.** (Breaching it in writing involves the wrongdoing called *libel*, which is discussed later.)

Legally, slander is the public uttering of a false statement that harms the good reputation of another. Slanderous public uttering means that the defamatory statements are made to, or within the hearing of, persons other than the defamed party. If one person calls another dishonest, manipulative, and incompetent when no one else is around, that does not constitute slander. The message is not communicated to a third party. If, however, a third party accidentally overhears defamatory statements, the courts have generally held that this constitutes a public uttering and therefore slander, which is prohibited.

The Supreme Court has prohibited types of speech that tend to incite an immediate breach of the peace. For example, public speakers may not use **fighting words.** These may include racial, religious, or ethnic slurs that are so inflammatory that they will provoke the "average" listener to fight. Members of a crowd listening to a speech are prohibited from exercising a **hecklers' veto.** The boisterous and disruptive behavior of hecklers poses the threat of disruption or violence, so hecklers are vetoing the essential rights of the speaker.

---

[24]495 U.S. 103 (1990).

Should the Internet Be Censored?

The Internet has become the greatest library ever. With the good, however, comes the bad. In particular, some citizens are worried that children can too easily access Web sites containing inappropriate materials, such as pornography. Also, those who prey on children might too easily come into contact with them through the Internet. Others are concerned about the use of the Web by groups that advocate violence, including terrorists.

Americans have conflicting views as to what, if anything, should be done to curb uses of the Internet that are perceived to be harmful to society. Some contend that the government should prohibit certain types of speech on the Internet. After all, they claim, restraints on speech are not new— for example, defamatory speech is not protected by the First Amendment; nor are "fighting words," obscene speech, and certain other forms of speech. Other groups argue that freedom of speech is one of our most important rights and that the government should let the Internet alone.

In fact, the federal government has already made two attempts to censor the Internet. The Communications Decency Act (CDA) of 1996 made it a criminal offense to make "patently offensive" and "indecent" speech available online to minors. Free speech advocates, including the American

Civil Liberties Union (ACLU), immediately challenged the law on First Amendment grounds. Ultimately, the Supreme Court ruled that the act was unconstitutional because it infringed too much on speech protected under the First Amendment.* In 1998, Congress made another attempt to regulate the Internet by passing the Child Online Protection Act. This act, which was popularly referred to as the "CDA II," made it a crime to make available online any material that is "harmful to minors" unless an age-verification system was used so that minor users could be separated from adult users. Like the 1996 CDA, the 1998 act was immediately blocked in court.†

Another question is whether it is even possible to effectively censor Internet speech. For example, even if Congress could pass a law prohibiting pornographic speech on the Web that would overcome the courts' objections, an army of federal "Internet watchers" would be needed to enforce the law. The number of Web sites is growing at a daunting rate. There is no way that a government, even the federal government, can check every potentially pornographic Web site every day. Additionally, our government could do little to regulate

Internet sites in other countries. After all, the U.S. government does not control the world but only what happens within its borders, more or less. Given the ease with which anyone can set up a home page on a server thousands of miles from U.S. shores, the possibility of truly stopping indecent material on the Web seems remote.

There is also the problem of defining what does or does not constitute pornography. Traditionally, the Supreme Court has held that this determination should be based on local community standards. What would happen if this same approach were used as a "base line" for censoring materials on the Internet, which can be accessed from any community in the United States (and the world)? In effect, the most restrictive community standards would apply to every U.S. user of the Internet. So, what could be viewed on the Internet would have to satisfy the decency and obscenity standards of our most restrictive community, wherever it may be in America.

FOR CRITICAL ANALYSIS

What is the difference between the regulation of obviously explicitly sexual material in magazines, which can be purchased in most jurisdictions by adults, and explictly sexual materials on the Web?

*Reno v. American Civil Liberties Union, 521 U.S. 844 (1997).
†American Civil Liberties Union v. Reno, 31 F.Supp.2d 473 (E.D.Pa. 1999).

Hate Speech

Some state universities have challenged the boundaries of the protection of free speech provided by the First Amendment with the issuance of campus speech and behavior codes. Such codes are designed to prohibit so-called hate speech—abusive speech attacking persons on the basis of their ethnicity, race, or other criteria. For example, a University of Michigan code banned "any behavior, verbal or physical, that stigmatizes or victimizes an individual on the basis of race, ethnicity, religion, sex, sexual orientation, creed, national origin, ancestry, age, marital status, handicap" or Vietnam-veteran status. A federal court found that the code violated students' First Amendment rights.[25] Although many people assert that such codes are necessary to stem violence on American campuses, the courts generally have held, as in the University of Michigan case, that they are unconstitutional restrictions on the right to free speech.

Campus speech and behavior codes raise a controversial issue: whether rights to free speech can (or should) be traded off to reduce violence in America. This issue extends to hate speech transmitted on the Internet as well, which is a growing concern for many Americans. Those who know how to navigate the online world can find information on virtually any topic, from how to build bombs to how to wage war against the government. Here again, the issue is whether free speech on the Internet should be restrained in the interests of protecting against violence.

At least one federal court has held that "hate speech" on the Internet is a criminal violation. That case, decided in 1998, involved an engineering student, Richard Machado, who had been attending the University of California's Irvine campus. After being expelled from the university for low grades, Machado sent e-mail messages to some sixty Asian students in which he threatened to "hunt down and kill" them. He was charged under a 1968 act making it a crime to interfere with federally protected activities, such as voting or attending a public school. The jury found that his actions violated that act.

FREEDOM OF THE PRESS

Freedom of the press can be regarded as a special instance of freedom of speech. Of course, at the time of the framing of the Constitution, the press meant only newspapers, magazines, and perhaps pamphlets. As technology has modified the ways in which we disseminate information, so too have the laws touching on freedom of the press been modified. What can and cannot be printed still occupies an important place in constitutional law, however.

Defamation in Writing

Libel is defamation in writing (or in pictures, signs, or films, or any other communication that has the potentially harmful qualities of written or printed words). As

---

[25]*Doe v. University of Michigan*, 721 F.Supp. 852 (1989).

with slander, libel occurs only if the defamatory statements are observed by a third party. If one person writes another a private letter wrongfully accusing her or him of embezzling funds, that does not constitute libel. It is interesting that the courts have generally held that dictating a letter to a secretary constitutes communication of the letter's contents to a third party, and therefore, if defamation has occurred, the wrongdoer can be sued. Newspapers are often involved in libel suits.

A Free Press versus a Fair Trial: Gag Orders

Another major issue relating to freedom of the press concerns media coverage of criminal trials. The Sixth Amendment to the Constitution guarantees the right of criminal suspects to a fair trial. In other words, the accused have rights. The First Amendment guarantees freedom of the press. What if the two rights appear to be in conflict? Which one prevails?

Jurors certainly may be influenced by reading news stories about the trial in which they are participating. In the 1970s, judges increasingly issued **gag orders,** which restricted the publication of news about a trial in progress or even a pretrial hearing. In a landmark 1976 case, *Nebraska Press Association v. Stuart,*[26] the Supreme Court unanimously ruled that a Nebraska judge's gag order had violated the First Amendment's guarantee of freedom of the press. Chief Justice Warren Burger indicated that even pervasive adverse pretrial publicity did not necessarily lead to an unfair trial and that prior restraints on publication were not justified. Some justices even went so far as to indicate that gag orders are never justified.

In spite of the *Nebraska Press Association* ruling, the Court has upheld certain types of gag orders. In *Gannett Company v. De Pasquale*[27] (1979), for example, the highest court held that if a judge found a reasonable probability that news publicity would harm a defendant's right to a fair trial, the court could impose a gag rule: "Members of the public have no constitutional right under the Sixth and Fourteenth Amendments to *attend* criminal trials."

Films, Radio, and TV

As has already been noted, in only a few cases has the Supreme Court upheld prior restraint of published materials. The Court's reluctance to accept prior restraint is less evident with respect to motion pictures. In the first half of the twentieth century, films were routinely submitted to local censorship boards. In 1968, the Supreme Court ruled that a film can be banned only under a law that provides for a prompt hearing at which the film is shown to be obscene. Today, few local censorship boards exist. Instead, the film industry regulates itself primarily through the industry's rating system.

Radio and television broadcasting has the most limited First Amendment protection. In 1934, the national government established the Federal Communications

---

[26]427 U.S. 539 (1976).
[27]443 U.S. 368 (1979).

Commission (FCC) to regulate electromagnetic wave frequencies. No one has a right to use the airwaves without a license granted by the FCC. The FCC grants licenses for limited periods and imposes numerous regulations on broadcasting. One of these regulations, called the **equal time rule,** requires any station that gives or sells airtime to a political candidate to make an equal amount of time available for purchase to all competing candidates. Another rule, sometimes referred to as the **personal attack rule,** provides that if a radio or television station is used to attack the honesty or integrity of a person, the station must see to it that the person attacked is afforded the fullest opportunity to respond. The FCC also can impose sanctions on those radio or TV stations broadcasting "filthy words," even if the words are not legally obscene. Also, the FCC has occasionally refused to renew licenses of broadcasters who presumably have not "served the public interest."

THE RIGHT TO ASSEMBLE AND TO PETITION THE GOVERNMENT

The First Amendment prohibits Congress from making any law that abridges "the right of the people peaceably to assemble and to petition the Government for a redress of grievances." Inherent in such a right is the ability of private citizens to communicate their ideas on public issues to government officials, as well as to other individuals. The Supreme Court has often put this freedom on a par with the freedom of speech and the freedom of the press. Nonetheless, it has allowed municipalities to require permits for parades, sound trucks, and demonstrations, so that public officials may control traffic or prevent demonstrations from turning into riots.

This became a major issue in 1977 when the American Nazi Party wanted to march through the largely Jewish suburb of Skokie, Illinois. The American Civil Liberties Union defended the Nazis' right to march (in spite of its opposition to the Nazi philosophy). The Supreme Court let stand a lower court's ruling that the city of Skokie had violated the Nazis' First Amendment guarantees by denying them a permit to march.[28]

An issue that has surfaced in recent years is whether communities can prevent gang members from gathering together on the streets without violating their right of assembly, or associational rights. Although some actions taken by cities to prevent gang members from gathering together or "loitering" in public places have passed constitutional muster, others have not.[29]

---

[28]*Smith v. Collin*, 439 U.S. 916 (1978).
[29]See, for example, *Gallo v. Acuna*, 14 Cal.4th 1090 (1997), in which the California Supreme Court upheld a court order preventing gang members from appearing in public together; and *City of Chicago v. Morales*, 527 U.S. 41 (1999), in which the United States Supreme Court held that Chicago's "anti-loitering" ordinance violated the constitutional right to due process of law because, among other things, it left too much power to the police to determine what constituted "loitering."

With their right to assemble and demonstrate protected by the Constitution, members of the modern Ku Klux Klan march in Wilmington, North Carolina. The police escort is charged with making sure that neither the marchers nor the observers provoke any violence.

PRIVACY RIGHTS

No explicit reference is made anywhere in the Constitution to a person's right to privacy. In the 1960s, however, the highest court began to infer such a right from various constitutional amendments in the Bill of Rights. For example, in 1965, in *Griswold v. Connecticut*,[30] the Supreme Court overthrew a Connecticut law that effectively prohibited the use of contraceptives, holding that the law violated the right to privacy. Justice William O. Douglas formulated a unique way of reading this right into the Bill of Rights. He claimed that the First, Third, Fourth, Fifth, and Ninth Amendments created "penumbras, formed by emanations from those guarantees that help give them life and substance," and he went on to talk about zones of privacy that are guaranteed by these rights.

When we read the Ninth Amendment, we can see the foundation for his reasoning: "The enumeration in the Constitution of certain rights, shall not be construed to deny or disparage others retained by the people." In other words, just because the Constitution, including its amendments, does not specifically talk about the right to privacy does not mean that this right is denied to the people.

During the past several years, a number of civil liberties that relate to the right to privacy have become important social issues. We look here at issues concerning abortion, the "right to die," and privacy rights in an information age.

---

[30]381 U.S. 479 (1965).

Privacy Rights and Abortion

"Abortion Trial, Again"

In *Roe v. Wade*[31] (1973), the United States Supreme Court accepted the argument that a Texas state law against abortion violated "Jane Roe's" right to privacy under the Constitution. (In 1973, performance of an abortion was a criminal offense in most states.) The Court did not answer the question about when life begins. It simply said that "the right to privacy is broad enough to encompass a woman's decision whether or not to terminate her pregnancy." The Court held that during the first trimester (three months) of pregnancy, abortion was an issue solely between a woman and her doctor. The state could not limit abortions except to require that they be performed by licensed physicians. During the second trimester, to protect the health of the mother, the state was allowed to specify the conditions under which an abortion could be performed. During the final trimester, the state could regulate or even out-law abortions except when necessary to preserve the life or health of the mother.

After *Roe*, the Supreme Court issued decisions in a number of cases defining and redefining the boundaries of state regulation of abortion. During the 1980s, the Court twice struck down laws that required a woman who wished to have an abor-tion to undergo counseling designed to discourage abortions. In the late 1980s and early 1990s, however, the Court took a more conservative approach. Although the Court did not explicitly overturn the *Roe* decision, it upheld state laws that place restrictions on abortion rights. For example, in *Webster v. Reproductive Health Services*[32] (1989), the Court upheld a Missouri statute that, among other things, banned the use of public hospitals or other taxpayer-supported facilities for perform-ing abortions. And, in *Planned Parenthood v. Casey*[33] (1992), the Court upheld a Pennsylvania law that required preabortion counseling, a waiting period of twenty-four hours, and, for girls under the age of eighteen, parental or judicial permission. As a result, abortions are now more difficult to obtain in some states than others.

Abortion continues to be a divisive issue. Antiabortion forces continue to push for laws banning abortion, to endorse political candidates who support their views, and to organize protests. Because of several episodes of violence attending protests at abortion clinics, in 1994 Congress passed the Freedom of Access to Clinic Entrances Act. The act prohibits protesters from blocking entrances to such clinics. In 1997, the Supreme Court upheld the constitutionality of prohibiting protesters from entering a fifteen-foot "buffer zone" around abortion clinics and from giving unwanted coun-seling to those entering the clinics.[34]

Privacy Rights and the "Right to Die"

In 1990, the Supreme Court took up the issue, of whether the right to privacy includes the right of a patient to refuse treatment and, if so, whether patients unable

[31]410 U.S. 113 (1973). Jane Roe was not the real name of the woman in this case. It is a common legal pseudonym used to protect a person's privacy.
[32]492 U.S. 490 (1989).
[33]505 U.S. 833 (1992).
[34]*Schenck v. ProChoice Network*, 519 U.S. 357 (1997).

to speak can exercise that right through a family member or guardian. In *Cruzan v. Director, Missouri Department of Health*,[35] the Court stated that a patient's life-sustaining treatment can be withdrawn at the request of a family member only if there is "clear and convincing evidence" that the patient did *not* want such treatment. Today, most states have laws permitting people to designate their wishes concerning life-sustaining procedures in "living wills" or durable health-care powers of attorney. These laws and the Supreme Court's *Cruzan* decision largely have resolved this aspect of the right-to-die controversy.

In the 1990s, however, another issue surfaced: Do privacy rights include the right of terminally ill people to end their lives through physician-assisted suicide? In 1997, in *Washington v. Glucksberg*,[36] the Supreme Court stated that the liberty interest protected by the Constitution does not include a right to commit suicide, with or without assistance. To hold otherwise, said the Court, would be "to reverse centuries of legal doctrine and practice, and strike down the considered policy choice of almost every state." In effect, the Supreme Court left the decision in the hands of the states. Since then, assisted suicide has been allowed in only one state—Oregon.

Privacy Rights in an Information Age

An important privacy issue, created in part by new technology, is the amassing of information on individuals by government agencies and private businesses, such as marketing firms. The average American citizen has personal information filed away in dozens of agencies—such as the Social Security Administration and the Internal Revenue Service. Because of the threat of indiscriminate use of private information by nonauthorized individuals, Congress passed the Privacy Act in 1974. This was the first law regulating the use of federal government information about private individuals. Under the Privacy Act, every citizen has the right to obtain copies of personal records collected by federal agencies and to correct inaccuracies in such records.

The ease with which personal information can be obtained by using the Internet for marketing and other purposes has led to unique challenges with regard to privacy rights. Not surprisingly, various government agencies and Congress have been considering proposals calling for government regulation of the Internet to protect privacy. To head off such regulation, most of the major online companies have agreed voluntarily to impose greater restrictions on access to such sensitive information. Privacy groups are not satisfied, however. They point out that voluntary agreements cannot provide for punishment if they are violated.

THE CONSTITUTION AND CRIMINAL PROCEDURES

The United States has one of the highest violent crime rates in the world. It is not surprising, therefore, that many citizens have extremely strong opinions about the rights of those accused of criminal offenses. When an accused person, especially one who has

---

[35]497 U.S. 261 (1990).
[36]521 U.S. 702 (1997).

confessed to some criminal act, is set free because of an apparent legal "technicality," many people may feel that the rights of the accused are being given more weight than the rights of society and of potential or actual victims. Why, then, give criminal suspects rights? The answer is partly to avoid convicting innocent people, but mostly because all criminal suspects have the right to due process of law and fair treatment.

The courts and the police must constantly engage in a balancing act of competing rights. At the center of all discussions about the appropriate balance is, of course, the U.S. Bill of Rights. The Fourth, Fifth, Sixth, and Eighth Amendments deal specifically with the rights of criminal defendants. These rights form the basis for criminal procedures in the United States.

Rights of the Accused

The basic rights of criminal defendants are outlined below. When appropriate, the specific constitutional provision or amendment on which a right is based also is given.

Limits on the Conduct of Police Officers and Prosecutors.
- No unreasonable or unwarranted searches and seizures (Amend. IV).
- No arrest except on probable cause (Amend. IV).
- No coerced confessions or illegal interrogation (Amend. V).
- No entrapment.
- Upon questioning, a suspect must be informed of his or her rights.

Defendant's Pretrial Rights.
- Writ of *habeas corpus* (Article I, Section 9).
- Prompt arraignment (Amend. VI).
- Legal counsel (Amend. VI).
- Reasonable bail (Amend. VIII).
- To be informed of charges (Amend. VI).
- To remain silent (Amend. V).

Trial Rights.
- Speedy and public trial before a jury (Amend. VI).
- Impartial jury selected from a cross section of the community (Amend. VI).
- Trial atmosphere free of prejudice, fear, and outside interference.
- No compulsory self-incrimination (Amend. V).
- Adequate counsel (Amend. VI).
- No cruel and unusual punishment (Amend. VIII).
- Appeal of convictions.
- No double jeopardy (Amend. V).

Extending the Rights of the Accused

During the 1960s, the Supreme Court, under Chief Justice Earl Warren, significantly expanded the rights of accused persons. In a case decided in 1963, *Gideon v.*

Wainwright,[37] the Court held that if a person is accused of a felony and cannot afford an attorney, an attorney must be made available to the accused person at the government's expense. Although the Sixth Amendment to the Constitution provides for the right to counsel, the Supreme Court had established a precedent twenty-one years earlier in *Betts v. Brady*,[38] when it held that only criminal defendants in capital cases automatically had a right to legal counsel.

Three years later, the Court issued its decision in *Miranda v. Arizona*.[39] The case involved Ernesto Miranda, who was arrested and charged with the kidnapping and rape of a young woman. After two hours of questioning, Miranda confessed and was later convicted. Miranda's lawyer appealed his conviction, arguing that the police had never informed Miranda that he had a right to remain silent and a right to be represented by counsel. The Court, in ruling in Miranda's favor, enunciated the *Miranda* rights that are now familiar to virtually all Americans:

[37]372 U.S. 335 (1963).
[38]316 U.S. 455 (1942).
[39]384 U.S. 436 (1966).

This individual is being read his Miranda *rights by the arresting officer. These rights were established in the 1966 case* Miranda v. Arizona. *The rights concern minimum procedural safeguards. They are also known as the* Miranda *warnings and include informing arrested persons prior to questioning (1) that they have the right to remain silent, (2) that anything they say may be used as evidence against them, and (3) that they have the right to the presence of an attorney.*

Prior to any questioning, the person must be warned that he has a right to remain silent, that any statement he does make may be used against him, and that he has a right to the presence of an attorney, either retained or appointed.

Congress and the courts subsequently have created several exceptions to the *Miranda* ruling. For example, Section 3501 of the Omnibus Crime Control and Safe Streets Act of 1968 provided that in federal cases, a voluntary confession could be used as evidence even if the accused person was not informed of his or her rights.[40] Even in cases that are not tried in federal courts, confessions have been allowed into evidence in certain circumstances. For example, in 1984 the Supreme Court held that when "public safety" required action (in this case, to find a loaded gun), police could interrogate the suspect before advising him of his right to remain silent.[41]

The Exclusionary Rule

INFOTRAC®

"Exclusionary Rule 20th Century Invention"

At least since 1914, judicial policy has prohibited the admission of illegally seized evidence at trials in federal courts. This is the so-called **exclusionary rule.** Improperly obtained evidence, no matter how telling, cannot be used by prosecutors. This includes evidence obtained by police in violation of a suspect's *Miranda* rights or of the Fourth Amendment. The Fourth Amendment protects against unreasonable searches and seizures and requires that a search warrant may be issued by a judge to a police officer only on probable cause (a demonstration of facts that permit a reasonable belief that a crime has been committed). The exclusionary rule was first extended to state court proceedings in a 1961 Supreme Court decision, *Mapp v. Ohio.*[42]

The reasoning behind the exclusionary rule is that it forces police officers to gather evidence properly, in which case their due diligence will be rewarded by a conviction. The exclusionary rule has always had critics who argue that it permits guilty persons to be freed because of innocent errors.

Over time, the Supreme Court has recognized several exceptions to the exclusionary rule, thus limiting its scope. For example, in 1984, the Supreme Court held that illegally obtained evidence could be admitted at trial if law enforcement personnel could prove that they would have obtained the evidence legally anyway.[43] In another case decided in the same year, the Court held that a police officer who used a technically incorrect search warrant form to obtain evidence had acted in good faith and therefore the evidence was admissible at trial. The Court thus created the "good faith" exception to the exclusionary rule.[44]

---

[40]The U.S. Department of Justice immediately disavowed Section 3501 as unconstitutional and continues to hold this position. In 1999, however, in *United States v. Dickerson*, 97 F.3d 4750 (4th Cir. 1999), a federal appellate court disagreed with the Justice Department's view and enforced the provision. The United States Supreme Court has agreed to review this decision.

[41]*New York v. Quarles*, 47 U.S. 649 (1984).

[42]367 U.S. 643 (1961).

[43]*Nix v. Williams*, 467 U.S. 431 (1984).

[44]*Massachusetts v. Sheppard*, 468 U.S. 981 (1984).

KEY TERMS

- bad-tendency rule 75
- civil liberties 68
- clear and present danger test 75
- commercial speech 77
- defamation of character 78
- equal time rule 82

- establishment clause 70
- exclusionary rule 88
- fighting words 78
- free exercise clause 73
- gag order 81
- hecklers' veto 78
- incorporation theory 69

- libel 80
- personal attack rule 82
- prior restraint 75
- slander 78
- symbolic speech 76
- writ of *habeas corpus* 86

CHAPTER SUMMARY

❶ To deal with American colonists' fears of a too-powerful national government, after the adoption of the U.S. Constitution, Congress proposed a Bill of Rights. These ten amendments to the Constitution were ratified by the states by the end of 1791. The amendments represent civil liberties—that is, they are limitations on the government.

❷ Originally, the Bill of Rights limited only the power of the national government, not that of the states. Gradually, however, the Supreme Court accepted the incorporation theory under which no state can violate the Bill of Rights.

❸ The First Amendment protects against government interference with the freedom of religion by requiring a separation of church and state and by guaranteeing the free exercise of religion. The separation of church and state is mandated in the establishment clause. Under this clause, the Supreme Court has ruled against officially sponsored prayer in public schools. The Court has also struck down laws forbidding the teaching of evolution or requiring the teaching of the biblical story of the creation. The government can provide financial aid to religious schools if the aid is secular in aim, the aid does not have the primary effect of advancing or inhibiting religion, and if the aid does not create "an excessive government entanglement with religion."

❹ The First Amendment protects against government interference with the freedom of speech, which includes symbolic speech (expressive conduct). Restrictions are permitted when expression presents a clear and present danger to the peace or public order, or when expression has a bad tendency (that is, when it might lead to some "evil"). Expression may be restrained before it occurs, but such prior restraint has a "heavy presumption" against its constitutionality. Commercial speech (advertising) by businesses has received limited First Amendment protection. Speech that has not received First Amendment protection includes expression judged to be obscene, utterances considered to be slanderous, and speech constituting fighting words or a hecklers' veto.

❺ The First Amendment protects against government interference with the freedom of the press, which can be regarded as a special instance of freedom of speech. Speech by the press that may not receive protection includes libelous statements. Publication of news about a criminal trial may be restricted by a gag order under unusual circumstances.

❻ The First Amendment protects the right to assemble peaceably and to petition the government. Permits may be required for parades, sound trucks, and demonstrations to maintain the public order, and a permit may be denied to protect the public safety.

❼ Under the Ninth Amendment, rights not specifically mentioned in the Constitution are not denied to the people. A constitutional right to privacy has been inferred from the First, Third, Fourth, Fifth, and Ninth Amendments. Questions concerning whether an individual's privacy rights include a right to have an abortion or a right to commit physician-assisted suicide continue to elicit controversy. The Supreme Court has held that individuals do not have a constitutional right to commit physician-assisted suicide and has upheld state laws banning the practice. A major privacy issue today concerns the problem of protecting privacy rights in cyberspace.

8 The Constitution includes protections for the rights of persons accused of crimes. Under the Fourth Amendment, no one may be subject to an unreasonable search or seizure or arrested except on probable cause. Under the Fifth Amendment, an accused person has the right to remain silent.

Under the Sixth Amendment, an accused person must be informed of the reason for his or her arrest. The accused also has the right to adequate counsel, even if he or she cannot afford an attorney, and the right to a prompt arraignment and a speedy and public trial before an impartial jury selected from a cross section of the community.

9 In *Miranda v. Arizona* (1966), the Supreme Court held that criminal suspects, prior to interrogation by law enforcement personnel, must be informed of certain constitutional rights, including the right to remain silent and the right to counsel. The exclusionary rule forbids the admission in court of illegally seized evidence. There is a "good faith exception" to the exclusionary rule: illegally seized evidence need not be thrown out owing to, for example, a technical defect in a search warrant.

SELECTED PRINT AND ELECTRONIC RESOURCES

Suggested Readings

Fiss, Owen M. *The Irony of Free Speech.* Cambridge, Mass.: Harvard University Press, 1996. The author, a professor at Yale Law School, argues that the state "might become the friend, rather than the enemy, of freedom" by suppressing certain types of speech, such as hate speech and pornography.

Foster, James C., and Susan M. Leeson. *Constitutional Law: Cases in Context.* Englewood Cliffs, N.J.: Prentice-Hall, 1998. This comprehensive collection of Supreme Court constitutional law cases traces the effects of each case on the American political system.

Lewis, Anthony. *Gideon's Trumpet.* New York: Vintage, 1964. This classic work discusses the background and facts of *Gideon v. Wainwright*, the 1963 Supreme Court case in which the Court held that the state must make an attorney available for any person accused of a felony who cannot afford a lawyer.

Neumann, Milton, et al., eds. *Hate Speech on Campus: Cases, Case Studies, and Commentary.* Boston: Northeastern University Press, 1997. This collection of essays examines free speech issues and cases, including hate speech on university campuses.

Media Resources

The Chamber—A movie, based on John Grisham's novel by the same name, about a young lawyer who defends a man (his grandfather) who has been sentenced to death and faces imminent execution.

Execution at Midnight—A video presenting the arguments and evidence on both sides of the controversial death-penalty issue.

Gideon's Trumpet—An excellent 1980 film about the *Gideon v. Wainwright* case; Henry Fonda plays the role of the convicted petty thief, Clarence Earl Gideon.

May It Please the Court: The First Amendment—A set of audiocassette recordings and written transcripts of the oral arguments made before the Supreme Court in sixteen key First Amendment cases. Participants in the recording include nationally known attorneys and several Supreme Court justices.

The People versus Larry Flynt—An R-rated 1996 film that clearly articulates the conflict between freedom of the press and how a community defines pornography.

LOGGING ON

At Project Vote Smart's Web site, you can find discussions of major issues, including those involving civil liberties, abortion, and crime. Go to

http://www.
vote-smart.org/issues

The American Civil Liberties Union (ACLU), the leading civil liberties organization, provides an extensive array of information and links concerning civil rights issues at

http://www.aclu.org

The Liberty Counsel describes itself as "a nonprofit religious civil liberties education and legal defense organization established to preserve religious freedom." The URL for its Web site is

http://www.lc.org

Summaries and the full text of Supreme Court constitutional law decisions, plus a virtual tour of the Supreme Court, are available at

http://oyez.nwu.edu

If you want to read historic Supreme Court decisions, you can find them, listed by name, at

http://supct.law.cornell.edu/supct

The Center for Democracy and Technology (CDT) focuses on how developments in communications technology are affecting the constitutional liberties of Americans. You can access the CDT's site at

http://www.cdt.org

For a copy of the statement by the American Library Association's Intellectual Freedom Committee concerning the use of filtering software and other issues relating to free speech on the Internet, use the search engine at:

http://www.ala.org

USING THE INTERNET FOR POLITICAL ANALYSIS

Explore the freedom of religious expression that is available to all through the Internet. Use a search engine, such as Yahoo or Alta Vista, to search for Web sites sponsored by "mainline" religious groups and for sites offered by groups that subscribe to less common religious or quasi-religious beliefs or doctrines, such as Scientology, Satanism, atheism, Heaven's Gate, and Zoroastrianism. Examine the home pages of at least three groups. List any of their views or beliefs that may violate current laws, be counter to current political practices, or otherwise have political implications. Do the groups acknowledge their differences with the state or with each other? How does an individual judge the validity or persuasiveness of this information?

CHAPTER 5

Civil Rights

Equality is at the heart of the concept of civil rights. Generally, the term **civil rights** refers to the rights of all Americans to equal treatment under the law, as provided for by the Fourteenth Amendment to the Constitution. Although the terms *civil rights* and *civil liberties* are sometimes used interchangeably, scholars tend to make a distinction between the two. As you learned in Chapter 4, civil liberties are basically *limitations on government*; they specify what the government *cannot* do. Civil rights, in contrast, specify what the government *must do*—to ensure equal protection and freedom from discrimination.

Essentially, the history of civil rights in America is the story of the struggle of various groups to be free from discriminatory treatment. In spite of the words set forth in the Declaration of Independence that "all Men are created equal," the majority of the population in the early years of this nation had no political rights. As you learned in Chapter 2, the framers of the Constitution permitted slavery to continue (although many of the founders would have liked to abolish it). Slaves thus were excluded from the political process. Women also were excluded for the most part, as were Native Americans, African Americans who were not slaves, and even white men who did not own property. Indeed, it has taken this nation more than two hundred years to approach even a semblance of equality among all Americans.

In this chapter, we look first at two movements that had significant consequences for the history of civil rights in America: the civil rights movement of the 1950s and 1960s and the women's movement, which began in the mid-1800s and continues today. Each of these movements resulted in legislation that secured important basic rights for all Americans—the right to vote and the right to equal protection under the laws. We then explore a question with serious implications for today's voters and policymakers: What should be the government's responsibility when equal protection under the law is not enough to ensure truly equal opportunities for Americans?

CIVIL RIGHTS FOR AFRICAN AMERICANS AND OTHER MINORITIES

Article I, Section 2, of the U.S. Constitution states that congressional representatives are to be apportioned among the states according to their respective numbers. These numbers were to be obtained by adding to the total number of free persons "three fifths of all other Persons." The "other persons" were, of course, slaves. A slave was thus equal to three-fifths of a white person. Before 1863, the Constitution thus protected slavery and made equality impossible in the sense we use the word today. African American leader Frederick Douglass pointed out that "Liberty and Slavery—opposite as Heaven and Hell—are both in the Constitution."

The constitutionality of slavery was confirmed just a few years before the outbreak of the Civil War in the famous *Dred Scott v. Sanford*[1] case of 1857. The Supreme Court held that slaves were not citizens of the United States, nor were they entitled to the rights and privileges of citizenship. The Court also ruled that the Missouri Compromise, which banned slavery in the territories north of 36° 30′ latitude (the southern border of Missouri), was unconstitutional. The *Dred Scott* decision had grave consequences. Most observers contend that the ruling contributed to making the Civil War inevitable.

The Civil War Amendments

With the emancipation of the slaves by President Lincoln's Emancipation Proclamation in 1863 and the passage of the Thirteenth, Fourteenth, and Fifteenth

---

[1] 19 Howard 393 (1857).

Abraham Lincoln reads the Emancipation Proclamation on July 22, 1862. The Emancipation Proclamation did not abolish slavery (that was done by the Thirteenth Amendment, in 1865), but it ensured that slavery would be abolished if and when the North won the Civil War. After the Battle of Antietam on September 17, 1862, Lincoln publicly announced the Emancipation Proclamation and declared that all slaves residing in states that were still in rebellion against the United States on January 1, 1863, would be freed once those states came under the military control of the Union Army.

Amendments (often called the Civil War Amendments) during the Reconstruction period following the Civil War, constitutional inequality was ended.

The Thirteenth Amendment (1865) states that neither slavery nor involuntary servitude shall exist within the United States. The Fourteenth Amendment (ratified on July 9, 1868) tells us that *all* persons born or naturalized in the United States are citizens of the United States. It states, furthermore, that "[n]o State shall make or enforce any law which shall abridge the privileges or immunities of the citizens of the United States; nor shall any State deprive any person of life, liberty or property, without due process of law; nor deny to any person within its jurisdiction the equal protection of the laws." (Note the use of the terms *citizen* and *person* in this amendment. *Citizens* have political rights, such as the right to vote and run for political office. All *persons*, however, including legal *and* illegal immigrants, have a right to due process of law and equal protection under the law.) The Fifteenth Amendment states that "[t]he right of citizens of the United States to vote shall not be denied or abridged by the United States or by any State on account of race, color, or previous condition of servitude."

Early Civil Rights Acts. From 1865 to 1875, Congress passed a series of civil rights acts that were aimed at enforcing these amendments. The Civil Rights Act of 1866 extended citizenship to anyone born in the United States and gave African Americans full equality before the law. The act further authorized the president to enforce the law with national armed forces. The Enforcement Act of May 31, 1870, set out specific criminal sanctions for interfering with the right to vote as protected by the Fifteenth Amendment and by the Civil Rights Act of 1866. Equally important was the Civil Rights Act of April 20, 1872, known as the Anti–Ku Klux Klan Act. This act made it a federal crime for anyone to use law or custom to deprive an individual of his or her rights, privileges, and immunities secured by the Constitution or by any federal law. Section 2 of that act imposed detailed penalties or damages for violation of the act. The last of these early civil rights acts, passed on March 1, 1875, and known as the Second Civil Rights Act, declared that everyone is entitled to full and equal enjoyment of public accommodations, theaters, and other places of public amusement. The act also imposed penalties for violators.

These early civil rights acts ultimately did little to secure equality for African Americans in their civil rights. The decisions in both the *Civil Rights Cases* of 1883 and the case of *Plessy v. Ferguson* effectively nullified these acts. Additionally, various voting barriers were erected that prevented African Americans from exercising their right to vote.

The *Civil Rights Cases*. The Supreme Court invalidated the 1875 Civil Rights Act when it held, in the *Civil Rights Cases*[2] of 1883, that the enforcement clause of the Fourteenth Amendment (which states that "[n]o State shall make or enforce any law which shall abridge the privileges or immunities of citizens") was limited to correcting actions by states in their *official* acts; thus, the discriminatory acts of *private* citi-

---

[2]109 U.S. 3 (1883).

zens were not illegal. The 1883 Supreme Court decision met with widespread approval throughout most of the United States.

Twenty years after the Civil War, the nation was all too willing to forget about the Civil War amendments and the civil rights legislation of the 1860s and 1870s. The other civil rights laws that the Court specifically did not invalidate became dead letters in the statute books, although they were never repealed by Congress. At the same time, many former proslavery secessionists had regained political power in the southern states. In the last decades of the nineteenth century, these racists enacted the Jim Crow laws, which will be discussed next in relation to the separate-but-equal doctrine.

Plessy v. Ferguson: **Separate but Equal.** A key decision during this period concerned Homer Plessy, a Louisiana resident who was one-eighth African American. In 1892, he was riding in a train from New Orleans when the conductor made him leave the car, which was restricted to whites, and directed him to a car for nonwhites. At that time, Louisiana had a statute providing for separate railway cars for whites and African Americans. Plessy claimed that such a statute was contrary to the Fourteenth Amendment's equal protection clause.

In 1896, the United States Supreme Court rejected Plessy's contention. The Court concluded that the Fourteenth Amendment "could not have been intended to abolish distinctions based upon color, or to enforce social . . . equality." The Court indicated that segregation alone did not violate the Constitution: "Laws permitting, and even requiring their separation in places where they are liable to be brought into contact do not necessarily imply the inferiority of either race to the other."[3] So was born the **separate-but-equal doctrine.**

Plessy v. Ferguson became the judicial cornerstone of racial discrimination throughout the United States. Even though *Plessy* upheld segregated facilities in railway cars only, it was assumed that the Supreme Court was upholding segregation everywhere as long as the separate facilities were equal. The result was a system of racial segregation, particularly in the South, that required separate drinking fountains; separate seats in theaters, restaurants, and hotels; separate public toilets; and separate waiting rooms for the two races—collectively known as Jim Crow laws.

Voting Barriers. The brief enfranchisement of African Americans ended after 1877, when the federal troops that occupied the South during the Reconstruction era were withdrawn. Southern politicians regained control of state governments and, using everything except race as a formal criterion, passed laws that effectively deprived African Americans of the right to vote. By using the ruse that political party primaries were private, southern whites were allowed to exclude African Americans. The white primary was upheld by the Supreme Court until 1944 when, in *Smith v. Allwright*,[4] the Court found it to be a violation of the Fifteenth Amendment.

Another barrier to African American voting was the **grandfather clause,** which restricted the voting franchise to those who could prove that their grandfathers had voted before 1867. **Poll taxes** required the payment of a fee to vote; thus, poor African

---

[3]*Plessy v. Ferguson*, 163 U.S. 537 (1896).
[4]321 U.S. 649 (1944).

Jim Crow laws required the segregation of the races, particularly in public facilities such as this theater. The name "Jim Crow" originates from a nineteenth-century vaudeville character who was called Jim (which was a common name) Crow (for a black-colored bird). Thus, the name "Jim Crow" was applied to laws and practices affecting African Americans.

Americans—as well as poor whites—who could not afford to pay the tax were excluded from voting. Not until the Twenty-fourth Amendment to the Constitution was ratified in 1964 was the poll tax eliminated as a precondition to voting. Literacy tests also were used to deny the vote to African Americans. Such tests asked potential voters to read, recite, or interpret complicated texts, such as a section of the state constitution, to the satisfaction of local registrars.

The End of the Separate-but-Equal Doctrine

A successful attack on the separate-but-equal doctrine began with a series of lawsuits in the 1930s to admit African Americans to state professional schools. By 1950, the Supreme Court had ruled that African Americans who were admitted to a state university could not be assigned to separate sections of classrooms, libraries, and cafeterias. In 1951, Oliver Brown decided that his eight-year-old daughter, Linda Carol Brown, should not have to go to an all-nonwhite elementary school twenty-one blocks from her home, when there was a white school only seven blocks away. The National Association for the Advancement of Colored People (NAACP), formed in 1909, decided to help Oliver Brown. The results were monumental in their impact on American society. Actually, a series of cases, first argued in 1952, contested state laws permitting or requiring the establishment of separate school facilities based on race. Following the death of Chief Justice Frederick M. Vinson and his replacement by Earl Warren, the Supreme Court asked for rearguments.

In 1954, in *Brown v. Board of Education of Topeka*,[5] the Supreme Court ruled that public school segregation of races violates the equal protection clause of the Fourteenth Amendment. The following year, in *Brown v. Board of Education*[6] (sometimes called the second *Brown* decision), the Supreme Court declared that the lower courts must ensure that African Americans would be admitted to schools on a nondiscriminatory basis "with all deliberate speed." The district courts were to consider devices in their desegregation orders that might include "the school transportation system, personnel, [and] revision of school districts and attendance areas into compact units to achieve a system of determining admission to the public schools on a nonracial basis."

The white South did not let the Supreme Court ruling go unchallenged. In some school districts, the public school population became 100 percent nonwhite when

INFOTRAC®

"Does School Integration Work"

---

[5] 347 U.S. 483 (1954).
[6] 349 U.S. 294 (1955).

white parents sent their children to newly established private schools, sometimes known as "segregation academies." Arkansas's Governor Orval Faubus used the state's National Guard to block the integration of Central High School in Little Rock in September 1957. The federal court demanded that the troops be withdrawn. Finally, President Dwight Eisenhower had to federalize the Arkansas National Guard and send it to quell the violence. Central High became integrated.

An Integrationist Attempt at a Cure: Busing

In most parts of the United States, residential concentrations by race have made it difficult to achieve racial balance in schools. Although it is true that a number of school boards in northern districts created segregated schools by drawing school district lines arbitrarily, the residential concentration of African Americans and other minorities in well-defined geographic locations has contributed to the difficulty of achieving racial balance. This concentration results in ***de facto* segregation.**

For a number of years after the Brown decision, whites reacted aggressively, particularly with respect to the attempt to desegregate the school system in Little Rock, Arkansas. After the local school board secured approval of the federal courts for desegregation, Governor Orval Faubus sent in the state's National Guard to preserve order when a handful of African American students entered Little Rock Central High School on September 2, 1957. The National Guard was withdrawn after a few weeks and replaced by a white mob. On September 24, President Dwight Eisenhower sent in five hundred soldiers, many of whom remained there for the rest of the school year.

The obvious solution to both *de facto* and **de jure segregation** (segregation that occurs as a result of laws or government policies) seemed to be transporting some African American schoolchildren to white schools and some white schoolchildren to African American schools. Increasingly, the courts ordered school districts to engage in such **busing across neighborhoods**. Busing led to violence in some northern cities, such as in south Boston, where African American students were bused into blue-collar Irish Catholic neighborhoods. Indeed, busing was unpopular with many groups. In the mid-1970s, almost 50 percent of African Americans interviewed were opposed to busing, and approximately three-fourths of the whites interviewed held the same opinion. Nonetheless, through the next decade, the Supreme Court fairly consistently upheld busing plans in the cases it decided.

By the 1990s, however, a number of major busing programs had either been cut back or terminated. In 1995, the Supreme Court ruled in *Missouri v. Jenkins*[7] that the state of Missouri could stop spending money to attract a multiracial student body in urban school districts through major educational improvements. This decision dealt a potentially fatal blow to the use of magnet schools for racial integration.

Generally, in the early 2000s Americans are taking another look at what desegregation means. The attempt to integrate the schools, particularly through busing, has largely failed to improve educational resources and achievement for African American children. The goal of racially balanced schools envisioned in the 1954 *Brown v. Board of Education of Topeka* decision now seems to be giving way to the goal of better educated children, even if that means educating them in schools populated primarily by minorities.

The Civil Rights Movement

The *Brown* decision applied only to public schools. Not much else in the structure of existing segregation was affected. In December 1955, a forty-three-year-old African American woman, Rosa Parks, boarded a public bus in Montgomery, Alabama. When the bus became crowded and several white people stepped aboard, Parks was asked to move to the rear of the bus, the "colored" section. She refused, was arrested, and was fined $10; but that was not the end of the matter. For an entire year, African Americans boycotted the Montgomery bus line. The protest was headed by a twenty-seven-year-old Baptist minister, Dr. Martin Luther King, Jr. During the protest period, he went to jail, and his house was bombed. In the face of overwhelming odds, however, King won. In 1956, the federal district court issued an injunction prohibiting the segregation of buses in Montgomery. The era of civil rights protests had begun.

King's Philosophy of Nonviolence. The following year, in 1957, King formed the Southern Christian Leadership Conference (SCLC). King advocated nonviolent civil disobedience as a means to achieve racial justice. He used tactics such as demonstrations and marches, as well as purposeful, public disobedience to unjust

---

[7]515 U.S. 70 (1995).

laws, while remaining nonviolent. King's followers successfully used these methods to widen public acceptance of their case.

For the next decade, African Americans and sympathetic whites engaged in sit-ins, freedom rides, and freedom marches. In the beginning, such demonstrations were often met with violence, but the contrasting image of nonviolent African Americans and violent, hostile whites created strong public support for the civil rights movement.

The civil rights movement gathered momentum in the 1960s. One of the most famous of the violence-plagued protests occurred in Birmingham, Alabama, in the spring of 1963, when Police Commissioner Eugene "Bull" Connor unleashed police dogs and used electric cattle prods against the protesters. The object of the protest had been to provoke a reaction by local officials so that the federal government would act. People throughout the country viewed the event on national television with indignation and horror. King himself was thrown in jail. The media coverage of the Birmingham protest and the violent response it elicited played a key role in the process of ending Jim Crow conditions in the United States. The ultimate result was the most important civil rights act in the nation's history, the Civil Rights Act of 1964 (to be discussed shortly).

In August 1963, King organized the massive March on Washington for Jobs and Freedom. Before nearly a quarter-million white and African American spectators and millions watching on television, King told the world his dream: "I have a dream," he said, "that my four little children will one day live in a nation where they will not be judged by the color of their skin but by the content of their character."

Police-dog attacks, cattle prods, high-pressure water hoses, beatings, bombings, and the March on Washington—all of these events helped to create an environment

Dr. Martin Luther King, Jr., at the August 1963 March on Washington for Jobs and Freedom.

in which Congress felt compelled to act on behalf of African Americans. The second era of civil rights acts, sometimes referred to as the second Reconstruction period, was under way.

Civil Rights Legislation. As the civil rights movement mounted in intensity, equality before the law came to be "an idea whose time has come," in the words of conservative Senate Minority Leader Everett Dirksen. The Civil Rights Act of 1964, the most far-reaching bill on civil rights in modern times, forbade discrimination on the basis of race, color, religion, gender, and national origin. The major provisions of the act were as follows:

INFOTRAC®

"Remove Confederate Flag Statehouse"

1. It outlawed arbitrary discrimination in voter registration.
2. It barred discrimination in public accommodations, such as hotels and restaurants, whose operations affect interstate commerce.
3. It authorized the federal government to sue to desegregate public schools and facilities.
4. It expanded the power of the Civil Rights Commission and extended its life.
5. It provided for the withholding of federal funds from programs administered in a discriminatory manner.
6. It established the right to equality of opportunity in employment and created the **Equal Employment Opportunity Commission,** which was charged with hearing and investigating claims of employment discrimination.

The Civil Rights Act of 1968 forbade discrimination in most housing and provided penalties for those attempting to interfere with individual civil rights (giving protection to civil rights workers, among others). Subsequent legislation added enforcement provisions to the federal government's rules pertaining to discriminatory mortgage-lending practices. Today, all lenders must report to the federal government the race, gender, and income of all mortgage-loan seekers, along with the final decision on their loan applications.

The Voting Rights Act of 1965 outlawed discriminatory voter-registration tests and authorized federal registration of persons and federally administered voting procedures in any political subdivision or state that discriminated electorally against a particular group. In part, the act provided that certain political subdivisions could not change their voting procedures and election laws without federal approval. The act targeted counties, mostly in the South, in which less than 50 percent of the eligible population was registered to vote. Federal voter registrars were sent to these areas to register African Americans who had been restricted by local registrars. Within one week after the act was passed, forty-five federal examiners were sent to the South. A massive voter-registration drive covered the country.

As a result of the Voting Rights Act of 1965, its amendments, and the large-scale voter-registration drives in the South, the number of African Americans registered to vote climbed dramatically. By 1980, 55.8 percent of African Americans of voting age in the South were registered. By the 1996 presidential elections, 63.5 percent of voting-age African Americans were registered to vote, which was just slightly less than the 67.7 percent of voting-age whites who were registered to vote.

Civil Rights for Other Minorities

Numerous minorities in this nation have suffered—and some continue to suffer—from discrimination. Hispanics, Native Americans, Asian Americans, Arab Americans from Middle Eastern countries, and persons from India have all had to struggle for equal treatment, as have people from various island nations and other countries. The fact that these groups are not singled out for special attention in this chapter should not be construed to mean that their struggle for equality is any less significant than the struggles of those groups that we do discuss.

Although the civil rights movement was primarily focused on the rights of African Americans, the legislation resulting from the movement ultimately has benefited virtually all minority groups. The Civil Rights Act of 1964, for example, prohibits discrimination against any person because of race, color, or national origin. Subsequent amendments to the Voting Rights Act of 1965 extended its protections to other minorities, including Hispanic Americans, Asian Americans, Native Americans, and Native Alaskans. To further protect the voting rights of minorities, the act now provides that states must make bilingual ballots available in counties where 5 percent or more of the population speaks a language other than English.

Political participation by minorities has increased dramatically since the 1960s. Nonetheless, the number of political offices held by members of minority groups remains disproportionately low compared to their numbers in the overall population.

WOMEN'S STRUGGLE FOR EQUAL RIGHTS

Like African Americans and other minorities, women also have had to struggle for equality. During the first phase of this struggle, the primary goal of women was to obtain the right to vote. Some women had hoped that the founders would provide such a right in the Constitution. In 1776, Abigail Adams wrote to her husband, John Adams, the following words in reference to new laws that would be necessary if a Declaration of Independence was issued:

> I desire you would remember the ladies. . . . If particular care and attention is not paid to the ladies, we are determined to foment a rebellion and will not hold ourselves bound by any laws in which we have no voice or representation.[8]

Despite this request, the founders did not include in the Constitution a provision guaranteeing women the right to vote. Nor did it deny to women—or to any others—this right. Rather, the founders left it up to the states to decide such issues, and, as mentioned earlier, by and large, the states limited the franchise to adult white males who owned property.

Early Women's Political Movements

In 1848, Lucretia Mott and Elizabeth Cady Stanton organized the first women's rights convention in Seneca Falls, New York. The three hundred people who

---

[8]As quoted in Lewis D. Eigen and Jonathan P. Siegel, *The Macmillan Dictionary of Political Quotations* (New York: Macmillan, 1993), p. 324.

attended approved a Declaration of Sentiments: "We hold these truths to be self-evident: that all men *and women* are created equal." In the following twelve years, groups of feminists held seven conventions in different cities in the Midwest and East. With the outbreak of the Civil War, however, advocates of women's rights were urged to put their support behind the war effort, and most agreed.

In 1869, Susan B. Anthony and Elizabeth Cady Stanton formed the National Woman Suffrage Association. According to their view, women's suffrage—the right to vote—was a means to achieve major improvements in the economic and social situation of women in the United States. In other words, the vote was to be used to obtain a larger goal.

By the early 1900s, gaining the right to vote had become the sole objective of the women's movement. Small radical splinter groups dedicted to this goal emerged, such as the Congressional Union, headed by Alice Paul. This organization worked solely for the passage of an amendment to the U.S. Constitution. Willing to use "unorthodox" means to achieve its goal, this group and others took to the streets. Parades, hunger strikes, arrests, and jailings ensued. Finally, in 1920, seventy-two years after the Seneca Falls convention, the Nineteenth Amendment was passed: "The right of citizens of the United States to vote shall not be denied or abridged by the United States or by any State on account of sex." Women were thus enfranchised. Although today it may seem that the United States was slow to give women the vote, it was really not too far behind the rest of the world (see Table 5.1).

The Modern Women's Movement

Although women gained the right to vote in 1920, there was little organized political activity by women until the 1960s. The civil rights movement of that decade resulted in a growing awareness of rights for all groups, including women. Additionally, the publication of Betty Friedan's *The Feminine Mystique* in 1963 focused national attention on the unequal status of women in American life. In 1966, Friedan and others formed the National Organization for Women (NOW). NOW immediately adopted a blanket resolution designed "to bring women into full participation in the mainstream of American society *now*, exercising all the privileges and responsibilities thereof in truly equal partnership with men." NOW has been in the forefront of what is often called the *feminist movement*.

The initial focus of the modern women's movement was not on expanding the political rights of women. Rather, leaders of NOW and other liberal women's rights

TABLE 5.1

Years, by Country, in Which Women Gained the Right to Vote

1893: New Zealand	1919: Germany	1945: Italy	1953: Mexico
1902: Australia	1920: United States	1945: Japan	1956: Egypt
1913: Norway	1930: South Africa	1947: Argentina	1963: Kenya
1918: Britain	1932: Brazil	1950: India	1971: Switzerland
1918: Canada	1944: France	1952: Greece	1984: Yemen

SOURCE: Center for the American Woman and Politics, 1995.

advocates sought to eradicate gender inequality through a constitutional amendment. The proposed amendment, called the Equal Rights Amendment (ERA), states as follows: "Equality of rights under the law shall not be denied or abridged by the United States or by any state on account of sex." To date, however, proponents of the ERA have not succeded in garnering enough political support for the amendment to secure both its adoption by Congress and its ratification by the necessary thirty-eight states. Although Congress adopted the ERA in 1972, the amendment was not ratified by the states within the necessary time period (see Chapter 2 for a discussion of the constitutional amendment process).

When the ERA failed to be ratified, women's rights organizations began to refocus their efforts. Although NOW continued to press for the ERA, other groups challenged discriminatory statutes and policies in the federal courts, contending that they violated the Fourteenth Amendment's equal protection clause. Since the 1970s, the Supreme Court has tended to scrutinize gender classifications closely and has invalidated a number of such statutes and policies. For example, in 1977 the Court held that police and firefighting units cannot establish arbitrary rules, such as height and weight requirements, that tend to preclude women from joining those occupations.[9] In 1983, the Court ruled that insurance companies cannot charge different rates for women and men.[10] In 1996, the Supreme Court held that the state-financed Virginia Military Institute's policy of accepting only males violated the equal protection clause.[11]

Women in Politics Today

Following the failure of the ERA, in addition to fighting discrimination in the courts, the women's movement began to work for increased representation in government. Several women's political organizations that are active today concentrate their efforts on getting women elected to political offices. These organizations include the national Women's Political Caucus, the Coalition for Women's Appointments, the Fund for a Feminist Majority, and Black Women Organized for Action.

A variety of women's political action committees, or PACs (see Chapter 7), have also been created and are now important sources of financial support for women candidates. The largest of these PACs is EMILY's List (EMILY stands for "Early Money Is Like Yeast—It Makes the Dough Rise"). This PAC supports Democratic women candidates for congressional offices and governorships. Founded in 1985, EMILY's List now has nearly 70,000 members who contribute funds to be used for political campaigns.

The efforts of women's rights advocates and organizations have helped to increase the number of women holding political offices in all areas of government. The men's club atmosphere still prevails in Congress, however, and no woman has yet held one of the major congressional leadership positions. But the number of

---

[9]*Dothard v. Rawlinson,* 433 U.S. 321 (1977).
[10]*Arizona v. Norris,* 463 U.S. 1073 (1983).
[11]*United States v. Virginia,* 518 U.S. 515 (1996).

women holding congressional seats has increased significantly in recent years. Elections during the 1990s brought more women to Congress than either the Senate or the House had seen before. After the 1998 elections, there were fifty-six women in the House and nine in the Senate.

For all their achievements in the political arena, however, the number of women holding political offices remains disproportionately low compared to their participation as voters. As Table 5.2 indicates, the absolute turnout of female voters nationally is higher than that of male voters.

Gender-Based Discrimination in the Workplace

Traditional cultural beliefs concerning the proper role of women in society continue to be evident not only in the political arena but also in the workplace. Since the 1960s, however, women have gained substantial protection against discrimination by laws mandating equal employment opportunities and equal pay.

"Mother Calls More Outreach"

Title VII of the Civil Rights Act of 1964. Title VII of the Civil Rights Act of 1964 prohibits gender discrimination in the employment context and has been used to strike down employment policies that discriminate against employees on the basis of gender. In 1978, Congress amended Title VII to expand the definition of gender discrimination to include discrimination based on pregnancy.

The Supreme Court has also held that Title VII prohibits sexual harassment in the workplace. Sexual harassment occurs when job opportunities, promotions, salary increases, and so on are given in return for sexual favors. A special form of sexual harassment, called hostile-environment harassment, occurs when an employee is subjected to sexual conduct or comments that interfere with the employee's job performance or are so pervasive or severe as to create an intimidating, hostile, or offensive environment.

Wage Discrimination. By 2000, women constituted close to 50 percent of the U.S. labor force, and that number continues to grow. By the year 2010, women will approach a majority of U.S. workers. Although Title VII and other legislation since

TABLE 5.2

Voting and Registration

Voting participation by females has recently been equal to, or greater than, voting participation by males. In both percentage and absolute terms, more females than males voted and registered in 1996.

	PERSONS OF VOTING AGE (MILLIONS)	PERSONS REPORTING THEY REGISTERED (MILLIONS)	PERSONS REPORTING THEY VOTED (PERCENTAGE)
Male	92.6	59.6	52.8
Female	101.0	68.0	55.5

SOURCE: U.S. Bureau of the Census.

the 1960s have mandated equal employment opportunities for men and women, women continue to earn less, on average, than men do. Currently, nationwide for every dollar earned by men, women earn about seventy-five cents.[12]

The issue of wage discrimination was first addressed during World War II (1941–1945), when the War Labor Board issued an "equal pay for women" policy. In implementing the policy, the board often evaluated jobs for their comparability and required equal pay for comparable jobs. The board's authority ended with the war. Supported by the next three presidential administrations, the Equal Pay Act was finally enacted in 1963 as an amendment to the Fair Labor Standards Act of 1938. Basically, the Equal Pay Act requires employers to pay equal pay for substantially equal work. In other words, males legally cannot be paid more than females who perform essentially the same job.

Although increased numbers of women are holding jobs in professions or business enterprises that were once dominated by men, few women hold top positions in their firms. Less than 10 percent of the Fortune 500 companies—America's leading corporations—have a woman as one of their five highest-paid executives. Because the barriers faced by women in the corporate world are subtle and not easily pinpointed, they have been referred to as "the glass ceiling." Clearly, age-old perceptions of the proper role of women in society continue to make it difficult for women to compete effectively in the corporate and professional world.

CIVIL RIGHTS: BEYOND EQUAL PROTECTION

As noted earlier, the Civil Rights Act of 1964 prohibited discrimination against any person on the basis of race, color, national origin, religion, or gender. The act also established the right to equal opportunity in employment. A basic problem remained, however: minority groups and women, because of past discrimination, often lacked the education and skills to compete effectively in the marketplace. In 1965, the federal government attempted to remedy this problem by implementing the concept of affirmative action. **Affirmative action** policies give special preferences in educational admissions and employment decisions to groups that have been discriminated against in the past.

Affirmative action policies, by giving special treatment to some groups and not others in an attempt to "level the playing field," go beyond a strict interpretation of the equal protection clause of the Fourteenth Amendment. So do a number of other laws and programs established by the government during and since the 1960s. In 1967, Congress passed legislation designed to assist older Americans in the workplace, who traditionally have suffered from discriminatory treatment. In 1990, Congress enacted a law mandating that the needs of persons with disabilities be

---

[12]According to some observers, this nationwide, "average" figure is misleading. For example, Diana Furchtgott-Roth, a journalist for the *Washington Post*, argues that if you compare "women who are in the same jobs as men, who have the same qualifications, and who don't cut back on their time in the work force because of child-rearing," women earn about the same as men—about 95 cents on the dollar. See Diana Furchtgott-Roth, "This Pay Gap Is a Phony," *The Washington Post*, January 31, 2000, p. A19.

accommodated in all public facilities as well as in the workplace. Some state and local governments have passed special laws protecting the rights of yet another group—gay males and lesbians.

Affirmative Action

In 1965, President Lyndon Johnson ordered that affirmative action policies be undertaken to remedy the effects of past discrimination. All government agencies, including those of state and local governments, were required to implement such policies. Additionally, affirmative action requirements were imposed on companies that sell goods or services to the federal government and on institutions that receive federal funds. Affirmative action policies were also required whenever an employer had been ordered to develop such a plan by a court or by the Equal Employment Opportunity Commission because of evidence of past discrimination. Finally, labor unions that had been found to discriminate against women or minorities in the past were required to establish and follow affirmative action plans.

Affirmative action programs have been controversial because they sometimes result in **reverse discrimination**—discrimination against majority groups, such as white males—or discrimination against other minority groups that may not be given preferential treatment under a particular affirmative action program. At issue in the current debate over affirmative action programs is whether such programs, because of their inherently discriminatory nature, violate the equal protection clause of the Fourteenth Amendment to the Constitution.

The *Bakke* Case. An early case addressing this issue involved an affirmative action program implemented by the University of California at Davis. Allan Bakke, a Vietnam War veteran and engineer who had been turned down for medical school at the Davis campus of the University of California, discovered that his academic record was better than those of some of the minority applicants who had been admitted to the program. He sued the University of California regents, alleging *reverse discrimination*. The UC–Davis Medical School had held sixteen places out of one hundred for educationally "disadvantaged students" each year, and the administrators at that campus admitted to using race as a criterion for admission for these particular minority slots. At trial, Bakke said that his exclusion from medical school violated his rights under the Fourteenth Amendment's provision for equal protection of the laws.

In 1978, the Supreme Court handed down its decision in *Regents of the University of California v. Bakke.*[13] The Court held that Bakke must be admitted to the UC–Davis Medical School because its admission policy had used race as the sole criterion for the sixteen "minority" positions. According to the Court, race could be one of many criteria for admission, but not the only one. So affirmative action programs, but not specific quota systems, were upheld as constitutional.

---

[13]438 U.S. 265 (1978).

Further Limitations on Affirmative Action. A number of cases decided during the 1980s and 1990s placed even further limits on affirmative action programs. In a landmark 1995 decision in *Adarand Constructors, Inc. v. Peña*,[14] the Supreme Court held that any federal, state, or local affirmative action program that uses racial or ethnic classifications as the basis for making decisions is subject to "strict scrutiny" by the courts. Under a strict-scrutiny analysis, to be constitutional, a discriminatory law or action must be narrowly tailored to meet a *compelling* government interest. In effect, the Court's opinion in *Adarand* means that an affirmative action program cannot make use of quotas or preferences for unqualified persons, and once the program has succeeded, it must be changed or dropped.

In 1996, a federal appellate court went even further. In *Hopwood v. State of Texas*,[15] two white law school applicants sued the University of Texas School of Law in Austin, alleging that they were denied admission because of the school's affirmative action program. The program allowed admissions officials to take race and other factors into consideration when determining which students would be admitted. The federal appellate court held that the program violated the equal protection clause because it discriminated in favor of minority applicants. Significantly, the court directly challenged the *Bakke* decision by stating that the use of race even as a means of achieving diversity on college campuses "undercuts the Fourteenth Amendment." The Supreme Court declined to hear the case, thus letting the lower court's decision stand.

State Ballot Initiatives. In 1996, by a ballot initiative known as Proposition 209, a majority of California voters approved a constitutional amendment that ended all state-sponsored affirmative action programs in that state. The law was immediately challenged in court by civil rights groups and others. These groups claimed that the law violated the Fourteenth Amendment by denying racial minorities and women the equal protection of the law. In 1997, however, a federal appellate court upheld the constitutionality of the amendment. Thus, affirmative action is now illegal in California in all state-sponsored institutions, including state agencies and educational institutions. Washington voters also approved a law banning affirmative action programs in 1998.

Special Protection for Older Americans

Americans are getting older. In colonial times, about half the population was under the age of sixteen. In 1990, the number of people under the age of sixteen was fewer than one in four, and half were thirty-three or older. By the year 2050, at least half could be thirty-nine or older. Today, more than 34 million Americans (over 12 percent of the population) are aged sixty-five or over. As can be seen in Figure 5.1 on the next page, by the year 2020, this figure is projected to reach about 53 million. Senior citizens face a variety of problems unique to their group. One problem that

---

[14]515 U.S. 200 (1995).
[15]84 F.3d 720 (5th Cir. 1996).

FIGURE 5.1

Population Projections: Persons Aged 65 or Older (in Millions)
As shown here, the number of Americans who will be sixty-five years of age or older will grow
dramatically during the next decade. The number will nearly double between 2005 and 2050. The
political power of these older Americans will increase as their numbers increase.

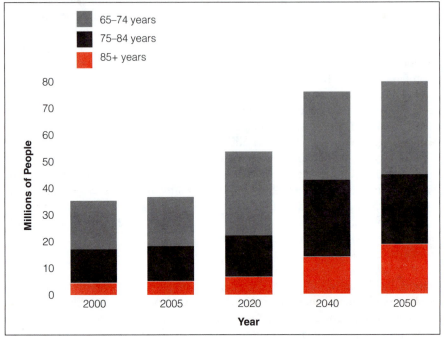

SOURCE: U.S. Department of Commerce, *Statistical Abstract of the United States* (Washington, D.C.: U.S. Government Printing Office, 1999), p. 17.

seems to endure, despite government legislation designed to prevent it, is age discrimination in employment. Others include health care and income security, topics tht we will discuss in Chapter 13.

Age discrimination is potentially the most widespread form of discrimination, because anyone—regardless of race, color, national origin, or gender—could be a victim at some point in life. The unstated policies of some companies not to hire or to demote or dismiss people they feel are "too old" have made it difficult for some older workers to succeed in their jobs or continue with their careers. Additionally, older workers have fallen victim at times to cost-cutting efforts by employers. To reduce operational costs, companies may replace older, higher-salaried workers with younger, lower-salaried workers.

In an attempt to protect older employees from such discriminatory practices, Congress passed the Age Discrimination in Employment Act (ADEA) in 1967. The act, which applies to employers, employment agencies, and labor organizations and covers individuals over the age of forty, prohibits discrimination against individuals on the basis of age. Specifically, it is against the law to discriminate by age in wages, benefits, hours worked, or availability of overtime. Employers and unions may not discriminate in providing fringe benefits, such as education or training programs, career development, sick leave, and vacations.

To succeed in a suit for age discrimination, an employee must prove that the employer's action, such as a decision to fire the employee, was motivated, at least in part, by age bias. Proof that qualified older employees are generally discharged before younger employees or that co-workers continually made unflattering age-related comments about the discharged worker may be enough. Even if an older worker is replaced by a younger worker falling under the protection of the ADEA—that is, by a younger worker who is also over the age of forty—the older worker is entitled to bring a suit under the ADEA. In all ADEA cases, the issue is whether age discrimination has in fact occurred, regardless of the age of the replacement worker.

In early 2000, the Supreme Court limited the ADEA's applicability somewhat in its decision in *Kimel v. Florida Board of Regents.*[16] The Court held that the sovereign immunity granted the states by the Eleventh Amendment precluded suits against them by private parties alleging violations of the ADEA. According to the Court, Congress had exceeded its constitutional authority when it included in the ADEA a provision stating that "all employers," includig state employers, were subject to the act. As a result of this decision, state employees, in effect, no longer fall under the protection of the ADEA.

Securing Rights for Persons with Disabilities

Like older Americans, persons with disabilities did not fall under the protective umbrella of the Civil Rights Act of 1964. Remember from earlier in this chapter that the 1964 act prohibited discrimination against any person on the basis of race, color, national origin, religion, or gender. As just noted, Congress addressed the problem of age discrimination in 1967. By the 1970s, Congress also began to pass legislation to protect Americans with disabilities. In 1973, Congress passed the Rehabilitation Act, which prohibited discrimination against persons with disabilities in programs receiving federal aid. A 1978 amendment to the act established the Architectural and Transportation Barriers Compliance Board. Regulations for ramps, elevators, and the like in all federal buildings were implemented. Congress passed the Education for All Handicapped Children Act in 1975. It guarantees that all children with disabilities will receive an "appropriate" education. The most significant federal legislation with respect to the rights of persons with disabilities, however, is the Americans with Disabilities Act (ADA), which Congress passed in 1990.

The ADA requires that all public buildings and public services be accessible to persons with disabilities. The act also mandates that employers must reasonably accommodate the needs of workers or potential workers with disabilities. Physical access means ramps; handrails; wheelchair-accessible restrooms, counters, drinking fountains, telephones, and doorways; and more accessible mass transit. In addition,

---

[16]120 S.Ct. 145 (2000).

other steps must be taken to comply with the act. Car-rental companies must provide cars with hand controls for disabled drivers. Telephone companies are required to have operators to pass on messages from speech-impaired persons who use telephones with keyboards.

The ADA requires employers to "reasonably accommodate" the needs of persons with disabilities unless to do so would cause the employer to suffer an "undue hardship." The ADA defines persons with disabilities as persons who have physical or mental impairments that "substantially limit" their everyday activities. Health conditions that have been considered disabilities under federal law include blindness, alcoholism, heart disease, cancer, muscular dystrophy, cerebral palsy, paraplegia, diabetes, acquired immune deficiency syndrome (AIDS), and, most recently, the human immunodeficiency virus (HIV) that causes AIDS.

The ADA does not require that *unqualified* applicants with disabilities be hired or retained. If a job applicant or an employee with a disability, with reasonable accommodation, can perform essential job functions, however, then the employer must make the accommodation. Required accommodations may include installing ramps for a wheelchair, establishing more flexible working hours, creating or modifying job assignments, and creating or improving training materials and procedures.

The Rights and Status of Gay Males and Lesbians

On June 27, 1969, patrons of the Stonewall Inn, a New York City bar popular with gays and lesbians, responded to a police raid by throwing beer cans and bottles because they were angry at what they felt was unrelenting police harassment. In the ensuing riot, which lasted two nights, hundreds of gays and lesbians fought with police. Before Stonewall, the stigma attached to homosexuality and the resulting fear of exposure had tended to keep most gays and lesbians quiescent. In the months immediately after Stonewall, however, "gay power" graffiti began to appear in New York City. The Gay Liberation Front and the Gay Activist Alliance were formed, and similar groups sprang up in other parts of the country. Thus, Stonewall has been called "the shot heard round the homosexual world."

The Stonewall incident marked the beginning of the movement for gay and lesbian rights. Since then, gay men and lesbians have formed thousands of organizations to exert pressure on legislatures, the media, schools, churches, and other organizations to recognize their right to equal treatment. One of the largest gay rights groups today is the Human Rights Campaign Fund, whose goal is to see federal gay rights laws passed. The American Civil Liberties Union also actively promotes laws protecting gays and lesbians, as do several other liberal civil rights organizations.

Prior to the Stonewall incident in 1969, forty-nine states had sodomy laws (Illinois, which had repealed its sodomy law in 1962, was the only exception). During the 1970s and 1980s, more than half of these laws were either repealed or

---

[17]California, Connecticut, Hawaii, Massachusetts, Minnesota, New Hampshire, New Jersey, Rhode Island, Vermont, and Wisconsin. Maine also had a law protecting gay and lesbian rights until February 1998, when the law was repealed in a referendum.

struck down by the courts. Several state and local governments have gone further in their efforts to protect gay and lesbian rights. Today, ten states[17] and 165 cities and counties have special laws protecting lesbians and gay men against discrimination in employment, housing, public accommodations, and credit.

In a 1996 case, *Romer v. Evans*,[18] the Supreme Court issued a decision that had a significant impact on the rights of gays and lesbians. The case involved a Colorado state constitutional amendment that invalidated all existing state and local laws protecting homosexuals from discrimination. The Supreme Court held that the amendment violated the equal protection clause of the Constitution because it denied to homosexuals in Colorado—but to no other Colorado residents—"the right to seek specific protection of the law." The Court stated that the equal protection clause simply does not permit Colorado to make homosexuals "unequal to everyone else." Despite the *Romer* decision, in 1998 the Supreme Court declined to review an appellate court decision that left standing an anti-gay amendment to the charter of Cincinnati.

To a great extent, lesbian and gay groups have succeeded in changing public opinion—and state and local laws—relating to their status and rights. Nevertheless, they continue to struggle against age-old biases against homosexuality, often rooted in deeply held religious beliefs, and the rights of gay men and lesbians remain an extremely divisive issue in American society. (See this chapter's *At Issue: Marriage Rights for Gays and Lesbians?* on page 112 for a discussion of perhaps one of the most sensitive issues with respect to the rights of gay and lesbian couples—whether they should have the right to legally marry.)

INFOTRAC®

"Courting Gay Vote"

[18]517 U.S. 620 (1996).

Gay men and lesbians demonstrate in New York City's Bryant Park in favor of same-sex marriages. They want the state of New York to legalize such marriages.

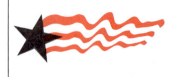

Marriage Rights for Gays and Lesbians?

Do gay and lesbian couples have the right to be legally married? Do laws banning such marriages violate the equal protection clause of the U.S. Constitution or state constitutional provisions guaranteeing equal rights? The controversy over this issue was fueled in 1993 when the Hawaii Supreme Court ruled that denying marriage licenses to gay couples might violate the equal protection clause of the Hawaii constitution. The court stated that unless Hawaii could offer a "compelling" reason for maintaining this discriminatory practice, it must be abandoned. The Hawaii Supreme Court then sent the case back to the trial court to determine if the state did indeed have a compelling reason. In 1996, the trial court ruled that the state had failed to meet this burden, and therefore the ban on same-sex marriages violated the state constitution.

In the wake of these events, other states began to worry about whether they would have to treat persons who were legally married in Hawaii as married couples in their states as well. Opponents of gay rights pushed for state laws banning same-sex marriages, and a number of states enacted such laws. At the federal level, Congress passed the Defense of Marriage Act of 1996, which bans federal recognition of lesbian and gay couples and allows state governments to ignore same-sex mar-

riages performed in other states. Ironically, the Hawaii court decisions that gave rise to these concerns have largely come to naught. In 1998, the residents in that state voted for a state constitutional amendment that allows the Hawaii legislature to ban same-sex marriages.

More recently, developments in Vermont have ignited further controversy. In 1999, the Vermont Supreme Court ruled that gay couples are entitled to the same benefits of marriage as opposite-sex couples. The unanimous ruling interpreted the state constitution's "Common Benefits Clause," which is similar to the U.S. Constitution's equal protection clause. The court said that it was up to the legislature to implement the decision. According to the court, the legislature may allow gay couples to marry, or it may allow them to register as "domestic partners," as long as they have all of the same rights and benefits as married couples have.* The Vermont legislature then enacted a historic law, in April 2000, that allowed gay couples to form "civil unions" that would entitle them to some three hundred state benefits available to married couples.

Polling data show that although a strong majority of Americans believe in equal political and economic rights for gays

*Baker v. State, 744 A.2d 864 (Vt. 1999).

and lesbians, only about 30 to 35 percent support legally sanctioned marriages for these groups. For example, surveys show that about 83 percent of Americans believe that gay and lesbian civil rights should be protected and that the government has not gone far enough to protect these rights. Between 57 and 59 percent of Americans also state that gay and lesbian spouses should be entitled to certain benefits received by heterosexual spouses—including inheritance rights, Social Security benefits, and job-related benefits, such as health insurance.[†]

Clearly, over the last several decades lesbian and gay groups have succeeded in bringing about significant changes in public opinion—and state and local laws— relating to their status and rights. Yet Americans seem reluctant to take the further step of extending symbolic equality to gays and lesbians with respect to the institution of marriage and the family.

FOR CRITICAL ANALYSIS

Would laws permitting gay and lesbian couples to be legally married help to establish family values and more stable relationships among these groups?

[†]Based on surveys reported in *Public Perspective,* January/February 2000, pp. 22–31.

KEY TERMS

affirmative action 105

busing 98

civil rights 92

de facto segregation 97

de jure segregation 98

Equal Employment
Opportunity Commission 100

gender discrimination 104

grandfather clause 95

literacy test 96

poll tax 95

reverse discrimination 106

separate-but-equal
doctrine 95

sexual harassment 104

white primary 95

CHAPTER SUMMARY

1 The civil rights movement started with the struggle by African Americans for equality. Before the Civil War, African Americans were slaves, and slavery was protected by the Constitution and the Supreme Court. African Americans were not considered citizens or entitled to the rights and privileges of citizenship. In 1863 and during the years after the Civil War, the Emancipation Proclamation and the Thirteenth, Fourteenth, and Fifteenth Amendments (the "Civil War amendments") legally and constitutionally ended slavery. From 1865 to 1875, to enforce the Civil War amendments, Congress passed a number of laws (civil rights acts). African Americans gained citizenship, the right to vote, equality before the law, and protection from deprivation of these rights.

2 Politically and socially, African American inequality continued. The *Civil Rights Cases* (1883) and *Plessy v. Ferguson* (1896) effectively nullified the civil rights acts of 1865 to 1875. In the *Civil Rights Cases*, the Supreme Court held that the Fourteenth Amendment did not apply to private invasions of individual rights. In *Plessy*, the Court upheld the separate-but-equal doctrine, declaring that segregation did not violate the Constitution. African Americans were excluded from the voting process through poll taxes, grandfather clauses, white primaries, and literacy tests.

3 Legal segregation was declared unconstitutional by the Supreme Court in *Brown v. Board of Education of Topeka* (1954), in which the Court

stated that separation implied inferiority. In *Brown v. Board of Education* (1955), the Supreme Court ordered federal courts to ensure that public schools were desegregated "with all deliberate speed." Segregationists resisted with legal tactics, violence, and "white flight." Integrationists responded with court orders, federal marshals, and busing. The civil rights movement began with a boycott of segregated public transportation in Montgomery, Alabama.

4 The Civil Rights Act of 1964 has had particular impact. The act bans discrimination on the basis of race, color, religion, gender, or national origin in employment and public accommodations. The act created the Equal Employment Opportunity Commission to administer the act. The Voting Rights Act of 1965 outlawed discriminatory voter-registration tests and authorized federal registration of persons and federally administered procedures in any state or political subdivision evidencing electoral discrimination or low registration rates. Subsequent amendments to this act extended its protections to other minorities. As a result of the Voting Rights Act, its amendments, and federal registration drives, African American political participation increased dramatically.

5 The protective legislation passed during and since the 1960s applies not only to African Americans but to other ethnic groups as well. Other minorities have also been increasingly represented in national and state politics, although they have yet to gain representation proportionate to their numbers in the U.S. population.

6 In the early history of the United States, women were considered citizens, but by and large they had no political rights. After the first women's rights convention in 1848, the women's movement gained momentum. Women's organizations continued to work toward the goal of the enfranchisement of women. In 1920, when the Nineteenth Amendment was ratified, women finally obtained the right to vote.

7 The modern women's movement began in the 1960s in the wake of the civil rights movement. The National Organization for Women (NOW) was formed in 1966 to bring about complete equality for women in all walks of life. Although women have found it difficult to gain positions of political leadership, their numbers in Congress and in state and local government bodies increased significantly in the 1990s.

8 Women continue to struggle against gender discrimination in the employment context. Federal government efforts to eliminate gender discrimination in the workplace include Title VII of the Civil Rights Act of 1964, which prohibits, among other things, gender-based discrimination. The Supreme Court has upheld the right of women to be free from sexual harassment on the job. Wage discrimination also continues to be a problem for women, as does the "glass ceiling" that prevents them from rising to the top of their business or professional firms.

9 Affirmative action programs have been controversial because they can lead to reverse discrimination against majority groups or even other minority groups. In an early case on the issue, *Regents of the University of California v. Bakke* (1978), the Supreme Court held that using race as the sole criterion for admission to a university is improper. Since *Bakke* a number of Supreme Court decisions have further limited affirmative action programs. Recent Supreme Court decisions, particularly *Adarand Constructors, Inc. v.*

Peña, and decisions by the lower courts that the Supreme Court has let stand, such as *Hopwood v. State of Texas*, have led some observers to conclude that it will be difficult in the future for any affirmative action program to pass constitutional muster. California voters banned state-sponsored affirmative action in that state in a 1996 ballot initiative known as Proposition 209, which was upheld as constitutional by a federal appellate court. Washington voters also rejected affirmative action in a ballot initiative.

10 Problems associated with aging and retirement are becoming increasingly important as the number of older persons in the United States increases. Many older Americans have lost their jobs due to age bias and cost-cutting efforts by business firms. The Age Discrimination in Employment Act of 1967 prohibits job-related discrimination against individuals over the age of forty on the basis of age, unless age is shown to be a bona fide occupational qualification reasonably necessary to the normal operation of the business.

11 In 1973, Congress passed the Rehabilitation Act, which prohibits discrimination against persons with disabilities in programs receiving federal aid. The Americans with Disabilities Act of 1990 prohibits job discrimination against persons with physical and mental disabilities, requiring that positive steps be taken to comply with the act's requirements. The act also requires expanded access to public facilities, including transportation, and to services offered by such private concerns as car-rental and telephone companies.

12 Gay and lesbian rights groups, which first began to form in 1969, now number in the thousands. These groups work to promote laws protecting gay men and lesbians from discrimination and to repeal anti-gay laws. Gay men and lesbians increasingly are protected by laws against discrimination. A controversial issue today is whether gay and lesbian couples should have the right to legally marry.

SELECTED PRINT AND ELECTRONIC RESOURCES

Suggested Readings

Lawrence, Charles R., III, and Mari J. Matsuda. *We Won't Go Back: Making the Case for Affirmative Action.* St. Charles, Ill.: Houghton Mifflin, 1997. The authors look at how affirmative action policies have benefited people. They focus on the human side of the debate over this divisive issue and include a variety of stories showing how these policies have affected the everyday lives of numerous Americans.

McGlen, Nancy E., and Karen O'Connor. *Women, Politics, and American Society.* 2d ed. Upper Saddle River, N.J.: Prentice Hall, 1998. This is an excellent history of the women's movement in the United States.

Roemer, John E. *Equality of Opportunity.* Cambridge, Mass.: Harvard University Press, 1998. Roemer examines the two positions in the affirmative action debate and concludes that both emphasize equal opportunity; they differ over whether equal opportunity should be required before or after the competition (such as for jobs) starts.

Woodward, C. Vann. *The Strange Career of Jim Crow.* New York: Oxford University Press, 1957. This is the classic study of segregation in the southern United States.

Media Resources

Affirmative Action: The History of an Idea—This program explores the historical roots of affirmative action and the current debate over its usefulness.

Beyond the Glass Ceiling—A CNN-produced program showing the difficulties women face in trying to rise to the top in corporate America.

Dr. Martin Luther King: A Historical Perspective—One of the best documentaries on the civil rights movement, focusing on the life and times of Martin Luther King, Jr.

Frederick Douglass—A documentary about the man who escaped slavery to become a world-famous orator, journalist, diplomat, abolitionist, and civil rights advocate in the mid-1800s.

Separate but Equal—A video focusing on Thurgood Marshall, the lawyer (and later Supreme Court justice) who took the struggle for equal rights to the Supreme Court, and on the rise and demise of segregation in America.

LOGGING ON

There are an incredible number of resources on the World Wide Web relating to civil rights—and particularly the problem of discrimination. One of the most active and visible civil rights organizations today is the American Civil Liberties Union. You can access its Web site at

http://www.aclu.org

An extensive collection of information on Martin Luther King, Jr., is offered by the Martin Luther King Papers Project at Stanford University. If you wish to check out these papers, go to

http://www.stanford.edu/group/King

If you are interested in learning more about the Equal Employment Opportunity Commission (EEOC) or want to find out how to file a complaint with that agency, go to

http://www.eeoc.gov

The National Association for the Advancement of Colored People (NAACP) is online at

http://www.naacp.org

For information on the League of Latin American Citizens (LULAC), go to

http://www.mundo.com/lulac.html

The URL for Women's Web World, which provides information on empowerment and equality for women, is

http://www.feminist.org

The Center for the American Woman and Politics maintains up-to-date records and files on women in political office and other facts about women's participation in politics. You can access its collection of fact sheets and files at

http://www.rci.rutgers.edu/~cawp

An excellent source for the most recent legal cases involving the rights of gays and lesbians is that of the Lambda Society at

http://www.lambdalegal.org

The National Organization for Women (NOW) offers online information and updates on the status of women's rights, including affirmative action cases involving women. Go to

http://www.now.org

You can find information on the Americans with Disabilities Act (ADA) of 1990, including the act's text, at

http://janweb.icdi.wvu.edu/kinder

USING THE INTERNET FOR POLITICAL ANALYSIS

Imagine that you are the owner of a new franchise business and are hiring your first employees. Several of the applicants are over the age of sixty-five, and one of them tells you that she has impaired hearing but has a good hearing aid to assist her.

Using one of the Web sites given in the next column, look up Labor and Employment Law and develop some guidelines for your hiring practices that will not violate laws prohibiting discrimination against older Americans and workers with disabilities. Consider the information that you find on the Web. To what extent would you rely on this information when you write an employ-

ment manual? What other resources might you also check?

FindLaw, at
http://www.findlaw.com

U.S. House of Representatives Law Library, at
http://law.house.gov

Legal Resource Guide, at
http://www.ilrg.com

PART TWO

THE
POLITICS
OF DEMOCRACY

CHAPTER 6

Public Opinion, Political Socialization, and the Media

Public opinion polls can give voice to the preferences of the people between elections. Public opinion, whether expressed through scientifically conducted opinion polls or directly over the Internet, can reflect the public's views on specific policy actions in a way that elections cannot. What role, then, does public opinion play in the changing American political system? Is it truly the voice of the people, or is it an instrument to be manipulated by politicians and interest groups? Can political leaders count on public opinion to provide guidance on their actions, or are the results of most opinion polls too ephemeral to be useful?

The very character of public opinion polls may limit their usefulness. After all, the pollster wrote the questions, called the respondents, and perhaps forwarded the results to the politicians. Public opinion, as gathered by polls, is not equivalent to constituents' letters to their representatives or to ballots cast in an election. In fact, polls may be flawed in a number of ways, as you will read later in this chapter. Nonetheless, polls have become a frequent component of the political and judicial process.

HOW POWERFUL IS PUBLIC OPINION?

At various times in the recent history of the United States, public opinion has played a powerful role in presidential politics. Beginning in 1965, public opinion became strongly divided over the Vietnam War (1964–1975). Numerous public expressions of opposition to the war took place, as measured by the polls and demonstrations in many cities. By 1968, when President Lyndon Johnson was preparing to run for another term, public opinion against the war was expressed through a surge of support for antiwar candidate Senator Eugene McCarthy in the New Hampshire primary. Faced with public disapproval, Johnson dropped out of the race.

Public opinion also played a significant role during President Richard Nixon's administration as the scandal surrounding the **Watergate break-in** unfolded. The scandal had to do with the 1972 illegal entry into the Democratic National Committee offices by participants in Nixon's reelection campaign. When Nixon's role was discovered, through congressional hearings and tape recordings from his office, a groundswell of opinion against the president occurred. In this case, the disastrous fall in Nixon's approval ratings to less than 25 percent coincided with the decision by the House Judiciary Committee to initiate impeachment proceedings against the president. Nixon, facing an impeachment trial, resigned from office in 1974.

Public opinion polls also can be seen as a measure of a president's strength. As charges about his personal life were debated openly in the media, President

Clinton's presidential approval rating climbed to the highest point in his presidency. Public approval of the president remained high throughout the impeachment proceedings and trial. It appeared that the public approved the president's job performance in part due to the strong economy. At the same time, public opinion polls showed a steady decline in the public's appraisal of President Clinton's character.

In most situations, legislators, politicians, and presidents use public opinion to shore up their own arguments. It provides a kind of evidence for their own point of view. If the results of polls do not support their positions, they can either commission their own polls or ignore the polls. Politicians find it more difficult to use public opinion on complex issues, such as changes in Medicare or welfare reform, because such complicated issues cannot be discussed fully in a poll. People will give opinions when asked, but poll questions do not really provide the opportunity for discussion and dialogue. Public opinion is more likely to be unfavorable when it comes to the use of troops overseas, but presidents who are able to limit the casualties among American troops sent on a military mission have much more freedom from the constraints of public opinion. President Clinton was able to secure such freedom with the almost casualty-free missions of American troops in both Haiti and Bosnia. Public opinion, then, is neither all powerful nor powerless.

DEFINING PUBLIC OPINION

There is no one public opinion, because there are many different "publics." In a nation of over 275 million people, there may be innumerable gradations of opinion on an issue. What we do is describe the distribution of opinions among the public about a particular question. Thus, we define public opinion as the aggregate of individual attitudes or beliefs shared by some portion of the adult population. Often, the public holds quite a range of opinions on a topic, making it difficult to discern what kinds of policies most Americans might support.

INFOTRAC®

"Public Opinion Toward Immigrants Immigration Policies"

How is public opinion made known in a democracy? In the case of the Vietnam War, it was made known by numerous antiwar protests, countless articles in magazines and newspapers, and continuing electronic media coverage of antiwar demonstrations. Normally, however, public opinion becomes known in a democracy through elections and, in some states, initiatives or referenda (discussed in Chapter 1). Other ways are through lobbying and interest group activities, which are also used to influence public opinion (see Chapter 7). In the age of the Internet, citizens increasingly are able to send their opinions to government officials electronically.

CONSENSUS AND DIVISION

There are very few issues on which most Americans agree. The more normal situation is for opinion to be distributed among several different positions. Looking at the distribution of opinion can tell us how divided the public is on a question and give us some indication of whether compromise is possible. The distribution of opinion can also tell us how many individuals have not thought enough about an issue to hold an opinion.

When a large proportion of the American public appears to express the same view on an issue, we say that a **consensus** exists, at least at the moment the poll was taken. Figure 6.1 shows the pattern of opinion that might be called consensual. Issues on which the public holds widely differing attitudes result in **divisive opinion** (Figure 6.2). If there is no possible middle position on such issues, we expect that the division will continue to generate political conflict.

Figure 6.3 shows a distribution of opinion indicating that most Americans either have no information about the issue or are not interested enough in the issue to formulate a position. Politicians may feel that the lack of knowledge gives them more room to maneuver, or they may be wary of taking any action for fear that opinion will crystallize after a crisis.

Public opinion can be defined most clearly by its effect. As political scientist V. O. Key, Jr., said, public opinion is what governments "find it prudent to heed."[1] This means that for public opinion to be effective, enough people have to hold a particular view with such strong conviction that a government feels its actions should be influenced by that view.

An interesting question arises as to when *private* opinion becomes *public* opinion. Everyone probably has a private opinion about the competence of the president, as well as private opinions about more personal concerns, such as the state of a neighbor's lawn. We say that private opinion becomes public opinion when the opinion is publicly expressed and if the opinion concerns public issues. When someone's private opinion becomes so strong that the individual is willing to go to the polls to vote

[1]V. O. Key, Jr., *Public Opinion and American Democracy* (New York: Knopf, 1961), p. 10.

FIGURE 6.1

Consensus Opinion
Question: Do you think it is morally acceptable to clone human beings?

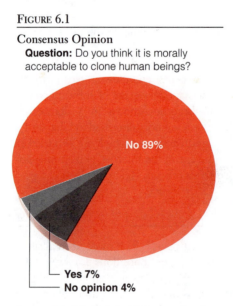

SOURCE: Survey by Yankelovich Partners, Inc., for *Time*/CNN, February 26–27, 1997.

FIGURE 6.2

Divisive Opinion
Question: Do you think it would be a good thing or a bad thing for the tobacco companies in this country to be driven out of business by a lawsuit?

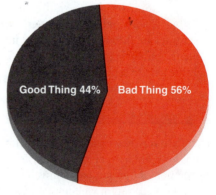

SOURCE: Gallup Organization for CNN/USA *Today*, May 6–7, 1997.

for or against a candidate or an issue—or is willing to participate in a demonstration, to discuss the issue at work, to speak out on local television or a radio talk show, or to participate in the political process in any one of a dozen other ways—then that opinion becomes public opinion.

MEASURING PUBLIC OPINION: POLLING TECHNIQUES

Although some idea of public opinion can be discovered by asking persons we know for their opinions or by reading the "Letters to the Editor" sections in newspapers, most descriptions of the distribution of opinions are based on **opinion polls.** An opinion poll is a method of systematically questioning a small, selected sample of respondents who are deemed representative of the total population. Opinion polls are widely used by government, business, university scholars, political candidates, and voluntary groups to provide reasonably accurate data on public attitudes, beliefs, expectations, and behavior.

During the 1800s, certain American newspapers and magazines spiced up their political coverage by doing face-to-face straw polls (unofficial polls indicating the trend of political opinion) or mail surveys of their readers' opinions. In the twentieth century, the magazine *Literary Digest* further developed the technique of opinion polls by mailing large numbers of questionnaires

FIGURE 6.3

Nonopinion

Question: Will it be good or bad for the United States if China becomes a member of the World Trade Organization?

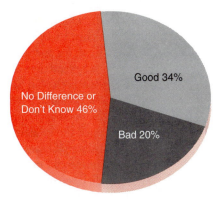

SOURCE: Survey by the Pew Center for the People and the Press, February 9–14, 2000.

Union members protest a cut in benefits. A strike can be seen as an expression of public opinion, but if the union does not get support from others, politicians will feel little effect.

to individuals, many of whom were its own subscribers. From 1916 to 1936, more than 70 percent of the magazine's election predictions were accurate.

Literary Digest's polling activities suffered a major setback in 1936, however, when the magazine predicted, based on more than two million returned questionnaires, that Republican candidate Alfred Landon would win over Democratic candidate Franklin D. Roosevelt. Landon won in only two states. A major problem with the *Digest's* polling technique was its continuing use of nonrepresentative respondents. In 1936, at the bottom of the Great Depression, the magazine's subscribers were, for one thing, considerably more affluent than the average American.

Several newcomers to the public opinion poll industry accurately predicted Roosevelt's landslide victory. The organizations of these newcomers are still active in the poll-taking industry today: the Gallup poll of George Gallup, and the Roper poll founded by Elmo Roper. Gallup and Roper, along with Archibald Crossley, developed the modern polling techniques of market research. Using personal interviews with small samples of selected voters (less than a few thousand), they showed that they could predict with accuracy the behavior of the total voting population. We shall see how this is possible.

Sampling Techniques

How can interviewing fewer than two thousand voters tell us what tens of millions of voters will do? Clearly, it is necessary that the sample of individuals be representative of all voters in the population.

The most important principle in sampling, or poll taking, is randomness. Every person should have a known chance, and especially an *equal chance,* of being sampled. If this happens, then a small sample should be representative of the whole group, both in demographic characteristics (age, religion, race, living area, and the like) and in opinions. The ideal way to sample the voting population of the United States would be to put all voter names into a jar—or a computer—and randomly sample, say, two thousand of them. Because this is too costly and inefficient, pollsters have developed other ways to obtain good samples. One of the most interesting techniques is simply to choose a random selection of telephone numbers and interview the respective households. This technique produces a relatively accurate sample at a low cost.

To ensure that the random samples include respondents from relevant segments of the population—rural, urban, Northeast, South, and so on—most survey organizations randomly choose, say, urban areas that they will consider as representative of all urban areas. Then they randomly select their respondents within those areas. A generally less accurate technique is known as *quota sampling.* For this type of poll, survey researchers decide how many persons of certain types they need in the survey—such as minorities, women, or farmers—and then send out interviewers to find the necessary number of these types. This method is often not only less accurate, but it also may be biased if, say, the interviewer refuses to go into certain neighborhoods or will not interview after dark.

Generally, the national survey organizations take great care to select their samples randomly, because their reputations rest on the accuracy of their results. Usually, the Gallup or Roper polls interview about 1,500 individuals, and their results have a very high probability of being correct—within a margin of 3 percent.

Similar sampling techniques are used in many other, nonpolitical situations. For the Nielsen ratings of television programs, for example, representative households

INFOTRAC®

"Iowa Clears Throat"

INFOTRAC®

"Sampling External Validity"

are selected by the A. C. Nielsen Company, and a machine is attached to each household's television set. The machine monitors viewing choices twenty-four hours a day and transmits this information to the company's central offices. A one-point drop in a Nielsen rating can mean a loss of revenue of millions of dollars to a television network. A one-point drop indicates that about 800,000 fewer viewers are watching a particular show. As a result, advertisers are unwilling to pay as much for viewing time. Indeed, in many cases advertising rates are based solely on Nielsen ratings. When you consider that only about three thousand families have that little machine attached to their television sets, it is apparent that the science of selecting representative samples has come a long way—at least far enough to convince major advertisers to accept advertising fees based on the results of those samples.

Problems with Polls

Public opinion polls are, as noted above, snapshots of the opinions and preferences of the people at a specific moment in time and as expressed in response to a specific question. Given that definition, it is fairly easy to understand situations in which the polls are wrong. For example, opinion polls leading up to the 1980 presidential election showed President Jimmy Carter defeating challenger Ronald Reagan. Only a few analysts noted the large number of "undecided" respondents to poll questions a week before the election. Those voters shifted massively to Reagan at the last minute, and Reagan won the election.

The famous photo of Harry Truman showing the front page that declared his defeat is another tribute to the weakness of polling. Again, the poll that predicted his defeat was taken more than a week before election day.

President Harry S. Truman holds up the front page of the Chicago Daily Tribune *issue that predicted his defeat on the basis of a Gallup poll. The poll had indicated that Truman would lose the 1948 contest for his reelection by a margin of 55.5 to 44.5 percent. Gallup's poll was completed more than two weeks before the election, so it missed the undecided voters. Truman won the election with 49.9 percent of the vote.*

Polls may also report erroneous results because the pool of respondents was not chosen in a scientific manner. That is, the form of sampling and the number of people sampled may be too small to overcome sampling error, which is the difference between the sample results and the true result if the entire population had been interviewed. The sample would be biased, for example, if the poll interviewed people by telephone and did not correct for the fact that more women than men answer the telephone and that some populations (college students and very poor individuals, for example) cannot be found so easily by telephone. Unscientific mail-in polls, telephone call-in polls, and polls completed by the workers in a campaign office are usually biased and do not give an accurate picture of the public's views.

As poll takers get close to election day, they become even more concerned about their sample of respondents. Some pollsters continue to interview eligible voters, meaning those over eighteen and registered to vote. Many others use a series of questions in the poll and other weighting methods to try to identify "likely voters" so that they can be more accurate in their election-eve predictions. When a poll changes its method from reporting the views of eligible voters to reporting those of likely voters, the results are likely to change dramatically.

Finally, it makes sense to expect that the results of a poll will depend on the questions that are asked. Depending on what question is asked, voters could be said either to support a particular proposal or to oppose it. Furthermore, respondents' answers are also influenced by the order in which questions are asked, by the types of answers they are allowed to choose, and, in some cases, by their interaction with the interviewer. To some extent, people try to please the interviewer. They answer questions about which they have no information and avoid some answers to try to measure up to the interviewer's expectations. Most recently, some campaigns have been using "push polls," in which the respondents are given misleading information in the questions asked to get them to vote against a candidate. Obviously, the answers given are likely to be influenced by such techniques. For a further discussion of push polls, see this chapter's *At Issue: Polls That Mislead.*

PUBLIC OPINION AND THE POLITICAL PROCESS

Surveys of public opinion, no matter what fascinating questions they ask or how quickly they get the answers, are not equivalent to elections in the United States. Because not all Americans are equally interested in politics or equally informed, public opinion polls can suggest only the general distribution of opinion on issues. Many times, only a few citizens have formulated preferences, and these preferences will be changed by events.

Politicians, whether in office or in the midst of a campaign, see public opinion as important to their careers. The president, members of Congress, governors, and other elected officials realize that strong support by the public as expressed in opinion polls is a source of power in dealing with other politicians. It is far more difficult for a senator to say no to the president if the president is immensely popular and if polls show approval of the president's policies. Public opinion also helps political candidates identify the most important concerns among the public and may help them shape their campaigns successfully.

AT ISSUE

Polls That Mislead

Pollsters have long known that the wording of questions can influence the response that a person gives. Different question wordings can provoke extensive political debate about the actual preferences of the public. When President Clinton and the congressional Republicans were unable to resolve their differences over the budget for more than six months, Democrats were cheered by poll results that showed that the majority of Americans opposed "cutting funding for Medicare."

Republicans countered by showing poll results that indicated that many Americans supported "decreasing the growth in funding for Medicare." Both parties were depending on question wording for building a case for their own positions.

A far more deliberate use of question wording has surfaced recently in election campaigns. In the weeks before a primary or general election, voters are interviewed in what seems to be a legitimate poll. One or more of the questions in the poll, however, give the respondent false or misleading information about the opposing candidate in an effort to influence the respondent's vote.

Such surveys have become known as "push polls," because they are intended to push the voter to the candidate whose campaign sponsored the poll. Sometimes the information given in the question is simply misleading, but on other occasions it has been closer to scandal or gossip. In another variation, push polls can be used to start rumors about a candidate at a time very close to the election when rebuttal of the information is almost impossible.

The prevalence of push polling prior to the 1996 presidential elec-tions led to a statement by the American Association for Public Opinion Research condemning such polls and labeling them marketing ploys. It also led to the introduction of legislation in Virginia to regulate polls by requiring the disclosure of the candidate sponsoring the polls. Subsequently, both major political parties issued a statement saying that they would not engage in such polls. Similar tactics may also be used by polls about commercial products or any other topic, however. The ultimate result will be a further weakening of public confidence in any poll.

FOR CRITICAL ANALYSIS

How can you tell whether a survey question is worded "neutrally" or whether it might be biased toward a particular response?

Although opinion polls cannot give exact guidance on what the government should do in a specific instance, the opinions measured in polls do set an informal limit on government action. For example, consider the highly controversial issue of abortion. Most Americans are moderates on this issue; they do not approve of abortion as a means of birth control, but they do feel that it should be available under certain circumstances. Yet sizable groups of people express very intense feelings both for and against abortion. Given this distribution of opinion, most elected officials would rather not try to change policy to favor either of the extreme positions. To do so would clearly violate the opinion of the majority of Americans. In this case, as in many others, public opinion does not make public policy; rather, it restrains officials from taking truly unpopular actions. If officials do act in the face of public opposition, the consequences of such actions will be determined at the ballot box.

Political Culture and Public Opinion

Americans are divided into a multitude of ethnic, religious, regional, and political subgroups. In many cases, members of these groups hold a particular set of opinions about government policies, about the goals of the society, and about the rights of their group and the rights of others. Given the diversity of American society and the wide range of opinions contained within it, how is it that the political process continues to function without being stalemated by conflict and dissension?

One explanation is rooted in the concept of the American political culture, which can be described as a set of attitudes and ideas about the nation and the government. As discussed in Chapter 1, our political culture is widely shared by Americans of many different backgrounds. To some extent, it consists of symbols, such as the American flag, the Liberty Bell, and the Statue of Liberty. The elements of our political culture also include certain shared beliefs about the most important values in the American political system, including (1) liberty, equality, and property; (2) support for religion; and (3) community service and personal achievement. The structure of the government—particularly federalism, the political parties, the powers of Congress, and popular rule—have also been found to be important values.[2]

The political culture provides a general environment of support for the political system. If the people share certain beliefs about the system and a reservoir of good feeling exists toward the institutions of government, the nation will be better able to weather periods of crisis, such as Watergate. This foundation of goodwill may combat cynicism and increase the level of participation in elections as well. During the 1960s and 1970s, survey research consistently showed a steep decline in the overall level of **political trust**—the degree to which individuals express trust in the government and political institutions, usually measured through a specific series of survey questions. A considerable proportion of Americans seemed to feel that they could not trust government officials and that they could not count on officials to care about the ordinary person. This index of political trust reached an all-time low in 1994, reflecting Americans' cynicism about the government and election campaign tactics (see Table 6.1).

[2]Donald Devine, *Political Culture of the United States* (Boston: Little, Brown, 1972).

TABLE 6.1

Trends in Political Trust

QUESTION: HOW MUCH OF THE TIME DO YOU THINK YOU CAN TRUST THE GOVERNMENT IN WASHINGTON TO DO WHAT IS RIGHT—JUST ABOUT ALWAYS, MOST OF THE TIME, OR ONLY SOME OF THE TIME?

	1964	1968	1972	1974	1976	1978	1980	1982	1984	1986	1988	1990	1992	1994	1996	1998	1999
Percentage saying: Always/Most of the time	76	61	53	36	33	29	25	32	46	42	44	27	23	20	25	34	29
Some of the time	22	36	45	61	63	67	73	64	51	55	54	73	75	79	71	66	63

SOURCE: *New York Times*/CBS News Surveys; the University of Michigan Survey Research Center, National Election Studies; Pew Research Center for the People and the Press; Council for Excellence in Government, May–June 1999.

Public Opinion about Government

A vital component of public opinion in the United States is the considerable ambivalence with which the public regards many major national institutions. Table 6.2 shows trends in Gallup public opinion polls asking respondents, at regularly spaced intervals over time, how much confidence they had in the institutions listed. Over the years, military and religious organizations have ranked highest, but note the decline in confidence in churches following the numerous scandals involving television evangelists in the late 1980s. Note also the heightened regard for the military after the war in the Persian Gulf in 1991. Not only did the Gulf War give a temporary boost to President Bush's popularity, but it also seemed to inspire patriotism and support for the military throughout the nation. Table 6.2 shows that in 1991, the public had more confidence in the military than it did in the church or organized religion, in newspapers, or in any institution of government. By 1999, confidence in the military increased again, possibly due to the successful military action in Kosovo and the attacks by American aircraft on terrorist camps in Afghanistan.

The United States Supreme Court, which many people do not see as a particularly political institution, although it is clearly involved in decisions with vitally important consequences for the nation, also scored well, as did banks and banking until recently. A series of unpopular Supreme Court decisions from 1989 to 1991 and the savings and loan scandals of about the same time caused the public's confidence in both of those institutions to drop significantly by 1991. Even less confidence is expressed in newspapers, big business, television, and organized labor, all of which certainly are involved directly or indirectly in the political process. In 1991, following a scandal involving congressional banking practices and other embarrassments,

TABLE 6.2

Confidence in Institutions Trend

QUESTION: I AM GOING TO READ A LIST OF INSTITUTIONS IN AMERICAN SOCIETY. WOULD YOU PLEAE TELL ME HOW MUCH CONFIDENCE YOU, YOURSELF, HAVE IN EACH ONE—A GREAT DEAL, QUITE A LOT, SOME, OR VERY LITTLE?

| | PERCENTAGE SAYNG "GREAT DEAL" OR "QUITE A LOT" | | | | | | | | | | | | | |
	1973	1975	1977	1979	1981	1983	1985	1987	1989	1991	1993	1995	1997	1999
Church or organized religion	66%	68%	65%	65%	64%	62%	66%	61%	52%	56%	53%	57%	56%	58%
Military	NA	58	57	54	50	53	61	61	63	69	67	64	60	68
U.S. Supreme Court	44	49	46	45	46	42	56	52	46	39	43	44	50	49
Banks and banking	NA	NA	NA	60	46	51	51	51	42	30	38	43	41	43
Public schools	58	NA	54	53	42	39	48	50	43	35	39	40	40	36
Congress	42	40	40	34	29	28	39	NA	32	18	19	21	22	26
Newspapers	39	NA	NA	51	35	38	35	31	NA	32	31	30	35	33
Big business	26	34	33	32	20	28	31	NA	NA	22	23	21	28	30
Television	37	NA	NA	38	25	25	29	28	NA	24	21	33	34	34
Organized labor	30	38	39	36	28	26	28	26	NA	22	26	26	23	28

NA = Not asked.

SOURCE: *The Gallup Report*, July 1999.

confidence in Congress fell to a record low of 18 percent. By 1999, it had climbed to 26 percent.

Although people may not have much confidence in government institutions, they nonetheless turn to government to solve what they perceive to be the major problems facing the country. Table 6.3, which is based on Gallup polls conducted over the years 1975 to 2000, shows that the leading problems clearly have changed over time. The public tends to emphasize problems that are immediate. It is not at all unusual to see fairly sudden, and even apparently contradictory, shifts in public perceptions of what government should do. In recent years, education, crime, morals, and family decline reached the top of the problems list.

This gives rise to a critically important question: Is government really responsive to public opinion? A study by political scientists Benjamin I. Page and Robert Y. Shapiro suggests that in fact the national government is very responsive to the public's demands for action.[3] In looking at changes in public opinion poll results over time, Page and Shapiro show that when the public supports a policy change, the following occurs: policy changes in a direction congruent with the change in public opinion 43 percent of the time, policy changes in a direction opposite to the change in opinion 22 percent of the time, and policy does not change at all 33 percent of the time. So, overall, the national government could be said to respond to changes in public opinion about two-thirds of the time. Page and Shapiro also show, as should be no surprise, that when public opinion changes more dramatically—say, by 20 percentage points rather than by just 6 or 7 percentage points—government policy is much more likely to follow changing public attitudes.

---

[3]See the extensive work of Page and Shapiro in Benjamin I. Page and Robert Y. Shapiro, *The Rational Public: Fifty Years of Trends in Americans' Policy Preferences* (Chicago: University of Chicago Press, 1992).

TABLE 6.3

Most Important Problems Trend, 1975 to Present

2000	Morals, family decline	1987	Unemployment, economy
1999	Education, crime, morals	1986	Unemployment, budget deficit
1998	Crime, violence	1985	Fear of war, unemployment
1997	Crime, violence	1984	Unemployment, fear of war
1996	Budget deficit	1983	Unemployment, high cost of living
1995	Crime, violence	1982	Unemployment, high cost of living
1994	Crime, violence, health care	1981	High cost of living, unemployment
1993	Health care, budget deficit	1980	High cost of living, unemployment
1992	Unemployment, budget deficit	1979	High cost of living, energy problems
1991	Economy	1978	High cost of living, energy problems
1990	War in Middle East	1977	High cost of living, unemployment
1989	War on drugs	1976	High cost of living, unemployment
1988	Economy, budget deficit	1975	High cost of living, unemployment

SOURCES: *New York Times*/CBS News Poll, January 1996; *Gallup Report*, 2000.

THE SPECTRUM OF POLITICAL BELIEFS

Political candidates and officeholders in the United States frequently are identified as liberals or conservatives. As discussed in Chapter 1, these terms refer loosely to a spectrum of political beliefs that commonly are arrayed on a continuum from left to right. Each of the terms has changed its meaning from its origins and continues to change as the issues of political debate change. In the United States, however, the terms most frequently refer to sets of political positions that date from the Great Depression.

Liberals are most commonly understood to embrace national government solutions to public problems, to believe that the national government should intervene in the economy to ensure its health, to support social-welfare programs to assist the disadvantaged, and to be tolerant of social change. Today, liberals are often identified with policies supporting women's rights and civil rights, and opposing increased defense spending.

In contrast, *conservatives* usually feel that the national government has grown too large, that the private sector needs less interference from the government, that social-welfare programs should be limited, that state and local governments should be able to make their own decisions, and that the nation's defense should be strengthened. Some conservatives express grave concerns about the decline of family life and traditional values in this country; they would not be tolerant of gay rights laws, for example.

When asked, Americans usually are willing to identify themselves on the liberal-conservative spectrum. More individuals (about 40 percent) are likely to consider themselves *moderates* than liberals (about 20 percent) or conservatives (about 33 percent). Although the number of moderates and conservatives has increased and the number of liberals has declined in the past two decades, there has not been a dramatic change in ideological self-identification since 1976.

Many political leaders, who are quite conscious of their philosophical views and who hold a carefully thought out and a more or less consistent set of political beliefs, can be described as **ideologues.** Partly because most citizens are not strongly interested in all political issues and partly because Americans have different stakes in politics, most people have mixed sets of opinions that do not fit into one ideological framework. Election research suggests that only a small percentage of all Americans, perhaps less than 10 percent, could be identified as ideologues. The rest of the public conceives of politics more in terms of the political parties or of economic well-being.

Some critics of the American political system have felt that elections would be more meaningful and that the nation could face important policy problems more effectively if Americans were more ideological in their thinking. Public opinion research suggests that for most Americans, political issues are not usually as important as events in their daily lives are. There is no evidence to suggest that forces are in place to turn Americans into highly motivated ideological voters.

POLITICAL SOCIALIZATION

Most Americans are willing to express opinions on political issues when asked. How do individuals acquire these opinions and attitudes? Most views that are expressed as political opinions are acquired through the process of political socialization. By *political socialization*, we mean that individuals acquire their political attitudes, often including their party identification, through relationships with their families, friends, and co-workers. We touched briefly on this process in Chapter 1. Here, we look at the process in more detail.

The most important influences in the political socialization process are the following: (1) the family, (2) the educational environment and achievement of the individual, (3) peers, (4) religion, (5) economic status and occupation, (6) political events, (7) opinion leaders, (8) race and other demographic traits, and (9) the media. We discuss each of these influences below, as well as the relatively recent phenomenon of the gender gap.

The Importance of the Family

The family is the most important force in political socialization. Not only do our parents' political attitudes and actions affect our adult opinions, but the family also links us to other socialization forces. We acquire our ethnic identity, our notion of social class, our educational opportunities, and our early religious beliefs from our families. Each of these factors can also influence our political attitudes.

How do parents transmit these attachments? Studies suggest that the influence of parents is due to two factors: communication and receptivity. Parents communicate their feelings and preferences to children constantly. Because children have such a strong need for parental approval, they are very receptive to their parents' views.[4] The clearest legacy of the family is partisan identification. If both parents identify with one party, there is a strong likelihood that the children will begin political life with the same party preference.

Educational Influence on Political Opinion

From the early days of the republic, schools were perceived to be important transmitters of political information and attitudes. Children in the primary grades learn about their country mostly in patriotic ways. They learn to salute the flag, to say the Pledge of Allegiance, and to celebrate national holidays. Later, in the middle grades, children learn more historical facts and come to understand the structure of government and the functions of the president, judges, and Congress. By high school, students have a more complex understanding of the political system, may identify with a political party, and may take positions on issues.

Generally, education is closely linked to political participation. The more education a person receives, the more likely that person will be interested in politics, be confident in his or her ability to understand political issues, and be an active participant in the political process.

---

[4]Barbara A. Bardes and Robert W. Oldendick, *Public Opinion: Measuring the American Mind* (Belmont, Calif.: Wadsworth Publishing Co., 2000), p. 73.

Peers and Peer Group Influence

Once a child enters school, the child's friends become an important influence on behavior and attitudes. For young children, and later for adults, friendships and associations in **peer groups**—groups whose members share common relevant social characteristics—are influential on political attitudes. We must, however, separate the effects of peer group pressure on opinions and attitudes in general from peer group pressure on political opinions. For the most part, associations among peers are non-political. Political attitudes are more likely to be shaped by peer groups when the peer groups are directly involved in political activities.

Individuals who join interest groups based on ethnic identity may find, for example, a common political bond through working for the group's civil liberties and rights. African American activist groups may consist of individuals who join together to support government programs that will aid the African American population. Members of a labor union may feel strong political pressure to support certain pro-labor candidates.

Religious Influence

Religious associations tend to create definite political attitudes. Surveys show that Roman Catholic respondents tend to be more liberal on economic issues than are Protestants. Jewish respondents tend to be more liberal on all fronts than either Catholics or Protestants. In terms of voting behavior, northern white Protestants are more likely to vote Republican, whereas northern white Roman Catholics more often vote Democratic; everywhere in the United States, Jews mostly vote Democratic. The increase in fundamentalist or evangelical Protestants has had a significant political impact in recent years. A study by the Pew Center for the People and the Press found that 42 percent of white evangelical Protestants are Republican. Less than ten years ago, this figure was 35 percent.

INFOTRAC®

"Americans' Belief in God"

The Influence of Economic Status and Occupation

How wealthy you are and the kind of job you hold are also associated with your political views. Social-class differences emerge on a wide range of issues. Poorer people are more inclined to favor government social-welfare programs but are likely to be conservative on social issues such as abortion. The upper middle class is more likely to hold conservative economic views but to be tolerant of social change. People in lower economic strata also tend to be more isolationist on foreign policy issues and are more likely to identify with the Democratic Party and vote for Democratic candidates. Support for civil liberties and tolerance of different points of view tend to be greater among those with higher social status and lower among those with lower social status. Probably, educational differences, more than the pattern of life at home or work, account for this.

The Influence of Political Events

People's political attitudes may be shaped by political events and the nation's reactions to them. When events produce a long-lasting political impact, **generational** effects result. Voters who grew up in the 1930s during the Great Depression were likely to form lifelong attachments to the Democratic Party, the party of Franklin D. Roosevelt.

In the 1960s and 1970s, the war in Vietnam and the Watergate break-in and subsequent cover-up fostered widespread cynicism toward government. In one study of the impact of the Watergate scandal of 1972, Christopher Arterton found that schoolchildren changed their image of President Nixon from a "benevolent" to a "malevolent" leader as the scandal unfolded. Negative views about other aspects of politics and politicians also increased. Members of that age group moderated their views, however, as they matured.[5]

There was some evidence that the years of economic prosperity under Ronald Reagan during the 1980s may have influenced young adults to identify with the Republican Party. A 1990 poll showed that 52 percent of thirteen- to seventeen-year-olds thought of themselves as Republicans, whereas 32 percent of this age group thought of themselves as Democrats. Although the number of younger voters identifying themselves as Republicans declined in 1992, members of the group that voted for the first time in 1995 were more likely to be Republican.[6]

Opinion Leaders' Influence

We are all influenced by those with whom we are closely associated or whom we hold in great respect—friends at school, family members and other relatives, teachers, and so on. In a sense, these people are **opinion leaders,** but on an informal level; that is, their influence over us is not necessarily intentional or deliberate. We are also influenced by formal opinion leaders, such as presidents, lobbyists, congresspersons, or news commentators, who have as part of their jobs the task of swaying people's views. Their interest lies in defining the political agenda in such a way that discussions about policy options will take place on their terms.

The Influence of Demographic Traits

African Americans show a much stronger commitment than do whites to steady or more rapid racial desegregation. African Americans tend to be more liberal than whites on social-welfare issues, civil liberties, and even foreign policy. Party preference and voting among African Americans since the 1930s have supported the Democrats very heavily.

It is somewhat surprising that a person's chronological age has comparatively little impact on political preferences. Still, young adults are somewhat more liberal than older people on most issues, and they are considerably more progressive on such issues as marijuana legalization, pornography, civil disobedience, and racial and sexual equality.

Finally, attitudes vary from region to region, although such patterns probably are accounted for mostly by social class and other differences. Regional differences are

---

[5]Christopher F. Arterton, "The Impact of Watergate on Children's Attitudes toward Authority," *American Political Science Review,* Vol. 89 (June 1974), pp. 269–288.
[6]*America at the Polls 1996* (Storrs, Conn.: Roper Center, 1997), pp. 56–57.

relatively unimportant today. There is still a tendency for the South and the East to be more Democratic than the West and the Midwest. More important than region is a person's residence—urban, suburban, or rural. Big cities tend to be more liberal and Democratic because of their greater concentration of minorities and newer ethnic groups. Smaller communities are more conservative and, outside the South, more Republican.

The Gender Gap

Until the 1980s, there was little evidence that men's and women's political attitudes were very different. The election of Ronald Reagan in 1980, however, soon came to be associated with a **gender gap.** In a May 1983 Gallup poll, 43 percent of the women polled approved of Reagan's performance in office and 44 percent disapproved, versus 49 percent of men who approved and 41 percent who disapproved.

In the 1988 election, the gender gap reappeared, but in a modified form. Although the Democrats hoped that women's votes would add significantly to their totals, a deep split between men and women did not occur. The final polls showed that 54 percent of the men voted for George Bush, as did 50 percent of the women. The 1992 presidential election again found women more likely than men to vote for the Democrats: 46 percent of women voted for Bill Clinton, compared with 41 percent of the men. Additionally, women were less likely to vote for independent candidate H. Ross Perot than were men. Throughout his first term, Clinton continued to get higher approval marks from women than from men, and women were more supportive of him through the personal scandal periods of his second term.

Women also appear to hold different attitudes from their male counterparts on a range of issues other than presidential preferences. They are much more likely to oppose capital punishment, as well as the use of force abroad. Studies have also shown that women are more concerned about risks to the environment, more supportive of social welfare, and more supportive of extending civil rights to gay men and lesbians than are men. These differences of opinion appear to be growing and may become an important factor in future elections at national and local levels.

Media Influence

Clearly, the **media**—newspapers, television, radio broadcasts, and Internet sources—strongly influence public opinion. This is because the media inform the public about the issues and events of our times and thus have an agenda-setting effect. In other words, to borrow from Bernard Cohen's classic statement on the media and public opinion, the media may not be successful in telling people what to think, but they are "stunningly successful in telling their audience what to think about."[7]

Today, many contend that the media's influence is increasing to the point that the media are as influential as the family in regard to public opinion. For example, in

---

[7]*The Press and Foreign Policy* (Princeton, N.J.: Princeton University Press, 1963), p. 81.

her analysis of the role played by the media in American politics,[8] media scholar Doris A. Graber points out that high school students, when asked where they obtain the information on which they base their attitudes, mention the mass media far more than their families, friends, and teachers. As we discuss next, the media play an important role in all areas of American political life.

THE MEDIA AND POLITICS

The study of people and politics—of how people gain the information that they need to be able to choose between political candidates, to organize for their own interests, and to formulate opinions on the policies and decisions of the government—needs to take into account the role played by the media in the United States. Historically, the printed media played the most important role in informing public debate. The printed media developed, for the most part, our understanding of how news is to be reported. Today, however, more than 90 percent of all Americans use television news as their primary source of information. In the future, the Internet may become the most important source of information and political debate for Americans.

Functions of the Media

The mass media perform a number of different functions in any country. In the United States, we can list at least six. Almost all of them can have political implications, and some are essential to the democratic process. These functions are as follows: (1) entertainment, (2) reporting the news, (3) identifying public problems, (4) socializing new generations, (5) providing a political forum, and (6) making profits. It is important to keep in mind that almost all newspapers and radio and television outlets are owned by private corporations.

Entertainment. By far the greatest number of radio and television hours are dedicated to entertaining the public. The battle for prime-time ratings indicates how important successful entertainment is to the survival of networks and individual stations.

Although there is no direct linkage between entertainment and politics, network dramas often introduce material that may be politically controversial and that may stimulate public discussion. Made-for-TV movies have focused on many controversial topics, including AIDS, incest, and wife battering.

Reporting the News. A primary function of the mass media in all their forms—newspapers and magazines, radio, television, cable, and online news services—is the reporting of news. The media convey words and pictures about events, facts, personalities, and ideas. The protections of the First Amendment are intended to keep the flow of news as free as possible, because it is an essential part of the democratic

---

[8]See Doris A. Graber, *Mass Media and American Politics*, 5th ed. (Washington, D.C.: Congressional Quarterly Books, 1997).

process. If citizens cannot get unbiased information about the state of their communities and their leaders' actions, how can they make voting decisions? Perhaps the most incisive comment about the importance of the media was made by James Madison, who said, "A people who mean to be their own governors must arm themselves with the power knowledge gives. A popular government without popular information or the means of acquiring it, is but a prologue to a farce or a tragedy or perhaps both."[9]

Identifying Public Problems. The power of information is important not only in revealing what the government is doing but also in determining what the government ought to do—in other words, in setting the public agenda. The mass media identify public issues, such as the placement of convicted sex offenders in new homes and neighborhoods. The media then influence the passage of legislation, such as "Megan's Law," which requires police to notify neighbors about the release and/or resettlement of certain offenders. American journalists also work in a long tradition of uncovering public wrongdoing, corruption, and bribery and of bringing such wrongdoing to the public's attention. Closely related to this investigative function is that of presenting policy alternatives. Public policy is often complex and difficult to make entertaining, but programs devoted to public policy increasingly are

---

[9]As quoted in "Castro vs. (Some) Censorship," editorial, *The New York Times*, November 22, 1983, p. 24.

The town meeting of yesterday has given way to the electronic town meeting of today. Here, Bill Clinton answers a question asked by a citizen in another location but whose image and voice were transmitted through video conferencing telecommunications equipment. As telecommunications that include video and voice become better and cheaper, politicians will be able to use the electronic town-meeting concept more and more.

being scheduled for prime-time television. Most networks produce shows with a "news magazine" format that sometimes include segments on foreign policy and other issues.

Because those who control the media are not elected representatives of the people, the agenda-setting role of the media necessarily is a controversial one. The relationship of the media to agenda setting remains complex, though, because politicians are able to manipulate media coverage to control some of its effects, as well as to exploit the media to further their agendas with the public. No one can predict the long-term effects of this interaction on the quality of American political life.

Socializing New Generations. As mentioned earlier, the media, and particularly television, strongly influence the beliefs and opinions of all Americans. Because of this influence, the media play a significant role in the political socialization of the younger generation, as well as immigrants to this country. Through the transmission of historical information (sometimes fictionalized), the presentation of American culture, and the portrayal of the diverse regions and groups in the United States, the media teach young people and immigrants about what it means to be an American. TV talk shows, such as *Oprah*, sometimes focus on controversial issues (such as abortion or assisted suicide) that relate to basic American values (such as liberty). Many children's shows are designed not only to entertain young viewers but also to instruct them in the traditional moral values of American society. In recent years, the public has become increasingly concerned about the level of violence depicted on children's programs and on other shows during prime time.

Providing a Political Forum. As part of their news function, the media also provide a political forum for leaders and the public. Candidates for office use news reporting to sustain interest in their campaigns, whereas officeholders use the media to gain support for their policies or to present an image of leadership. Presidential trips abroad are an outstanding way for the chief executive to get colorful, positive, and exciting news coverage that makes the president look "presidential." The media also offer a way for citizens to participate in public debate, through letters to the editor, televised editorials, or electronic mail.

Making Profits. Most of the news media in the United States are private, for-profit corporate enterprises. One of their goals is to make profits—for employee salaries, for expansion, and for dividends to the stockholders who own the companies. Profits are made, in general, by charging for advertising. Advertising revenues usually are related directly to circulation or to listener/viewer ratings.

Several well-known outlets are publicly owned—public television stations in many communities and National Public Radio. These operate without extensive commercials and are locally supported and often subsidized by the government and corporations.

Added up, these factors form the basis for a complex relationship among the media, the government, and the public. Throughout the rest of this chapter, we examine some of the many facets of this relationship. Our purpose is to set a foundation for understanding how the media influence the political process.

The Primacy of Television

Television is the most influential medium. It also is big business. National news TV personalities such as Peter Jennings may earn in excess of several million dollars per year from their TV news–reporting contracts alone. They are paid so much because they command large audiences, and large audiences command high prices for advertising on national news shows. Indeed, news per se has become a major factor in the profitability of TV stations. In 1963, the major networks—ABC, CBS, and NBC—devoted only eleven minutes daily to national news. Today, the networks devote about three hours to news-type programming. In addition, a twenty-four-hour-a-day news cable channel—CNN—started operating in 1980. News is obviously good business.

Television's influence on the political process today is recognized by all who engage in it. Its special characteristics are worthy of attention. Television news is often criticized for being superficial, particularly compared with the detailed coverage available in the *New York Times*, for example. In fact, television news is constrained by its peculiar technical characteristics, the most important being the limitations of time; stories must be reported in only a few minutes.

The most interesting aspect of television is, of course, the fact that it relies on pictures rather than words to attract the viewer's attention. Therefore, the videotapes or slides that are chosen for a particular political story have exaggerated importance. Viewers do not know what other photos may have been taken or events recorded—they see only those appearing on their screens. Television news can also be exploited for its drama by well-constructed stories. Some critics suggest that there is pressure to produce television news that has a "story line," like a novel or movie. The story should be short, with exciting pictures and a clear plot. In the extreme case, the news media are satisfied with a **sound bite,** a several-second comment selected or crafted for its immediate impact on the viewer.

It has been suggested that these formatting characteristics—or necessities—of television increase its influence on political events. (Newspapers and news magazines are also limited by their formats, but to a lesser extent.) As you are aware, real life is usually not dramatic, nor do all events have a neat or an easily understood plot. Political campaigns are continuing events, lasting perhaps two years or more. The significance of their daily turns and twists is only apparent later. The "drama" of Congress, with its 535 players and dozens of important committees and meetings, is also difficult for the media to present. What television needs is dozens of daily three-minute stories.

The Revolution in the Electronic Media

Technology is increasing the number of alternative news sources today. The advent of pay TV, cable TV, subscription TV, satellite TV, and the Internet has completely changed the electronic media landscape. When there were basically only three TV networks, it was indeed a "wasteland," as former Federal Communications Commission chairman Newton Minnow once claimed. But now, with hundreds, if not thousands, of potential outlets for specialized programs, the electronic media are becoming more and more like the printed media in catering to specialized tastes. This is sometimes referred to as **narrowcasting.** Both cable television and the Internet offer the public unparalleled access to specialized information on everything from gardening and home repair to sports and religion. Most viewers are able to choose among several sources for their favorite type of programming.

In recent years, narrowcasting has become increasingly prevalent. Consumers watch only those shows and channels that they like, and the networks' audiences are declining. Between 1982 and 2000, network television's share of the audience fell from 72 percent to 52 percent. At the same time, the percentage of households having access to the Internet grew from zero to more than 40 percent, with 20 percent of all households subscribing to an online service.

In the realm of politics, the multiple news outlets have given rise to literally thousands of talk shows, whether on television, radio, or the Internet. By 2000, there were more than two dozen national television talk shows; their hosts ranged from Jerry Springer, who is regarded as a sensationalist, to Larry King, whose show has become a political necessity for candidates. Ross Perot actually announced his candidacy for the presidency in the 1992 election on *Larry King Live.*

The real blossoming of "talk" has occurred on the radio. The number of radio stations that program only talk shows has increased from about 300 in 1989 to more than 1,200 today. The subjects of talk shows range from business and investment to psychology to politics. There has been considerable criticism of the political talk shows, especially those hosted by Rush Limbaugh, G. Gordon Liddy, and other conservatives. Critics contend that such shows increase the level of intolerance and irrationality in American politics. The listeners to those shows are self-selected and tend to share the viewpoint of the host. Similarly, the Internet makes it possible for a Web site to be highly ideological or partisan and to encourage chat with others of the same persuasion. One of the potential hazards of narrowcasting of this kind is that people will be less open to dialogue with those whose opinions differ from their own and that more extremism in politics may result.

THE MEDIA AND POLITICAL CAMPAIGNS

All forms of the media—television, newspapers, radio, and magazines—have an enormous political impact on American society. Media influence is most obvious during political campaigns. News coverage of a single event, such as the results of the Iowa caucuses or the New Hampshire primary, may be the most important factor in having a candidate be referred to in the media as the "front-runner" in presidential campaigns. It is not too much of an exaggeration to say that almost all national political figures, starting with the president, plan all public appearances and statements to snag media coverage.

Because television is the primary news source for the majority of Americans, candidates and their consultants spend much of their time devising strategies to use television to their benefit. Three types of TV coverage are generally used in campaigns for the presidency and other offices: advertising, management of news coverage, and campaign debates.

Advertising

Perhaps one of the most effective political ads of all time was a short, thirty- second spot created by President Lyndon Johnson's media adviser. In this ad, a little girl stood in a field of daisies. As she held a daisy, she pulled the petals off and quietly counted to herself. Suddenly, when she reached number ten, a deep bass voice cut in and began a countdown: "10, 9, 8, 7, 6 . . ." When the voice intoned "zero," the unmistakable mushroom cloud of an atomic bomb began to fill the screen. Then President Johnson's voice was heard: "These are the stakes. To make a world in which all of God's children can live, or to go into the dark. We must either love each other or we must die." At the end of the commercial, the message read, "Vote for President Johnson on November 3."

To understand how effective this daisy girl commercial was, you must know that Johnson's opponent was Barry Goldwater, a Republican conservative candidate known for his expansive views on the role of the U.S. military. The ad's implication was that Goldwater would lead the United States into nuclear war. Although the ad was withdrawn within a few days, it has a place in political campaign history as the classic negative campaign announcement.

Since the daisy girl advertisement, negative advertising has come into its own. Candidates vie with one another to produce "attack" ads and then to counterattack when the opponent responds. The public claims not to like negative advertising, but as one consultant put it, "Negative advertising works." Any advertising "works" when viewers or listeners remember an ad. It is clear that negative ads are more memorable than ones that praise the candidate's virtues.

Too many blatantly negative ads by the candidates, of course, can alienate viewers and subject the candidates to criticism by the press and other media. Nonetheless, at least at the national level, negative ads continue to be used extensively.

Management of News Coverage

Using political advertising to get a message across to the public is very expensive. Coverage by the news media, however, is free; it simply demands that the campaign ensure that coverage takes place. In recent years, campaign managers have shown increasing sophistication in creating newsworthy events for journalists to cover. As Doris Graber points out, "To keep a favorable image of their candidates in front of the public, campaign managers arrange newsworthy events to familiarize potential voters with their candidates' best aspects."[10]

To take advantage of the media's interest in campaign politics, whether at the presidential level or perhaps in a Senate race, the campaign staff tries to influence the quantity and type of coverage the campaign receives. First, it is important for the campaign staff to understand the technical aspects of media coverage—camera angles, necessary equipment, timing, and deadlines—and to plan their political events to accommodate the press. Second, the campaign organization learns that political reporters and their sponsors—networks or newspapers—are in competition

---

[10]Graber, *Mass Media and American Politics*, p. 59.

for the best stories and can be manipulated through the granting of favors, such as a personal interview with the candidate. Third, an important task for the scheduler in the campaign is the planning of events that will be photogenic and interesting enough for the evening news.

A related goal, although one that is more difficult to attain, is to convince reporters that a particular interpretation of an event is correct. Today, the art of putting the appropriate spin on a story or event is highly developed. Each presidential candidate's press advisers, often referred to as spin doctors, try to convince the journalists that their interpretations of the political events are correct.

Going for the Knockout Punch—Presidential Debates

Perhaps of equal importance to political advertisements is the performance of the candidate in a televised presidential debate. After the first such debate in 1960, in which John Kennedy, the young senator from Massachusetts, took on the vice president of the United States, Richard Nixon, candidates became aware of the great potential of television for changing the momentum of a campaign. In general, challengers have much more to gain from debating than do incumbents. Challengers hope that the incumbent may make a mistake in the debate and undermine the "presidential" image. Incumbent presidents are loath to debate their challengers, because it puts their opponents on an equal footing with them.

The crucial fact about the practice of televising debates is that, although debates are justified publicly as an opportunity for the voters to find out how candidates dif-

A family watches the 1960 Kennedy-Nixon debates on television. After the debate, TV viewers thought Kennedy had won, whereas radio listeners thought Nixon had won.

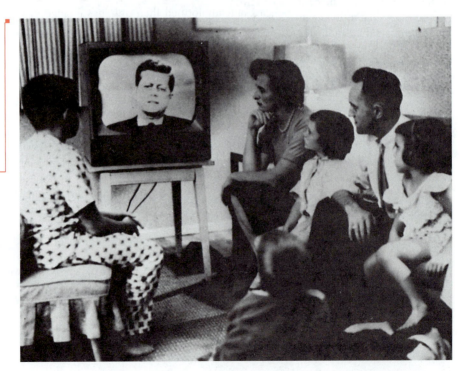

fer on the issues, what the candidates want is to capitalize on the power of television to project an image. They view the debate as a strategic opportunity to improve their own images or to point out the failures of their opponents. Candidates are very aware not only that the actual performance is important but also that the morning-after interpretation of the debate by the news media may play a crucial role in what the public thinks. Regardless of the risks of debating, the potential for gaining votes is so great that candidates undoubtedly will continue to seek televised debates.

The Media's Impact on the Voters

The question of how much influence the media have on voting behavior is difficult to answer. Generally, individuals watch television or read newspapers with certain preconceived ideas about political issues and candidates. These attitudes and opinions act as a kind of perceptual screen that filters out information that makes people feel uncomfortable or that does not fit with their own ideas.

Voters watch campaign commercials and news about political campaigns with "selective attentiveness." That is, they tend to watch those commercials that support the candidates they favor and tend to pay attention to news stories about their own candidates. This selectivity also affects their perceptions of the content of the news story or commercial and whether it is remembered. Apparently, the media are most influential with those persons who have not formed an opinion about political candidates or issues. Studies have shown that the flurry of television commercials and debates immediately before election day has the most impact on those voters who are truly undecided. Few voters who have already formed their opinions change their minds under the influence of the media.

THE MEDIA AND THE GOVERNMENT

The mass media not only wield considerable power when it comes to political campaigns, but they also, in one way or another, can wield power over the affairs of government and over government officials. Perhaps the most notable example in modern times concerns the activities of *Washington Post* reporters Bob Woodward and Carl Bernstein. Assigned to cover the Watergate break-in, these two reporters undertook an investigation that eventually led to the resignation of President Richard Nixon.

A love-hate relationship clearly exists between the president and the media. During the administration of John F. Kennedy, the president was seen in numerous photos scanning the *New York Times*, the *Washington Post*, and other newspapers each morning to see how the press tallied his successes and failures. This led to frequent jocular comments about his speed-reading ability.

In the United States, the prominence of the president is cultivated by a **White House press corps** composed of reporters assigned full-time to cover the presidency. These reporters even have a lounge in the White House where they spend their days, waiting for a story to break. Most of the time, they simply wait for the daily or twice-daily briefing by the president's **press secretary.** Because of the press corps's physical proximity to the president, the chief executive cannot even take a brief stroll around the presidential swimming pool without its becoming news. Perhaps no other nation allows the press such access to its highest government official. Consequently, no other nation has its airwaves and print media so filled with absolute trivia regarding the personal lives of the chief executive and his family.

President Franklin D. Roosevelt brought new spirit to a demoralized country and led it through the Great Depression through his effective use of the media, particularly through his radio broadcasts. His "fireside chats"—warm, informal talks via radio to a few million intimate friends—brought hope to millions. Roosevelt's speeches were masterful in their ability to forge a common emotional bond among his listeners. His decisive announcement in 1933 on the reorganization of the banks, for example, calmed a jittery nation and prevented the collapse of the banking industry, which was threatened by a run on banks, from which nervous depositors were withdrawing their assets. His famous Pearl Harbor speech, following the Japanese attack on the U.S. Pacific fleet on December 7, 1941 ("a day that will live in infamy"), mobilized the nation for the sacrifices and effort necessary to win World War II.

Perhaps no president exploited the electronic media more effectively than did Ronald Reagan. The "great communicator," as he was called, was never more dramatic than in his speech to the nation following the October 1983 U.S. invasion of the Caribbean island of Grenada. In this address, the president, in an almost flawless performance, appeared to many to have decisively laid to rest the uncertainty and confusion surrounding the event.

President Franklin D. Roosevelt, the first president to fully exploit the airwaves for his benefit, reported to the nation through radio "fireside chats."

Key Terms

consensus 120	narrowcasting 138	public opinion 119
divisive opinion 120	opinion leader 132	sampling error 124
"fireside chats" 142	opinion poll 121	sound bite 137
gender gap 133	peer group 131	spin 140
generational effect 131	political trust 126	spin doctor 140
ideologue 129	press secretary 141	Watergate break-in 118
media 133	public agenda 135	White House press corps 141

Chapter Summary

1 Public opinion is the aggregate of individual attitudes or beliefs shared by some portion of the adult population. Consensus issues are those on which most people agree, whereas divisive issues are those about which people strongly disagree.

2 Most descriptions of public opinion are based on the results of opinion polls. The accuracy of polls is based on sampling techniques that ensure randomness in the selection of respondents. Polls only measure opinions held on the day they are taken and will not reflect rapidly changing opinions. Certain methodological problems may reduce the accuracy of polls.

3 A political culture exists in the United States because so many Americans hold similar attitudes and beliefs about how the government and the political system should work.

4 Public opinion can play an important part in the political system by providing information to candidates, by indicating support or opposition to the president and Congress, and by setting limits on government action through public pressure.

5 Opinions and attitudes are produced by a combination of socialization, information, and experience. Young people, for example, are likely to be influenced by their parents' political party identification. Education has an effect on opinions and attitudes, as do peer groups, religious affiliation, and economic status. Political events may have generational effects, shaping the opinions of a par-

ticular age group. Opinion leaders, ethnicity, gender, and the media also affect political views.

6 The media play an important role in American politics today. They perform a number of functions, including (a) entertainment, (b) news reporting, (c) identifying public problems, (d) socializing new generations, (e) providing a political forum, and (f) making profits.

7 The electronic media (television and radio) are growing in significance in the area of communications. New technologies, such as cable television and the Internet, are giving broadcasters the opportunity to air a greater number of specialized programs.

8 The media wield significant political power during political campaigns and over the affairs of government and government officials by focusing attention on their actions. Today's political campaigns use political advertising and expert management of news coverage. Of equal importance for presidential candidates is how they appear in presidential debates.

9 The relationship between the media and the president is close; each has used the other—sometimes positively, sometimes negatively. The media play an important role in investigating the government and in getting government officials to better understand the needs and desires of American society.

SELECTED PRINT AND ELECTRONIC RESOURCES

Suggested Readings

Cook, Timothy E. *Governing with the News: The News Media as Political Institution.* Chicago: University of Chicago Press, 1998. Cook reviews the history of the media and examines their position today as a powerful part of government. He looks at the interactions of the various offices and branches of government with the news media and suggests reforms to make the media more accountable in their role as a political partner in government.

Delli Carpini, Michael X., and Scott Keeter. *What Americans Know about Politics and Why It Matters.* New Haven, Conn.: Yale University Press, 1996. The authors provide an extensive discussion of all the known data about the amount of political knowledge possessed by Americans and how they come to possess it.

Erikson, Robert S., and Kent L. Tedin. *American Public Opinion: Its Origins, Content, and Impact.* 5th ed. New York: Macmillan, 1995. This book gives an overview of public opinion, its formation, and its distribution within the public. It also explores how public opinion influences public policy.

Kurtz, Howard. *Spin Cycle: Inside the Clinton Propaganda Machine.* New York: Free Press, 1998. Kurtz, a member of the Washington press corps, writes about the ways that the Clinton administration tried to manipulate press coverage of its activities. Kurtz portrays the press corps as fundamentally distrustful of the president.

Media Resources

Campaigns and Elections Video Library—A series of videos, made available in 1998 by the periodical *Campaigns and Elections,* that include the best campaign ads of specific election cycles, the best overall ads, and the classic ads of all time.

Citizen Kane—A film, based on the life of William Randolph Hearst and directed by Orson Welles, that has been acclaimed as one of the best movies ever made. Welles himself stars as the newspaper tycoon. The film also stars Joseph Cotten and Alan Ladd. Oscar-winning best film in 1941.

All the President's Men—A film, produced by Warner Brothers in 1976, starring Dustin Hoffman and Robert Redford as the two *Washington Post* reporters, Bob Woodward and Carl Bernstein, who broke the story on the Watergate scandal. The film is an excellent portrayal of the *Washington Post* newsroom and the decisions that editors make in such situations.

LOGGING ON

According to its home page, the mission of National Election Studies (NES) "is to produce high quality data on voting, public opinion, and political participation that serves the research needs of social scientists, teachers, students, and policymakers concerned with understanding the theoretical and empirical foundations of mass politics in a democratic society." This is a good place to obtain information related to public opinion. Find it at

http://www.umich.edu/~nes

There are quite a few Web sites dealing with public opinion that are worth a look. One of the best is that maintained by the Gallup polling organization at

http://www.gallup.com

The Gallup organization posts all of its own reports and polling results. The archive of past polls is excellent.

To view *Slate,* the e-zine of politics and culture published by Microsoft, go to

http://www.slate.msn.com

An AP-like system for college newspapers is Uwire, offered by Northwestern University and

intended to provide college papers with a reliable source of information that directly affects their readers. You can access Uwire at

http://www.uwire.com

USING THE INTERNET FOR POLITICAL ANALYSIS

To sharpen your skills in using public opinion data, point your browser to one of the sites noted in the *Logging on* or to one maintained by one of the national newspapers. Pick a subject or topic on which the site maintains public opinion polling results (often you must use the Contents button for this). Then try to identify and consider the following types of information: First, how large was the sample, and how big is the "confidence" interval cited in the study? Do you know who commissioned the poll and to whom the results were given? Second, examine at least three questions and responses, and answer the following questions: How might the wording of the question have influenced the responses? How can you tell if the survey respondents had any information about the question asked? Was the number of respondents who couldn't answer the question significant? Can you tell if respondents could answer the question without much information? Finally, consider how much a political leader may or may not learn from this poll.

CHAPTER 7

Interest Groups and Political Parties

T he American system of government and politics provides a wealth of opportunities for citizens to voice their views and to try to influence policymakers. One way to do this is to join an **interest group**—defined as an organized group of individuals sharing common objectives who actively attempt to influence policymakers at all levels of government. Interest groups take many forms. They include ordinary people who make their points in Congress and the statehouses of America. When a businessperson contacts her state representative about a proposed change in the law, she **is lobbying**—attempting to influence—the government. When farmers descend on Washington, D.C., on tractors or Americans with disabilities gather in the corridors of city hall, they are also interest groups lobbying their representatives. Protected by the First Amendment's guarantee of the right to assemble and petition the government for the redress of grievances, individuals have joined together in voluntary associations to try to influence the government ever since the Boston Tea Party (see Chapter 2), which involved, after all, an eighteenth-century trade issue.

The governmental system has many points of access or places in the decision-making process where interest groups may focus an attack. If a bill opposed by a group passes the Senate, the lobbying efforts shift to the House of Representatives or to the president to seek a veto. If, in spite of all efforts, the legislation passes, the group may even lobby the executive agency or bureau that is supposed to implement the law and hope to influence the way in which the legislation is applied. In some cases, interest groups carry their efforts into the court system, either by filing lawsuits or by filing briefs as "friends of the court." The constitutional features of separation of powers and checks and balances encourage interest groups in their efforts.

Another way to attempt to influence policymaking is to become an active member of a political party and participate in the selection of political candidates, who, if elected, will hold government positions. A **political party** might be formally defined as a group of political activists who organize to win elections, to operate the government, and to determine public policy. This definition explains the difference between an interest group and a political party. Interest groups do not want to operate government, and they do not put forth political candidates—even though they support candidates who will promote their interests if elected or reelected. Another important distinction is that interest groups tend to sharpen issues, whereas American political parties tend to blur their issue positions to attract voters.

A NATION OF JOINERS?

Alexis de Tocqueville observed in 1834 that "in no country of the world has the principle of association been more successfully used or applied to a greater multitude of objectives than in America."[1] The French traveler was amazed at the degree to which Americans formed groups to solve civic problems, establish social relationships, and speak for their economic or political interests. Perhaps James Madison, when he wrote *Federalist Paper* No. 10, had already judged the character of his country's citizens similarly. He supported the creation of a large republic with several states to encourage the formation of many interests. The multitude of interests, in Madison's view, would work to discourage the formation of an oppressive larger minority or majority interest.

Surely, neither Madison nor Tocqueville foresaw the formation of more than a hundred thousand associations in the United States. Polling data show that more than two-thirds of all Americans belong to at least one group or association. While the majority of these affiliations could not be classified as "interest groups" in the political sense, Americans do understand the principles of working in groups. As noted in Chapter 1, some scholars maintain that this penchant for group action supports a pluralist interpretation of American politics, in which most government policies are worked out through group conflict and compromise. Some critics might say that the drive to organize interests can go too far, resulting in "hyperpluralism," meaning that so many powerful interests are competing that no real policy change can take place. Furthermore, it is possible that interest groups can become so powerful that the needs and demands of ordinary citizens can be ignored.

Recently, American society has been faulted for a perceived decline in participation in group activities, a decline that may threaten society's ability to maintain itself. The debate over this issue is discussed in this chapter's *At Issue: Is America's Social Fabric Coming Apart at the Seams?* on page 148.

TYPES OF INTEREST GROUPS

Thousands of groups exist to influence government. Among the major types of interest groups are those that represent the main sectors of the economy—business, agricultural, government, and labor groups. In more recent years, a number of "public-interest" organizations, including some "single-issue" groups, have been formed to represent the needs of the general citizenry. The interests of foreign governments and foreign businesses are also represented in the American political arena.

Economic Interest Groups

Numerous interest groups have been formed to promote economic interests. These groups include business, agricultural, labor, public employee, and professional organizations.

---

[1]Alexis de Tocqueville, *Democracy in America*, Vol. 1, edited by Phillips Bradley (New York: Knopf, 1980), p. 191.

Is America's Social Fabric Coming Apart at the Seams?

During the 1990s, a common lament was that Americans were becoming apathetic about politics and disinterested in civic participation. Voter turnout was low. Surveys showed that Americans were increasingly distrustful of government officials and that confidence in major institutions, such as Congress, was declining.

In 1995, Robert D. Putnam of Harvard University published an influential essay in which he argued that Americans were becoming increasingly disconnected from their communities and from each other. Just as more people were "bowling alone" rather than joining bowling leagues, so were more Americans retreating into private spaces rather than getting involved in their communities. To bolster his thesis, Putnam pointed to the declining participation in such organizations as the PTA, the Red Cross, and the Girl Scouts.[*]

Civic participation has always been the thread that holds our nation's social fabric together, and

worried commentators echoed Putnam's fear that declining civic involvement could have dire results for our nation. Despite these alarms, however, recent studies have shown that America is not falling apart at the seams. On the contrary, membership in organizations appears to be higher than previously reported, according to a study of civic involvement conducted by the University of Virginia's Center for Survey Research under the direction of the American Association of Retired Persons (AARP).[†]

The results of the AARP study clearly showed that "we're not a nation of civic slugs," as Constance Swank, who directed the project for the AARP, commented. In fact, 98 percent of those surveyed were involved in at least one activity that connected them to people outside their households: 78 percent visit with friends, 64 percent are engaged in religious activities, 61 percent pursue hobbies outside their households, 57 percent perform activities with teens and children, and 53 percent volunteer time. The average respondent

claimed more than four memberships in more than three types of organizations, including religious organizations, health and sports clubs, professional trade groups, school groups, and neighborhood groups. One-third of the respondents reported that they had worked with others to solve local problems, and eight out of ten respondents believed that they could solve local problems by acting in concert with others.

A not-too-rosy finding was that the youngest adults surveyed—those between the ages of eighteen and twenty-six—exhibited the least confidence in the government's ability to do what is right and the least involvement in their communities. A big unknown is whether the opinions and actions of this age group will change in the coming years.

FOR CRITICAL ANALYSIS

If a person stays informed on political issues and votes regularly at the polls, why should society be concerned if that person does not participate in any group activities?

---

[*]See the following articles by Robert Putnam: "Tuning In, Tuning Out: The Strange Disappearance of Social Capital in America," *PS: Political Science and Politics*, December 1995, pp. 664–683; and "Bowling Alone, Revisited," *The Responsive Community*, Vol. 18 (Spring 1995), p. 33.

[†]Thomas M. Guterbock and John C. Fries, *Maintaining America's Social Fabric: The AARP Survey of Civic Involvement* (University of Virginia: Center for Survey Research, December 1997).

Business Interest Groups.
Thousands of trade and business organizations attempt to influence government policies. Some groups target a single regulatory unit, whereas others try to effect major policy changes. Three large business groups are consistently effective: (1) the National Association of Manufacturers (NAM), (2) the U.S. Chamber of Commerce, and (3) the Business Roundtable. The annual budget of the NAM is more than $22 million, which it collects in dues from about 14,000 relatively large corporations. Sometimes called the National Chamber, the U.S. Chamber of Commerce represents more than 200,000 businesses. Dues from its members, which include

Northwest Airline pilots picket at the Minneapolis airport during their most recent strike.

about 4,000 local chambers of commerce, exceed $30 million a year. Separately, two hundred of the largest corporations in the United States send their chief executive officers to the Business Roundtable. This organization is based in New York, but it does its lobbying in Washington, D.C. Established in 1972, the Roundtable was designed to promote a more aggressive view of business interests in general, cutting across specific industries. Dues paid by the member corporations are determined by the companies' wealth.

Agricultural Interest Groups. American farmers and their workers represent about 2 percent of the U.S. population. In spite of this, farmers' influence on legislation beneficial to their interests has been enormous. Farmers have succeeded in their aims because they have very strong interest groups. They are geographically dispersed and therefore have many representatives and senators to speak for them. The American Farm Bureau Federation, established in 1919, has over 4.7 million members. It was instrumental in getting government guarantees of "fair" prices during the Great Depression in the 1930s.[2] Another important agricultural special interest organization is the National Farmers' Union (NFU).

Labor Interest Groups. Interest groups representing the labor movement—the expression and organization of working-class interests—date back to at least 1886 when the American Federation of Labor (AFL) was formed. In 1955, the AFL joined forces with the Congress of Industrial Organizations (CIO). Today, the combined AFL-CIO is an enormous union with a membership exceeding 13 million workers. In a sense, the AFL-CIO is a union of unions.

---

[2]The Agricultural Adjustment Act of 1933 (declared unconstitutional) was replaced by the 1937 Agricultural Adjustment Act and later changed and amended several times.

The political arm of the AFL-CIO is the Committee on Political Education (COPE). COPE's activities are funded by voluntary contributions from union members. COPE has been active in state and national campaigns since 1956.

The role of unions in American society has weakened in recent years, as witnessed by a decline in union membership. In the age of automation and with the rise of the **service sector,** blue-collar workers in basic industries (autos, steel, and the like) represent a smaller and smaller percentage of the total working population. Because of this decline in the industrial sector of the economy, national unions are looking to nontraditional areas for their membership, including migrant farm workers, service workers, and, most recently, public employees—such as police officers; firefighting personnel; and teachers, including college professors. Successful strikes by the Teamsters against United Parcel Service and by the UAW against General Motors in recent years strengthened the resolve of unions to recruit new members.

Public Employee Interest Groups. The degree of unionization in the private sector has declined since 1965, but this has been offset partially by growth in the unionization of public employees. With a total work force of more than 6.6 million, these unions are likely to continue expanding.

Both the American Federation of State, County, and Municipal Employees and the American Federation of Teachers are members of the AFL-CIO's Public Employee Department. Originally, the public employee unions started out as social and professional organizations. Over the years, they have become quite militant and are often involved in strikes. Many of these strikes are illegal, because certain public employees do not have the right to strike and essentially sign a contract so stating. In August 1981, the Professional Air Traffic Controllers Organization (PATCO) went on strike in defiance of a court order. President Ronald Reagan, convinced that public opinion was on his side, fired the strikers. Supervisors, nonstrikers, military personnel, and new trainees were rounded up to handle the jobs vacated by the 16,000 terminated air traffic controllers.

A powerful interest group lobbying on behalf of public employees is the National Education Association (NEA), a nationwide organization of about 2.3 million administrators, teachers, and others connected with education. The NEA lobbies intensively for increased public funding of education. The NEA sponsors regional and national conventions each year and has an extensive program of electronic media broadcasts, surveys, and the like.

Interest Groups of Professionals. Numerous professional organizations exist, including the American Bar Association, the Association of General Contractors of America, the Institute of Electrical and Electronic Engineers, the Screen Actors Guild, and others. Some professional groups, such as lawyers and doctors, are more influential than others due to their social status. Lawyers have a unique advantage—a large number of members of Congress share their profession. In terms of money spent on lobbying, however, one professional organization stands head and shoulders above the rest—the American Medical Association (AMA). Founded in 1947, it is now affiliated with more than 2,000 local and state medical societies and has a total membership of 285,000 and an administrative staff of 1,100. The AMA spends heavily on presidential campaign contributions in its efforts to influence legislation.

Environmental Groups

Environmental interest groups are not new. The National Audubon Society was founded in 1905 to protect the snowy egret from the commercial demand for hat decorations, and the patron of the Sierra Club, John Muir, worked for the creation of national parks more than ninety years ago. But the blossoming of national environmental groups with mass memberships is a relatively recent phenomenon. Since the first Earth Day, organized in 1972, many interest groups have sprung up to protect the environment in general or unique ecological niches. The groups range from the National Wildlife Federation, with a membership of more than 4.4 million and an emphasis on education, to the fairly elite Environmental Defense Fund, with a membership of 300,000 and a focus on influencing federal policy. Other groups include the Nature Conservancy, which seeks members' contributions so the organization can buy up threatened natural areas and either give them to state or local governments or manage them itself, and the more radical Greenpeace Society and Earth First.

Public-Interest Groups

Public interest is a difficult term to define because, as we noted earlier, there are many publics in our nation of over 275 million. It is almost impossible for one particular public policy to benefit everybody, which makes it practically impossible to define the public interest. Nonetheless, over the past few decades, a variety of law and lobbying organizations have been formed "in the public interest."

The Rainbow Warrior, *the flagship of Greenpeace, is both a symbol for the environmental interest group and a resource that can be used for actions at sea to protect the environment. The* Rainbow Warrior *has acted to save dolphins, to protest oil spills, and to stop Japanese and Russian whaling.*

Ralph Nader began the movement to create public-interest groups through the publication, in 1965, of his book Unsafe at Any Speed, *which criticized General Motors for underplaying the dangers of its Corvair automobile. Since that time, he has founded a number of not-for-profit public-interest groups that track business and governmental actions in specific policy arenas.*

The most well-known and perhaps the most effective public-interest groups are those organized under the leadership of consumer activist Ralph Nader. Partly in response to the Nader organizations, numerous conservative public-interest law firms have sprung up that are often pitted against the consumer groups in court. Some of these are the Mountain States Legal Defense Foundation, the Pacific Legal Foundation, the National Right-to-Work Legal Defense Foundation, the Washington Legal Foundation, and the Mid-Atlantic Legal Foundation.

One of the largest public-interest groups is Common Cause, founded in 1968, whose goal is to reorder national priorities toward "the public" and to make governmental institutions more responsive to the needs of the public. Anyone willing to pay dues of $20 a year can become a member. Other public-interest groups are active on a wide range of issues. The goal of the League of Women Voters, founded in 1920, is to educate the public on political matters. Although generally nonpartisan, it has lobbied for the Equal Rights Amendment and for government reform. The Consumer Federation of America is an alliance of about two hundred local and national organizations interested in consumer protection. The American Civil Liberties Union dates back to World War I, when, under a different name, it defended draft resisters. It generally enters into legal disputes related to Bill of Rights issues.

Special Interest Groups

Special interest groups, being narrowly focused, may be able to call more attention to their respective causes because they have simple and straightforward goals and because their members tend to care intensely about the issues. Thus, such groups can easily motivate their members to contact legislators or to organize demonstrations in support of their policy goals.

The job of lobbyists never stops. These Washington lobbyists are scrutinizing news reports to ascertain the positions of members of Congress on policy issues that will have an impact on the interests that the lobbyists represent. Although many critics of lobbyists and interest groups argue that they distort the actions of our government, the First Amendment prohibits the government from regulating their speech.

A number of interest groups focus on just one issue. The abortion debate has created various groups opposed to abortion (such as Right to Life) and groups in favor of abortion (such as the National Abortion Rights Action League). Other single-issue groups are the National Rifle Association, the Right to Work Committee (an anti-union group), and the Hudson Valley PAC (a pro-Israel group).

Other groups represent particular groups of Americans who share a common characteristic, such as age or ethnicity. Such interest groups lobby for legislation that may benefit their members in terms of rights or just represent a viewpoint.

The American Association of Retired Persons (AARP), which works on behalf of older Americans, is one of the most powerful interest groups in Washington, D.C., and, according to some, the strongest lobbying group in the United States. It is certainly the nation's largest interest group, with a membership of over thirty-three million. The AARP has accomplished much for its members over the years. It played a significant role in the creation of Medicare and Medicaid, as well as in obtaining cost-of-living increases in Social Security payments.

Foreign Governments

Home-grown interests are not the only players in the game. Washington, D.C., is also the center for lobbying by foreign governments as well as private foreign interests. Large research and lobbying staffs are maintained by governments of the largest U.S. trading partners, such as Japan, South Korea, Canada, and the European Union (EU) countries. Even smaller nations, such as those in the Caribbean, engage lobbyists when vital legislation affecting their trade interests is considered. Frequently,

"How Become Top
Banana"

these foreign interests hire former representatives or former senators to promote their positions on Capitol Hill. There is growing concern over the influence of foreign interests on U.S. politics.

Interest Group Strategies

Interest groups employ a wide range of techniques and strategies to promote their policy goals. The techniques used by interest groups may be divided into **direct techniques,** in which the interest group and its lobbyists approach government officials personally to press their case, and **indirect techniques** in which the interest group uses the general public or individuals to influence the government for the group.

Direct Techniques

Lobbying, publicizing ratings of legislative behavior, and providing campaign assistance are the three main direct techniques used by interest groups.

Lobbying Techniques. As might be guessed, the term *lobbying* comes from the activities of private citizens regularly congregating in the lobbies of legislative chambers before a session to petition legislators. In the latter part of the nineteenth century, railroad and industrial groups openly bribed state legislators to pass legislation beneficial to their interests, giving lobbying a well-deserved bad name. Today, standard lobbying techniques still include buttonholing (detaining and engaging in conversation) senators and representatives in state capitols and in Washington, D.C., while they are moving from their offices to the voting chambers. Lobbyists, however, do much more than that.

Lobbyists engage in an array of activities to influence legislation and government policy. These include, at a minimum, the following:

1. Engaging in private meetings with public officials, including the president's advisers, to make known the interests of the lobbyist's clients. Although acting on behalf of a client, often lobbyists furnish needed information to senators and representatives (and government agency appointees) that they could not hope to obtain on their own. It is to the lobbyist's advantage to provide accurate information so that the policymaker will rely on this source in the future.

2. Testifying before congressional committees for or against proposed legislation being considered by Congress.

3. Testifying before executive rulemaking agencies—such as the Federal Trade Commission or the Consumer Product Safety Commission—for or against proposed rules.

4. Assisting legislators or bureaucrats in drafting legislation or prospective regulations. Often lobbyists furnish legal advice on the specific details of legislation.

5. Inviting legislators to social occasions, such as cocktail parties, boating expeditions, and other events, including conferences at exotic locations. Most lobbyists feel that contacting legislators in a more relaxed social setting is effective.

6. Providing political information to legislators and other government officials. Often the lobbyists will have better information than the party leadership about how other legislators are going to vote. In this case, the political information they furnish may be a key to legislative success.

7. Supplying nominations for federal appointments to the executive branch.

The Ratings Game. Many interest groups attempt to influence the overall behavior of legislators through their rating systems. Each year, the interest group selects those votes on legislation that it feels are most important to the organization's goals. Each legislator is given a score based on the percentage of times that he or she voted in favor of the group's position. The usual scheme ranges from 0 to 100 percent. If a legislator has a score of, for example, 90 percent on the Americans for Democratic Action (ADA) rating, it means that he or she supported that group's position to a high degree. A legislator with such a high ADA score is usually considered to be very liberal. The groups that use rating systems range from the American Conservative Union to the League of Conservation Voters (an environmental group). Each year, the latter group identifies the twelve legislators having what it sees as the worst records on environmental issues and advertises them as the "Dirty Dozen."

Campaign Assistance. Interest groups have additional strategies to use in their attempts to influence government policies. Groups recognize that the greatest concern of legislators is to be reelected, so they focus on the legislators' campaign needs. Associations with large memberships, such as labor unions or the National Education Association, are able to provide workers for political campaigns, including precinct workers to get out the vote, volunteers to put up posters and pass out literature, and people to staff telephone banks for campaign headquarters.

In many states where membership in certain interest groups is large, candidates vie for the groups' endorsements in the campaign. Gaining those endorsements may be automatic, or it may require that the candidates participate in a debate or interview with the interest groups. Endorsements are important because an interest group usually publicizes its choices in its membership publication and because the candidate can use the endorsement in her or his campaign literature. Traditionally, labor unions such as the AFL-CIO and the Teamsters have endorsed Democratic Party candidates. Republican candidates, however, often try to persuade union locals at least to refrain from any endorsement. Making no endorsement can then be perceived as disapproval of the Democratic Party candidate.

PACs and Political Campaigns. In the last two decades, the most important form of campaign help from interest groups has become the political contribution from a group's **political action committee (PAC)**, a committee set up by and representing a corporation, labor union, or special interest group. The Federal Election Campaign Act of 1971 and its amendments, which will be discussed in detail in Chapter 8, allow corporations, labor unions, and other interest groups to set up PACs to raise money for candidates.

The number of PACs has grown astronomically, as has the amount they spend on elections. There were about 1,000 political action committees in 1976; by the late 1990s, there were more than 4,500. The total amount of spending by PACs grew

INFOTRAC®

"Mother's Milk Elections"

from $19 million in 1973 to an estimated $500 million in the 2000 presidential elections. Of all of the campaign money spent by House candidates, about 30 percent came from PACs.[3]

Interest groups funnel PAC money to the candidates they think can do the most good for them. Frequently, they make the maximum contribution of $5,000 per election to candidates who face little or no opposition. The great bulk of campaign contributions goes to incumbent candidates rather than to challengers. Some PACs balance their contributions between Democratic and Republican candidates. Corporations are particularly likely to give money to Democrats in Congress as well as to Republicans, because Democratic incumbents may again chair important committees or subcommittees. Why, might you ask, would business leaders give to Democrats who may be more liberal than themselves? Interest groups see PAC contributions as a way to ensure access to powerful legislators, even though the groups may disagree with the legislators some of the time. PAC contributions are, in a way, an investment in a relationship.

The campaign-finance regulations (see Chapter 8) clearly limit the amount that a PAC can give to any one candidate, but there is no limit on the amount that a PAC can spend on an independent campaign, either on behalf of a candidate or party or in opposition to one.

Indirect Techniques

Interest groups can also try to influence government policy by working through third parties—who may be constituents, the general public, or other groups. Indirect techniques mask the interest group's own activities and make the effort appear to be spontaneous. Furthermore, legislators and government officials are often more impressed by contacts from constituents than from an interest group's lobbyist.

In some instances, interest groups try to produce a "groundswell" of public pressure to influence the government. Such efforts may include advertisements in national magazines and newspapers, mass mailings, television publicity, and demonstrations. Interest groups may commission polls to find out what the public's sentiments are and then publicize the results. The intent of this activity is to convince policymakers that public opinion overwhelmingly supports the group's position.

INFOTRAC®

"Letters, We Get Letters Grassroot Lobbying"

One of the most effective interest group activities is the use of constituents to lobby for the group's goals. The interest group mobilizes large numbers of constituents to write, phone, or send e-mail to their legislators or the president. These efforts are only effective on Capitol Hill when there is an extraordinary number of responses, however, because legislators know that the voters did not initiate the communications on their own. A more influential variation of this technique uses only important constituents. For example, an interest group might ask the manager of a local plant in Utah to contact the senator from Utah.[4] Because the manager is seen as being responsible for many jobs or other resources, the legislator is more likely to listen carefully to his or her concerns about legislation than to a paid lobbyist.

---

[3]Norman Ornstein, Thomas E. Mann, and Michael J. Malbin, *Vital Statistics on Congress, 1995–1996* (Washington, D.C.: Congressional Quarterly Press, 1996), p. 95.

Another indirect technique used by interest groups is to form an alliance with other groups concerned about the same legislation to share expenses and multiply the influence of their individual groups. Often, these groups will set up a paper organization with an innocuous name, such as the Citizens Trade Campaign, to represent their joint concerns. These alliances are efficient devices for keeping like-minded groups from duplicating one another's lobbying efforts.

REGULATING LOBBYISTS

Congress made its first attempt to control lobbyists and lobbying activities through Title III of the Legislative Reorganization Act of 1946, otherwise known as the Federal Regulation of Lobbying Act. The act actually provided for public disclosure more than for regulation, and it neglected to specify which agency would enforce its provisions. The 1946 legislation defined a lobbyist as any person or organization that received money to be used principally to influence legislation before Congress. Such persons and individuals were supposed to "register" their clients and the purposes of their efforts, and report quarterly on their activities.

The legislation was tested in a 1954 Supreme Court case, *United States v. Harriss*,[5] and was found to be constitutional. The Court agreed that the lobbying law did not violate due process, freedom of speech or of the press, or the freedom to petition. The Court narrowly construed the act, however, holding that it applied only to lobbyists who were influencing federal legislation *directly*.

The result of the act was that a minimal number of individuals registered as lobbyists. National interest groups, such as the National Rifle Association and the American Petroleum Institute, could employ hundreds of staff members who were, of course, working on legislation but only register one or two lobbyists who were engaged *principally* in influencing Congress. There were no reporting requirements for lobbying the executive branch, federal agencies, the courts, or congressional staff. Approximately seven thousand individuals and organizations registered annually as lobbyists, although most experts estimated that ten times that number were actually employed in Washington to exert influence on the government.

The reform-minded Congress of 1995–1996 overhauled the lobbying legislation, fundamentally changing the ground rules for those who seek to influence the federal government. Lobbying legislation, passed in 1995, included the following provisions:

1. A lobbyist is defined as anyone who spends at least 20 percent of his or her time lobbying members of Congress, their staffs, or executive branch officials.
2. Lobbyists must register with the clerk of the House and the secretary of the Senate within forty-five days of being hired or of making their first contact. The registration requirement applies to organizations that spend more than $20,000 in one year or to individuals who are paid more than $5,000 annually for their work.

---

[4]Kay Lehman Schlozman and John T. Tierney, *Organized Interests and American Democracy* (New York: Harper & Row, 1986), p. 293.
[5]347 U.S. 612 (1954).

3. Semiannual reports must disclose the general nature of the lobbying effort, specific issues and bill numbers, the estimated cost of the campaign, and a list of the branches of government contacted. The names of the individuals contacted need not be reported.

4. Representatives of U.S.-owned subsidiaries of foreign-owned firms and lawyers who represent foreign entities also are required to register for the first time.

5. The requirements exempt "grassroots" lobbying efforts and those of tax-exempt organizations, such as religious groups.

The 1995 law was expected to increase the number of registered lobbyists by three to ten times what it was then. It made the connections between organizations and specific issues much clearer in the reporting process. The major exemption for grassroots campaigns, however, was expected to cause interest groups to divert major resources to organizing the folks back home so that they can exert pressure on Congress.

Concurrently with the debate on the 1995 law, both the House and the Senate adopted new rules on gifts and travel expenses: the House adopted a flat ban on gifts, and the Senate limited gifts to $50 in value and to no more than $100 in gifts from a single source in a year. There are exceptions for gifts from family members and for home-state products and souvenirs, such as T-shirts and coffee mugs. Both chambers ban all-expenses-paid trips, golf outings, and other such junkets. An exception applies for "widely attended" events, however, or if the member is a primary speaker at an event. The new gift rules stop the broad practice of taking members of Congress to lunch or dinner, but the various exemptions and exceptions undoubtedly will cause much controversy as individual cases are decided by the Senate and House Ethics Committees in future years.

POLITICAL PARTIES VERSUS INTEREST GROUPS AND FACTIONS

Around election time, the polls and the media concentrate on the state of the political parties. Every poll asks the question, "Do you consider yourself to be a Republican, a Democrat, or an independent?" Most Americans are able to answer that question, and the number of persons who identify themselves as **independents**—that is, voters or candidates who do not identify with a political party—now exceeds 30 percent.

In the United States, being a member of a political party does not require paying dues, passing an examination, or swearing an oath of allegiance. If nothing is really required to be a member of a political party, what, then, is a political party?

As mentioned earlier in this chapter, a political party is a group that seeks to win elections, operate the government, and determine public policy. Political parties are thus quite different from interest groups, which seek to influence, not run, the government.

Political parties also differ from **factions**, which are smaller groups that are trying to obtain certain benefits for themselves. Factions generally preceded the formation of political parties in American history, and the term is still used to refer to groups within parties that follow a particular leader or share a regional identification or an ideological viewpoint. The Republican Party sometimes is seen as having a northeastern "moderate" faction. The supporters of the late Robert Kennedy and Senator Edward (Ted) Kennedy might be described as a liberal faction within the Democratic Party. Factions are subgroups within parties that may try to capture a nomination or get a position adopted by the party. The key difference between factions and parties is that factions do not have a permanent organization, whereas political parties do.

FUNCTIONS OF POLITICAL PARTIES IN THE UNITED STATES

Political parties in the United States engage in a wide variety of activities, many of which are discussed in this chapter. Through these activities, parties perform a number of functions for the political system. These functions include the following:

1. *Recruiting candidates for public office.* Because it is the goal of parties to gain control of government, they must work to recruit candidates for all elective offices. Often this means recruiting candidates to run against powerful incumbents or for unpopular jobs. Yet if parties did not search out and encourage political hopefuls, far more offices would be uncontested, and voters would have limited choices.

Democratic National Convention delegates in 1996 show their support for the Clinton/Gore ticket. The costumes they wear are part of the convention culture and may attract television cameras. Does the often circus-like atmosphere of national party conventions detract from the seriousness of the decisions made at these conventions?

2. *Organizing and running elections*. Although elections are a government activity, political parties actually organize the voter-registration drives, recruit the volunteers to work at the polls, provide most of the campaign activity to stimulate interest in the election, and work to increase participation.

3. *Presenting alternative policies to the electorate*. In contrast to factions, which are often centered on individual politicians, parties are focused on a set of political positions. The Democrats or Republicans in Congress who vote together do so because they represent constituencies that have similar expectations and demands.

4. *Accepting responsibility for operating the government*. When a party elects the president or governor and members of the legislature, it accepts the responsibility for running the government. This includes staffing the executive branch with loyal party supporters and developing linkages among the elected officials to gain support for policies and their implementation.

5. *Acting as the organized opposition to the party in power*. The "out" party, or the one that does not control the government, is expected to articulate its own policies and oppose the winning party when appropriate. By organizing the opposition to the "in" party, the opposition party forces debate on the policy alternatives.

Students of political parties, such as Leon D. Epstein, point out that the major functions of American political parties are carried out by a small, relatively loose-knit **cadre,** or nucleus, of party activists.[6] This is quite a different arrangement from the more highly structured, mass-membership party organization typical of certain European working-class parties. American parties concentrate on winning elections rather than on signing up large numbers of deeply committed, dues-paying members who believe passionately in the party's program.

A SHORT HISTORY OF POLITICAL PARTIES IN THE UNITED STATES

Political parties in the United States have a long tradition dating back to the 1790s. The function and character of these political parties, as well as the emergence of the two-party system itself, have much to do with the unique historical forces operating from this country's beginning as an independent nation.

Generally, we can divide the evolution of our nation's political parties into six periods:

1. The creation of parties, from 1789 to 1812.
2. The era of one-party rule, or personal politics, from 1816 to 1824.
3. The period from Andrew Jackson's presidency to just prior to the Civil War, from 1828 to 1860.
4. The post–Civil War period, from 1864 to 1892.
5. The progressive period, from 1896 to 1928.
6. The modern period, from 1932 to the present.

---

[6]*Political Parties in Western Democracies* (New Brunswick, N.J.: Transaction, 1980).

The Formative Years: Federalists and Anti-Federalists

The first partisan political division in the United States occurred prior to the adoption of the Constitution. Recall from Chapter 2 that the Federalists pushed for the adoption of the Constitution, whereas the Anti-Federalists were against ratification.

In September 1796, George Washington, who had served as president for almost two full terms, decided not to run again. In his farewell address, he warned of "baneful effects of the spirit of party." He viewed parties as a threat to both national unity and the concept of popular government. Early in his career, Thomas Jefferson did not like political parties either. In 1789, he stated, "If I could not go to heaven but with a party, I would not go there at all."[7]

What Americans found out during the first decade or so after the ratification of the Constitution was that even a patriot-king (as George Washington has been called) could not keep everyone happy. There is no such thing as a neutral political figure who is so fair minded that everyone agrees with him or her. During this period, it became obvious to many that something more permanent than a faction would be necessary to identify candidates for the growing number of citizens who would be participating in elections. Thus, according to many historians, the world's first democratic political parties were established in this country. Also, in 1800, when the Federalists lost the presidential election to the Democratic Republicans (also known as the Jeffersonian Republicans), one of the first peaceful transfers of power from one party to another was achieved.

The Era of Personal Politics

From 1816 to 1828, a majority of U.S. voters regularly elected Democratic Republicans to the presidency and to Congress. Two-party competition did not really exist. This was the so-called **era of personal politics,** when attention centered on the character of individual candidates rather than on party identification. Although during elections the Democratic Republicans opposed the Federalists' call for a stronger, more active central government, they acquired the Louisiana Territory and Florida, established a national bank, enforced a higher tariff (tax on imports), and resisted European intrusion into the Western Hemisphere. Because there was no real political opposition to the dominant Democratic Republicans and thus little political debate, the administration of James Monroe (1817–1825) came to be known as the **era of good feeling.**

National Two-Party Rule: Democrats and Whigs

During the era of personal politics, one-party rule did not prevent the Democratic Republican factions from competing against each other. Indeed, there was quite a bit of intraparty rivalry. Finally, in 1824 and 1828, Democratic Republicans who belonged to the factions of Henry Clay and John Quincy Adams split with the rest of the party to oppose Andrew Jackson in those elections. Jackson's supporters and the Clay-Adams bloc formed separate parties, the **Democratic Party** and the **Whig**

---

[7]Letter to Francis Hopkinson written from Paris while Jefferson was minister to France. In John P. Foley, ed., *The Jeffersonian Cyclopedia* (New York: Russell & Russell, 1967), p. 677.

Andrew Jackson earned the name "Old Hickory" for his exploits during the War of 1812. In 1828, Jackson was elected president as the candidate of the new Democratic Party.

Party, respectively. That same Democratic Party is now the oldest continuing political party in the Western world. The Whig Party, one of the foremost political organizations in the United States during the first half of the nineteenth century was able to elect two presidents—William Henry Harrison in 1840 and Zachary Taylor in 1848. The Whigs, however, were unable to maintain a common ideological base when the party became increasingly divided over the issue of slavery in the late 1840s. During the 1850s, the Whigs fell apart as a national party.

The Post–Civil War Period

The existing two-party system was disrupted by the election of 1860, in which there were four major candidates. Abraham Lincoln, the candidate of the newly formed Republican Party, was the victor with a majority of the electoral vote, although with only 39.9 percent of the popular vote. This newly formed Republican Party—not to be confused with the Democratic Republicans—was created in the mid-1850s from the various groups that sought to fill the vacuum left by the disintegration of the Whigs. It took the label of Grand Old Party, or GOP.

After the end of the Civil War, the South became heavily Democratic (the Solid South), and the North became heavily Republican. This era of Republican dominance was highlighted by the election of 1896, when the Republicans, emphasizing economic development and modernization under William McKinley, resoundingly defeated the Democratic and Populist candidate, William Jennings Bryan. The Republicans' control was solidified by winning over the urban working-class vote in northern cities. From the election of Abraham Lincoln in 1860 until the election of Franklin D. Roosevelt in 1932, the Republicans won all but four presidential elections.

The Progressive Movement

In 1912, a major schism occurred in the Republican Party when former Republican president Theodore Roosevelt ran for the presidency as a Progressive. Consequently, there were three significant contenders in that presidential contest. Woodrow Wilson was the Democratic candidate, William Howard Taft was the regular Republican candidate, and Roosevelt was the Progressive candidate. The Republican split allowed Wilson to be elected. The Wilson administration, although Democratic, ended up enacting much of the Progressive Party's platform. Left without any reason for opposition, the Progressive Party collapsed in 1921.

Republican Warren Harding's victory in 1920 reasserted Republican domination of national politics until the Republicans' defeat by Franklin D. Roosevelt in 1932, in the depths of the Great Depression.

The Modern Era: From the New Deal to the Present

Franklin D. Roosevelt was elected in 1932 and reelected in 1936, 1940, and 1944. The impact of his successive Democratic administrations and the New Deal that he crafted is still with us today. Roosevelt used his enormous personal appeal to unify Democrats under his leadership, and he established direct communication between the president and the public through his radio fireside chats.

In April 1945, Roosevelt died; Vice President Harry Truman became president through succession and, in 1948, through election. The New Deal coalition, under Truman's revised theme of the Fair Deal, continued. It was not until Republican Dwight Eisenhower won the 1952 election that the Democrats lost their control of the presidency. Eisenhower was reelected in 1956.

From 1960 through 1968, the Democrats, led first by John F. Kennedy and then by Lyndon B. Johnson, held national power. Republicans again gained control of the presidency with Richard Nixon's victory in 1968 and retained it in 1972, but they lost prestige after the Watergate scandal forced Nixon's resignation on August 8, 1974. For

William McKinley campaigns in 1896 on a platform draped with the flag. Similar decorations would be used by candidates a century later.

this and other reasons, the Democrats were back in power after the presidential elections in 1976. But Democratic president Jimmy Carter was unable to win reelection against Ronald Reagan in 1980. The Republicans also gained control of the Senate in 1980 and retained it in the elections of 1982 and 1984. The 1984 reelection of Ronald Reagan appeared to some pollsters to signal the resurgence of the Republican Party as a competitive force in American politics as more people declared themselves to be Republicans than had done so in the previous several decades.

The election of George Bush in 1988 may have signaled the beginning of a true era of **divided government**. Divided government occurs when one major political party controls the presidency and the other controls the chambers of Congress, or when one party controls a state governorship and the other controls the state legislature. Republican Bush won the presidency, but his Republican Party lost seats in the House and Senate to Democrats. In 1992, Democrat Bill Clinton won the presidency, with Democratic control of the House and Senate, but his party actually lost congressional seats, presaging the Democrats' debacle in 1994 when the Republicans took control of both the House and the Senate. In 1996, Bill Clinton was reelected, but the voters returned Republicans to control in Congress. Republicans also controlled most of the governorships in the states. Divided government can lead to stalemate, but to many American voters it is a way to avoid the excesses of both parties.

PARTY ORGANIZATION AND IDEOLOGY

The two major American political parties are often characterized as being too much like Tweedledee and Tweedledum, the twins in Lewis Carroll's *Through the Looking Glass*. When both parties nominate moderates for the presidency, the similarities between the parties seem to outweigh their differences. Yet the political parties do generate strong conflict for political offices throughout the United States, and there are significant differences between the parties, both in the characteristics of their members and in their platforms. Here, we examine how the parties organize their efforts to win elections and look at some of the ideological differences between the two major parties in the United States.

Party Organization

In theory, each of the American political parties has a standard, pyramid-shaped **party organization,** with the national chairperson and national committee at the top of the pyramid and the local (precinct) chairperson and committee at the bottom. The pyramid, however, does not accurately reflect the relative power and strengths of the individual parts of the party organization. If it did, the national chairperson of the Democratic Party or the Republican Party, along with the national committee, could simply dictate how the organization was to be run, just as if it were ExxonMobil Corporation or Ford Motor Company.

In reality, the formal structure of the political parties resembles a layer cake with autonomous strata more than it does a pyramid. Malcolm E. Jewell and David M.

Olson point out that "there is no command structure within political parties. Rather, each geographic unit of the party tends to be autonomous from the other units at its same geographic level."[8]

The National Party Organization. Each party has a national organization, the most clearly institutional part of which is the national convention, held every four years. The convention is used to nominate the presidential and vice presidential candidates. In addition, the party platform is written, ratified, and revised at the national convention. The platform sets forth the party's position on the issues and makes promises to initiate certain policies if the party wins the presidency.

INFOTRAC®

"Both Parties Rake Record Cash"

After the convention, the platform frequently is neglected or ignored by party candidates who disagree with it. Because candidates are trying to win votes from a wide spectrum of voters, it is counterproductive to emphasize the fairly narrow and sometimes controversial goals set forth in the platform. The work of Gerald M. Pomper has shown, however, that once elected, the parties do try to carry out platform promises and that roughly three-fourths of the promises eventually become law.[9] Of course, some general goals, such as economic prosperity, are included in the platforms of both parties.

At the national convention, each of the parties formally chooses a national standing committee, elected by the individual state parties. This national committee is established to direct and coordinate party activities during the following four years. One of the jobs of the national committee is to ratify the presidential nominee's choice of a national chairperson, who in principle acts as the spokesperson for the party. (If that candidate loses, however, the chairperson is often changed.) Basically, the national chairperson and the national committee simply plan the next campaign and the next convention, obtain financial contributions, and publicize the national party. They also attempt to maintain some sort of liaison among the different levels of the party organization. The fact is that the real strength and power of a national party are at the state level.

The State Party Organization. Because every state party is unique, it is impossible to describe what an "average" state political party is like. Nonetheless, state parties have several organizational features in common: each state party has a chairperson, a committee, and a number of local organizations. In principle, each state central committee—the principal organized structure of each political party within each state—has a similar role in the various states. The committee, usually composed of those members who represent congressional districts, state legislative districts, or counties, has responsibility for carrying out the policy decisions of the party's state convention, and in some states the state committee will direct the state chairperson with respect to policymaking.

---

[8]Malcolm E. Jewell and David M. Olson, *American State Political Parties and Elections*, rev. ed. (Homewood, Ill.: Dorsey Press, 1982), p. 73.

[9]Gerald M. Pomper and Susan S. Lederman, *Elections in America: Control and Influence in Democratic Politics*, 2d ed. (New York: Longman, 1980).

Also, like the national committee, the state central committee has control over the use of party campaign funds during political campaigns. Usually, the state central committee has little, if any, influence on party candidates once they are elected. In fact, state parties are fundamentally loose alliances of local interests and coalitions of often bitterly opposed factions.

State parties are also important in national politics because of the **unit rule,** which awards electoral votes in presidential elections as an indivisible bloc (except in Maine and Nebraska). Presidential candidates concentrate their efforts in states in which voter preferences seem to be evenly divided or in which large numbers of electoral votes are at stake.

Local Party Machinery: The Grassroots. The lowest layer of party machinery is the local organization, supported by district leaders, precinct or ward captains, and party workers. Much of the work is coordinated by county committees and their chairpersons. At the end of the nineteenth century, the institution of **patronage**—rewarding the party faithful with government jobs or contracts—held the local organization together. For immigrants and the poor, the political machine often furnished important services and protections. The big-city machine was the archetypal example, and Tammany Hall, or the Tammany Society, which dominated New York City government for nearly two centuries, was perhaps the highest refinement of this political form.

The last big-city local political machine to exercise a great deal of power was run by Chicago's Mayor Richard J. Daley, who was also an important figure in national Democratic politics. Daley, as mayor, ran the Chicago Democratic machine from 1955 until his death in 1976. The Daley organization, largely Irish in candidate origin and voter support, was split by the successful candidacy of African American Democrat Harold Washington in the racially divisive 1983 mayoral election. The current mayor of Chicago, Richard M. Daley, son of the former mayor, today heads a party organization that includes many different groups in the electorate.

City machines are now dead, mostly because their function of providing social services (and reaping the reward of votes) has been taken over by state and national agencies. This trend began in the 1930s, when the social legislation of the New Deal established Social Security and unemployment insurance. The local party machine has little, if anything, to do with deciding who is eligible to receive these benefits.

Local political organizations, whether located in cities, in townships, or at the county level, still can contribute a great deal to local election campaigns. These organizations are able to provide the foot soldiers of politics—individuals who pass out literature and get out the vote on election day, which can be crucial in local elections. In many regions, local Democratic and Republican organizations still exercise some patronage, such as awarding courthouse jobs, contracts for street repair, and other lucrative construction contracts. Local party organizations are also the most important vehicles for recruiting young adults into political work, because political involvement at the local level offers activists many opportunities to gain experience.

Differences between the Parties

Although Democrats and Republicans are not divided along religious or class lines to the extent that some European parties are, certain social groups are more likely to identify with each party. Since the New Deal of Franklin D. Roosevelt, the Democratic Party has appealed to the more disadvantaged groups in society. African American voters are far more likely to identify with the Democrats, as are members of union households, Jewish voters, and individuals who have less than a high school education. Republicans draw more of their support from college graduates, upper-income families, and professionals or businesspersons. In recent years, more women than men have tended to identify themselves as Democrats than as Republicans.

The coalition of minorities, the working class, and various ethnic groups has been the core of Democratic Party support since the presidency of Franklin D. Roosevelt. The social programs and increased government intervention in the economy that were the heart of Roosevelt's New Deal were intended to ease the strain of economic hard times on these groups. This goal remains important for many Democrats today. In general, Democratic identifiers are more likely to approve of social-welfare spending, to support government regulation of business, to approve of measures to improve the situation of minorities, and to support assistance to the elderly with their medical expenses. Republicans are more supportive of the private marketplace, and many Republicans feel that the federal government should be involved in fewer social programs.

According to polling data, a majority of Americans think that Republicans are likely to do a better job on national defense, foreign affairs, balancing the budget, handling crime and the drug problem, and changing campaign-finance laws. Democrats are seen as having an advantage with respect to protecting Social Security and Medicare, improving the schools, protecting the environment, and helping the poor. These are the issues that are most attractive to Democratic voters.

Note that by the early 2000s, Democrats and Republicans were viewed as about equally trustworthy on issues of keeping the economy strong and taxes low. This is a bit of a reversal from the years of Ronald Reagan and George Bush, when Republicans were perceived to have an advantage on economic issues. The strong performance of the nation's economy during the Clinton presidency apparently increased voters' confidence in the ability of the Democratic Party to address economic issues effectively.

The Party in Government

After the election is over and the winners are announced, the focus of party activity shifts from getting out the vote to organizing and controlling the government. As you will see in Chapter 9, party membership plays an important role in the day-to-day operations of Congress, with partisanship determining everything from office space to committee assignments and power on Capitol Hill. For the president, the political party furnishes the pool of qualified applicants for political appointments to run the government. Although it is uncommon to do so, presidents can and occasionally do appoint executive personnel, such as cabinet secretaries, from the opposition party. As we note in Chapter 11, there are not as many of these appointed positions as presidents might like, and presidential power is limited by the permanent bureaucracy. Judicial appointments, however, offer a great opportunity to the winning party. For the most part, presidents are likely to appoint federal judges from their own party.

All of these party appointments suggest that the winning political party, whether at the national, state, or local level, has a great deal of control in the American system. Because of the checks and balances and the relative lack of cohesion in American parties, however, such control is an illusion. In fact, many Americans, at least implicitly, prefer a "divided government," with the executive and legislative branches controlled by different parties.

THE AMERICAN TWO-PARTY SYSTEM

Many democratic systems around the globe have three-party, four-party, or even ten-party systems. In contrast, the United States has a **two-party system,** and that system has been around from about 1800 to the present. Considering the range of political ideology among voters and the variety of local and state party machines, the fact that we still have just two major political parties is somewhat unusual.

Why Do We Have a Two-Party System?

There are several reasons why two major parties have dominated the political landscape in the United States for almost two centuries. These reasons have to do with (1) the historical foundations of the system, (2) the self-perpetuation of the parties, (3) the commonality of views among Americans, (4) the winner-take-all electoral system, and (5) state and federal laws favoring the two-party system.

The Historical Foundations of the Two-Party System. As we have seen, the first two opposing groups in U.S. politics were the Federalists and the Anti-Federalists. The Federalists, who remained in power and solidified their identity as a political party, represented those with commercial interests, including merchants, shipowners, and manufacturers. The Federalists supported the principle of a strong national government. The Anti-Federalists, who gradually became known as the Democratic Republicans, represented artisans and farmers. They strongly supported states' rights. These interests were also fairly well split along geographic lines, with the Federalists dominant in the North and the Democratic Republicans dominant in the South.

Two relatively distinct sets of interests continued to characterize American politics. During Andrew Jackson's time in power, eastern commercial interests were pitted against western and southern agricultural and frontier interests. Before the Civil War, the major split again became North versus South. The split was ideological (over the issue of slavery), as well as economic (the Northeast's industrial interests versus the agricultural interests of the South). After the Civil War, the Republicans found most of their strength in the Northeast, and the Democrats, among white voters in the Solid South. The period from the Civil War to the 1920s has been called one of **sectional politics.**

Sectional politics gave way to **national politics** as the entire nation became more urban and industrialized. The contemporary period can also be described as one of **class politics,** with the Republicans generally finding support among groups of higher economic status and the Democrats appealing more to working-class constituencies and the poor.

Self-Perpetuation of the Two-Party System. As we saw in Chapter 6, most children identify with the political party of their parents. Children learn at a fairly young age to think of themselves as either Democrats or Republicans. Relatively few are taught to think of themselves as libertarians or socialists or even independents. This generates a built-in mechanism to perpetuate a two-party system. Also, many politically oriented people who aspire to work for social change consider that the only realistic way to capture political power in this country is to be either a Republican or a Democrat.

A Commonality of Goals. Another determining factor in the perpetuation of our two-party system is the commonality of goals among Americans. Most Americans want continuing material prosperity. There has never been much support for the idea of limiting the ownership of private property or equalizing everyone's income. Most Americans take a dim view of such proposals. Private property is considered a basic American value, and the ability to acquire and use it the way one wishes commonly is regarded as a basic American right. Thus, socialist parties have found limited support.

This handbill was used in the election campaign of 1860. Handbills served the same purpose as today's direct-mail advertisements, appealing directly to the voters with the candidate's message.

Another reason we have had a basic consensus about our political system and the two major parties is that we have managed largely to separate religion from politics. Religion was an issue in 1928, when Governor Alfred Smith of New York became the first Roman Catholic to be nominated for the presidency (he was defeated by Republican Herbert Hoover), and again in 1960, when John F. Kennedy was running for president. But religion has never been a dividing force triggering splinter parties. There has never been a major Catholic party or a Protestant party or a Jewish party or a Muslim party.

The major division in American politics has been economic. As we mentioned earlier, the Democrats have been known—at least since the 1920s—as the party of the working class. They have been in favor of government intervention in the economy and more government redistribution of income from the wealthy to those with lower incomes. The Republican Party has been known in modern times as the party of the middle and upper classes and commercial interests, in favor of fewer constraints on the market system and less redistribution of income.

Not only does the political culture support the two-party system, but also the parties themselves are adept at making the necessary shifts in their platforms or electoral appeal to gain new members. Because the general ideological structure of the parties is so broad, it has been relatively easy for them to change their respective platforms or to borrow popular policies from the opposing party or from minor parties to attract voter support. Both parties perceive themselves as being broad enough to accommodate every group in society.

The Winner-Take-All Electoral System. At virtually every level of government in the United States, the outcome of elections is based on the plurality, winner-take-all principle. A plurality system is one in which the winner is the person who obtains the most votes, even if a majority is not obtained. Whoever gets the most votes gets everything. Because most legislators in the United States are elected from single-member districts in which only one person represents the constituency, the candidate who finishes second in such an election receives nothing for the effort.

Many countries do not use the plurality, winner-take-all electoral system. Some hold run-off elections until a candidate obtains at least one vote over 50 percent of the votes. Such a system also may be used in countries with multiple parties. Small parties hope to be able to obtain a sufficient number of votes at least to get into a run-off election. Many other nations use a system of proportional representation with multi-member districts. If, during the national election, party X obtains 12 percent of the vote, party Y gets 43 percent of the vote, and party Z gets the remaining 45 percent of the vote, then party X gets 12 percent of the seats in the legislature, party Y gets 43 percent of the seats, and party Z gets 45 percent of the seats. Because even a minor party may still obtain at least a few seats in the legislature, the smaller parties have a greater incentive to organize under such electoral systems than they do in the United States.

State and Federal Laws Favoring the Two Parties. Many state and federal election laws offer a clear advantage to the two major parties. In some states, the established major parties need to gather fewer signatures to place their candidates on the ballot than minor parties or independent candidates do. The criterion for determining how many signatures will be required is often based on the total party vote in the last general election, thus penalizing a new political party that did not compete in that election.

At the national level, minor parties face different obstacles. All of the rules and procedures of both houses of Congress divide committee seats, staff members, and other privileges on the basis of party membership. A legislator who is elected on a minor-party ticket, such as the Liberal Party of New York, must choose to be counted with one of the major parties to get a committee assignment. The Federal Election Commission (FEC) rules for campaign financing also place restrictions on minor-party candidates. Such candidates are not eligible for federal matching funds in either the primary or the general election. In the 1980 election, John Anderson, running for president as an independent, sued the FEC for campaign funds. The commission finally agreed to repay part of his campaign costs after the election in proportion to the votes he received.

The Role of Minor Parties

For the reasons just discussed, minor parties have a difficult, if not impossible, time competing within the American two-party political system. Nonetheless, minor parties have played an important role in our political life. Frequently, dissatisfied groups have split from major parties and formed so-called third parties, which have acted as barometers of changes in the political mood.[10] Such barometric indicators have forced the major parties to recognize new issues or trends in the thinking of

---

[10]The term *third party* is erroneous, because sometimes there have been third, fourth, fifth, and even sixth parties. Because it has endured, however, we will use the term here.

Americans. Political scientists also believe that third parties have acted as a safety valve for dissident political groups, perhaps preventing major confrontations and political unrest. Additionally, parties may be formed to represent a particular ethnic group, such as Hispanics, or groups such as gays and lesbians.

Historically Important Minor Parties. Most minor parties that have endured have had a strong ideological foundation that is typically at odds with the majority mind-set. Some of the notable third parties include the following:

1. The Socialist Labor Party, started in 1877.
2. The Socialist Party, founded in 1901.
3. The Communist Party, started in 1919 as the radical left wing that split from the Socialist Party.
4. The Socialist Workers' Party, formerly a Trotskyite group, started in 1938.
5. The Libertarian Party, formed in 1972 and still an important minor party.
6. The Reform Party, founded in 1996.

As we can see from their labels, several of these minor parties have been Marxist oriented. The most successful was Eugene Debs's Socialist Party, which captured 6 percent of the popular vote for president in 1912 and elected more than a thousand candidates at the local level. About eighty mayors were affiliated with the Socialist Party at one time or another. It owed much of its success to the corruption of big-city machines and to antiwar sentiment. At the other end of the ideological spectrum, the Libertarian Party supports a *laissez-faire* capitalist economic program, combined with a hands-off policy on regulating matters of moral conduct.

Splinter Minor Parties. The most successful minor parties have been those that split from major parties. The impetus for these **splinter parties,** or factions, has usually been a situation in which a particular personality was at odds with the major party. The most famous spin-off was the Bull Moose Progressive Party, which split from the Republican Party in 1912 over the candidate chosen to run for president. Theodore Roosevelt rallied his forces and announced the formation of the Bull Moose Progressive Party, leaving the regular Republicans to support William Howard Taft. Although the party was not successful in winning the election for Roosevelt, it did succeed in splitting the Republican vote so that Democrat Woodrow Wilson won.

Among the Democrats, there have been three splinter third parties since the late 1940s: (1) the Dixiecrat (States' Rights) Party of 1948, (2) Henry Wallace's Progressive Party of 1948, and (3) the American Independent Party supporting George Wallace in 1968. The strategy employed by Wallace in the 1968 election was to deny Richard Nixon or Hubert Humphrey the necessary majority in the electoral college. Many political scientists believe that Humphrey still would have lost to Nixon in 1968 even if Wallace had not run, because most Wallace voters would probably have given their votes to Nixon. The American Independent Party emphasized mostly racial issues and, to a lesser extent, foreign policy. Wallace received 9.9 million popular votes and 46 electoral votes.

Theodore Roosevelt, president of the United States from 1901 to 1909, became president after William McKinley was assassinated. Roosevelt was reelected in 1904. In 1912, unable to gain the nomination of the Republican Party, Roosevelt formed a splinter group named the Bull Moose Progressive Party but was unsuccessful in his efforts to win the presidency.

Other Minor Parties. Numerous minor parties have coalesced around specific issues or aims. The Free Soil Party, active from 1848 to 1852, was dedicated to preventing the spread of slavery. The goal of the Prohibition Party, started in 1869, was to ban the sale of liquor.

Some minor parties have had specific economic interests as their reason for being. When those interests are either met or made irrelevant by changing economic conditions, these minor parties disappear. Such was the case with the Greenback Party, which lasted from 1876 to 1884. It was one of the most prominent farmer-labor parties that favored government intervention in the economy. Similar to the Greenbacks, but with broader support, was the Populist Party, which lasted from about 1892 to 1908. Farmers were the backbone of this party, and agrarian reform was its goal. In 1892, it ran a presidential candidate, James Weaver, who received one million popular votes and twenty-two electoral votes. The Populists, for the most part, joined with the Democrats in 1896, when both parties endorsed the Democratic presidential candidate, William Jennings Bryan.

The Impact of Minor Parties. Minor parties clearly have had an impact on American politics. What is more difficult to ascertain is how great that impact has been. Simply by showing that third-party issues were taken over some years later by a major party really does not prove that the third party instigated the major party's change. The case for the importance of minor parties may be strongest for the splinter parties. These parties do indeed force a major party to reassess its ideology and organization. There is general agreement that Teddy Roosevelt's Progressive Party in 1912 and Robert La Follette's Progressive Party in 1924 caused the major parties to take up business regulation as one of their major issues.

Minnesota governor Jesse Ventura introduces his $23 billion, two-year budget Thursday, January 28, 1999, at the World Trade Center in St. Paul, Minnesota. The budget calls for cuts in both income tax rates and auto registration fees, and sets up endowments for the tobacco settlement.

Minor parties can also have a serious impact on the outcome of an election. Although Bill Clinton might well have won the 1992 election in any case, the campaign of H. Ross Perot left its imprint on American politics. In 1992, Perot was not the candidate of a third party; rather, he was antiparty, attacking both major political parties for being ineffective and beholden to special interests. Perot had a very strong appeal to young voters, to independent voters, and to disaffected party identifiers.

Carol Miller, a member of the Green Party, recently won 17 percent of the vote in a special election for New Mexico's Third District congressional seat. Using a populist and environmentalist platform, the Green Party has garnered enough votes in New Mexico elections since 1994 to allow the Republicans to win three major races in a state having a Democratic majority.

In 1996, as the Reform Party candidate, Perot received only 8 percent of the national vote. This total was enough to affect the margins of both Dole and Clinton, but because Perot drew votes from Republicans, Democrats, and independents, his campaign did not keep Clinton from being reelected. In 1998, Jesse Ventura became the first Reform Party candidate to gain a statewide office. The success of Ventura, a former wrestler who was largely ignored by the press and his opponents as a serious contender, was one of the great surprises of the 1998 elections. During his campaign, Ventura had struck a largely antiparty, antiestablishment pose. Ventura regarded his victory as a "wake-up call" to the major parties. A few months after the election, he stated, "If these parties don't wake up from their bipartisan bickering, there will be more Jesse Venturas on the horizon."[11] In 2000, Ventura announced his decision to leave the Reform Party and establish an independent party.

INFOTRAC®

"McCain's Next Big Move"

The Uncertain Future of Party Identification

Calling the U.S. system a two-party system is an oversimplification. The nature and names of the major parties have changed over time, and smaller parties have almost always enjoyed a moderate degree of success. What is evident in recent years is the rise of the independent voter combined with a relative strengthening of support for the Republican Party, so that the traditional Democratic advantage in party identification is relatively small today. Trends in **party identification,** as measured by standard polling techniques over time, show that in the 1940s, only about 20 percent of voters classified themselves as independents. By 1975, this percentage had increased to about 33 percent, and more recent polls show it holding steady at about that level. At times, the Democrats have captured the loyalty of about half the electorate, and the Republicans, until 1960, had more than 30 percent support. By the 1990s, the Democrats could count on less than 40 percent of the electorate and the Republicans, on about 30 percent.

Not only have ties to the two major parties weakened in the last three decades, but also voters are less willing to vote a straight ticket—that is, to vote for all the candidates of one party. The percentage of voters who do not vote a straight ticket has increased from 12 percent in 1952 to more than 38 percent in the presidential election of 1996. This trend, along with the increase in the number of voters who call themselves independents, suggests that parties have lost much of their hold on the loyalty of the voters.

[11]"Ventura Muscles Up a Warning," *Tulsa World*, February 23, 1999, p. 5.

KEY TERMS

CHAPTER SUMMARY

❶ An interest group is an organization whose members share common objectives and who actively attempt to influence government policy. Interest groups proliferate in the United States because they can influence government at many points in the political structure. A political party, in contrast, is a group of political activists who organize to win elections, operate the government, and determine public policy.

❷ Major types of interest groups include business, agricultural, labor, public employee, professional, and environmental groups. Other important groups may be considered public-interest groups. In addition, special interest groups and foreign governments lobby the government.

❸ Interest groups use direct and indirect techniques to influence government. Direct techniques include testifying before committees and rulemaking agencies, providing information to legislators, rating legislators' voting records, and making campaign contributions. Contributions are often made through political action committees, or PACs. Indirect techniques to influence government include campaigns to rally public sentiment, letter-writing campaigns, and using constituents to lobby for the group's interest.

❹ The 1946 Legislative Reorganization Act was the first attempt to control lobbyists and their activities through registration requirements. The Supreme Court narrowly construed the act as applying only to lobbyists who directly seek to influence federal legislation. In 1995, Congress approved new legislation requiring anyone who spends 20 percent of his or her time influencing legislation to register. Also, any organization spending $20,000 or more and any individual who is paid more than $5,000 annually for his or her work must register. Grassroots lobbying and the lobbying efforts of tax-exempt organizations are exempt from the new rules.

❺ Political parties perform a number of functions for the political system. These functions include recruiting candidates for public office, organizing and running elections, presenting alternative policies to the voters, assuming responsibility for operating the government, and acting as the opposition to the party in power.

❻ The evolution of our nation's political parties can be divided into six periods: (a) the creation and formation of political parties from 1789 to 1812; (b) the era of one-party rule, or personal politics, from 1816 to 1824; (c) the period from Andrew Jackson's presidency to the Civil War, from 1828 to 1860; (d) the post–Civil War period, from 1864 to 1892, ending with solid control by the modern Republican Party; (e) the progressive period, from 1896 to 1928; and (f) the modern period, from 1932 to the present.

❼ In theory, each of the political parties has a pyramid-shaped organization with a hierarchical command structure. In reality, each level of the party—local, state, and national—has considerable autonomy. The national party organization is responsible for holding the national convention in presidential election years, writing the party platform, choosing the national committee, and conducting party business.

8 Although it may seem that the two major American political parties do not differ substantially on the issues, each has a different core group of supporters. The general shape of the parties' coalitions reflects the party divisions of Franklin Roosevelt's New Deal. It is clear, however, that party leaders are much further apart in their views than are the party followers. The party in government comprises all of the elected and appointed officeholders of a party.

9 Two major parties have dominated the political landscape in the United States for almost two centuries. The reasons for this include (a) the historical foundations of the system, (b) the self-perpetuation of the parties, (c) the commonality of views among Americans, (d) the winner-take-all electoral system, and (e) state and federal laws favoring the two-party system. Minor parties have emerged from time to time, often as dissatisfied splinter groups from within major parties, and have acted as barometers of changes in political moods. Splinter parties, or factions, usually have emerged when a particular personality was at odds with the major party, as when Teddy Roosevelt's differences with the Republican Party resulted in the formation of the Bull Moose Progressive Party. Numerous other minor parties, such as the Prohibition Party, have formed around single issues.

10 Minor parties have sometimes had a serious impact on the outcome of elections. In 1992, for example, the candidacy of H. Ross Perot drew enough support to change the outcome of the presidential election. In 1998, Jesse Ventura became the first Reform Party candidate to win a statewide office—the governorship of Minnesota. From the 1940s to the present, independent voters have formed an increasing proportion of the electorate, with a consequent decline of strongly Democratic or strongly Republican voters.

SELECTED PRINT AND ELECTRONIC RESOURCES

Suggested Readings

Beck, Paul Allen. *Party Politics in America*. 8th ed. New York: Longman, 1998. This excellent text covers the role of parties in the late twentieth century, the changes in campaign financing, and the role of parties in the life of the voter.

Berry, Jeffrey M. *The Interest Group Society*. 3d ed. New York: Longman, 1997. This is an excellent overview and discussion of the ways in which interest groups and lobbies participate in the political system.

Dionne, E. J., Jr. *They Only Look Dead: Why Progressives Will Dominate the Next Political Era*. New York: Simon & Schuster, 1995. A commentary on the state of American politics by a noted *Washington Post* journalist. Dionne predicts the possible creation of a third party out of the middle class that is dissatisfied with both parties.

Wilson, James Q. *Political Organizations* (with a new introduction to the 1974 edition). Princeton, N.J.: Princeton University Press, 1995. This is one of the classic works on the formation and membership of interest groups in American society. Wilson looks closely at the motivations of a group's members and the relationship of the members to the leaders of a group.

Media Resources

A Third Choice—A film that examines America's experience with third parties and independent candidates throughout American political history.

Norma Rae—A 1979 film about an attempt by a northern union organizer to unionize workers in the southern textile industry; stars Sally Field.

Silkwood—A 1983 film focusing on the story of a nuclear plant worker who attempted to investigate safety issues at the plant and ended up losing her job; stars Meryl Streep and Cher.

Washington under the Influence—A segment of the PBS series On the Issues, produced in 1993, in which ABC news correspondent Jeff Greenfield follows the trail of lobbyists, press leaks, and PAC money as a corporation faces Senate hearings following allegations that the company's popular product causes injury.

LOGGING ON

Interest groups have established literally hundreds of sites that you can investigate. A good starting point is the Web site of Internet Public Library (IPL) Associations on the Net, which provides efficient access to more than six hundred professional and trade associations. Go to

http://www.ipl.org/ref/AON

The Democratic Party is online at

http://www.democrats.org

The Republican National Committee is at

http://www.rnc.org

The Libertarian Party has a Web site at

http://www.lp.org/lp.html

The Socialist Party in the United States can be found at

http://sp-usa.org

The Pew Research Center for the American People and the Press offers survey data online on how the parties fared during the most recent elections, voter typology, and numerous other issues. To access this site, go to

http://www.people-press.org

USING THE INTERNET FOR POLITICAL ANALYSIS

Access the home pages of both the Democratic and Republican Parties using the URLs given in the *Logging on*. List at least three major differences in the policies and approaches to government of the two parties. Then look at the home page for one of the other parties—such as the Libertarian, Socialist Workers, Green, or Populist Party—and compare the policy positions you find there with those of the major parties. What other kinds of information truly differentiate the major parties from the minor ones? To what extent do the two major parties manage to ignore or minimize the importance of any other parties? How do the goals of the major parties differ from those of the minor parties?

CHAPTER 8

Campaigns, Elections and Voting Behavior

Political campaigns are at the heart of a democratic political system. When voters go to the polls and choose between candidates who have presented their views on leadership and policy, the citizens are exercising the fundamental right to choose the leadership of the nation and, thus, to direct national policy. The same process is repeated at every level of government in the United States: on election day, voters choose members of the town council, the county prosecuting attorney, state legislators, governors, and members of Congress, depending on the year in the political cycle. In each of these venues, candidates depend on their campaigns to sway the voters and win the election.

THE PEOPLE WHO RUN FOR OFFICE

For democracy to work, there must be candidates for office, and for voters to have a choice, there must be competing candidates for most offices. The presidential campaign provides the most colorful and exciting look at these candidates and how they prepare to compete for the highest office in the land. In fact, soon after President Bill Clinton was reelected in 1996, men and women who wanted to be candidates in the 2000 presidential campaign began to assess their chances of winning. They faced a long and obstacle-filled path: first, they needed to raise enough money to tour the nation, particularly the early primary states, to see if they had enough local supporters. Then, they needed funds to start up an organization, devise a plan to win primary votes, and win the party's nomination at the national convention. Finally, they needed funds to finance a successful campaign for president. Always, at every turn, was the question of whether they would have enough money to wage a campaign.

Who Is Eligible?

There are few constitutional restrictions on who can become a candidate in the United States. As detailed in the Constitution, the formal requirements for a national office are as follows:

1. *President.* Must be a natural-born citizen, have attained the age of thirty-five years, and be a resident of the country for fourteen years by the time of inauguration.

2. *Vice president.* Must be a natural-born citizen, have attained the age of thirty-five years, and not be a resident of the same state as the candidate for president.

3. *Senator.* Must be a citizen for at least nine years, have attained the age of thirty by the time of taking office, and be a resident of the state from which elected.

4. *Representative.* Must be a citizen for at least seven years, have attained the age of twenty-five by the time of taking office, and be a resident of the state from which elected.

The qualifications for state legislators are set by the state constitutions and likewise relate to age, place of residence, and citizenship. (Usually, the requirements for the upper chamber of a legislature are somewhat higher than those for the lower chamber.) The legal qualifications for running for governor or other state office are similar.

Who Runs?

In spite of these minimal legal qualifications for office at both the national and state levels, a quick look at the slate of candidates in any election—or at the current members of the U.S. House of Representatives—will reveal that not all segments of the population take advantage of these opportunities. Holders of political office in the United States are overwhelmingly white and male. Until the twentieth century, politicians were also predominantly of northern European origin and predominantly Protestant. Laws enforcing segregation in the South and many border states, as well as laws that effectively denied voting rights, made it impossible to elect African American public officials in many areas in which African Americans constituted a significant portion of the population. As a result of the passage of major civil rights

Dwight D. Eisenhower campaigns for president in 1952. Why do few presidential candidates take the time to ride in parades today?

legislation in the last several decades, the number of African American public officials has increased throughout the United States.

Until recently, women generally were considered to be appropriate candidates only for lower-level offices, such as state legislator or school board member. The last ten years have seen a tremendous increase in the number of women who run for office, not only at the state level but for the U.S. Congress as well. In 1998, 134 women ran for Congress, and 60 were elected. Whereas African Americans were restricted from running for office by both law and custom, women generally were excluded by the agencies of recruitment—parties and interest groups—because they were thought to have no chance of winning or because they had not worked their way up through the party organization. Women also had a more difficult time raising campaign funds. Today, it is clear that women are just as likely as men to participate in many political activities, and a majority of Americans say they would vote for a qualified woman or for an African American for president of the United States.

Professional Status

Not only are candidates for office more likely to be male and white than female or African American, but they are also likely to be professionals, particularly lawyers. Political campaigning and officeholding are simply easier for some occupational and economic groups than for others, and political involvement can make a valuable contribution to certain careers. Lawyers, for example, have more flexible schedules than do other professionals, can take time off for campaigning, and can leave their jobs to hold public office full-time. Perhaps most important, many jobs that lawyers aspire to—federal or state judgeships, state attorney offices, or work in a federal agency—can be attained by political appointment.

THE MODERN CAMPAIGN MACHINE

American political campaigns are extravagant, year-long events that produce campaign buttons and posters for collectors, hours of film and sound to be relayed by the media, and, eventually, winning candidates who become the public officials of the nation. Campaigns are also enormously expensive; the total expenditures for all congressional and local races in 2000 were estimated to be several billion dollars. Political campaigns exhaust candidates, their staff members, and the journalists covering the campaign—to say nothing of the public's patience.

The Changing Campaign

Campaigns seem to be getting longer and more excessive each year. The goal of all the frantic activity of campaigns is the same for all of them—to convince voters to choose a candidate or a slate of candidates for office. Part of the reason for the increased intensity of campaigns in the last decade is that they have changed from being centered on the party to being centered on the candidate. The candidate-centered campaign emerged in response to changes in the electoral system, to the importance of television in campaigns, to technological innovations such as computers, and to the increased cost of campaigning.

To run a successful and persuasive campaign, the candidate's organization must be able to raise funds for the effort, get coverage from the media, produce and pay for political commercials and advertising, schedule the candidate's time effectively with constituent groups and prospective supporters, convey the candidate's position on the issues, conduct research on the opposing candidate, and get the voters to go to the polls. When party identification was stronger among voters and before the advent of television campaigning, a strong party organization on the local, state, or national level could furnish most of the services and expertise that the candidate needed. Until the 1970s, political parties provided the funds for campaigning. Parties used their precinct organizations to distribute literature, register voters, and get out the vote on election day. Less effort was spent on advertising for a single candidate's positions and character, because the party label communicated that information to many of the voters.

One of the reasons that campaigns no longer depend on parties is that fewer people identify with them (see Chapter 7), as is evident from the increased number of independent voters. In 1952, about 22 percent of the voters were independent voters; in 2000, between 26 and 33 percent classified themselves as independents, depending on the survey. Independent voters include not only well-educated and issue-oriented voters but also many voters who are not very interested in politics or well informed about candidates or issues.

The Professional Campaign

Whether the candidate is running for the state legislature, for the governor's office, for the U.S. Congress, or for the presidency, every campaign must accomplish some fundamental tasks. What is most striking about today's campaigns is that most of these tasks are now put into the hands of paid professionals rather than volunteers or amateur politicians.

The most sought-after and possibly the most criticized campaign expert is the **political consultant,** who, for a large fee, devises a campaign strategy, thinks up a campaign theme, and possibly chooses the campaign colors and candidate's portrait for all literature to be distributed. Political consultants began to displace volunteer campaign managers in the 1960s, about the same time that television became a force in campaigns. The paid consultant monitors the campaign's progress, plans all media appearances, and coaches the candidate for debates. The consultants and the firms they represent are not politically neutral; most will work only for candidates from one party or only for candidates of a particular ideological persuasion.

THE STRATEGY OF WINNING

The goal of every political campaign is the same: to win the election. In the United States, unlike some European countries, there are no rewards for a candidate who comes in second; the winner takes all. The campaign organization must plan a

"Trump's Top Op"

strategy to maximize the candidate's chances of winning. The basic wisdom that guides a campaign strategy in American politics is this: candidates seek to capture all the votes of their party members, to convince a majority of the independent voters to vote for them, and to gain a few votes from members of the other party. To accomplish these goals, candidates must consider their visibility, their message, and their campaign strategy.

Candidate Visibility and Appeal

One of the most important concerns is how well known the candidate is. If he or she is a highly visible incumbent, there may be little need for campaigning except to remind the voters of the officeholder's good deeds. If, however, the candidate is an unknown challenger or a largely unfamiliar character attacking a well-known public figure, the campaign must devise a strategy to get the candidate before the public.

In the case of an independent candidate or a candidate representing a minor party, the problem of name recognition is serious. There are usually a number of third-party candidates in each presidential election. Such candidates must present an overwhelming case for the voter to reject the major-party candidate. Both the Democratic and the Republican candidates use the strategic ploy of labeling third-party candidates as "not serious" and therefore not worth the voter's time.

George W. Bush, governor of Texas, greets a crowd as he begins his campaign for the 2000 Republican nomination for president.

The Use of Opinion Polls and Focus Groups

One of the major sources of information for both the media and the candidates is opinion polls. Poll taking is widespread during the primaries. Presidential hopefuls have private polls taken to make sure that there is at least some chance they could be nominated and, if nominated, elected. Also, because the party nominees depend on polls to fine-tune their campaigns, during the presidential campaign itself continual polls are taken. Polls are taken not only by the regular pollsters—Roper, Harris, Gallup, and others—but also privately by each candidate's campaign organization. These private polls, as opposed to the independent public polls conducted by Gallup and others, are for the exclusive and secret use of the candidate and her or his campaign organization.

As the election approaches, many candidates use **tracking polls,** which are polls taken almost every day, to find out how well they are competing for votes. Tracking polls, by indicating how well the campaign is going, enable consultants to fine-tune the advertising and the candidate's speeches in the last days of the campaign.

Another tactic is the use of **focus groups** to gain insights into public perceptions of the candidate. Professional consultants organize a discussion of the candidate or of certain political issues among ten to fifteen ordinary citizens. The citizens are selected from certain target groups in the population—for example, working men, blue-collar men, senior citizens, or young voters. The group discusses personality traits of the candidate, political advertising, and other candidate-related issues. The conversation is videotaped (and often observed from behind a mirrored wall). Focus groups are expected to reveal more emotional responses to candidates or the deeper anxieties of voters—expressions that consultants believe often are not tapped by more impersonal telephone surveys. The campaign then can shape its messages to respond to these feelings and perceptions.

FINANCING THE CAMPAIGN

In a book published in 1932 entitled *Money in Elections,* Louise Overacker had the following to say about campaign financing:

> The financing of elections in a democracy is a problem which is arousing increasing concern. Many are beginning to wonder if present-day methods of raising and spending campaign funds do not clog the wheels of our elaborately constructed mechanism of popular control, and if democracies do not inevitably become plutocracies.[1]

Although writing almost seventy years ago, Overacker touched on a sensitive issue in American political campaigns—the connection between money and elections. It is estimated that over $2.7 billion was spent at all levels of campaigning in the 1995–1996 election cycle. At the federal level alone, a total of more than $478 million is estimated to have been spent in races for the House of Representatives, $288 million in senatorial races, and $600 million in the presidential campaign. Except for the presidential campaign in the general election, all of the other money had to

---

[1]Louise Overacker, *Money in Elections* (New York: Macmillan, 1932), p. vii.

be provided by the candidates and their families, borrowed, or raised by contributions from individuals or PACs (as discussed in Chapter 7). For the general presidential campaign, much of the money comes from the federal government.

Regulating Campaign Financing

The way in which campaigns are financed has changed dramatically in the last two and a half decades, and today candidates and political parties, when trying to increase their funding sources, must operate within the constraints imposed by complicated laws regulating campaign financing.

There have been a variety of federal **corrupt practices acts** designed to regulate campaign financing. The first, passed in 1925, limited primary and general election expenses for congressional candidates. In addition, it required disclosure of election expenses and, in principle, put controls on contributions by corporations. Numerous loopholes were found in the restrictions on contributions, and the acts proved to be ineffective.

The Hatch Act. The **Hatch Act** (Political Activities Act) of 1939 was passed in another attempt to control political influence buying. That act forbade a political group to spend more than $3 million in any campaign and limited individual contributions to a political group to $5,000. Of course, such restrictions were easily circumvented by creating additional political groups.

The Federal Election Campaign Act. The Federal Election Campaign Act of 1971 essentially replaced all past laws and instituted a major reform. The act placed no limit on overall spending but restricted the amount that could be spent on mass-media advertising, including television. It limited the amount that candidates and their families could contribute to their own campaigns and required disclosure of all contributions and expenditures in excess of $100. In principle, the act limited the role of labor unions and corporations in political campaigns. It also provided for a voluntary $1 check-off on federal income tax returns for general campaign funds to be used by major-party presidential candidates (first applied in the 1976 campaign).

For many, however, the act did not go far enough. In 1974, Congress passed amendmens to the act that did the following:

1. *Created the Federal Election Commission.* This commission consists of six nonpartisan administrators whose duties are to enforce compliance with the requirements of the act.
2. *Provided public financing for presidential primaries and general elections.* Any candidate running for president who is able to obtain sufficient contributions in at least twenty states can obtain a subsidy from the U.S. Treasury to help pay for primary campaigns. Each major party was given $12.4 million for its national convention in 1996. The major-party candidates have federal support for almost all of their expenses, provided they are willing to accept campaign-spending limits.
3. *Limited presidential campaign spending.* Any candidate accepting federal support has to agree to limit campaign expenditures to the amount prescribed by federal law.

4. *Limited contributions.* Citizens can contribute up to $1,000 to each candidate in each federal election or primary; the total limit of all contributions from an individual to all candidates is $25,000 per year. Groups can contribute up to a maximum of $5,000 to a candidate in any election.

5. *Required disclosure.* Each candidate must file periodic reports with the Federal Election Commission, listing who contributed, how much was spent, and for what the money was spent.

In a significant 1976 case, *Buckley v. Valeo*,[2] the Supreme Court declared unconstiutional the provision in the 1971 act that limited the amount congressional candidates or their immediate families could spend on their own behalf: "The candidate, no less than any other person, has a First Amendment right to engage in the discussion of public issues and vigorously and tirelessly to advocate his own election."

The 1971 act, as further amended in 1976, allows corporations, labor unions, and special interest groups to set up PACs to raise money for candidates. For a PAC to be legitimate, the money must be raised from at least fifty volunteer donors and must be given to at least five candidates in the federal election. Each corporation or each union is limited to one PAC. As you might imagine, corporate PACs obtain funds from executives, employees, and stockholders in their firms, and unions obtain PAC funds from their members.[3]

Campaign Financing beyond the Limits

Within a few years after the establishment of the tight limits on contributions, new ways to finance campaigns were developed that skirt the reforms and make it possible for huge sums of money to be raised, especially by the major political parties.

Contributions to Political Parties. Candidates, PACs, and political parties have found ways to generate **soft money**—that is, campaign contributions to political parties that escape the rigid limits of federal election law. Although federal law limits contributions that are spent on elections, there are no limits on contributions to political parties for party activities such as voter education or voter-registration drives. This loophole has enabled the parties to raise millions of dollars from corporations and individuals. It has not been unusual in the past for such corporations as Time Warner (now AOL Time Warner) to give more than half a million dollars to the Democratic National Committee and for the tobacco companies to send more than a million dollars to the Republican Party.[4] The parties then spend this money for the convention, for registering voters, and for advertising to promote the general party position. The parties also send a great deal of the money to state and local party organizations, which use it to support their own tickets. (For a discussion of the use of soft money in recent campaigns, see this chapter's *At Issue: Should "Soft Money" Be Banned?*)

INFOTRAC®

"Long Shadow Soft Money Issue Advocacy"

INFOTRAC®

"Follow Money Hard Money Soft Money"

---

[2]424 U.S. 1 (1976).
[3]See Paul Allen Beck, *Party Politics in America*, 8th ed. (New York: Longman Publishers, 1997), p. 285.
[4]Beck, *Party Politics in America*, pp. 293–294.

Should "Soft Money" Be Banned?

The 1971 Federal Election Campaign Act, as amended, set strict limits on campaign contributions: $1,000 per election per individual and $5,000 per election per political action committee (PAC). In addition, annual limits on donations were also established. Such regulated contributions must be reported to the Federal Election Commission and are known as "hard money." Contributions that are not subject to the regulations are called "soft money." Soft money contributions to state and local parties were legitimized by a decision of the Federal Election Commission in 1978 and an amendment to the law in 1979.

During the 1996 and 1998 election cycles, the unprecedented amounts of "soft money" contributed to political parties became a contentious issue. In the 1997–1998 federal election cycle, for example, more than $2.7 billion was spent on campaign expenses. Of that total, more than $220 million was in soft money contributions. Some contend that soft money should be banned or restricted significantly.

Should soft money be banned? What effects would such a ban have, if implemented?

One effect of banning soft money would be, of course, that parties and party committees would have fewer funds to spend on campaigns. Because soft money must be spent on "party-building" efforts—such as getting voters to register, encouraging turnout, and, in the case of state and local parties, preparing campaign materials—expenditures on these activities would decline. Candidates might, in fact, be asked to share some of their own campaign funds with the parties to pay for such activities, as was the case before soft money was legalized in 1978.

The rationale for allowing soft money was to strengthen political parties, especially at the local and state levels. The federal campaign limits were seen as being so restrictive that after individuals had exhausted their annual giving limit, they could give no additional funds to help support local activities. The national parties, needing every penny of the legal contributions, no longer were interested in helping, or able to help, state and local parties. The banning of soft money contributions would thus probably weaken local and state parties and reduce their ability to help local candidates because there would be few "big money" sources for them to tap. Unless other sources of funding were provided to support political parties, they would likely return to the fragmented state characteristic of the mid-1970s.

Even if the practice of giving unregulated contributions to political parties and campaign committees were banned, it is doubtful that unregulated expenditures would disappear from the system. There are other ways to spend money on campaigns outside the parties—ways that are protected by the courts and the First Amendment. For example, unregulated political funds can be spent freely for "issue advertising."

In the 1996 campaign, both the AFL-CIO and the U.S. Chamber of Commerce developed and paid for national advertising campaigns that were supportive of their respective choices for president. Interest groups such as the tobacco industry can sponsor issue advertising, as can the Sierra Club. In fact, there are no limits on funds spent for advertising on issues so long as those expenditures are not, in the words of the Federal Election Commission, "coordinated with a candidate."

If soft money were banned, the amount of money spent on these "independent" campaign tactics would likely increase. As a result, there would be an even greater variety of voices in the political arena, and voters would find it even more difficult to identify the economic and political interests behind each advertisement.

FOR CRITICAL ANALYSIS

What kinds of funding could be provided to support the activities of state and local political parties so that they would no longer need soft money?

Independent Expenditures. Business corporations, labor unions, and other interest groups discovered that it was legal to make **independent expenditures** in an election campaign so long as the expenditures were not coordinated with those of the candidate or political party. Hundreds of unique committees and organizations blossomed to take advantage of this campaign tactic. Although a 1990 United States Supreme Court decision, *Austin v. Michigan State Chamber of Commerce,*[5] upheld the right of the states and the federal government to limit independent, direct corporate expenditures (such as for advertisements) on behalf of *candidates,* the decision did not stop business and other types of groups from making independent expenditures on *issues.*

Indeed, issue advocacy—spending unregulated money on advertising that promotes positions on issues rather than candidates—has become a prevalent tactic in recent years. Consider some examples. Prior to the 1996 campaign, Clinton's candidacy was greatly enhanced by a series of issue ads that accused the Republicans of wanting to damage Medicare if they were elected. These ads were developed and paid for by unregulated funds and were sponsored by organizations that were not directly connected with the president's own campaign. The Christian Coalition, which is incorporated, annually raises millions of dollars to produce and distribute voter guidelines and other direct-mail literature to describe candidates' positions on various issues and to promote its agenda. Although promoting issue positions is very close to promoting candidates who support those positions, the courts repeatedly

------

[5]494 U.S. 652 (1990).

Vice President Al Gore takes to the podium at a rally supporting his bid for the presidency in the 2000 campaign.

have held, in accordance with the *Buckley v. Valeo* decision mentioned earlier, that interest groups have a First Amendment right to advocate their positions.

The Supreme Court clarified, in a 1996 decision,[6] that political parties may also make independent expenditures on behalf of candidates—as long as the parties do so *independently* of the candidates. In other words, the parties must not coordinate such expenditures with the candidates' campaigns or let the candidates know the specifics of how party funds are being spent.

Bundling. Yet another way to maximize contributions to a candidate or a party is through the practice of **bundling**—collecting $1,000 contributions from a number of individuals in the same firm or family and then sending the quite large check to the candidate of choice. While this practice is in complete compliance with the law, it makes the candidate or party more aware of the source of the funding.

The effect of all of these strategies is to increase greatly the amount of money spent for campaigns and party activities. Critics of the system continue to wonder whether the voice of the individual voter or the small contributor is drowned in the flood of big contributions.

RUNNING FOR PRESIDENT: THE LONGEST CAMPAIGN

The American presidential election is the culmination of two different campaigns linked by the parties' national conventions. First comes the primary campaign in which candidates compete in **presidential primaries,** or statewide primary elections of delegates to a political party's national convention to help the party determine its presidential nominee. The primary campaign lasts officially from January until June of the election year, and the final presidential campaign heats up around Labor Day.

Primary elections were first mandated in 1903 in Wisconsin. The purpose of the primary was to open the nomination process to ordinary party members and to weaken the influence of party bosses in the nomination process. Until 1968, however, there were fewer than twenty primary elections for the presidency. They were generally **"beauty contests"** in which the contending candidates for the nomination competed for popular votes, but the results had little or no impact on the selection of delegates to the national convention. National conventions were meetings of the party elite—legislators, mayors, county chairpersons, and loyal party workers—who were mostly appointed to their delegations. National conventions saw numerous trades and bargains among competing candidates, and the leaders of large blocs of delegate votes could direct their delegates to support a favorite candidate.

Reforming the Primaries

In recent decades, the character of the primary process and the make-up of the national convention have changed dramatically. The mass public, rather than party

---

[6]*Colorado Republican Federal Campaign Committee v. Federal Election Commission,* 518 U.S. 604 (1996).

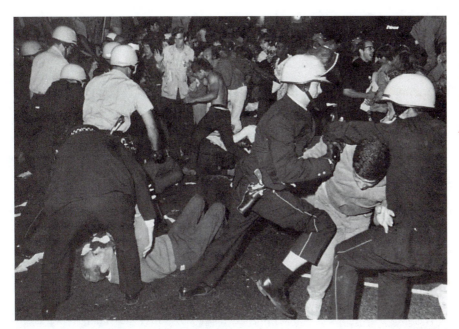

Riots outside the 1968 Democratic convention in Chicago. The riots influenced the party to reform its delegate selection rules.

elites, now generally controls the nomination process, owing to extraordinary changes in the party rules. After the massive riots outside the doors of the 1968 Democratic convention in Chicago, many party leaders pushed for serious reforms of the convention process. They saw the general dissatisfaction with the convention, and the riots in particular, as stemming from the inability of the average party member to influence the nomination system.

The Democratic National Committee appointed a special commission to study the problems of the primary system. Referred to as the McGovern-Fraser Commission, the group over the next several years formulated new rules for delegate selection that had to be followed by state Democratic Parties.

The reforms instituted by the Democratic Party, which were imitated in most states by the Republicans, revolutionized the nomination process for the presidency. The most important changes require that most convention delegates in both parties be elected by the voters in primary elections, in caucuses—meetings of party members to select candidates and propose policies—held by local parties, or at state conventions, rather than being nominated by the elites. Delegates are mostly pledged to a particular candidate, although the pledge is not always formally binding at the convention. The delegation from each state must also include a proportion of women, younger party members, and representatives of the minority groups within the party. At first, virtually no special privileges were given to elected party officials, such as senators or governors. In 1984, however, many of these officials returned to the Democratic convention as superdelegates, who are not elected at the state level but nonetheless are given the right to vote at the convention.

Types of Primaries

The states and state parties may hold different types of primary elections. Among the most likely to be seen are the following.

Closed Primary. In a *closed primary*, the selection of a party's candidates in an election is limited to avowed or declared party members. In other words, voters must declare their party affiliation, either when they register or at the primary election. A closed-primary system tries to make sure that registered voters cannot cross over into the other party's primary in order to nominate the weakest candidate of the opposing party or to affect the ideological direction of that party.

Open Primary. In an *open primary*, voters can vote in either party primary without disclosing their party affiliation. Basically, the voter makes the choice in the privacy of the voting booth. The voter must, however, choose one party's list from which to select candidates. Open primaries place no restrictions on independent voters.

Blanket Primary. A *blanket primary* is one in which the voter may vote for candidates of more than one party. Alaska, Louisiana, Washington, and California all have blanket primaries. Blanket-primary campaigns may be much more costly because each candidate for every office is trying to influence all the voters, not just those in his or her party.

Run-off Primary. Some states have a two-primary system. If no candidate receives a majority of the votes in the first primary, the top two candidates must compete in another primary, called a *run-off primary.*

The Primary as a Springboard to the White House

As soon as politicians and potential presidential candidates realized that winning as many primary elections as possible guaranteed the party's nomination for president, their tactics changed dramatically. Candidates realized that winning early primaries, such as the New Hampshire election in February, or finishing first in the Iowa caucus meant that the media instantly would label the winner as the **front-runner,** thus increasing the candidate's media exposure and increasing the pace of contributions to his or her campaign fund.

The states and state political parties began to see that early primaries had a much greater effect on the outcome of the presidential election and, accordingly, began to hold their primaries earlier in the season to secure that advantage. While New Hampshire held on to its claim as the "first" primary, other states moved to the next week. The southern states decided to hold their primaries on the same date, known as **Super Tuesday,** in the hopes of nominating a moderate southerner at the Democratic convention. When California, which had held the last primary (in June), moved its election to March, the primary season was curtailed drastically. Due to this process of **front-loading** the primaries, today the presidential nominating process is largely over by late March.

On to the National Convention

Presidential candidates have been nominated by the convention method in every election since 1832. The delegates are sent from each state and are apportioned on the basis of state representation. Extra delegates are allowed to attend from states that had voting majorities for the party in the preceding elections. Parties also accept delegates from the District of Columbia, the territories, and certain overseas groups.

At the convention, each political party uses a **credentials committee** to determine which delegates may participate. The credentials committee usually prepares a roll of all delegates entitled to be seated. Because delegates generally arrive at the convention committed to presidential candidates, no convention since 1952 has required more than one ballot to choose a nominee. Since 1972, candidates have usually come into the convention with enough committed delegates to win.

The typical convention lasts only a few days. The first day consists of speech making, usually against the opposing party. During the second day, there are committee reports, and during the third day, there is presidential balloting. On the fourth day, a vice presidential candidate is usually nominated, and the presidential nominee gives the acceptance speech.

THE ELECTORAL COLLEGE

Most voters who vote for the president and vice president think that they are voting directly for a candidate. In actuality, they are voting for **electors** who will cast their ballots in the electoral college. The graphic in Figure 8.1 on the next page shows how the electoral votes are apportioned by state. Article II, Section 1, of the Constitution outlines in detail the number and choice of electors for president and vice president. The framers of the Constitution wanted to avoid the selection of president and vice president by the excitable masses. Rather, they wished the choice to be made by a few supposedly dispassionate, reasonable men (but not women).

The Choice of Electors

Each state's electors are selected during each presidential election year. The selection is governed by state laws and by the applicable party apparatus. After the national party convention, the electors are pledged to the candidates chosen. The total number of electors today is 538, equal to 100 senators, 435 members of the House, plus 3 electors for the District of Columbia (subsequent to the Twenty-third Amendment, ratified in 1961). Each state's number of electors equals that state's number of senators (two) plus its number of representatives.

The Electors' Commitment

If a **plurality** (more than vote for any other candidate but not necessarily a majority) of voters in a state chooses one slate of electors, then those electors are pledged to cast their ballots on the first Monday after the second Wednesday in December in

FIGURE 8.1

State Electoral Votes

The map of the United States shown here is distorted to show the relative weight of the states in terms of electoral votes. Considering that 270 electoral votes are needed for election, the candidates plan their visits around the nation to maximize exposure in the most important states.

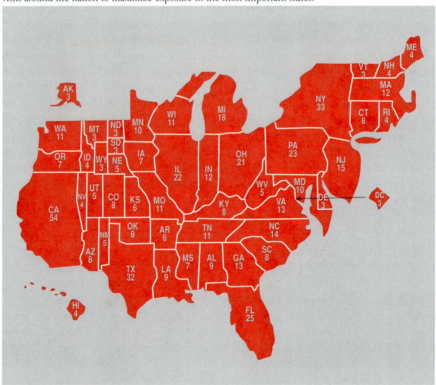

the state capital for the presidential and vice presidential candidates for the winning party.[7] The Constitution does not, however, require the electors to cast their ballots for the candidate of their party.

The ballots are counted and certified before a joint session of Congress early in January. The candidates who receive a majority of the electoral votes (270) are certified as president-elect and vice president–elect. According to the Constitution, if no candidate receives a majority of the electoral votes, the election of the president is decided in the House from among the candidates with the three highest number of votes (decided by a plurality of each state delegation), each state having one vote. The selection of the vice president is determined by the Senate in a choice between the two highest candidates, each senator having one vote. Congress was required to choose the president and vice president in 1801 (Thomas Jefferson and Aaron Burr), and the House chose the president in 1825 (John Quincy Adams).

[7]In Maine and Nebraska, electoral votes are based on congressional districts. Each district chooses one elector. The remaining two electors are chosen statewide.

It is possible for a candidate to become president without obtaining a majority of the popular vote. There have been numerous minority presidents in our history, including Abraham Lincoln, Woodrow Wilson, Harry S. Truman, John F. Kennedy, Richard Nixon (in 1968), and Bill Clinton. Such an event can always occur when there are third-party candidates.

Perhaps more distressing is the possibility of a candidate's being elected when the opposing candidate receives a larger share of the popular vote. This occurred on three occasions—in the elections of John Quincy Adams in 1824, Rutherford B. Hayes in 1876, and Benjamin Harrison in 1888, all of whom won elections without obtaining a plurality of the popular vote.

Criticisms of the Electoral College

Besides the possibility of a candidate's becoming president even though his or her major opponent obtains more popular votes, there are other complaints about the electoral college. The idea of the Constitution's framers was to have electors use their own discretion to decide who would make the best president. But electors no longer perform the selecting function envisioned by the founders, because they are committed to the candidate who has a plurality of popular votes in their state in the general election.[8]

One can also argue that the current system, which gives all of the electoral votes to the candidate who has a statewide plurality, is unfair to other candidates and their supporters. The unit system of voting also means that presidential campaigning will be concentrated in those states that have the largest number of electoral votes and in those states where the outcome is likely to be close. All of the other states generally get second-class treatment during the presidential campaign.

It can also be argued that there is something of a less-populous-state bias in the electoral college, because including Senate seats in the electoral vote total partly offsets the edge of the more populous states in the House. A state such as Alaska (with two senators and one representative) gets an electoral vote for roughly each 183,000 people (based on the 1990 census), whereas Iowa gets one vote for each 397,000 people, and New York has a vote for every 545,000 inhabitants.

HOW ARE ELECTIONS CONDUCTED?

The United States uses the **Australian ballot**—a secret ballot that is prepared, distributed, and counted by government officials at public expense. Since 1888, all states have used the Australian ballot. Before that, many states used the alternatives of oral voting and differently colored ballots prepared by the parties. Obviously, knowing which way people were voting made it easy to apply pressure to change their votes, and vote buying was common.

---

[8]Note, however, that there have been revolts by so-called *faithless electors*—in 1796, 1820, 1948, 1956, 1960, 1968, 1972, 1976, and 1988.

Office-Block and Party-Column Ballots

Two types of ballots are in use in the United States in general elections. The first, called an **office-block ballot,** or sometimes a **Massachusetts ballot,** groups all the candidates for each elective office under the title of each office. Politicians dislike the office-block ballot, because it places more emphasis on the office than on the party; it discourages straight-ticket voting and encourages split-ticket voting.

A **party-column ballot** is a form of general election ballot in which the candidates are arranged in one column under their respective party labels and symbols. It is also called the **Indiana ballot.** In some states, it allows voters to vote for all of a party's candidates for local, state, and national offices by simply marking a single "X" or by pulling a single lever. Most states use this type of ballot. As it encourages straight-ticket voting, majority parties favor this form. When a party has an exceptionally strong presidential or gubernatorial candidate to head the ticket, the **coattail effect** is increased by the use of the party-column ballot.

Voting by Mail

Although voting by mail has been accepted for absentee ballots for many decades, particularly for those who are doing business away from home or for members of the armed forces, only recently have several states begun to try offering mail ballots to all of their voters. The rationale for going to the mail ballot is to make voting easier and more accessible to the voters, particularly in an era when voters are likely to hold jobs and commute some distance from home to work.

There are arguments both for and against mail balloting across the nation. Some commentators, including Norman Ornstein,[9] suggest that mail balloting subverts the whole process. In part, this is because the voter casts his or her ballot at any time, perhaps before any debates or other dialogues are held between candidates. Thus, the voter may be casting an uninformed ballot. Furthermore, Ornstein believes that although the elections so far have shown no evidence of corruption, balloting by mail presents an exceptional opportunity for vote fraud. Others, however, see the mail ballot as the best way to increase voter participation in a time when many are too busy to vote or have little interest in the process.

Vote Fraud

Vote fraud is regularly suspected but seldom proved. Voting in the nineteenth century, when secret ballots were rare and people had a cavalier attitude toward the open buying of votes, was probably much more conducive to fraud than modern elections are. A recent investigation by Larry J. Sabato and Glenn R. Simpson, however, revealed that the potential for vote fraud is high in many states, particularly through the use of phony voter registrations and absentee ballots.[10]

---

[9]Norman Ornstein, "Vote-by-Mail: Is It Good for Democracy?" *Campaigns and Elections,* May 1996, p. 47.

[10]Larry J. Sabato and Glenn R. Simpson, *Dirty Little Secrets: The Persistence of Corruption in American Politics* (New York: Random House, 1996).

Recent changes in the election laws of California, for example, make it very difficult to remove a name from the polling list even if the person has not cast a ballot for the prior two years. Thus, many persons are still on the rolls even though they no longer reside in California. Enterprising political activists can use these names for absentee ballots. Other states have registration laws that are meant to encourage easy registration and voting. Such laws can be taken advantage of by those who seek to vote more than once. Since the passage of the "motor voter" law in 1993, all states have been required to allow voters to register by mail. It may be necessary to develop new processes to verify that registrations or ballots sent by mail come from legitimate voters.

VOTING IN NATIONAL, STATE, AND LOCAL ELECTIONS

In 1996, there were 196.5 million eligible voters. Of that number, 151.7 million, or 77 percent, actually registered to vote in the general presidential election. Of those who registered, 95.8 million actually went to the polls. The participation rate during the 1996 presidential election was only 63 percent of registered voters, down from 76 percent in 1992, and 48.8 percent of eligible voters (see Table 8.1).

TABLE 8.1

Elected by a Majority?

Most presidents have won a majority of the votes cast in the election. We generally judge the extent of their victory by whether they have won more than 51 percent of the votes. Some presidential elections have been proclaimed *landslides*, meaning that the candidates won by an extraordinary majority of votes cast. As indicated below, however, no modern president has been elected by more than 38 percent of the total voting-age electorate.

YEAR—WINNER (PARTY)	PERCENTAGE OF TOTAL POPULAR VOTE	PERCENTAGE OF VOTING-AGE POPULATION
1932—Roosevelt (D)	57.4	30.1
1936—Roosevelt (D)	60.8	34.6
1940—Roosevelt (D)	54.7	32.2
1944—Roosevelt (D)	53.4	29.9
1948—Truman (D)	49.6	25.3
1952—Eisenhower (R)	55.1	34.0
1956—Eisenhower (R)	57.4	34.1
1960—Kennedy (D)	49.7	31.2
1964—Johnson (D)	61.1	37.8
1968—Nixon (R)	43.4	26.4
1972—Nixon (R)	60.7	33.5
1976—Carter (D)	50.1	26.8
1980—Reagan (R)	50.7	26.7
1984—Reagan (R)	58.8	31.2
1988—Bush (R)	53.4	26.8
1992—Clinton (D)	43.3	23.1
1996—Clinton (D)	49.2	23.2

SOURCES: *Congressional Quarterly Weekly Report*, January 31, 1989, p. 137; *The New York Times*, November 5, 1992; and *The New York Times*, November 7, 1996.

Figure 8.2 shows **voter turnout** in the United States for presidential and congressional elections from 1896 to 1998. The last "good" year of turnout for the presidential elections was 1960, when almost 65 percent of the eligible voters actually voted. Each of the peaks in the figure represents voter turnout in a presidential election. Thus, we can also see that voting for U.S. representatives is greatly influenced by whether there is a presidential election in the same year.

The same is true at the state level. When there is a race for governor, more voters participate both in the general election for governor and in the election for state representatives. Voter participation rates in gubernatorial elections are also greater in presidential election years. The average turnout in state elections is about 14 percentage points higher when a presidential election is held.

Now consider local elections. In races for mayor, city council, county auditor, and the like, it is fairly common for only 25 percent or less of the electorate to vote. Is something amiss here? It would seem obvious that people would be more likely to vote in elections that directly affect them. At the local level, each person's vote counts more (because there are fewer voters). Furthermore, the issues—crime control, school bonds, sewer bonds, and so on—touch the immediate interests of the voters. The facts, however, do not fit the theory. Potential voters are most interested in national elections, when a presidential choice is involved. Otherwise, voter participation in our representative government is very low (and, as we have seen, it is not overwhelmingly great even at the presidential level).

The Effect of Low Voter Turnout

"Delirium Democracy"

There are two schools of thought concerning low voter turnout. Some view the decline in voter participation as a clear threat to our representative democratic government. Fewer and fewer individuals are deciding who wields political power in our society. Also, low voter participation presumably signals apathy about our political system in general. It also may signal that potential voters simply do not want to take the time to learn about the issues. When only a handful of people do take the time, it will be easier, say the alarmists, for an authoritarian figure to take over our government.

Others are less concerned about low voter participation. They believe that a decline in voter participation simply indicates more satisfaction with the status quo. Also, they believe that representative democracy is a reality even if a very small percentage of eligible voters vote. If everyone who does not vote believes that the outcome of the election will accord with his or her own desires, then representative democracy is working. The nonvoters are obtaining the type of government—with the type of people running it—that they want to have anyway.

Factors Influencing Who Votes

A clear association exists between voter participation and the following characteristics: age, educational attainment, minority status, income level, and the existence of two-party competition.

FIGURE 8.2

Voter Turnout for Presidential and Congressional Elections, 1896 to Present

The peaks represent turnout in presidential election years; the troughs represent turnout in off-presidential election years.

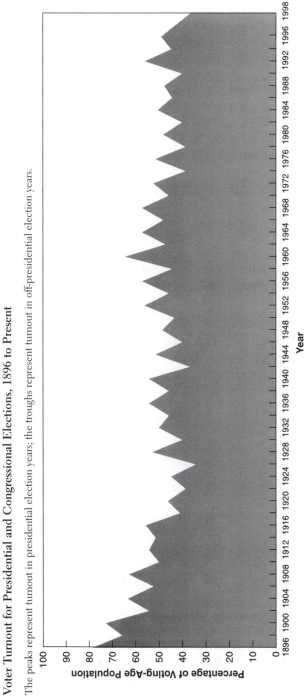

SOURCES: Historical Data Archive, Inter-university Consortium for Political and Social Research; U.S. Department of Commerce, *Statistical Abstract of the United States: 1980*, 101st ed. (Washington, D.C.: U.S. Government Printing Office, 1980), p. 515; William H. Flanigan and Nancy H. Zingale, *Political Behavior of the American Electorate*, 5th ed. (Boston: Allyn and Bacon, 1983), p. 20; *Congressional Quarterly*, various issues; and authors' update.

1. *Age.* Age is a strong factor in determining voter turnout on election day. The reported turnout increases with older age groups. Greater participation with age is very likely due to the fact that older voters are more settled in their lives, are already registered, and have had more time to experience voting as an expected activity.

2. *Educational attainment.* Education also influences voter turnout. In general, the more education you have, the more likely you are to vote. This pattern is clearly evident in the 1996 election results. Reported turnout was over 30 percentage points higher for those who had some college education than it was for people who had never been to high school.

3. *Minority status.* Race is important, too, in determining the level of voter turnout. Whites in 1996 voted at a 56.0 percent rate, whereas the African American turnout rate was 50.6 percent.

4. *Income levels.* Differences in income can also lead to differences in voter turnout. Wealthier people tend to be overrepresented in the electorate. In 1996, turnout among whites with annual family incomes under $15,000 was about half of that for people with annual family incomes of $50,000 or more.

5. *Two-party competition.* Another factor in voter turnout is the extent to which elections are competitive within a state. More competitive states generally have higher turnout rates, although the highest average percentage turnout for the past two decades has been in states in which Republicans were elected to most state offices.

The foregoing statistics reinforce one another. White voters are likely to be wealthier than African American voters, who are also less likely to have obtained a college education.

LEGAL RESTRICTIONS ON VOTING

Legal restrictions on voter registration have existed since the founding of the nation. Most groups in the United States have been concerned with the suffrage issue at one time or another.

Historical Restrictions

In colonial times, only white males who owned property with a certain minimum value were eligible to vote, leaving a far greater number of Americans ineligible than eligible to take part in the democratic process. Because many government functions are in the economic sphere and concern property rights and the distribution of income and wealth, some of the founders of our nation felt it was appropriate that only people who had an interest in property should vote on these issues. The idea of extending the vote to all citizens was, according to South Carolina delegate Charles Pinckney, merely "theoretical nonsense."

The logic behind this restriction of voting rights to property owners was questioned seriously by Thomas Paine in his pamphlet *Common Sense:*

> Here is a man who today owns a jackass, and the jackass is worth $60. Today the man is a voter and goes to the polls and deposits his vote. Tomorrow the jackass dies. The next day

Voter registration is an important part of our political process. These workers are helping a citizen register to vote in the next election. The requirements for voter registration vary across states.

the man comes to vote without his jackass and cannot vote at all. Now tell me, which was the voter, the man or the jackass?[11]

The writers of the Constitution allowed the states to decide who should vote. Thus, women were allowed to vote in Wyoming in 1870 but not in the entire nation until the Nineteenth Amendment was ratified in 1920.

By about 1850, most white adult males in virtually all the states could vote without any property qualification. North Carolina was the last state to eliminate its property test for voting—in 1856.

Extension of the franchise to black males occurred with the passage of the Fifteenth Amendment in 1870. This enfranchisement was short-lived, however, as the "redemption" of the South by white racists rolled back these gains by the end of the century. As discussed in Chapter 5, it was not until the 1960s that African Americans, both male and female, were able to participate in large numbers in the electoral process. Women received full national voting rights with the Nineteenth Amendment in 1920. The most recent extension of the franchise occurred when the voting age was reduced to eighteen by the Twenty-sixth Amendment in 1971.

Current Eligibility and Registration Requirements

Voting requires **registration,** and registration requires satisfying voter qualifications, or legal requirements. These requirements are the following: (1) citizenship, (2) age (eighteen or older), and (3) residency—the duration varying widely from state to state and with the type of election. Since 1972, states cannot impose residency requirements

---

[11]Thomas Paine, *Common Sense* (London: H. D. Symonds, 1792), p. 28.

of more than thirty days. In addition, most states disqualify people who are mentally incompetent, prison inmates, convicted felons, and election-law violators.

In 1993, Congress passed the "motor voter" bill, which requires that states provide voter-registration materials when people receive or renew driver's licenses, that all states allow voters to register by mail, and that voter-registration forms be made available at a wider variety of public places and agencies. In general, a person must register well in advance of an election, although voters in Maine, Minnesota, Oregon, and Wisconsin are allowed to register up to, and on, election day.

Some argue that registration requirements are responsible for much of the nonparticipation in our political process. Certainly, since their introduction in the late nineteenth century, registration laws have had the effect of reducing the voting participation of African Americans and immigrants. There also is a partisan dimension to the debate over registration and nonvoting. Republicans generally fear that an expanded electorate would help to elect more Democrats.

HOW DO VOTERS DECIDE?

Political scientists and survey researchers have collected much information about voting behavior. This information sheds some light on which people vote and why people decide to vote for particular candidates. We have already discussed factors influencing voter turnout. Generally, the factors that influence voting decisions can be divided into two groups: (1) socioeconomic and demographic factors and (2) psychological factors.

Socioeconomic and Demographic Factors

As Table 8.2 indicates, a number of socioeconomic and demographic factors appear to influence voting behavior: (1) education; (2) income and **socioeconomic status**, which groups people with similar levels of income and types of occupations; (3) religion; (4) ethnic background; (5) gender; (6) age; and (7) geographic region. These influences all reflect the voter's personal background and place in society. Clearly, many of these factors are related. People who have more education are likely to have higher incomes and to hold professional jobs. Similarly, children born into wealthier families are far more likely to complete college than children from poorer families.

Education. Having a college education tends to be associated with voting for Republicans. An exception to the rule that more educated voters vote Republican occurred in 1964, when college graduates voted 52 percent for Democrat Lyndon Johnson and 48 percent for Republican Barry Goldwater. Typically, those with less education are more inclined to vote for the Democratic nominee. In 1984, Democrat Walter Mondale received 43 percent and Republican Ronald Reagan, 57 percent of the vote from high school graduates, whereas those with only a grade school education voted 51 percent for Mondale and 49 percent for Reagan. This pattern held in 1996, when 46 percent of college graduates voted for Republican Bob Dole, compared with 28 percent of those who had not completed high school.

TABLE 8.2

Vote by Groups in Presidential Elections since 1988 (in Percentages)

	1988		1992			1996		
	DUKAKIS (DEM.)	BUSH (REP.)	CLINTON (DEM.)	BUSH (REP.)	PEROT (IND.)	CLINTON (DEM.)	DOLE (REP.)	PEROT (REF.)
National	45	53	43	38	19	49	41	8
Sex								
Male	41	57	41	38	21	43	44	10
Female	49	50	46	37	17	54	38	7
Race								
White	40	59	39	41	20	43	46	9
Nonwhite	86	12	NA	NA	NA	NA	NA	NA
Education								
College	43	56	44	39	18	44	46	8
High school	49	50	43	36	20	51	35	13
Grade school	56	43	56	28	NA	59	28	11
Occupation								
Professional	40	59	NA	NA	NA	NA	NA	NA
White collar	42	57	NA	NA	NA	NA	NA	NA
Manual	50	49	NA	NA	NA	NA	NA	NA
Age (Years)								
Under 30	47	52	44	34	22	54	34	10
30–49	45	54	42	38	20	48	41	9
50 and older	49	50	50	38	12	48	44	7
Religion								
Protestants	33	66	33	46	21	36	53	10
Catholics	47	52	44	36	20	53	37	9
Politics								
Republicans	8	91	10	73	17	13	80	6
Democrats	82	17	77	10	13	84	10	5
Independents	43	55	38	32	30	43	35	17
Region								
East	49	50	47	35	NA	55	34	9
Midwest	47	52	42	37	NA	48	41	10
South	41	58	42	43	NA	46	46	7
West	46	52	44	34	NA	48	40	8
Members of Labor Union Families	57	42	55	24	NA	59	30	9

NOTE: Results do not include votes for all minor-party candidates.
SOURCE: *The New York Times*, November 10, 1988, p. 18; *The New York Times*, November 15, 1992, p. B9; *The New York Times*, November 10, 1996, p. 16.

Income and Socioeconomic Status. If we measure socioeconomic status by profession, then those of higher socioeconomic status—professionals and businesspersons, as well as white-collar workers—tend to vote Republican more than Democratic. Manual laborers, factory workers, and especially union members are more likely to vote Democratic. The effects of income are much the same. The higher the income, the more likely it is that a person will vote Republican. But there are no hard and fast rules. Some very poor individuals are devoted Republicans, just as some extremely wealthy individuals support the Democratic Party. In a number of recent elections, the traditional pattern did not hold. In 1980, for example, many blue-collar Democrats voted for Ronald Reagan, although the 1996 election showed those votes going to Bill Clinton.

Religion. In the United States, Protestants have traditionally voted Republican, and Catholics and Jews have voted Democratic. As with the other patterns discussed, however, this one is somewhat fluid. Republican Richard Nixon obtained 52 percent of the Catholic vote in 1972, and Democrat Lyndon Johnson won 55 percent of the Protestant vote in 1964. The Catholic vote was evenly split between Democrat Jimmy Carter and Republican Ronald Reagan in 1980 but went heavily for Reagan in 1984. In 1996, Republican candidate Bob Dole obtained fewer votes from Catholics than did Democratic candidate Bill Clinton.

Ethnic Background. Traditionally, the Irish have voted for Democrats. So, too, have voters of Slavic, Polish, and Italian heritages. But Anglo-Saxon and northern European ethnic groups have voted for Republican presidential candidates. These patterns were disrupted in 1980, when Ronald Reagan obtained much of his support from several of the traditionally Democratic ethnic groups, with the help of funda-mentalist religious groups.

African Americans voted principally for Republicans until Democrat Franklin Roosevelt's New Deal in the 1930s. Since then, they have largely identified with the Democratic Party. Indeed, Democratic presidential candidates have received, on average, more than 80 percent of the African American vote since 1956.

Gender. As discussed in Chapter 6, until relatively recently there seemed to be no fixed pattern of voter preference by gender in presidential elections. One year, more women than men would vote for the Democratic candidate; another year, more men than women would do so. Some political analysts believe that a "gender gap" became a major determinant of voter decision making in the 1980 presidential elec-tion. Ronald Reagan obtained 15 percentage points more than Jimmy Carter among male voters, whereas women gave about an equal number of votes to each candidate. In 1984, the gender gap amounted to 9 percentage points nationally, with 64 percent of male voters casting their ballots for Ronald Reagan and 55 percent of female vot-ers doing the same. In 1996, women cast 54 percent of their votes for Bill Clinton, the Democrat. The gender gap rarely appears in congressional elections.

Age. Age clearly seems to relate to an individual's voting behavior. Younger voters have tended to vote Democratic, whereas older voters have tended to vote Republican. It was only the voters under age thirty who clearly favored Jimmy Carter during the Carter-Reagan election in 1980. This trend was reversed in 1984, when voters under thirty voted heavily for Ronald Reagan and again voted Republican in

1988. In 1992, Bill Clinton won back the young voters by 10 percentage points, a margin that expanded to 20 percentage points in 1996.

Geographic Region. As we noted in Chapter 7, the former Solid (Democratic) South has crumbled in national elections. In 1972, Republican Richard Nixon obtained 71 percent of the southern vote, whereas Democrat George McGovern obtained only 29 percent. Ronald Reagan drew 52 percent of the southern vote in 1980, however, and 63 percent in 1984.

Democrats still draw much of their strength from large northern and eastern cities. Rural areas tend to be Republican (and conservative) throughout the country except in the South, where the rural vote still tends to be heavily Democratic. On average, the West has voted Republican in presidential elections. Except for the 1964 election between Barry Goldwater and Lyndon Johnson, and again in the 1992 and 1996 elections, the Republicans have held the edge in western states in every presidential election since 1956.

Psychological Factors

In addition to socioeconomic and demographic explanations for the way people vote, at least three important psychological factors play a role in voter decision making. These factors, which are rooted in attitudes and beliefs held by voters, are (1) party identification, (2) perception of the candidates, and (3) issue preferences.

Party Identification. With the possible exception of race, party identification has been the most important determinant of voting behavior in national elections. As we pointed out in Chapter 6, party affiliation is influenced by family and peer groups, by age, by the media, and by psychological attachment. During the 1950s, independent voters were a little more than 20 percent of the eligible electorate. In the middle to late 1960s, however, party identification began to weaken, and by the mid-1990s, independent voters constituted over 30 percent of all voters. In 1998, the proportion of independent voters was between 26 and 33 percent. Independent voting seems to be concentrated among new voters, particularly among new young voters. Thus, we can still say that party identification for established voters is an important determinant in voter choice.

Perception of the Candidates. The image of the candidate also seems to be important in a voter's choice for president. To some extent, voter attitudes toward candidates are based on emotions (such as trust) rather than on any judgment about experience or policy. In 1996, voters' decisions were largely guided by their perceptions of who they could trust to run the economy. Bob Dole tried to reduce the voters' trust in Bill Clinton but failed to make an impact.

Issue Preferences. Issues make a difference in presidential and congressional elections. Although personality or image factors may be very persuasive, most voters have some notion of how the candidates differ on basic issues or at least know that the candidates want a change in the direction of government policy.

Historically, economic issues have the strongest influence on voters' choices. When the economy is doing well, it is very difficult for a challenger, particularly at the presidential level, to defeat the incumbent. In contrast, increasing inflation, rising unemployment, or high interest rates are likely to work to the disadvantage of the incumbent. Studies of how economic conditions affect the vote differ in their conclusions. Some indicate that people vote on the basis of their personal economic well-being, whereas other studies seem to show that people vote on the basis of the nation's overall economic health.

Foreign policy issues become more prominent in a time of crisis. Although the parties and candidates have differed greatly over policy toward trade with China, for example, foreign policy issues are truly influential only when armed conflict is a possibility. Clearly, public dissension over the war in Vietnam had an effect on elections in 1968 and 1972.

Some of the most heated debates in American political campaigns take place over the social issues of abortion, the role of women, the rights of lesbians and gay males, and prayer in the public schools. In general, presidential candidates would prefer to avoid such issues, because voters who care about these questions are likely to be offended if a candidate does not share their views.

From time to time, drugs, crime, and corruption become important campaign issues. The Watergate affair cost the Republicans a number of congressional seats in 1974, but Clinton and the Democrats were not touched by Clinton's impeachment and trial in late 1998 and early 1999. If the president or high officials are involved in truly criminal or outrageous conduct, the issue will undoubtedly influence voters.

All candidates try to set themselves apart from their opposition on crucial issues in order to attract voters. What is difficult to ascertain is the extent to which issues overshadow partisan loyalty or personality factors in the voters' minds. It appears that some campaigns are much more issue oriented than others. Some research has shown that **issue voting** was most important in the presidential elections of 1964, 1968, and 1972, was moderately important in 1980, and was less important in the 1990s and 2000s.

KEY TERMS

Australian ballot 193	front-runner 190	presidential primary 188
"beauty contest" 188	Hatch Act 184	registration 199
bundling 188	independent expenditures 187	socioeconomic status 200
caucus 189	issue voting 204	soft money 185
coattail effect 194	office-block, or Massachusetts, ballot 194	superdelegate 189
corrupt practices acts 184		Super Tuesday 190
credentials committee 191	party-column, or Indiana, ballot 194	tracking poll 183
elector 191	plurality 191	voter turnout 196
focus group 183	political consultant 181	
front-loading 190		

CHAPTER SUMMARY

1 People may choose to run for political office to further their careers, to carry out specific political programs, or in response to certain issues or events. The legal qualifications for holding political office are minimal at both the state and local levels, but holders of political office still are predominantly white and male and are likely to be from the professional class.

2 American political campaigns are lengthy and extremely expensive. In the last decade, they have become more candidate centered rather than party centered in response to technological innovations and decreasing party identification. Candidates have begun to rely less on the party and more on paid professional consultants to perform the various tasks necessary to wage a political campaign. The crucial task of professional political consultants is image building. The campaign organization devises a campaign strategy to maximize the candidate's chances of winning. Candidates use public opinion polls to gauge their popularity and to test the mood of the country.

3 The amount of money spent in financing campaigns is steadily increasing. A variety of corrupt practices acts have been passed to regulate campaign finance. The Federal Election Campaign Act of 1971, as amended, instituted major reforms by limiting spending and contributions; the act allowed corporations, labor unions, and interest groups to set up political action committees (PACs) to raise money for candidates. New techniques, including contributions to the parties, independent expenditures, and bundling, have been created to raise money.

4 Following the Democratic convention of 1968, the McGovern-Fraser Commission was appointed to study the problems of the primary system. It formulated new rules, which were adopted by all Democrats and by Republicans in many states. These reforms opened up the nomination process for the presidency to all voters.

5 A presidential primary is a statewide election to help a political party determine its presidential nom-

inee at the national convention. Types of primaries include the closed primary, the open primary, the blanket primary, and the run-off primary. Some states use the caucus method of choosing convention delegates. The primary campaign recently has been shortened to the first few months of the election year.

6 In making a presidential choice on election day, the voter technically does not vote directly for a candidate but chooses between slates of presidential electors. The slate that wins the most popular votes throughout the state gets to cast all the electoral votes for the state. The candidate receiving a majority (270) of the electoral votes wins. Both the mechanics and the politics of the electoral college have been sharply criticized. There have been many proposed reforms, including a proposal that candidates be elected on a popular-vote basis in direct elections.

7 The United States uses the Australian ballot, a secret ballot that is prepared, distributed, and counted by government officials. The office-block ballot groups candidates according to office. The party-column ballot groups candidates according to their party labels and symbols.

8 Voter participation in the United States is low (and generally declining). Some view the decline in voter turnout as a threat to representative democracy, whereas others believe it simply indicates greater satisfaction with the status quo. There is an association between voting and a person's age, education, minority status, and income level.

9 In colonial times, only white males with a certain minimum amount of property were eligible to vote. The suffrage issue has concerned, at one time or another, most groups in the United States. Current voter eligibility requires registration, citizenship, and specified age and residency requirements. Each state has different qualifications. It is argued that these requirements are responsible for much of the nonparticipation in the political process in the United States.

⑩ Socioeconomic or demographic factors that influence voting decisions include (a) education, (b) income and socioeconomic status, (c) religion, (d) ethnic background, (e) gender, (f) age, and (g) geographic region. Psychological factors that influence voting decisions include (a) party identification, (b) perception of candidates, and (c) issue preferences.

SELECTED PRINT AND ELECTRONIC RESOURCES

Suggested Readings

Bike, William S. *Winning Political Campaigns: A Comprehensive Guide to Electoral Success.* New York: Denali Press, 1998. This is a guide to politics for any aspiring officeholder or candidate.

Conway, M. Margaret, Gertrude A. Steuernagel, and David W. Ahern. *Women and Political Participation.* Washington, D.C.: CQ Press, 1997. This volume examines the changing role of women in the political system, including the increase in participation and officeholding by women.

Davis, James W. *U.S. Presidential Primaries and the Caucus-Convention System: A Sourcebook.* New York: Greenwood Press, 1997. A comprehensive source book on the history of the American electoral system, this work provides analyses of primaries, polls, and campaign-finance regulations.

Jackson, John S., III, and William Crotty. *The Politics of Presidential Selection.* New York: Longman Publishers, 1996. This account of how we elect the president and the members of Congress is based on theories of rational decision making by voters and dis-

cusses the limits to such decision making for those voters without information.

Media Resources

The Candidate—Starring the young Robert Redford, this 1972 film produced by Warner Brothers effectively investigates and satirizes the decisions that a candidate for the U.S. Senate must make. It's a political classic.

The War Room—Using video coverage taped throughout Bill Clinton's 1992 campaign for the presidency, this 1993 documentary shows the strategic decisions behind the scenes in the campaign. Footage shows Clinton's strategists, including James Carville and George Stephanopoulos, pulling out all the stops for their candidate.

All the King's Men—A classic film, produced in 1949 and based on a best-selling novel by Robert Penn Warren, that traces the rise to power of a southern politician (played by Broderick Crawford) and parallels the life of Huey Long, the governor of Louisiana during the Great Depression of the 1930s.

LOGGING ON

For detailed information about current campaign election laws and for the latest filings of finance reports, see the site maintained by the Federal Election Commission at

http://www.fec.gov

To find excellent reports on where the money comes from and how it is spent in campaigns, be sure to view the

site maintained by the Center for Responsive Politics at

http://www.opensecrets.org/home/index.asp

Another excellent site for investigating voting records and campaign-finance information is that of Project VoteSmart. Go to

http://www.vote-smart.org

USING THE INTERNET FOR POLITICAL ANALYSIS

Point your browser at either the Federal Election Commission site (http://www.fec.org) or the Center for Responsive Politics site at the URL given above. Choose the campaign-finance records of at least three individual candidates or members of Congress. Print out those records, and then compare the types of donors that are listed. Can you find enough information about campaign donations to have some idea of what policy positions are held by the candidates? What does the donor list tell you about each person's role and importance in Congress?

CHAPTER 9

The Congress

Most Americans spend little time thinking about the Congress of the United States, and when they do, their opinions are frequently unflattering. For many years, the public's approval rating of Congress as a whole was about 30 percent. With the strong economy of the late 1990s, Congress's approval ratings climbed to between 40 percent and 50 percent in most polls, although this rating dropped precipitously during the impeachment proceedings against President Clinton in late 1998 and early 1999. Most voters, however, expressed even higher approval ratings (in the range of 60 percent to 70 percent) for the members of Congress from their districts. This is one of the paradoxes of the relationship between the people and Congress. Members of the public hold the institution in relatively low regard while expressing satisfaction with their individual representatives.

Part of the explanation for these seemingly contradictory appraisals is that members of Congress spend considerable time and effort serving their **constituents**—those who elected them. If the federal bureaucracy makes a mistake, the senator's or representative's office tries to resolve the issue. What most Americans see of Congress, therefore, is the work of their own representatives in their home states.

Congress, however, was created to work not just for local constituents but also for the nation as a whole. Understanding the nature of the institution and the process of lawmaking is an important part of understanding how the policies that shape our lives are made.

WHY WAS CONGRESS CREATED?

The founders of the American republic believed that the bulk of the power that would be exercised by a national government should be in the hands of the legislature. As you will recall from Chapter 2, the authors of the Constitution were strongly influenced by their fear of tyrannical kings and powerful, unchecked rulers. They were also aware of how ineffective the confederal Congress had been during its brief existence under the Articles of Confederation.

The leading role envisioned for Congress in the new government is apparent from its primacy in the Constitution. Article I deals with the structure, the powers, and the operation of Congress, beginning in Section 1 with an application of the basic principle of separation of powers: "All legislative Powers herein granted shall be vested in a Congress of the United States, which shall consist of a Senate and House of

Representatives." These legislative powers are spelled out in detail in Article I and elsewhere.

The **bicameralism** of Congress—its division into two legislative houses—was in part an outgrowth of the Connecticut Compromise, which tried to balance the large-state population advantage, reflected in the House, and the small-state demand for equality in policymaking, which was satisfied in the Senate. Beyond that, the two chambers of Congress also reflected the social class biases of the founders. They wished to balance the interests and the numerical superiority of the common citizens with the property interests of the less numerous landowners, bankers, and merchants. This goal was achieved by providing in Sections 2 and 3 of Article I that members of the House of Representatives should be elected directly by "the People," whereas members of the Senate were to be chosen by the elected representatives sitting in state legislatures, who were more likely to be members of the elite. (The latter provision was changed in 1913 by the passage of the Seventeenth Amendment, which provides that senators also are to be elected directly by the people.)

The logic of separate constituencies and separate interests underlying the bicameral Congress was reinforced by differences in length of tenure. Members of the House were required to face the electorate every two years, whereas senators could serve for a much more secure term of six years—even longer than the four-year term provided for the president. Furthermore, the senators' terms were staggered so that only one-third of the senators would face the electorate every two years, along with all of the House members.

THE POWERS OF CONGRESS

The Constitution is both highly specific and extremely vague about the powers that Congress may exercise. The first seventeen clauses of Article I, Section 8, specify most of the **enumerated powers** of Congress—that is, powers expressly given to that body.

Enumerated Powers

The enumerated, or expressed, powers of Congress include the right to impose taxes and import tariffs; borrow money; regulate interstate commerce and international trade; establish procedures for naturalizing citizens; make laws regulating bankruptcies; coin (and print) money and regulate its value; establish standards of weights and measures; punish counterfeiters; establish post offices and postal routes; regulate copyrights and patents; establish the federal court system; punish pirates and others committing illegal acts on the high seas; declare war; raise and regulate an army and a navy; call up and regulate the state militias to enforce laws, to suppress insurrections, and to repel invasions; and govern the District of Columbia.

The most important of the domestic powers of Congress, listed in Article I, Section 8, are the rights to collect taxes, to spend, and to regulate commerce, whereas the most important foreign policy power is the power to declare war. Other sections of the Constitution give Congress a wide range of further powers. Generally, Congress is also able to establish rules for its own members, to regulate the electoral college, and to override a presidential veto.

Some functions are restricted to only one chamber. Under Article II, Section 2, the Senate must advise on, and consent to, the ratification of treaties and must accept or reject presidential nominations of ambassadors, Supreme Court justices, and "all other Officers of the United States." But the Senate may delegate to the president, the courts, or department heads the power to make lesser appointments. Congress may regulate the extent of the Supreme Court's authority to review cases decided by the lower courts, regulate relations between states, and propose amendments to the Constitution.

The amendments to the Constitution provide for other congressional powers. Congress must certify the election of a president and a vice president or itself choose these officers if no candidate has a majority of the electoral vote (Twelfth Amendment). It may levy an income tax (Sixteenth Amendment) and determine who will be acting president in case of the death or incapacity of the president or vice president (Twentieth Amendment, Sections 3 and 4, and Twenty-fifth Amendment, Sections 2, 3, and 4). In addition, Congress explicitly is given the power to enforce, by appropriate legislation, the provisions of several other amendments.

The Necessary and Proper Clause

Beyond these numerous specific powers, Congress enjoys the right under Article I, Section 8 (the "elastic," or "necessary and proper," clause), "[t]o make all Laws which shall be necessary and proper for carrying into Execution the foregoing Powers [of Article I], and all other Powers vested by this Constitution in the Government of the United States, or in any Department or Officer thereof." As discussed in Chapter 3, this vague statement of congressional responsibilities set the stage for a greatly expanded role for the national government relative to the states. It also constitutes, at least in theory, a check on the expansion of presidential powers.

THE FUNCTIONS OF CONGRESS

Congress, as an institution of government, is expected by its members, by the public, and by other centers of political power to perform a number of functions for the American political system. Our perceptions of how good a job Congress is doing overall are tied closely to evaluations of whether and how it fulfills certain specific tasks. These tasks include lawmaking, service to constituents, representation, oversight, public education, and conflict resolution.

The Lawmaking Function

The principal and most obvious function of any legislature is **lawmaking**—the process of deciding the legal rules that govern society. Congress is the highest elected body in the country charged with making binding rules for all Americans. Lawmaking requires decisions about the size of the federal budget, about health-care reform and gun control, and about the long-term prospects for war or peace. This does not mean, however, that Congress initiates most of the ideas for legislation that it eventually considers. Most of the bills that Congress acts on originate in the executive branch, and many other bills are traceable to interest groups and political party organizations. Through the processes of compromise and **logrolling** (offering to support a fellow member's bill in exchange for that member's promise to support your bill in the future), as well as debate and discussion, backers of legislation attempt to fashion a winning majority coalition.

Service to Constituents

Individual members of Congress are expected by their constituents to act as brokers between private citizens and the imposing, often faceless federal government. **Casework** is the usual form taken by this function of providing service to constituents. The legislator and his or her staff spend a considerable portion of their time in casework activity, such as tracking down a missing Social Security check, explaining the meaning of particular bills to people who may be affected by them, promoting a local business interest, or interceding with a regulatory agency on behalf of constituents who disagree with proposed agency regulations.

Legislators and many analysts of congressional behavior regard this **ombudsperson** role as an activity that strongly benefits the members of Congress. (An ombudsperson is a person who hears and investigates complaints by private individuals against public officials or agencies.) A government characterized by a large, confusing bureaucracy and complex public programs offers innumerable opportunities for legislators to come to the assistance of (usually) grateful constituents. Morris P. Fiorina suggests, somewhat mischievously, that senators and representatives prefer to maintain bureaucratic confusion in order to maximize their opportunities for performing good deeds on behalf of their constituents:

> Some poor, aggrieved constituent becomes enmeshed in the tentacles of an evil bureaucracy and calls upon Congressman St. George to do battle with the dragon. . . . In dealing with the bureaucracy, the congressman is not merely one vote of 435. Rather, he is a nonpartisan power, someone whose phone call snaps an office to attention. He is not kept on hold. The constituent who receives aid believes that his congressman and his congressman alone got results.[1]

The Representation Function

If constituency service carries with it nothing but benefits for most members of Congress, the function of **representation**—representing the views of their constituents—is less certain and even carries with it some danger that the legislator will lose her or his bid for reelection. Generally, representation means that the many competing interests in society should be represented in Congress. It follows that Congress should be a body acting slowly and deliberately and that its foremost

---

[1] Morris P. Fiorina, *Congress: Keystone of the Washington Establishment,* 2d ed. (New Haven, Conn.: Yale University Press, 1989), pp. 44, 47.

concern should be to maintain a carefully crafted balance of power among competing interests.

How is representation to be achieved? There are basically two points of view on this issue.

The Trustee View of Representation. The first approach to the question of how representation should be achieved is that legislators should act as **trustees** of the broad interests of the entire society and that they should vote against the narrow interests of their constituents as their conscience and their perception of national needs dictate. For example, some Republican legislators supported strong laws regulating the tobacco industry in spite of the views of some of their constituents.

The Instructed-Delegate View of Representation. Directly opposed to the trustee view of representation is the notion that the members of Congress should behave as **instructed delegates.** That is, they should mirror the views of the majority of the constituents who elected them to power in the first place. On the surface, this approach is plausible and rewarding. For it to work, however, we must assume that constituents actually have well-formed views on the issues that are decided in Congress and, further, that they have clear-cut preferences about these issues. Neither condition is likely to be satisfied very often. Most people generally do not have well-articulated views on major issues.

In a major study of the attitudes held by members of Congress about their proper role as representatives, Roger Davidson found that most legislators held neither a pure trustee view nor a pure instructed-delegate view. Davidson's sampling of members of Congress showed that about the same proportion endorsed the trustee approach (28 percent) and delegate approach (23 percent) to representation. The clear preference, however, was for the **politico** position, which combines both perspectives in a pragmatic mix, depending on the issue under consideration.[2]

The Oversight Function

INFOTRAC®

"Report Criticizes Federal Oversight"

Oversight of the bureaucracy is essential if the decisions made by Congress are to have any force. **Oversight** is the process by which Congress follows up on the laws it has enacted to ensure that they are being enforced and administered in the way Congress intended. This is done by holding committee hearings and investigations, changing the size of an agency's budget, and cross-examining high-level presidential nominees to head major agencies.

Senators and representatives increasingly see their oversight function as a critically important part of their legislative activities. In part, oversight is related to the concept of constituency service, particularly when Congress investigates alleged arbitrariness or wrongdoing by bureaucratic agencies.

The Public-Education Function

Educating the public is a function that is exercised whenever Congress holds public hearings, exercises oversight over the bureaucracy, or engages in committee and floor

---

[2]Roger Davidson, *The Role of the Congressman* (New York: Pegasus, 1969), p. 117.

debate on such major issues and topics as political assassinations, aging, illegal drugs, or the concerns of small businesses. In so doing, Congress presents a range of viewpoints on pressing national questions. Congress also decides what issues will come up for discussion and decision; **agenda setting**—determining which public-policy questions it will debate or consider—is a major facet of its public-education function.

The Conflict-Resolution Function

Congress is commonly seen as an institution for resolving conflicts within American society. Organized interest groups and representatives of different racial, religious, economic, and ideological interests look on Congress as an access point for airing their grievances and seeking help. This puts Congress in the role of trying to resolve the differences among competing points of view by passing laws to accommodate as many interested parties as possible. To the extent that Congress meets pluralist expectations in accommodating competing interests, it tends to build support for the entire political process by all branches of government.

HOUSE-SENATE DIFFERENCES

Congress is composed of two markedly different—but coequal—chambers. Although the Senate and the House of Representatives exist within the same legislative institution, each has developed certain distinctive features that clearly distinguish life on one end of Capitol Hill from conditions on the other (the Senate wing is on the north side of the Capitol building, and the House wing is on the south side). A summary of these differences is given in Table 9.1.

TABLE 9.1

Differences between the House and the Senate

HOUSE*	SENATE*
Members chosen from local districts	Members chosen from an entire state
Two-year term	Six-year term
Originally elected by voters	Originally (until 1913) elected by state legislatures
May impeach (indict) federal officials	May convict federal officials of impeachable offenses
Larger (435 voting members)	Smaller (100 members)
More formal rules	Fewer rules and restrictions
Debate limited	Debate extended
Less prestige and less individual notice	More prestige and more media attention
Originates bills for raising revenues	Has power to advise the president on, and to consent to, presidential appointments and treaties
Local or narrow leadership	National leadership
More partisan	Less party loyalty

*Some of these differences, such as the term of office, are provided for in the Constitution. Others, such as debate rules, are not.

Size and Rules

The central difference between the House and the Senate is simply that the House is much larger than the Senate. The House has 435 representatives, plus delegates from the District of Columbia, Puerto Rico, Guam, American Samoa, and the Virgin Islands, compared with just 100 senators. This size difference means that a greater number of formal rules are needed to govern activity in the House, whereas correspondingly looser procedures can be followed in the less crowded Senate. This difference is most obvious in the rules governing debate on the floors of the two chambers.

The Senate normally permits extended debate on all issues that arise before it. In contrast, the House operates with an elaborate system. Its **Rules Committee,** a standing (permanent) committee, provides special rules under which specific bills can be debated, amended, and considered by the House. This committee normally proposes time limitations on debate for any bill, and a majority of the entire body accepts or modifies those suggested time limits. As a consequence of its stricter time limits on debate, the House, despite its greater size, often is able to act on legislation more quickly than the Senate.

Debate and Filibustering

According to historians, the Senate tradition of unlimited debate, which is known as **filibustering,** dates back to 1790, when a proposal to move the U.S. capital from New York to Philadelphia was stalled by such time-wasting tactics. This unlimited-debate tradition—which also existed in the House until 1811—is not absolute, however.

Under Senate Rule 22, debate may be ended by invoking **cloture,** or shutting off discussion on a bill. Amended in 1975 and 1979, Rule 22 states that debate may be closed off on a bill if sixteen senators sign a petition requesting it and if, after two days have elapsed, three-fifths of the entire membership (sixty votes, assuming no vacancies) vote for cloture. After cloture is invoked, each senator may speak on a bill for a maximum of one hour before a vote is taken.

In 1979, the Senate extended Rule 22 to provide that a final vote must take place within one hundred hours of debate after cloture has been imposed. It further limited the use of multiple amendments to stall postcloture final action on a bill.

Prestige

As a consequence of the greater size of the House, representatives generally cannot achieve as much individual recognition and public prestige as can members of the Senate. Senators, especially those who openly express presidential ambitions, are better able to gain media exposure and to establish careers as spokespersons for large national constituencies. To obtain recognition for his or her activities, a member of the House generally must do one of two things. He or she might survive in office long enough to join the ranks of the leadership on committees or within the party. Alternatively, the representative could become an expert on some specialized aspect of legislative policy—such as tax laws, the environment, or education.

The Impeachment Process

Another difference between the House and the Senate has to do with the roles played by the two chambers in the **impeachment** process. The Constitution of the United States refers to the impeachment process several times. Article II, Section 4, states as follows: "The President, Vice President and all civil Officers of the United States, shall be removed from Office on Impeachment for, and Conviction of Treason, Bribery, or other high Crimes and Misdemeanors." Article I, Sections 2 and 3, specify how the process of impeachment and conviction is to be carried out. In this process, the House and the Senate play different, but clearly defined roles.

INFOTRAC®

"Need Twenty-Eighth Amendment"

The authority to impeach (that is, to accuse, or charge) is vested in the House of Representatives, and formal impeachment proceedings are initiated there. In the House, a representative must list the charges against the president, vice president, or other civil officer. The impeachment charges are referred either to the Judiciary Committee or to a special investigating committee. If, as in the case of the Clinton impeachment in late 1998, a majority in the House votes for impeachment, then articles of impeachment are drawn up, which set forth the basis for the removal of the executive-branch officer.

The actual trial of impeachment is conducted in the Senate, with all members sitting in judgment. The chief justice of the United States Supreme Court presides over the Senate trial. A two-thirds vote of the senators present is required for conviction. The only punishment that Congress can mete out is removal from office and disqualification from holding any other federal office. Of course, the convicted official is subject to further punishment according to law. At the end of the Senate trial of President Clinton in 1999, neither of the two impeachment charges received the required two-thirds vote.

The different roles for the House and the Senate reflect the founders' views of the two chambers. Because House members were expected to represent the volatile will of the people, the founders did not give that chamber the final authority to convict and remove a federal officer. Rather, this authority was given to the Senate. The founders viewed the Senate as the more stable chamber—because of its longer terms and because it was further removed from popular influence (remember that until the passage of the Seventeenth Amendment in 1913, senators were elected by members of their state legislatures—not directly by the voters).

CONGRESSPERSONS AND THE CITIZENRY: A COMPARISON

Government institutions are given life by the people who work in them and shape them as political structures. Who, then, are the members of Congress, and how are they elected?

Members of the U.S. Senate and the U.S. House of Representatives are not typical American citizens. As can be seen in Table 9.2 on page 218, members of Congress are older than most Americans, partly because of constitutional age requirements and partly because a good deal of political experience normally is an advantage in running for national office. Members of Congress are also disproportionately white, male, Protestant, and trained in higher-status occupations. Lawyers

TABLE 9.2

Characteristics of the 106th Congress (1999–2001)

CHARACTERISTIC	U.S. POPULATION (1990)	HOUSE	SENATE
Age (median)	33.0	52.6	58.3
Percentage minority	28.0	14.4	3
Religion			
Percentage church members	61.0	98	99
Percentage Roman Catholic	39.0	28.9	25
Percentage Protestant	56.0	63	63
Percentage Jewish	4.0	5.3	11
Percentage female	51.9	13	9
Percentage with college degrees	21.4	94	96
Occupation			
Percentage lawyers	2.8	39	57
Percentage blue-collar workers	20.1	0	0
Family income			
Percentage of families earning over $50,000 annually	22.0	100	100
Personal wealth			
Percentage of population with assets over $1 million	0.7	16	33

are by far the largest occupational group among congresspersons, although the proportion of lawyers in the House is lower now than it was in the past.

CONGRESSIONAL ELECTIONS

The process of electing members of Congress is decentralized. Congressional elections are operated by the individual state governments, which must conform to the rules established by the U.S. Constitution and by national statutes. The Constitution states that representatives are to be elected every second year by popular ballot, and the number of seats awarded to each state is to be determined by the results of the decennial census. Each state has at least one representative, with most congressional districts having about half a million residents. Senators are elected by popular vote (since the passage of the Seventeenth Amendment) every six years; approximately one-third of the seats are chosen every two years. Each state has two senators. Under Article I, Section 4, of the Constitution, state legislatures are given control over "[T]he Times, Places and Manner of holding Elections for Senators and Representatives"; however, "the Congress may at any time by Law make or alter such Regulations."

Candidates for Congressional Elections

Candidates for congressional seats may be self-selected, or, in districts where one party is very strong, they may be recruited by the local minority party leadership.[3]

---

[3]See the work of Gary Jacobson, *The Politics of Congressional Elections*, 4th ed. (New York: Longman Publishers, 1997).

Candidates may resemble the voters of the district in terms of ethnicity or religion, but they are also likely to be very successful individuals who have been active in politics before. Additionally, with respect to House seats, they are likely to have local ties to their districts. Candidates most likely choose to run because they believe they would enjoy the job and its accompanying status. They also may be thinking about a House seat as a stepping stone to future political office as a senator, governor, or presidential candidate.

Congressional campaigns have changed considerably in the past two decades. Like all other campaigns, they are much more expensive, with the average cost of a winning Senate campaign now being $4.7 million and a winning House campaign averaging more than $675,000. Campaign funds include direct contributions regulated by law (as discussed in Chapter 8), political action committee (PAC) contributions, and "soft money" funneled through the national and state party committees. Once in office, legislators spend some time almost every day raising funds for their next campaign.

Most candidates for Congress must win the nomination through a **direct primary,** an intraparty election in which the voters select the candidates who will run on a party's ticket in the subsequent general election. In a direct primary, **party identifiers**—those who identify with a particular political party—cast their votes for the candidate of their choice. To win the primary, candidates may take more liberal or more conservative positions to get the votes of party identifiers. In the general election, they may moderate their views to attract the votes of independents and voters from the other party.

Congressional candidates are always hopeful that a strong presidential candidate on the ticket will have "coattails" that will sweep in senators and representatives of the same party. In fact, coattail effects have been quite limited in this century, appearing only in landslide elections such as Lyndon Johnson's victory over Barry Goldwater in 1964. Members of Congress who are from contested districts or who are in their first term are more likely to experience the effect of midterm elections, which are held in the even-numbered years in between presidential contests. In these years, voter turnout falls sharply, and the party controlling the White House normally loses seats in Congress. Additionally, voters in midterm elections often are responding to incumbency issues, because there is no presidential campaign. The result is a fragmentation of party authority and a loosening of ties between Congress and the president. Table 9.3 shows the pattern for midterm elections since 1942.

The Power of Incumbency

The power of incumbency in the outcome of congressional elections cannot be overemphasized. Table 9.4 on the next page shows that the overwhelming majority of representatives and a smaller proportion of senators who decide to run for reelection are successful. This conclusion holds for both presidential-year and midterm elections. Even in the "shakeup" elections of 1994, the power of incumbency was evident. The 1994 midterm

TABLE 9.3

Midterm Losses by the Party of the President, 1942 to 1998

SEATS LOST BY THE PARTY OF THE PRESIDENT IN THE HOUSE OF REPRESENTATIVES	
1942	−45 (D.)
1946	−55 (D.)
1950	−29 (D.)
1954	−18 (R.)
1958	−47 (R.)
1962	−4 (D.)
1966	−47 (D.)
1970	−12 (R.)
1974	−48 (R.)
1978	−15 (D.)
1982	−26 (R.)
1986	−5 (R.)
1990	−8 (R.)
1994	−52 (D.)
1998	+5 (D.)

TABLE 9.4

The Power of Incumbency

	PRESIDENTIAL-YEAR ELECTIONS						MIDTERM ELECTIONS						
	1976	1980	1984	1988	1992	1996	1974	1978	1982	1986	1990	1994	1998
House													
Number of incumbent candidates	384	398	409	409	368	382	391	382	393	393	407	382	401
Reelected	368	361	390	402	325	359	343	358	352	385	391	347	394
Percentage of total	95.8	90.7	95.4	98.3	88.9	93.4	87.7	93.7	90.1	98.0	96.1	90.8	98.2
Defeated	16	37	19	7	43	23	48	24	39	8	16	35	8
In primary	3	6	3	1	19	2	8	5	10	2	1	1	1
In general election	13	31	16	6	24	21	40	19	29	6	15	34	7
Senate													
Number of incumbent candidates	25	29	29	27	28	21	27	25	30	28	32	26	29
Reelected	16	16	26	23	23	19	23	15	28	21	31	24	26
Percentage of total	64.0	55.2	89.6	85	82.1	90	85.2	60.0	93.3	75.0	96.9	92.3	89.6
Defeated	9	13	3	4	5	2	4	10	2	7	1	2	6
In primary	0	4	0	0	1	1	2	3	0	0	0	0	3
In general election	9	9	3	4	4	1	2	7	2	7	1	2	3

SOURCES: Norman Ornstein, Thomas E. Mann, and Michael J. Malbin, *Vital Statistics on Congress, 1993–1994* (Washington, D.C.: Congressional Quarterly Press, 1994), pp. 56–57; *Congressional Quarterly Weekly Report*, November 7, 1992, pp. 3551, 3576; and authors' update.

elections swept the Democratic majority in both chambers of Congress out of power and brought in a Republican majority in a nationwide change of government that surprised and shocked the members of Congress and the parties themselves. Notably, the speaker of the House, Tom Foley, was also defeated, the first speaker to be denied reelection since 1862. Nonetheless, as you can see in Table 9.4, over 90 percent of congressional incumbents were reelected in 1994.

David R. Mayhew argues that the pursuit of reelection is the strongest motivation behind the activities of members of Congress. The reelection goal is pursued in three major ways: by *advertising*, by *credit claiming*, and by *position taking*.[4] Advertising includes using the mass media, making personal appearances with constituents, and sending newsletters—all to produce a favorable image and to make the incumbent's name a household word. Members of Congress try to present themselves as informed, experienced, and responsive to people's needs. Credit claiming focuses on the things a legislator claims to have done to benefit her or his constituents—by fulfilling the congressional casework function or bringing money for

[4]David R. Mayhew, *Congress: The Electoral Connection* (New Haven, Conn.: Yale University Press, 1974).

Former lieutenant governor of Ohio Nancy Hollister campaigns in Ohio's Sixth District, in southeastern Ohio. Hollister ran against Democrat Ted Strickland, who won the seat in 1992 after campaigning for it in three previous elections. This district is almost evenly divided between Republicans and Democrats, making election outcomes difficult to predict. Strickland lost his seat in 1994 but won it back again in 1996 and retained it in 1998.

mass transit to the district, for example. Position taking occurs when an incumbent explains his or her voting record on key issues; makes public statements of general support for presidential decisions; or indicates that he or she specifically supports positions on key issues, such as gun control or anti-inflation policies. Position taking carries with it certain risks, as the incumbent may lose support by disagreeing with the attitudes of a large number of constituents.

CONGRESSIONAL REAPPORTIONMENT

By far the most complicated aspects of the mechanics of congressional elections are the issues of **reapportionment** (the allocation of seats in the House to each state after each census) and **redistricting** (the redrawing of the boundaries of the districts within each state).[5] In a landmark six-to-two vote in 1962, the Supreme Court made reapportionment a **justiciable**[6] (that is, a reviewable) **question** in the Tennessee case

INFOTRAC®

"Congressional Reapportionment"

---

[5]For an excellent discussion of these issues, see *Congressional Districts in the 1990s* (Washington, D.C.: Congressional Quarterly Press, 1993).

[6]Pronounced juhs-*tish*-a-buhl.

Citizens display signs that show their support for term limits for members of Congress. The movement toward establishing term limits gathered steam in the early 1990s, and by 1994 more than twenty states had passed laws imposing such limits on members of Congress elected in those states. In 1995, however, the Supreme Court held that these laws were unconstitutional. Because the Constitution did not provide for limiting the number of terms a congressperson could serve, term limits could be established only by a constitutional amendment. The Court's decision did not end the controversy over this issue, however, as this photo indicates.

of *Baker v. Carr*[7] by invoking the Fourteenth Amendment principle that no state can deny to any person "the equal protection of the laws." This principle was applied directly in the 1964 ruling, *Reynolds v. Sims,*[8] when the Court held that *both* cham-

[7]369 U.S. 186 (1962).
[8]377 U.S. 533 (1964).

bers of a state legislature must be apportioned with equal populations in each district. This "one person, one vote" principle was applied to congressional districts in the 1964 case of *Wesberry v. Sanders,*[9] based on Article I, Section 2, of the Constitution, which requires that congresspersons be chosen "by the People of the several States."

Severe malapportionment of congressional districts prior to *Wesberry* had resulted in some districts containing two or three times the populations of other districts in the same state, thereby diluting the effect of a vote cast in the more populous districts. This system generally had benefited the conservative populations of rural areas and small towns and harmed the interests of the more heavily populated and liberal urban areas. In fact, suburban areas have benefited the most from the *Wesberry* ruling, as suburbs account for an increasingly larger proportion of the nation's population, and cities include a correspondingly smaller segment of the population.

Gerrymandering

Although the general issue of reapportionment has been dealt with fairly successfully by the one person, one vote principle, the **gerrymandering** issue has not yet been resolved. This term refers to the legislative boundary-drawing tactics that were used by Elbridge Gerry, the governor of Massachusetts, in the 1812 elections (see Figure 9.1 on the next page). A district is said to have been gerrymandered when its shape is altered substantially by the dominant party in a state legislature to maximize its electoral strength at the expense of the minority party. This can be achieved either by concentrating the opposition's voter support in as few districts as possible or by diffusing the minority party's strength by spreading it thinly across many districts.

In 1986, the Supreme Court heard a case that challenged gerrymandered congressional districts in Indiana. The Court ruled for the first time that redistricting for the political benefit of one group could be challenged on constitutional grounds. In this specific case, *Davis v. Bandemer,*[10] however, the Court did not agree that the districts were drawn unfairly, because it could not be proved that a group of voters would consistently be deprived of its influence at the polls as a result of the new districts.

"Minority-Majority" Districts

The Supreme Court had declared as unconstitutional districts that are uneven in population or that violate norms of size and shape to maximize the advantage of one party. In the early 1990s, however, the federal government encouraged another type of gerrymandering that made possible the election of a minority representative from a "minority-majority" area. Under the mandate of the Voting Rights Act of 1965, the Justice Department issued directives to states after the 1990 census instructing them to create congressional districts that would maximize the voting power of minority groups—that is, create districts in which minority voters were the majority. One such district—the Twelfth District of North Carolina—was 165 miles long, following Interstate 85 for the most part (see Figure 9.2 on page 226). According to a local joke,

---

[9]376 U.S. 1 (1964).
[10]478 U.S. 109 (1986).

FIGURE 9.1

The Original Gerrymander

The practice of "gerrymandering"—the excessive manipulation of the shape of a legislative district to benefit a certain incumbent or party—is probably as old as the republic, but the name originated in 1812. In that year, the Massachusetts legislature carved out of Essex County a district that historian John Fiske said had a "dragonlike contour." When the painter Gilbert Stuart saw the misshapen district, he penciled in a head, wings, and claws and exclaimed, "That will do for a salamander!" Editor Benjamin Russell replied, "Better say a Gerrymander" (after Elbridge Gerry, then governor of Massachusetts).

SOURCE: *Congressional Quarterly's Guide to Congress*, 3d ed. (Washington, D.C.: Congressional Quarterly Press, 1982), p. 695.

the district was so narrow that a car traveling down the interstate highway with both doors open would kill most of the voters in the district. Many of these "minority-majority" districts were challenged in court by citizens who claimed that to create districts based on race or ethnicity alone violates the equal protection clause of the Constitution. (See this chapter's *At Issue: Racial Gerrymandering* for a further discussion of this issue.)

PAY, PERKS, AND PRIVILEGES

Compared with the average American citizen, members of Congress are well paid. In 2001, annual congressional salaries were $136,700. Legislators also have many benefits that are not available to most workers.

Racial Gerrymandering

The concept of equality is a basic American value. The meaning of equality, though, depends to a great extent on how the United States Supreme Court interprets such laws as the equal protection clause of the Constitution.

In the 1990s, the Supreme Court's views on equal protection clearly came into conflict with those of the Justice Department with respect to racial gerrymandering—the creation of "minority-majority" congressional districts to enhance the representation of minority groups. After the 1990 census, the Justice Department issued a directive to the states requiring them to create such districts. The motivation for this directive was a desire to ensure more equal treatment for minorities by allowing them a stronger voice in Congress.

As a result of the directive, in the early 1990s a number of states created "minority-majority" districts, some of which had extraordinarily odd shapes (see Figure 9.2 on page 226, for example) so that they could include more minority residents. Ironically, state compliance with the Justice Department's requirements resulted in several of these new districts being challenged in the courts. White plain-

tiffs contended that race-based districting was unconstitutional because it violated the equal protection clause. In 1993, the United States Supreme Court declared that racially gerrymandered districts were subject to strict scrutiny under the equal protection clause— which means that they can be justified only by a "compelling state interest" and must be "narrowly tailored" by the state to serve that interest.[*]

In 1995, the Supreme Court attacked race-based redistricting even more aggressively when it declared that Georgia's new Eleventh District was unconstitutional. The district stretched from Atlanta to the Atlantic, splitting eight counties and five municipalities along the way. The Court referred to the district as a "monstrosity" linking "widely spaced urban centers that have absolutely nothing to do with each other." The Court went on to say that when a state assigns voters on the basis of race, "it engages in the offensive and demeaning assumption that voters of a particular race, because of their race, think alike, share the same political interests, and will prefer the same candidates at the polls." The

Court also chastised the Justice Department for concluding that race-based districting was mandated under the Voting Rights Act of 1965: "When the Justice Department's interpretation of the Act compels race-based districting, it by definition raises a serious constitutional question."[†]

In subsequent rulings, the Court affirmed its position that when race is the dominant factor in the drawing of congressional district lines, the districts are unconstitutional. In two 1996 cases, the Court ruled that the Twelfth District in North Carolina (see Figure 9.2) and three Texas districts were unconstitutional for this reason.[‡] In 1997, the Court ruled Virginia's Third District unconstitutional as well, while approving a map for Georgia's Eleventh District drawn up by a three-judge panel after the Court's 1995 decision.

FOR CRITICAL ANALYSIS

Is the Supreme Court's position on racial gerrymandering consistent with its position on affirmative action programs? Why or why not?

---

[*]*Shaw v. Reno*, 509 U.S. 630 (1993).

[†]*Miller v. Johnson*, 515 U.S. 900 (1995).
[‡]*Shaw v. Hunt*, 517 U.S. 899 (1996);
Bush v. Vera, 517 U.S. 952 (1996).

FIGURE 9.2

The Twelfth District of North Carolina

The Twelfth District, which was declared unconstitutional by the United States Supreme Court in 1996, was created to facilitate the election of a minority representative. It snaked through North Carolina along Interstate 85.

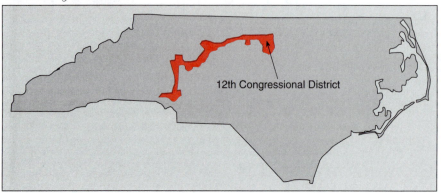

12th Congressional District

Special Benefits

Members of Congress benefit in many ways from belonging to a select group. They have access to private Capitol Hill gymnasium facilities; get low-cost haircuts; receive free, close-in parking at the National and Dulles Airports near Washington; and get six free parking spaces per member in Capitol Hill garages—plus one free outdoor Capitol parking slot. They also avoid parking tickets because of their congressional license plates and, until 1994, were not required to comply with most labor laws in dealing with their staffs. They eat in a subsidized dining room and take advantage of free plants from the Botanical Gardens for their offices, free medical care, an inexpensive but generous pension plan, liberal travel allowances, and special tax considerations.

Members of Congress are also granted generous **franking** privileges that permit them to send material through the mail by substituting their facsimile signature (frank) for postage. The annual cost of congressional mail has risen from $11 million in 1971 to almost $60 million today. Typically, the costs for these mailings rise enormously during election years.

Congresspersons have the assistance of permanent professional staffs. More than 35,000 people are employed in the Capitol Hill bureaucracy. About half of this total consists of personal and committee staff members. The personal staff includes office clerks and secretaries; professionals who deal with media relations, draft legislation, and satisfy constituency requests for service; and staffers who maintain local offices in the member's home district or state. Congress also benefits from the expertise of the professional staffs of agencies that were created to produce information for members of the House and Senate. For example, the Congressional Research Service (CRS), a section of the Library of Congress, furnishes a computer-based record of the contents and current legislative status of major bills that are under consideration. This record can be reviewed by staff members using computer terminals available in most offices.

Members of Congress also benefit from a number of special constitutional protections. Under Article I, Section 6, of the Constitution, they "shall in all Cases, except Treason, Felony and Breach of the Peace, be privileged from Arrest during their Attendance at the Session of their respective Houses, and in going to and returning from the same; and for any Speech or Debate in either House, they shall not be questioned in any other Place." The arrest immunity clause is not really an important provision today. The "speech or debate" clause, however, means that a member may make any allegations or other statements he or she wishes in connection with official duties and normally not be sued for libel or slander or otherwise be subject to legal action.

THE COMMITTEE STRUCTURE

Most of the actual work of legislating is performed by the committees and subcommittees within Congress. Thousands of bills are introduced in every session of Congress, and no single member can possibly be adequately informed on all the issues that arise. The committee system is a way to provide for specialization, or a division of the legislative labor. Members of a committee can concentrate on just one area or topic—such as taxation or energy—and develop sufficient expertise to draft appropriate legislation when needed. The flow of legislation through both the House and the Senate is determined largely by the speed with which the members of these committees act on bills and resolutions.

Commonly known as "little legislatures," committees usually have the final say on pieces of legislation.[11] Committee actions may be overturned on the floor by the House or Senate, but this rarely happens. Legislators normally defer to the expertise of the chairperson and other members of the committee who speak on the floor in defense of a committee decision. Chairpersons of committees exercise control over the scheduling of hearings and formal action on a bill. They also decide which subcommittee will act on legislation falling within their committee's jurisdiction.

Types of Congressional Committees

Over the past two centuries, Congress has created several different types of committees, each of which serves particular needs of the institution.

Standing Committees. By far the most important committees in Congress are the **standing committees**—permanent bodies that are established by the rules of each chamber of Congress and that continue from session to session. A list of the standing committees of the 106th Congress is presented in Table 9.5 on the next page. In addition, most of the standing committees have created several subcommittees to carry

---

[11]The term *little legislatures* is from Woodrow Wilson, *Congressional Government* (New York: Meridian Books, 1956 [first published in 1885]).

TABLE 9.5

Standing Committees of the 106th Congress, 1999–2001

HOUSE COMMITTEES	SENATE COMMITTEES
Agriculture	Agriculture, Nutrition, and Forestry
Appropriations	Appropriations
Armed Services	Armed Services
Banking and Financial Service	Banking, Housing, and Urban Affairs
Budget	Budget
Commerce	Commerce, Science, and Transportation
Education and the Workforce	Energy and Natural Resources
Government Reform and House	Environment and Public Works
Administration	Finance
International Relations	Foreign Relations
Judiciary	Governmental Affairs
Resources	Health, Education, Labor, and Pensions
Rules	Indian Affairs
Science	Judiciary
Small Business	Rules and Administration
Standards of Official Conduct	Small Business
Transportation and Infrastructure	Veterans' Affairs
Veterans' Affairs	
Ways and Means	

out their work. In the 106th Congress, there were 68 subcommittees in the Senate and 85 in the House.[12] Each standing committee is given a specific area of legislative policy jurisdiction, and almost all legislative measures are considered by the appropriate standing committees.

Select Committees. A **select committee** normally is created for a limited period of time and for a specific legislative purpose. For example, a select committee may be formed to investigate a public problem, such as child nutrition or aging. Select committees are disbanded when they have reported to the chamber that created them. They rarely create original legislation.

Joint Committees. A **joint committee** is formed by the concurrent action of both chambers of Congress and consists of members from each chamber. Joint committees, which may be permanent or temporary, have dealt with the economy, taxation, and the Library of Congress.

Conference Committees. Special types of joint committees—**conference committees**—are formed for the purpose of achieving agreement between the House and the Senate on the exact wording of legislative acts when the two chambers pass legislative proposals in different forms. No bill can be sent to the White House to be signed into law unless it first passes both chambers in identical form. Sometimes called the "third house" of Congress, conference committees are in a position to

---

[12]*Congressional Directory* (Washington, D.C.: U.S. Government Printing Office, various editions).

make significant alterations in legislation and frequently become the focal point of policy debates.

The House Rules Committee. Because of its special "gatekeeping" power over the terms on which legislation will reach the floor of the House of Representatives, the House Rules Committee holds a uniquely powerful position. A special committee rule sets the time limit on debate and determines whether and how a bill may be amended. The Rules Committee has the unusual power to meet while the House is in session, to have its resolutions considered immediately on the floor, and to initiate legislation on its own.

The Selection of Committee Members

In the House, representatives are appointed to standing committees by the Steering and Policy Committee (for Democrats) and by the Committee on Committees (for Republicans). Committee chairpersons normally are appointed according to seniority. The rule regarding seniority specifies that majority party members with longer terms of continuous service on the committee will be given preference when committee chairpersons—as well as holders of other significant posts in Congress—are selected. This is not a law but an informal, traditional process. The **seniority system,** although deliberately unequal, provides a predictable means of assigning positions of power within Congress.

THE FORMAL LEADERSHIP

The limited amount of centralized power that exists in Congress is exercised through party-based mechanisms. Congress is organized by party. When the Democratic Party, for example, wins a majority of seats in either the House or the Senate, Democrats control the official positions of power in that chamber, and every important committee has a Democratic chairperson and a majority of Democratic members. The same process holds when Republicans are in the majority.

We consider the formal leadership positions in the House and Senate separately, but you will note some broad similarities in the way leaders are selected and in the ways they exercise power in the two chambers.

Leadership in the House

The House leadership is made up of the speaker, the majority and minority leaders, and the party whips.

The Speaker. The presiding officer and foremost power holder in the House of Representatives is the **speaker of the House.** The speaker's position is technically a nonpartisan one, but in fact, for the better part of two centuries, the speaker has been the official leader of the majority party in the House. When a new Congress convenes in January of odd-numbered years, each party nominates a candidate for speaker. In one of the very rare instances of perfect party cohesion, all Democratic members of the House ordinarily vote for their party's nominee, and all Republicans support their alternative candidate.

The influence of modern-day speakers is based primarily on their personal prestige, persuasive ability, and knowledge of the legislative process—plus the acquiescence or active support of other representatives. The major formal powers of the speaker include the following:

1. Presiding over meetings of the House.
2. Appointing members of joint committees and conference committees.
3. Scheduling legislation for floor action.
4. Deciding points of order and interpreting the rules with the advice of the House parliamentarian.
5. Referring bills and resolutions to the appropriate standing committees of the House.

A speaker may take part in floor debate and vote, as can any other member of Congress, but recent speakers usually have voted only to break a tie.

INFOTRAC®

"Just Man GOP Needed"

The Majority Leader. The **majority leader of the House** is elected by a caucus of party members to foster cohesion among party members and to act as a spokesperson for the party. The majority leader influences the scheduling of debate and generally acts as the chief supporter of the speaker. The majority leader cooperates with the speaker and other party leaders, both inside and outside Congress, to formulate the party's legislative program and to guide that program through the legislative process in the House. The Democrats recruit future speakers from that position.

The Minority Leader. The **minority leader of the House** is the candidate nominated for speaker by a caucus of the minority party. Like the majority leader, the leader of the minority party has as his or her primary responsibility the maintaining of cohesion within the party's ranks. The minority leader works for cohesion among the party's members and speaks on behalf of the president if the minority party controls the White House. In relations with the majority party, the minority leader consults with both the speaker and the majority leader on recognizing members who wish to speak on the floor, on House rules and procedures, and on the scheduling of legislation. Minority leaders have no actual power in these areas, however.

Whips. The formal leadership of each party includes assistants to the majority and minority leaders, who are known as **whips.** The whips assist the party leaders by passing information down from the leadership to party members and by ensuring that members show up for floor debate and cast their votes on important issues. Whips conduct polls among party members about the members' views on major pieces of legislation, inform the leaders about whose vote is doubtful and whose is certain, and may exert pressure on members to support the leaders' positions.

Leadership in the Senate

The Senate is less than one-fourth the size of the House. This fact alone probably explains why a formal, complex, and centralized leadership structure is less necessary in the Senate than it is in the House.

The two highest-ranking formal leadership positions in the Senate are essentially ceremonial in nature. Under the Constitution, the vice president of the United States is the president (that is, the presiding officer) of the Senate and may vote to break a tie. The vice president, however, only rarely is present for a meeting of the Senate. The Senate elects instead a **president *pro tempore*** ("pro tem") to preside over the Senate in the vice president's absence. Ordinarily, the president pro tem is the member of the majority party with the longest continuous term of service in the Senate. The president pro tem is mostly a ceremonial position. Junior senators take turns actually presiding over the sessions of the Senate.

The real leadership power in the Senate rests in the hands of the **majority floor leader,** the **minority floor leader,** and their respective whips. The Senate majority and minority leaders have the right to be recognized first in debate on the floor and generally exercise the same powers available to the House majority and minority leaders. They control the scheduling of debate on the floor in conjunction with the majority party's Policy Committee, influence the allocation of committee assignments for new members or for senators attempting to transfer to a new committee, influence the selection of other party officials, and participate in selecting members of conference committees. The leaders are expected to mobilize support for partisan legislative initiatives or for the proposals of a president who belongs to the same party. The leaders act as liaisons with the White House when the president is of their party, try to get the cooperation of committee chairpersons, and seek to facilitate the smooth functioning of the Senate through the senators' unanimous consent. Floor leaders are elected by their respective party caucuses.

Senate party whips, like their House counterparts, maintain communication within the party on platform positions and try to ensure that party colleagues are present for floor debate and important votes. The Senate whip system is far less elaborate than its counterpart in the House, simply because there are fewer members to track.

HOW A BILL BECOMES LAW

Each year, Congress and the president propose and approve many laws. Some are budget and appropriation laws that require extensive bargaining but must be passed for the government to continue to function. Other laws are relatively free of controversy and are passed with little dissension between the branches of government. Still other proposed legislation is extremely controversial and reaches to the roots of differences between Democrats and Republicans and between the executive and legislative branches.

As detailed in Figure 9.3, each law begins as a bill, which must be introduced in either the House or the Senate. Often, similar bills are introduced in both chambers.

FIGURE 9.3

How a Bill Becomes Law

This illustration shows the most typical way in which proposed legislation is enacted into law. Most legislation begins as similar bills introduced into each chamber of Congress. The process is illustrated here with two hypothetical bills. House bill No. 100 (HR 100) and Senate bill No. 200 (S 200). The path of HR 100 is shown on the left, and that of S 200, on the right.

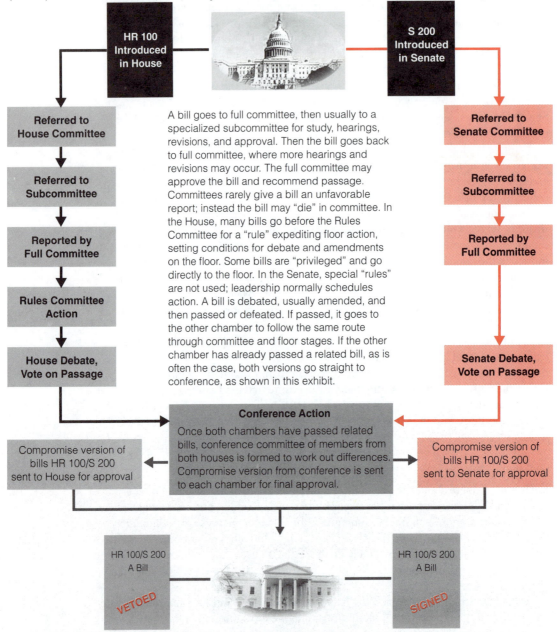

HR 100 Introduced in House

S 200 Introduced in Senate

Referred to House Committee

Referred to Senate Committee

Referred to Subcommittee

Referred to Subcommittee

Reported by Full Committee

Reported by Full Committee

Rules Committee Action

House Debate, Vote on Passage

Senate Debate, Vote on Passage

A bill goes to full committee, then usually to a specialized subcommittee for study, hearings, revisions, and approval. Then the bill goes back to full committee, where more hearings and revisions may occur. The full committee may approve the bill and recommend passage. Committees rarely give a bill an unfavorable report; instead the bill may "die" in committee. In the House, many bills go before the Rules Committee for a "rule" expediting floor action, setting conditions for debate and amendments on the floor. Some bills are "privileged" and go directly to the floor. In the Senate, special "rules" are not used; leadership normally schedules action. A bill is debated, usually amended, and then passed or defeated. If passed, it goes to the other chamber to follow the same route through committee and floor stages. If the other chamber has already passed a related bill, as is often the case, both versions go straight to conference, as shown in this exhibit.

Conference Action

Once both chambers have passed related bills, conference committee of members from both houses is formed to work out differences. Compromise version from conference is sent to each chamber for final approval.

Compromise version of bills HR 100/S 200 sent to House for approval

Compromise version of bills HR 100/S 200 sent to Senate for approval

HR 100/S 200 A Bill

VETOED

HR 100/S 200 A Bill

SIGNED

A compromise bill approved by both houses is sent to the president, who can sign it into law or veto it and return it to Congress. Congress may override a veto by a two-thirds majority vote in both houses; the bill then becomes law without the president's signature.

If it is a "money bill," however, it must start in the House. In each chamber, the bill follows similar steps. It is referred to a committee and its subcommittees for study, discussion, hearings, and rewriting. When the bill is reported out to the full chamber, it must be scheduled for debate (by the Rules Committee in the House and by the leadership in the Senate). After the bill has been passed in each chamber, if it contains different provisions, a conference committee is formed to write a compromise bill, which must be approved by both chambers before it is sent to the president to sign or veto.

How Much Will the Government Spend?

The Constitution is extremely clear about where the power of the purse lies in the national government: all money bills, whether for taxing or spending, must originate in the House of Representatives. Today, much of the business of Congress is concerned with approving government expenditures through the budget process and with raising the revenues to pay for government programs.

From 1922, when Congress required the president to prepare and present to the legislature an executive budget, until 1974, the congressional budget process was so disjointed that it was difficult to visualize the total picture of government finances. The president presented the executive budget to Congress in January. It was broken down into thirteen or more appropriations bills. Some time later, after all of the bills were debated, amended, and passed, it was more or less possible to estimate total government spending for the next year.

Frustrated by the president's ability to impound funds and dissatisfied with the entire budget process, Congress passed the Budget and Impoundment Control Act of 1974 to regain some control over the nation's spending. The act required the president to spend the funds that Congress had appropriated, frustrating the president's ability to kill programs of which the president disapproved by withholding funds. The other major accomplishment of the act was to force Congress to examine total national taxing and spending at least twice in each budget cycle.

The budget cycle of the federal government is described in the following subsections. (See Figure 9.4 on page 234 for a graphic illustration of the budget cycle.)

Preparing the Budget

The federal government operates on a fiscal year (FY) cycle. The fiscal year runs from October through September, so that fiscal 2001, or FY01, runs from October 1, 2000, through September 30, 2001. Eighteen months before a fiscal year starts, the executive branch begins preparing the budget. The Office of Management and Budget (OMB) receives advice from the Council of Economic Advisers (CEA) and the Treasury Department. The OMB outlines the budget and then sends it to the various departments and agencies. Bargaining follows, in which—to use only two of many examples—the Department of Health and Human Services argues for more welfare spending, and the armed forces argue for fewer defense spending cuts.

Even though the OMB has only six hundred employees, it is known as one of the most powerful agencies in Washington. It assembles the budget documents and

FIGURE 9.4

The Budget Cycle

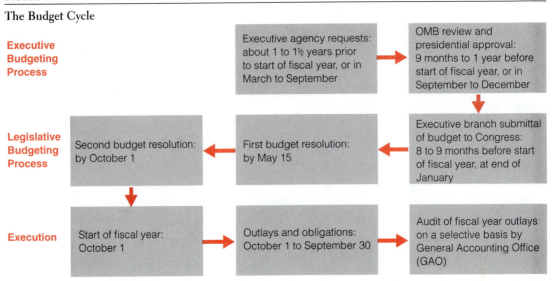

monitors the agencies throughout each year. Every year, it begins the budget process with a **spring review,** in which it requires all of the agencies to review their programs, activities, and goals. At the beginning of each summer, the director of the OMB sends out a letter instructing agencies to submit their requests for funding for the next fiscal year. By the end of the summer, each agency must submit a formal request to the OMB.

In actuality, the "budget season" begins with the **fall review.** At this time, the OMB looks at budget requests and, in almost all cases, routinely cuts them back. Although the OMB works within guidelines established by the president, specific decisions often are left to the director and the director's associates. By the beginning of November, the director's review begins. The director meets with cabinet secretaries and budget officers. Time becomes crucial. The budget must be completed by January so that it can go to the printer to be included in the *Economic Report of the President.*

Congress Faces the Budget

In January, nine months before the fiscal year starts, the president takes the OMB's proposed budget, approves it, and submits it to Congress. Then the congressional budgeting process takes over. Congressional committees and subcommittees look at the proposals from the executive branch. The Congressional Budget Office (CBO) advises the different committees on economic matters, just as the OMB and the CEA advise the president. The **first budget resolution** by Congress is supposed to be passed in May. It sets overall revenue goals and spending targets.

During the summer, bargaining among all the concerned parties takes place. Spending and tax laws that are drawn up during this period are supposed to be guided by the May congressional budget resolution. By September, Congress is supposed to pass its **second budget resolution,** one that will set "binding" limits on taxes and spending for the fiscal year beginning October 1. Bills passed before that date that do not fit within the limits of the budget resolution are supposed to be changed.

In actuality, between 1978 and 1996, Congress did not pass a complete budget by October 1. In other words, generally, Congress does not follow its own rules. Budget resolutions are passed late, and when they are passed, they are not treated as binding. In each fiscal year that starts without a budget, every agency operates on the basis of **continuing resolutions,** which enable the agencies to keep on doing whatever they were doing the previous year with the same amount of funding. Even continuing resolutions have not always been passed on time.

THE QUESTION OF CONGRESSIONAL ETHICS

Ethics is the most serious public relations problem confronting Congress today. Perhaps nothing has so tarnished the public's perception of Congress as the revelations concerning the abuse of staff members, the misuse of public funds, and the personal indiscretions and corruption of members of that institution.

Congress's response to revelations of member misconduct has been mixed. The House Democratic caucus in June 1980 voted 160 to 0 to require that chairpersons of committees or subcommittees be stripped of their posts automatically if they have been censured or indicted on a felony charge carrying a prison sentence of at least two years. This rule can be waived, however, by the same caucus.

Among the cases that received widespread publicity were those of Senator Bob Packwood (R., Ore.) who was accused of sexually harrassing a number of women, and of Representative Dan Rostenkowski (D., Ill.), who was convicted of several fraud charges. Packwood resigned from the Senate after its ethics committee voted his expulsion. Former speaker Newt Gingrich was also found to have violated House rules in the funding of his PAC.

Public financing of congressional campaigns may offer a partial solution to recurring problems of financial misconduct. Nonetheless, Congress has refused to use tax money for, or to impose spending limits on, its members' campaigns, even though it adopted such provisions for presidential campaigns in 1974. Part of the campaign-funding problem is illustrated by the former member of Congress who used leftover campaign funds to make a down payment on a fifty-five-foot houseboat in Florida and to finance a limousine carrying the congressional seal. The practice of diverting unused campaign funds to personal use was outlawed in January 1980, but members of Congress were exempted from coverage by the law until 1992. By the 1990s, the public's regard for Congress had reached an all-time low.

KEY TERMS

agenda setting 215

bicameralism 211

casework 213

cloture 216

conference committee 228

constituent 210

continuing resolution 235

direct primary 219

enumerated power 211

executive budget 233

fall review 234

filibustering 216

first budget resolution 235

fiscal year (FY) 233

franking 226

gerrymandering 223

impeachment 217

instructed delegate 214

joint committee 228

justiciable question 221

lawmaking 212

logrolling 213

majority floor leader 231

majority leader of the House 230

minority floor leader 231

minority leader of the House 230

ombudsperson 213

oversight 214

party identifier 219

politico 214

president *pro tempore* 231

reapportionment 221

redistricting 221

representation 213

Rules Committee 216

second budget resolution 235

select committee 228

seniority system 229

speaker of the House 229

spring review 234

standing committee 227

trustee 214

whip 230

CHAPTER SUMMARY

1 The authors of the Constitution, believing that the bulk of national power should be in the legislature, set forth the structure, power, and operation of Congress. The Constitution states that Congress will consist of two chambers. Partly an outgrowth of the Connecticut Compromise, this bicameral structure established a balanced legislature, with the membership in the House of Representatives based on population and the membership in the Senate based on the equality of states.

2 The first seventeen clauses of Article I, Section 8, of the Constitution specify most of the enumerated, or expressed, powers of Congress, including the right to impose taxes, to borrow money, to regulate commerce, and to declare war. Besides its enumerated powers, Congress enjoys the right to "make all Laws which shall be necessary and proper for carrying into Execution the foregoing Powers, and all other Powers vested by this Constitution in the

Government of the United States, or in any Department or Officer thereof." This is called the elastic, or necessary and proper, clause.

3 The functions of Congress include (a) lawmaking, (b) service to constituents, (c) representation, (d) oversight, (e) public education, and (f) conflict resolution.

4 There are 435 members in the House of Representatives and 100 members in the Senate. Owing to its larger size, the House has a greater number of formal rules. The Senate tradition of unlimited debate, or filibustering, dates back to 1790 and has been used over the years to frustrate the passage of bills. Under Senate Rule 22, cloture can be used to shut off debate on a bill.

5 Members of Congress are not typical American citizens. They are older than most Americans; disproportionately white, male, and Protestant; and trained in professional occupations.

6 Congressional elections are operated by the individual state governments, which must abide by rules established by the Constitution and national statutes. The process of nominating congressional candidates has shifted from party conventions to the direct primaries currently used in all states. The overwhelming majority of incumbent representatives and a smaller proportion of senators who run for reelection are successful. The most complicated aspect of the mechanics of congressional elections is reapportionment—the allocation of legislative seats to constituencies. The Supreme Court's "one person, one vote" rule has been applied to equalize the populations of state legislative and congressional districts.

7 Members of Congress are well paid and enjoy other benefits, including franking privileges. Members of Congress have personal and committee staff members available to them and also benefit from a number of legal privileges and immunities.

8 Most of the actual work of legislating is performed by committees and subcommittees within Congress. Legislation introduced into the House or Senate is assigned to the appropriate standing committees for review. Select committees are created for a limited period of time for a specific legislative purpose. Joint committees are formed by the concurrent action of both chambers and consist of members from each chamber. Conference committees are special joint committees set up to achieve agreement between the House and the Senate on the exact wording of legislative acts passed by both chambers in different forms. The seniority rule specifies that longer-serving members will be given preference when committee chairpersons and holders of other important posts are selected.

9 The foremost power holder in the House of Representatives is the speaker of the House. Other leaders are the House majority leader, the House minority leader, and the majority and minority whips. Formally, the vice president is the presiding officer of the Senate, with the majority party choosing a senior member as the president pro tempore to preside when the vice president is absent. Actual leadership in the Senate rests with the majority floor leader, the minority floor leader, and their respective whips.

10 A bill becomes law by progressing through both chambers of Congress and their appropriate standing and joint committees to the president.

11 The budget process for a fiscal year begins with the preparation of an executive budget by the president. This is reviewed by the Office of Management and Budget and then sent to Congress, which is supposed to pass a final budget by the end of September. Since 1978, Congress has not followed its own time rules.

12 Ethics is the most serious public relations problem facing Congress. Financial misconduct, sexual improprieties, and other unethical behavior on the part of several House and Senate members have resulted in a significant lowering of the public's regard for the institution of Congress. Despite congressional investigations of ethical misconduct and, in some cases, reprimands of members of Congress, the overall view of the public is that Congress has little control over the actions of its members with respect to ethics.

SELECTED PRINT AND ELECTRONIC RESOURCES

Suggested Readings

Barone, Michael, and Grant Ujifusa. *The Almanac of American Politics, 1999.* Washington, D.C.: National Journal, 1998. This is a comprehensive summary of current political information on each member of Congress, his or her state or congressional district, recent congressional election results, key votes and ratings of roll-call votes by various organizations, sources of campaign contributions, and records of campaign expenditures.

Davidson, Roger H., and Walter J. Oleszek. *Congress and Its Members.* 6th ed. Washington, D.C.:

Congressional Quarterly Press, 1997. This updated classic looks carefully at the "two Congresses," the one in Washington and the role played by congresspersons at home.

Deering, Christopher J., and Steven S. Smith. *Committees in Congress.* 3d ed. Washington, D.C.: Congressional Quarterly Press, 1997. This new edition of a classic work on committees expands its coverage of reforms in Congress and now includes those that have been initiated by the Republican majority since 1995.

Martin, Fenton S., and Robert U. Goehlert. *How to Research Congress.* Washington, D.C.: Congressional Quarterly Press, 1996. This easy-to-use guide provides information on researching bills, procedures in Congress, investigations, and the inner workings of Congress.

Media Sources

Mr. Smith Goes to Washington—A 1939 film in which Jimmy Stewart plays the naive congressman who is quickly educated in Washington. A true American political classic.

The Seduction of Joe Tynan—A 1979 film in which Alan Alda plays a young senator who must face serious decisions about his political role and his private life.

LOGGING ON

To find out about the schedule of activities taking place in Congress, use the following Web sites:

http://www.senate.gov

http://www.house.gov

http://thomas.loc.gov

The Congressional Budget Office is online at

http://www.cbo.gov

The URL for the Government Printing Office is

http://www.access.gpo.gov

For the real inside facts on what's going on in Washington, D.C., you can look at *RollCall*, the newspaper of the Capitol:

http://www.rollcall.com

Congressional Quarterly, a publication that reports on Congress:

http://www.cq.com

The Hill, which investigates various activities of Congress:

http://www.hillnews.com

Another site, organized by two Washington firms, that includes a wealth of data on Congress is

http://www.congress.org

One site, sponsored by C-SPAN, features online answers to questions about Congress. Past questions and answers about virtually any aspect of Congress are also posted at

http://www.c-span.org/questions

USING THE INTERNET FOR POLITICAL ANALYSIS

Point your browser to one of the general guides to Congress given at the following Web sites:

http://www.house.gov

http://www.senate.gov/

Look up the Web pages of at least three different members of the House or the Senate. Try to pick members from each of the major parties. Compare the Web pages on the following issues:

1. Which page appears to provide the most assistance to constituents?

2. How much partisan information is included on the Web page?

3 To what extent is the member of Congress giving information about his or her policy stands?

4. To what extent is the member trying to build trust and loyalty through providing personal information and services?

CHAPTER 10

The Presidency

T he writers of the Constitution created the presidency of the United States without any models on which to draw. Nowhere else in the world was there a democratically selected chief executive. What the founders did not want was a king. In fact, given their previous experience with royal governors in the colonies, many of the delegates to the Constitutional Convention wanted to create a very weak executive who could not veto legislation. Other delegates, especially those who had witnessed the need for a strong leader in the Revolutionary Army, believed a strong executive to be necessary for the republic. The delegates, after much debate, created a chief executive who was granted enough powers in the Constitution to balance those of the Congress.[1] In this chapter, after looking at who can become president and at the process involved, we examine closely the nature and extent of the constitutional powers held by the president.

WHO CAN BECOME PRESIDENT?

The requirements for becoming president, as outlined in Article II, Section 1, of the Constitution, are not overwhelmingly stringent:

> No person except a natural born Citizen, or a Citizen of the United States, at the time of the Adoption of this Constitution, shall be eligible to the Office of President; neither shall any Person be eligible to that Office who shall not have attained to the Age of thirty-five Years, and been fourteen Years a Resident within the United States.

Although the great American dream is symbolized by the statement that "anybody can become president of this country," in fact, out of forty-two presidents, twenty-six have been lawyers, and many have been relatively wealthy.

Although the Constitution states that the minimum-age requirement for the presidency is thirty-five years, most presidents have been much older than that when they assumed office. John F. Kennedy, at the age of forty-three, was the youngest elected president, and the oldest was Ronald Reagan, at age sixty-nine. The average age at inauguration has been fifty-four. There has clearly been a demographic bias in the selection of presidents. All have been male, white, and Protestant, except for John F.

[1]Forrest McDonald, *The American Presidency: An Intellectual History* (Lawrence, Kans.: University Press of Kansas, 1994), p. 179.

Kennedy, a Roman Catholic. Presidents have been men of great stature—such as George Washington—and men in whom leadership qualities were not so pronounced—such as Warren Harding.

THE PROCESS OF BECOMING PRESIDENT

Major and minor political parties nominate candidates for president and vice president at national conventions every four years. As discussed in Chapter 8, the nation's voters do not elect a president and vice president directly but rather cast ballots for presidential electors, who then vote for a president and a vice president in the electoral college.

Because the election is governed by a majority in the electoral college, it is conceivable that someone could be elected to the office of the presidency without having a plurality of the popular vote cast. Indeed, in three cases, candidates won elections even though their major opponents received more popular votes. In cases when more than two candidates were running for office, many presidential candidates have won the election with less than 50 percent of the total popular votes cast for all candidates—including Abraham Lincoln, Woodrow Wilson, Harry S. Truman, John F. Kennedy, and Richard Nixon. In the 1992 election, Bill Clinton, with only 43 percent of the vote, defeated incumbent George Bush. Independent candidate H. Ross Perot garnered a surprising 19 percent of the vote. Remember from Chapter 8 that no president has won a majority of votes from the entire voting-age population.

On occasion, the electoral college has failed to give any candidate a majority. At this point, the election is thrown into the House of Representatives. The president is then chosen from among the three candidates having the most electoral college votes. Only two times in our past has the House had to decide on a president. Thomas Jefferson and Aaron Burr tied in the electoral college in 1800. This happened because the Constitution had not been explicit in indicating which of the two electoral votes was for president and which was for vice president. In 1804, the **Twelfth Amendment** clarified the matter by requiring the president and vice president to be chosen separately. In 1824, the House again had to make a choice, this time among William H. Crawford, Andrew Jackson, and John Quincy Adams. It chose Adams, even though Jackson had more electoral and popular votes.

THE MANY ROLES OF THE PRESIDENT

The Constitution speaks briefly about the duties and obligations of the president. Based on a brief list of powers and the precedents of history, the presidency has grown into a very complicated job that requires balancing at least five constitutional roles. These are (1) chief of state, (2) chief executive, (3) commander in chief of the armed forces, (4) chief diplomat, and (5) chief legislator of the United States. Here we examine each of these significant presidential functions, or roles. It is worth noting that one person plays all these roles simultaneously and that the needs of these roles may at times come into conflict.

Chief of State

Every nation has at least one person who is the ceremonial head of state. In most democratic governments, the role of **chief of state** is given to someone other than the chief executive, who is the head of the executive branch of government. In Britain, for example, the chief of state is the queen. In France, the prime minister is the chief executive, and the chief of state is the president. But in the United States, the president is both chief executive and chief of state. According to William Howard Taft, as chief of state the president symbolizes the "dignity and majesty" of the American people.

As chief of state, the president engages in a number of activities that are largely symbolic or ceremonial, such as decorating war heroes, throwing out the first ball to open the baseball season, and dedicating parks and post offices.

Chief Executive

According to the Constitution, "The executive Power shall be vested in a President of the United States of America. . . . [H]e may require the Opinion, in writing, of the principal Officer in each of the executive Departments, upon any Subject relating to the Duties of their respective Offices . . . and he shall nominate, and by and with the Advice and Consent of the Senate, shall appoint . . . Officers of the United States. . . . [H]e shall take Care that the Laws be faithfully executed."

As **chief executive,** or the head of the executive branch of the government, the president is constitutionally bound to enforce the acts of Congress, the judgments of federal courts, and treaties signed by the United States. The duty to "faithfully execute" the laws has been a source of constitutional power for presidents. To assist in the various tasks of the chief executive, the president has a federal bureaucracy (see Chapter 11), which currently consists of over 2.7 million federal civilian employees.

The Powers of Appointment and Removal. You might think that the president, as head of the largest bureaucracy in the United States, wields enormous power. The president, however, only nominally runs the executive bureaucracy, for most government positions are filled by civil service employees.[2] Therefore, even though the president has **appointment power,** it is not very extensive, being limited to cabinet and subcabinet jobs, federal judgeships, agency heads, and about two thousand lesser jobs. This means that most of the 2.7 million federal employees owe no political allegiance to the president. They are more likely to owe loyalty to congressional committees or to interest groups representing the sector of the society that they serve. Less than 1 percent of the total employment in each executive department is available for political appointment by the president.

The president's power to remove from office officials who are not doing a good job or who do not agree with the president is not explicitly granted by the Constitution and has been limited. In 1926, however, a Supreme Court decision

---

[2]See Chapter 11 for a further discussion of the civil service.

prevented Congress from interfering with the president's ability to fire those executive-branch officials whom the president had appointed with Senate approval.[3]

Harry Truman spoke candidly of the difficulties a president faces in trying to control the executive bureaucracy. On leaving office, he referred to the problems that Dwight Eisenhower, as a former general of the army, was going to have: "He'll sit here and he'll say do this! do that! and nothing will happen. Poor Ike—it won't be a bit like the Army. He'll find it very frustrating."[4]

The Power to Grant Reprieves and Pardons. Section 2 of Article II of the Constitution gives the president the power to grant **reprieves** and **pardons** for offenses against the United States except in cases of impeachment. All pardons are administered by the Office of the Pardon Attorney in the Department of Justice. In principle, pardons are granted to remedy a mistake made in a conviction.

The Supreme Court upheld the president's power to grant reprieves and pardons in a 1925 case concerning the pardon granted by the president to an individual convicted of contempt of court. The judiciary had contended that only judges had the authority to convict individuals for contempt of court when court orders were violated and that the courts should be free from interference by the executive branch. The Supreme Court simply stated that the president could grant reprieves or pardons for all offenses "either before trial, during trial, or after trial, by individuals, or by classes, conditionally or absolutely, and this without modification or regulation by Congress."[5]

Commander in Chief

The president, according to the Constitution, "shall be Commander in Chief of the Army and Navy of the United States, and of the Militia of the several States, when called into the actual Service of the United States." In other words, the armed forces are under civilian, rather than military, control.

Certainly, those who wrote the Constitution had George Washington in mind when they made the president the **commander in chief**—the supreme commander of the military forces of the United States and of the state National Guard units when they are called into federal service. Although we no longer expect our president to lead the troops to battle, presidents as commanders in chief have wielded dramatic power. Harry Truman made the awesome decision to drop atomic bombs on Hiroshima and Nagasaki in 1945 to force Japan to surrender and thus bring to an end World War II. Lyndon Johnson ordered bombing missions against North Vietnam in the 1960s, and he personally selected some of the targets. Richard Nixon decided to invade Cambodia in 1970. Ronald Reagan sent troops to Lebanon and Grenada in 1983 and ordered U.S. fighter planes to attack Libya in 1986. George Bush sent troops to Panama in 1989 and to the Middle East in 1990. Bill Clinton sent troops to Haiti in 1994 and to Bosnia in 1995, and later to Kosovo. He ordered missile attacks on suspected terrorist bases in Afghanistan and the Sudan in 1998.

---

[3]*Meyers v. United States*, 272 U.S. 52 (1926).

[4]Quoted in Richard E. Neustadt, *Presidential Power: The Politics of Leadership* (New York: Wiley, 1960), p. 9.

[5]*Ex parte Grossman*, 267 U.S. 87 (1925).

President Bill Clinton and Mrs. Clinton visit U.S. troops stationed in Macedonia in June 1999.

The president is the ultimate decision maker in military matters. Everywhere he goes, so too goes the "football"—a briefcase filled with all the codes necessary to order a nuclear attack. Only the president has the power to order the use of nuclear force.

As commander in chief, the president has probably exercised more authority than in any other role. Constitutionally, Congress has the sole power to declare war, but the president can send the armed forces into a country in situations that are certainly the equivalent of war. When William McKinley ordered troops into Peking to help suppress the Boxer Rebellion in 1900, he was sending them into a combat situation. Harry Truman dispatched troops to Korea as part of a "police action" in 1950. Kennedy, Johnson, and Nixon waged an undeclared war in Southeast Asia, where more than 58,000 Americans were killed and 300,000 were wounded. In none of these situations did Congress declare war.

In an attempt to gain more control over military activities ordered by the president, in 1973 Congress passed a **War Powers Resolution**—over President Nixon's veto—requiring that the president consult with Congress when sending American forces into action. Once they are sent, the president must report to Congress within forty-eight hours. Unless Congress has passed a declaration of war within sixty days or has extended the sixty-day time limit, the forces must be withdrawn. Nonetheless, the powers of the president as commander in chief are more extensive today than they were in the past (see this chapter's *At Issue: Should the War Powers Resolution Be Repealed?* for a further discussion of this topic). These powers are linked closely to the president's powers as chief diplomat, or chief crafter of foreign policy.

Should the War Powers Resolution Be Repealed?

When the framers crafted the U.S. Constitution over two hundred years ago, they created a balance of powers among the three branches of the national government. Today, some people claim that Congress has upset this balance by yielding too many powers to the presidency that rightfully should be exercised by the legislative branch—including the power to wage war.

According to the U.S. Constitution, only Congress has the ability to declare war. Nonetheless, numerous presidents have sent American troops into action without a congressional declaration of war. The War Powers Resolution of 1973 marked an attempt by Congress to exercise some control over presidential military activities. As mentioned elsewhere in this chapter, the resolution requires the president to consult with Congress when sending American troops into action. After they are sent, the president has to report to Congress within two days. Congress then has to pass a declaration of war within sixty days or extend the sixty-day limit. Otherwise, the U.S. forces must be withdrawn.

The War Powers Resolution has had little effect on presidential use of the military throughout the world. The president today seems to take for granted, according to some, his unlimited use of the military for humanitarian reasons, as when troops were sent to Somalia, Haiti, Bosnia, and Kosovo, for example.

Some critics, including political scientists Louis Fisher and David Gray Adler, argue that the resolution should be repealed. These scholars suggest that although the resolution was intended to curb presidential powers, in effect, it allows the president to engage in war for up to at least sixty days without congressional approval. According to these authors, "Seldom has a statute misfired to such an extent on a basic purpose. The resolution does violence to the intent of the Framers and has not in any sense insured the collective judgment of Congress and the president in the use of military force."*

FOR CRITICAL ANALYSIS

What role, if any, does public opinion play in presidential decisions to send U.S. troops to trouble spots around the globe, such as Kosovo?

—————

*Louis Fisher and David Gray Adler, "The War Powers Resolution: Time to Say Goodbye," *Political Science Quarterly*, No. 113 (Spring 1998).

Chief Diplomat

The Constitution gives the president the power to recognize foreign governments; to make treaties, with the **advice and consent** of the Senate; and to make special agreements with other heads of state that do not require congressional approval. In addition, the president nominates ambassadors. As **chief diplomat,** the president can recognize foreign governments, make treaties, and make executive agreements. This allows the president to dominate American foreign policy, a role that has been supported numerous times by the Supreme Court.

Diplomatic Recognition. An important power of the president as chief diplomat is that of **diplomatic recognition,** or the power to recognize—or refuse to recognize— foreign governments. In the role of ceremonial head of state, the president has always received foreign diplomats. In modern times, the simple act of receiving a foreign

President Clinton is shown here working in the Oval Office. This oval-shaped office in the White House, with its immense seal of the United States in the carpet, is often used to represent the power of the presidency and of the United States. Indeed, common references to "the Oval Office" mean specifically the president who is in power at that time.

diplomat has been equivalent to accrediting the diplomat and officially recognizing his or her government. Such recognition of the legitimacy of another country's government is a prerequisite to diplomatic relations or negotiations between that country and the United States.

"National Security Rejects Test Ban"

Proposal and Ratification of Treaties. The president has the sole power to negotiate treaties with other nations. These treaties must be presented to the Senate, where they may be modified and must be approved by a two-thirds vote. After ratification, the president can approve the senatorial version of the treaty. Approval poses a problem when the Senate has tacked on substantive amendments or reservations to a treaty, particularly when such changes may require reopening negotiations with the other signatory governments. Sometimes a president may decide to withdraw a treaty if the senatorial changes are too extensive—as Woodrow Wilson did with the Versailles Treaty in 1919. Wilson felt that the senatorial reservations would weaken the treaty so much that it would be ineffective. His refusal to accept the senatorial version of the treaty led to the eventual refusal of the United States to join the League of Nations.

Executive Agreements. Presidential power in foreign affairs is enhanced greatly by the use of **executive agreements** made between the president and other heads of

President Bill Clinton (left) and Chinese President Jiang Zemin walk to a welcoming ceremony during Clinton's visit to China in June 1998.

state. Such agreements do not require Senate approval, although the House and Senate may refuse to appropriate the funds necessary to implement them. Whereas treaties are binding on all succeeding administrations, executive agreements are not binding without each new president's consent.

Among the advantages of executive agreements are speed and secrecy. The former is essential during a crisis; the latter is important when the administration fears that open senatorial debate may be detrimental to the best interests of the United States or to the interests of the president.[6] There have been far more executive agreements (about 9,000) than treaties (about 1,300). Many executive agreements contain secret provisions calling for American military assistance or other support.

INFOTRAC®

"First Black Speechwriting Director"

Chief Legislator

Constitutionally, presidents must recommend to Congress legislation that they judge necessary and expedient. Not all presidents have wielded their powers as **chief legislator** in the same manner. President John Tyler was almost completely unsuccessful in getting his legislative programs implemented by Congress. Presidents Theodore Roosevelt, Franklin Roosevelt, and Lyndon Johnson, however, saw much of their proposed legislation put into effect.

---

[6]The Case Act of 1972 requires that all executive agreements be transmitted to Congress within sixty days after the agreement takes effect. Secret agreements are transmitted to the foreign relations committees as classified information.

In modern times, the president has played a dominant role in creating the congressional agenda. In the president's annual **State of the Union message,** which is required by the Constitution (Article II, Section 3) and is usually given in late January shortly after Congress reconvenes, the president as chief legislator presents his program. The message gives a broad, comprehensive view of what the president wishes the legislature to accomplish during its session. It is as much a message to the American people and to the world as it is to Congress. Its impact on public opinion can determine the way in which Congress responds to the president's agenda.

Getting Legislation Passed. The president can propose legislation. Congress, however, is not required to pass any of the administration's bills. How, then, does the president get those proposals made into law? One way is by exercising the power of persuasion. The president writes to, telephones, and meets with various congressional leaders; makes public announcements to force the weight of public opinion onto Congress in favor of a legislative program; and, as head of the party, exercises legislative leadership through the congresspersons of the president's party.

To be sure, a president whose party represents a majority in both chambers of Congress may have an easier time getting legislation passed than does a president who faces a hostile Congress. But one of the ways in which a president who faces a hostile Congress still can wield power is through the ability to veto legislation.

Saying No to Legislation. The president has the power to say no to legislation through use of the veto, by which the White House returns a bill unsigned to the legislative body with a **veto message** attached.[7] Because the Constitution requires that every bill passed by the House and the Senate must be sent to the president before it becomes law, the president must act on each bill:

1. If the bill is signed, it becomes law.
2. If the bill is not sent back to Congress after ten congressional working days, it becomes law without the president's signature.
3. The president can reject the bill and send it back to Congress with a veto message setting forth objections. Congress then can change the bill, hoping to secure presidential approval and repass it. Or it can simply reject the president's objections by overriding the veto with a two-thirds roll-call vote of the members present in each chamber.
4. If the president refuses to sign the bill and Congress adjourns within ten working days after the bill has been submitted to the president, the bill is killed for that session of Congress. This is called a **pocket veto.** If Congress wishes the bill to be reconsidered, the bill must be reintroduced during the following session.

Presidents employed the veto power infrequently until the administration of Andrew Johnson, but it has been used much more vigorously since then (see Table 10.1).

---

[7]*Veto* in Latin means "I forbid."

TABLE 10.1

Presidential Vetoes, 1789 to Present

YEARS	PRESIDENT	REGULAR VETOES	VETOES OVERRIDDEN	POCKET VETOES	TOTAL VETOES
1789–1797	Washington	2	0	0	2
1797–1801	J. Adams	0	0	0	0
1801–1809	Jefferson	0	0	0	0
1809–1817	Madison	5	0	2	7
1817–1825	Monroe	1	0	0	1
1825–1829	J. Q. Adams	0	0	0	0
1829–1837	Jackson	5	0	7	12
1837–1841	Van Buren	0	0	1	1
1841–1841	Harrison	0	0	0	0
1841–1845	Tyler	6	1	4	10
1845–1849	Polk	2	0	1	3
1849–1850	Taylor	0	0	0	0
1850–1853	Fillmore	0	0	0	0
1853–1857	Pierce	9	5	0	9
1857–1861	Buchanan	4	0	3	7
1861–1865	Lincoln	2	0	4	6
1865–1869	A. Johnson	21	15	8	29
1869–1877	Grant	45	4	48	93
1877–1881	Hayes	12	1	1	13
1881–1881	Garfield	0	0	0	0
1881–1885	Arthur	4	1	8	12
1885–1889	Cleveland	304	2	110	414
1889–1893	Harrison	19	1	25	44
1893–1897	Cleveland	42	5	128	170
1897–1901	McKinley	6	0	36	42
1901–1909	T. Roosevelt	42	1	40	82
1909–1913	Taft	30	1	9	39
1913–1921	Wilson	33	6	11	44
1921–1923	Harding	5	0	1	6
1923–1929	Coolidge	20	4	30	50
1929–1933	Hoover	21	3	16	37
1933–1945	F. Roosevelt	372	9	263	635
1945–1953	Truman	180	12	70	250
1953–1961	Eisenhower	73	2	108	181
1961–1963	Kennedy	12	0	9	21
1963–1969	L. Johnson	16	0	14	30
1969–1974	Nixon	26*	7	17	43
1974–1977	Ford	48	12	18	66
1977–1981	Carter	13	2	18	31
1981–1989	Reagan	39	9	39	78
1989–1993	Bush	29	1	15	44
1993–1999	Clinton	27	4	0	27
TOTAL		1,475	108	1,064	2,539

*Two pocket vetoes, overruled in the courts, are counted here as regular vetoes.

SOURCES: Louis Fisher, *The Politics of Shared Power: Congress and the Executive,* 2d ed. (Washington, D.C.: Congressional Quarterly Press, 1987), p. 30; *Congressional Quarterly Weekly Report,* October 17, 1992, p. 3249; and authors' update.

Congress's Power to Override Presidential Vetoes. A veto is a clear-cut indication of the president's dissatisfaction with congressional legislation. Congress, however, can override a presidential veto, although it rarely exercises this power. Consider that two-thirds of the members of each chamber who are present must vote to override the president's veto in a roll-call vote. This means that if only one-third plus one of the members voting in one of the chambers of Congress do not agree to override the veto, the veto holds. Table 10.1 on page 249 tells us that it was not until the administration of John Tyler that Congress overrode a presidential veto. In the first sixty-five years of American federal government history, out of thirty-three regular vetoes, Congress overrode only one, or about 3 percent. Overall, only about 7 percent of all regular vetoes have been overridden.

Other Presidential Powers

The powers of the president just discussed are called **constitutional powers,** because their basis lies in the Constitution. In addition, Congress has established by law, or statute, numerous other presidential powers—such as the ability to declare national emergencies. These are called **statutory powers.** Both constitutional and statutory powers have been labeled the **expressed powers** of the president, because they are expressly written into the Constitution or into law.

Presidents also have what have come to be known as **inherent powers.** These depend on the loosely worded statement in the Constitution that "the executive Power shall be vested in a President" and that the president should "take Care that the Laws be faithfully executed." The most common example of inherent powers is the use of emergency powers by the president during wartime.

THE PRESIDENT AS PARTY CHIEF AND SUPERPOLITICIAN

Presidents are by no means above political partisanship, and one of their many roles is that of chief of party. Although the Constitution says nothing about the function of the president within a political party (the mere concept of political parties was abhorrent to most of the authors of the Constitution), today presidents are the actual leaders of their parties.

The President as Chief of Party

As party leader, the president chooses the national committee chairperson and can try to discipline party members who fail to support presidential policies. One way of exerting political power within the party is by **patronage**—appointing individuals to government or public jobs. This power was more extensive in the past, before the establishment of the civil service in 1883 (see Chapter 11), but the president still retains impressive patronage power. As we noted earlier, the president can appoint several thousand individuals to jobs in the cabinet, the White House, and the federal regulatory agencies.

Perhaps the most important role that the president has played for his party in recent years is that of fund-raiser. Because of the ability of political parties to accept unregulated contributions in the form of "soft money" (see Chapter 8 for details on these contributions), the president is able to raise large amounts of money for the political party through appearances at dinners, speaking engagements, and other social occasions.

"Does Macroeconomics Matter"

Presidents have a number of other ways of exerting influence as party chief. The president may make it known that a particular congressperson's choice for federal judge will not be appointed unless that member of Congress is more supportive of the president's legislative program.[8] The president may agree to campaign for a particular program or for a particular candidate. Presidents also reward loyal supporters in Congress with funding for local projects, tax breaks for regional industries, and other forms of "pork."

Constituencies and Public Approval

All politicians worry about their constituencies, and presidents are no exception. Presidents, however, have numerous constituencies. In principle, they are beholden to the entire electorate—the public of the United States—even to those who did not vote. They are certainly beholden to their party constituency, because its members put them in office. The president's constituencies also include members of the opposing party whose cooperation the president needs. Finally, the president has to take into consideration a constituency that has come to be called the **Washington community.** This community consists of individuals who—whether in or out of political office—are intimately familiar with the workings of government, thrive on gossip, and measure on a daily basis the political power of the president.

---

[8]"Senatorial courtesy" (see Chapter 12) often puts the judicial appointment in the hands of the Senate, however.

Soon after his videotaped admission of a relationship with Monica Lewinsky, President Clinton visited a school in Silver Spring, Maryland, to talk about improving the nation's education system. He was met by protesters along the route.

All of these constituencies are impressed by presidents who maintain a high level of public approval, partly because this is very difficult to accomplish. Presidential popularity, as measured by national polls, gives the president an extra political resource to use in persuading legislators or bureaucrats to pass legislation. After all, refusing to do so might be going against public sentiment. President Reagan showed amazing strength in the public opinion polls for a second-term chief executive, as Figure 10.1 indicates. President Clinton began his term in office with a 58 percent approval rating and then saw it plummet to 38 percent six months later. By the end of his first year, his rating returned to 48 percent approving his performance, although in the following year, it dropped to 38 percent again. Before the 1996 elections, it had climbed to 51 percent, however, and to the surprise of his critics, after news of a potential scandal involving a White House intern (Monica Lewinsky) broke, President Clinton's job approval ratings improved. His ratings remained high throughout the impeachment debate and Senate trial. The public's ratings of his moral character, however, declined steadily.

The presidential preoccupation with public opinion has been criticized by at least one scholar as changing the balance of national politics. Beginning in the early twentieth century, presidents have spoken more to the public and less to Congress. In the previous century, only 7 percent of presidential speeches were addressed to the public; since 1900, 50 percent have been addressed to the public.[9] Samuel Kernell has proposed that the style of presidential leadership has changed since World War II, owing partly to the influence of television.[10] Presidents frequently go over the heads

---

[9]Jeffrey Tulis, *The Rhetorical Presidency* (Princeton, N.J.: Princeton University Press, 1987), p. 138.
[10]Samuel Kernell, *Going Public: New Strategies of Presidential Leadership*, 3d ed. (Washington, D.C.: Congressional Quarterly Press, 1997).

FIGURE 10.1

Public Popularity of U.S. Presidents, 1953 to the Present

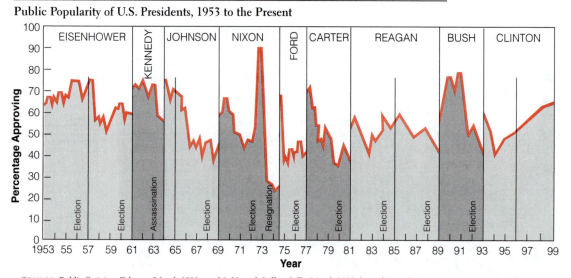

SOURCE: *Public Opinion*, February/March 1988, pp. 36–39; and Gallup Polls, March 1992 through March 1999.

of Congress and the political elites, taking their cases directly to the people. This strategy, which Kernell dubbed "going public," gives the president additional power through the ability to persuade and manipulate public opinion. By identifying their own positions so clearly, presidents make compromises with Congress much more difficult and weaken the legislators' positions. Given the increasing importance of the media as the major source of political information for citizens and elites, presidents will continue to use public opinion as part of their arsenal of weapons to gain support from Congress and to achieve their policy goals.

SPECIAL USES OF PRESIDENTIAL POWER

Presidents have at their disposal a variety of special powers and privileges not available in other branches of the U.S. government. These include (1) emergency powers, (2) executive orders, and (3) executive privilege.

Emergency Powers

If you were to read the Constitution, you would find no mention of the additional powers that the executive office may exercise during national emergencies. Indeed, the Supreme Court has indicated that an "emergency does not create power."[11] But it is clear that presidents have used their inherent powers during times of emergency, particularly in the realm of foreign affairs. The **emergency powers** of the president were first enunciated in the Supreme Court's decision in *United States v. Curtiss-Wright Export Corp.*[12] In that case, President Franklin Roosevelt, without authorization by Congress, ordered an embargo on the shipment of weapons to two warring South American countries. The Court recognized that the president may exercise inherent powers in foreign affairs and that the national government has primacy in foreign affairs.

Examples of emergency powers are abundant, coinciding with real or contrived crises in domestic and foreign affairs. Abraham Lincoln's suspension of civil liberties at the beginning of the Civil War, his calling of the state militias into national service, and his subsequent governance of conquered areas and even of areas of northern states were justified by claims that such actions were essential to preserve the Union. Franklin Roosevelt declared an "unlimited national emergency" following the fall of France in 1940 at the beginning of World War II in Europe and mobilized the federal budget and the economy for war.

President Harry Truman authorized the federal seizure of steel plants and their operation by the national government in 1952 during the Korean War. Truman claimed that he was using his inherent emergency power as chief executive and commander in chief to safeguard the nation's security, as the ongoing steel mill strike threatened the supply of weapons to the armed forces. The Supreme Court did not agree, holding that the president had no authority under the Constitution to seize

---

[11]*Home Building and Loan Association v. Blaisdell*, 290 U.S. 398 (1934).
[12]229 U.S. 304 (1936).

private property or to legislate such action.[13] According to legal scholars, this was the first time a limit was placed on the exercise of the president's emergency powers.

Executive Orders

Congress allows the president (as well as administrative agencies) to issue **executive orders** that have the force of law. These executive orders can do the following: (1) enforce legislative statutes, (2) enforce the Constitution or treaties with foreign nations, and (3) establish or modify rules and practices of executive administrative agencies.

An executive order, then, represents the president's legislative power. The only apparent requirement is that under the Administrative Procedure Act of 1946, all executive orders must be published in the *Federal Register,* a daily publication of the U.S. government. Executive orders have been used to establish some procedures for appointing noncareer administrators, to implement national affirmative action regulations, to restructure the White House bureaucracy, to ration consumer goods and to administer wage and price controls under emergency conditions, to classify government information as secret, and to regulate the export of restricted items.

Executive Privilege

"Clinton Misuse Executive Privilege"

Another inherent executive power that has been claimed by presidents concerns the ability of the president and the president's executive officials to refuse to appear before, or to withhold information from, Congress or the courts. This is called **executive privilege,** and it relies on the constitutional separation of powers for its basis. Critics of executive privilege believe that it can be used to shield from public scrutiny actions of the executive branch that should be open to Congress and to the American public.

Limits to executive privilege went untested until the Watergate affair in the early 1970s. Five men had broken into the headquarters of the Democratic National Committee and were caught searching for documents that would damage the candidacy of the Democratic nominee, George McGovern. Later investigation showed that the break-in was planned by members of Richard Nixon's campaign committee and that Nixon and his closest advisers had devised a strategy for impeding the investigation of the crime, using the Central Intelligence Agency for illegal activities. After it became known that all of the conversations held in the Oval Office had been tape-recorded on a secret system, Nixon was ordered to turn over the tapes to the special prosecutor. Nixon refused to do so, claiming executive privilege. He argued that "no president could function if the private papers of his office, prepared by his personal staff, were open to public scrutiny." In 1974, in one of the Supreme Court's most famous cases, *United States v. Nixon,*[14] the justices unanimously ruled that Nixon had to hand over the tapes to the Court. The Court held that executive privilege could not be used to prevent evidence from being heard in criminal proceedings.

---

[13]*Youngstown Sheet and Tube Co. v. Sawyer,* 343 U.S. 579 (1952).
[14]318 U.S. 683 (1974).

The claim of executive privilege was also raised by the Clinton administration as a defense against the aggressive investigation of Clinton's relationship with White House intern Monica Lewinsky by Independent Counsel Kenneth Starr—an investigtaion that ultimately led to the president's impeachment in late 1998. The Clinton administration claimed executive privilege for several presidential aides who might have discussed the situation with the president. In addition, President Clinton asserted that his White House counsel did not have to testify before the Starr grand jury due to attorney-client privilege. Finally, the Department of Justice claimed that members of the Secret Service who guard the president could not testify about his activities due to a "protective function privilege" inherent in their duties.

The federal judge overseeing the case denied both the claim of protective function privilege and that of attorney-client privilege in this investigation, so both sides appealed to the Supreme Court for an expedited hearing. The Court refused to accept the case and sent it to a federal appeals court for a hearing. The appellate court upheld the lower court's decision.

ABUSES OF EXECUTIVE POWER AND IMPEACHMENT

Presidents normally leave office either because their first term has expired and they do not seek (or win) reelection or because, having served two full terms, they are not allowed to be elected for a third term (owing to the Twenty-second Amendment, passed in 1951). Eight presidents have died in office. But there is still another way for a president to leave office—by *impeachment*.

The Impeachment Process

Articles I and II of the Constitution authorize the House and Senate to remove the president, the vice president, or other civil officers of the United States for crimes of "Treason, Bribery, or other high Crimes and Misdemeanors." Remember from Chapter 9 that according to the Constitution, the impeachment process begins in the House, which impeaches (accuses) the federal officer involved. If the House votes to impeach the officer, it draws up articles of impeachment and submits them to the Senate, which conducts the actual trial.

The Cases against Johnson and Nixon

In the history of the United States, no president has ever been impeached and also convicted—and thus removed from office—by means of this process. President Andrew Johnson, who succeeded to the office after the assassination of Abraham Lincoln, was seen by the Radical Republicans as too lenient toward the southern states. When Congress passed a law denying the president the right to remove cabinet officers, Johnson defied the law by firing his secretary of war. The House voted to impeach him and submitted eleven articles of impeachment to the Senate. After a three-month trial in the Senate, Johnson was acquitted by one vote. Seven Republicans, convinced that the impeachment articles were politically motivated, crossed party lines to vote for acquittal.

More than a century later, the House Judiciary Committee investigated President Richard Nixon for his involvement in the cover-up of the Watergate break-in of 1972 (when Republican operatives broke into the Democratic headquarters at the Watergate Hotel). After months of testimony, including the discovery of tapes made of presidential conversations in the Oval Office, the House committee approved three articles of impeachment against President Nixon. The charges were obstruction of justice, the abuse of power, and the failure to respond to the committee's subpoenas. Six Republicans voted with the committee's Democrats to approve the articles. Convinced that he had little hope of surviving a trial in the Senate, Nixon resigned on August 9, 1974, before the full House voted on the articles.

In both cases, charges that the process was totally political were common. The Nixon case, because of the taped evidence, became more clearly one of provable offense.

The Impeachment of Bill Clinton

The second president to be impeached but not convicted by the Senate was President Bill Clinton. In September 1998, Independent Counsel Kenneth Starr sent the findings of his investigation on the charges of perjury and obstruction of justice to Congress. The Republican majority in the House of Representatives then began to organize itself for the possible impeachment of the president, releasing some of the documents to the public. After the 1998 elections, in which the Republicans lost five House seats, the House Judiciary Committee presented four charges to the House for consideration. The House approved two of the charges against Clinton: lying to the grand jury about his affair with Monica Lewinsky (by a vote of 228 to 206); and obstruction of justice (by a vote of 221 to 212). Two of the four charges were rejected by the House.

Soon after the new Congress convened in 1999, the Senate received the articles of impeachment from the House of Representatives. The Senate then moved to the historic old Senate chambers for the trial. Chief Justice Rehnquist presided over the trial, although he had virtually no power to make any procedural or substantive decisions. All senators were sworn to act impartially and do justice. Soon after the House team of prosecutors and the president's defense team made their opening presentations, a motion was made to dismiss the charges for lack of evidence. When forty-one senators, all Democrats, voted to dismiss, it was clear to all that it would be impossible to obtain the two-thirds vote of the Senate required for conviction. The House team requested the right to call witnesses, and the Senate, unwilling to completely constrain their colleagues, allowed them to interview several witnesses on videotape, tapes that were shown on the Senate floor.

On several occasions during the trial and for three days before the final vote, the Senate debated behind closed doors. Although many liberals and members of the media decried this secrecy, no public outcry against it arose. Finally, on February 12, 1999, the Senate voted on the articles of impeachment: Article I, which charged perjury, was defeated by a vote of forty-five to fifty-five, and Article II, which charged obstruction of justice, was defeated by a fifty-fifty vote (thus falling far short of the two-thirds vote needed for conviction). On both votes, Republican senators joined Democrats to defeat the charges. The president was acquitted.

During the trial, several alternatives to impeachment were debated by the Senate. One alternative was to vote for a "finding of fact," which might allow the president to stay in office even though the Senate believed that he was guilty of the crimes with which he had been charged. Another alternative was to dismiss the charges by a simple majority vote. The Senate, however, after debating and considering each alternative, decided to follow the constitutional process to the end, thus preserving that process for use in the future. How history will treat the impeachment of President Clinton in relationship to his accomplishments in office will be answered in the years after he leaves office.

THE EXECUTIVE ORGANIZATION

Gone are the days when presidents answered their own mail, as George Washington did. It was not until 1857 that Congress authorized a private secretary for the president, to be paid by the federal government. Woodrow Wilson typed most of his correspondence, even though he did have several secretaries. At the beginning of Franklin Roosevelt's long tenure in the White House, the entire staff consisted of thirty-seven employees. It was not until the New Deal and World War II that the presidential staff became a sizable organization.

Today, the Executive Office of the President includes a staff of about 1,600. Not all of these employees have equal access to the president, nor are all of them likely to be equally concerned about the administration's political success. The 385 employees who work in the White House Office itself are closest to the president. They often include many individuals who worked in the president's campaign. These assistants are most concerned with preserving the president's reputation. Also included in the president's staff are a number of councils and advisory organizations, such as the National Security Council. Although the individuals who hold staff positions in these offices are appointed by the president, they are really more concerned with their own area than with the president's overall success. The group of appointees who perhaps are least helpful to the president is the cabinet, each member of which is the principal officer of a government department.

The Cabinet

Although the Constitution does not include the word *cabinet*, it does state that the president "may require the Opinion, in writing, of the principal Officer in each of the executive Departments." Since the time of George Washington, there has been an advisory group, or **cabinet,** to which the president turns for counsel. Originally, the cabinet consisted of only four officials—the secretaries of state, treasury, and war, and the attorney general. Today, the cabinet numbers thirteen secretaries and the attorney general. (Refer to Chapter 11 for a detailed discussion of these units.)

The cabinet may consist of more than the secretaries of the various departments. The president at his or her discretion can, for example, ascribe cabinet rank to the National Security Council adviser, to the ambassador to the United Nations, or to others. Because neither the Constitution nor statutory law requires the president to consult with the cabinet, its use is purely discretionary. Some presidents have relied on the counsel of their cabinets more than others. Dwight Eisenhower frequently turned to his cabinet for advice on a wide range of governmental policies—perhaps because he was used to the team approach to solving problems from his experience in the U.S. Army. Other presidents solicited the opinions of their cabinets and then did what they wanted to do anyway. Lincoln supposedly said—after a cabinet meeting in which a vote was seven nays against his one aye—"Seven nays and one aye, the ayes have it."[15] In general, few presidents have relied heavily on the advice of their cabinet members.

Often, a president will use a **kitchen cabinet** to replace the formal cabinet as a major source of advice. The term *kitchen cabinet* originated during the presidency of Andrew Jackson, who relied on the counsel of close friends who often met with him in the kitchen of the White House. A kitchen cabinet is a very informal group of advisers, such as Bill Clinton's Arkansas friends, who may or may not otherwise be connected with the government.

It is not surprising that presidents meet with their cabinet heads only reluctantly. Often, the departmental heads are more responsive to the wishes of their own staffs or to their own political ambitions than they are to the president. They may be more concerned with obtaining resources for their departments than with helping presidents achieve their goals. So there is often a strong conflict of interest between presidents and their cabinet members. It is likely that formal cabinet meetings are held more out of respect for the cabinet tradition than for their problem-solving value.

The Executive Office of the President

When President Franklin Roosevelt appointed a special committee on administrative management, he knew that the committee would conclude that the president needed help. Indeed, the committee proposed a major reorganization of the executive branch. Congress did not approve the entire reorganization, but it did create the **Executive Office of the President (EOP)** to provide staff assistance for the chief executive and to help coordinate the executive bureaucracy. Since that time, a number of agencies within the EOP have been created to supply the president with advice and staff help. These agencies are as follows:

- White House Office (1939).
- Council of Economic Advisers (1946).
- National Security Council (1947).
- Office of the United States Trade Representative (1963).
- Council on Environmental Quality (1969).
- Office of Management and Budget (1970).
- Office of Science and Technology Policy (1976).
- Office of Administration (1977).
- Office of National Drug Control Policy (1988).
- Office of Policy Development (1993).

---

[15]Quoted in Thomas E. Cronin, *The State of the Presidency*, 2d ed. (Boston: Little, Brown, 1980), p. 11.

Several of the offices within the EOP are especially important, including the White House Office, the Council of Economic Advisers, the Office of Management and Budget, and the National Security Council.

The White House Office. One of the most important of the agencies within the EOP is the **White House Office,** which includes most of the key personal and political advisers to the president. Among the jobs held by these aides are those of legal counsel to the president, secretary, press secretary, and appointments secretary. Often, the individuals who hold these positions are recruited from the president's campaign staff. Their duties—mainly protecting the president's political interests—are similar to campaign functions. In all recent administrations, one member of the White House Office has been named **chief of staff.** This person, who is responsible for coordinating the office, is one of the president's chief advisers.

The Council of Economic Advisers. The Employment Act of 1946 created a three-member **Council of Economic Advisers (CEA)** to advise the president on economic matters. The council's advice serves as the basis for the president's annual economic report to Congress. Each of the three members is appointed by the president and can be removed at will. In principle, the CEA was also created to advise the president on economic policy, but for the most part the function of the CEA has been to prepare the annual report.

The Office of Management and Budget. The **Office of Management and Budget (OMB)** was originally the Bureau of the Budget, which was created in 1921 within the Department of the Treasury. Recognizing the importance of this agency, Franklin Roosevelt moved it into the White House Office in 1939. Richard Nixon reorganized the Bureau of the Budget in 1970 and changed its name to reflect its new managerial function. It is headed by a director, who must make up the annual federal budget that the president presents to Congress each January for approval. In principle, the director of the OMB has broad fiscal powers in planning and estimating various parts of the federal budget, because all agencies must submit their proposed budget to the OMB for approval. In reality, it is not so clear that the OMB truly can affect the greater scope of the federal budget. The OMB may be more important as a clearinghouse for legislative proposals initiated in the executive agencies.

The National Security Council. The **National Security Council (NSC)** is a link between the president's key foreign and military advisers and the president. Its members consist of the president, the vice president, and the secretaries of state and defense, plus other informal members. The NSC has the resources of the National Security Agency (NSA) at its disposal in giving counsel to the president. (The NSA protects U.S. government communications and produces foreign intelligence information.)

THE VICE PRESIDENCY

The Constitution does not give much power to the vice president. The only formal duty is to preside over the Senate—which is rarely necessary. This obligation is

Vice President Al Gore. After taking office in 1993, Vice President Gore became known for his aggressive efforts to strengthen environmental-protection policies on a global basis. He also took special interest in areas of emerging technology and was instrumental in encouraging Congress to provide for Internet use in public schools.

fulfilled when the Senate organizes and adopts its rules and when the vice president is needed to decide a tie vote. In all other cases, the president pro tem manages parliamentary procedures in the Senate. The vice president is expected to participate only informally in senatorial deliberations, if at all.

The Vice President's Job

Vice presidents have traditionally been chosen by presidential nominees to balance the ticket to attract groups of voters or appease party factions. If a presidential nominee is from the North, it is not a bad idea to have a vice presidential nominee who is from the South or the West. If the presidential nominee is from a rural state, perhaps someone with an urban background would be most suitable as a running mate. Presidential nominees who are strongly conservative or strongly liberal would do well to have vice presidential nominees who are more in the middle of the political road. The job of vice president is not extremely demanding, even when the president gives some specific task to the vice president. Typically, vice presidents spend their time supporting the president's activities.

Vice presidents infrequently have become elected presidents in their own right.

Presidential Succession

Eight vice presidents have become president because of the death of the president. John Tyler, the first to do so, took over William Henry Harrison's position after only one month. No one knew whether Tyler should simply be a caretaker until a new president could be elected three and a half years later or whether he actually should be president. Tyler assumed that he was supposed to be the chief executive and he acted as such—although he was commonly referred to as "His Accidency." On all occasions since then, vice presidents taking over the position of the presidency because of the incumbent's death have assumed all of the presidential powers.

But what should a vice president do if a president becomes incapable of carrying out necessary duties while in office? This question was not addressed in the original Constitution. Article II, Section 1, says only that "in Case of the Removal of the President from Office, or of his Death, Resignation, or Inability to discharge the Powers and Duties of the said Office, the same shall devolve on the Vice President." There have been many instances of presidential disability. When Dwight Eisenhower became ill a second time in 1958, he entered into a pact with Richard Nixon that provided that the vice president could determine whether the president was incapable of carrying out his duties if the president could not communicate. John Kennedy and Lyndon Johnson entered into similar agreements with their vice presidents. Finally, in 1967, the **Twenty-fifth Amendment** was passed, establishing procedures in case of presidential incapacity.

According to the Twenty-fifth Amendment, when the president believes that he is incapable of performing the duties of office, he must inform the Congress in writing. Then the vice president serves as acting president until the president can resume his normal duties. When the president is unable to communicate, a majority of the cabinet, including the vice president, can declare that fact to Congress. Then the vice president serves as acting president until the president resumes his normal duties. If a dispute arises over the return of the president's ability to discharge his normal functions, a two-thirds vote of Congress is required to decide whether the vice president shall remain acting president or whether the president shall resume his duties.

The Twenty-fifth Amendment also addresses the issue of how the president should fill a vacant vice presidency. Section 2 of the amendment simply states, "Whenever there is a vacancy in the office of the Vice President, the President shall nominate a Vice President who shall take office upon confirmation by a majority vote of both Houses of Congress." The question of who shall be president if both the president and vice president die is answered by the Succession Act of 1947. If the president and vice president die, resign, or are disabled, the speaker of the House will act as president, after resigning from Congress. Next in line is the president pro tem of the Senate, followed by the cabinet officers in the order of the creation of their departments (see Table 10.2).

TABLE 10.2

Line of Succession to the Presidency of the United States

1. Vice president
2. Speaker of the House of Representatives
3. Senate president *pro tempore*
4. Secretary of state
5. Secretary of the treasury
6. Secretary of defense
7. Attorney general
8. Secretary of the interior
9. Secretary of agriculture
10. Secretary of commerce
11. Secretary of labor
12. Secretary of health and human services
13. Secretary of housing and urban development
14. Secretary of transportation
15. Secretary of energy
16. Secretary of education
17. Secretary of veterans affairs

KEY TERMS

advice and consent 245

appointment power 242

cabinet 257

chief diplomat 245

chief executive 242

chief legislator 247

chief of staff 259

chief of state 242

commander in chief 243

constitutional power 250

Council of Economic Advisers (CEA) 259

diplomatic recognition 245

emergency power 253

executive agreement 246

Executive Office of the President (EOP) 258

executive order 254

executive privilege 254

expressed power 250

Federal Register 254

inherent power 250

kitchen cabinet 258

National Security Council (NSC) 259

Office of Management and Budget (OMB) 259

pardon 243

patronage 250

pocket veto 248

reprieve 243

State of the Union message 248

statutory power 250

Twelfth Amendment 241

Twenty-fifth Amendment 261

veto message 248

War Powers Resolution 244

Washington community 251

White House Office 259

CHAPTER SUMMARY

❶ The office of the presidency in the United States, combining as it does the functions of chief of state and chief executive, is unique. The framers of the Constitution were divided over whether the president should be a weak executive controlled by the legislature or a strong executive.

❷ The requirements for the office of the presidency are outlined in Article II, Section 1, of the Constitution. The president's roles include both formal and informal duties. The president is chief of state, chief executive, commander in chief, chief diplomat, chief legislator, and party chief.

❸ As chief of state, the president is ceremonial head of the government. As chief executive, the president is bound to enforce the acts of Congress, the judgments of the federal courts, and treaties. The chief executive has the power of appointment and the power to grant reprieves and pardons.

❹ As commander in chief, the president is the ultimate decision maker in military matters. As chief diplomat, the president recognizes foreign

governments, negotiates treaties, signs agreements, and nominates and receives ambassadors.

❺ The role of chief legislator includes recommending legislation to Congress, lobbying for the legislation, approving laws, and exercising the veto power. The president also has statutory powers written into law by Congress. The president is also leader of his or her political party. Presidents use their power to persuade and their access to the media to fulfill this function.

❻ Presidents have a variety of special powers not available to other branches of the government. These include emergency power, executive power, and executive privilege.

❼ Abuses of executive power are dealt with by Articles I and II of the Constitution, which authorize the House and Senate to impeach and remove the president, vice president, or other officers of the federal government for crimes of "Treason, Bribery or other high Crimes and Misdemeanors."

8 The president gets assistance from the cabinet and from the Executive Office of the President (including the White House Office).

9 The vice president is the constitutional officer assigned to preside over the Senate and to assume the presidency in case of the death, resignation, removal, or disability of the president. The Twenty-fifth Amendment, passed in 1967, established procedures to be followed in case of presidential incapacity and when filling a vacant vice presidency.

SELECTED PRINT AND ELECTRONIC RESOURCES

Suggested Readings

Kernell, Samuel. *Going Public: New Strategies of Presidential Leadership.* 3d ed. Washington, D.C.: Congressional Quarterly Press, 1997. Kernell focuses on how presidents go "over the head of Congress" to the people and includes examples from the Clinton presidency.

Pfiffner, James P. *The Modern Presidency.* 2d ed. New York: St. Martin's Press, 1997. This examination of the presidency looks carefully at the importance of the White House staff, the media, and the president's role in foreign policy in the contemporary political scene.

Pious, Richard M. *The Presidency.* Boston: Allyn and Bacon, 1996. In this comprehensive look at the presidency, the author uses examples from many presidencies to illustrate his discussions of presidential influence.

Reich, Robert B. *Locked in the Cabinet.* New York: Random House, 1998. This memoir is a lively, anecdote-filled account of life in Washington, D.C., during Reich's four years as secretary of labor.

Media Resources

Sunrise at Campobello—An excellent portrait of one of the greatest presidents, Franklin Delano Roosevelt, produced in 1960 and starring Ralph Bellamy.

LBJ: A Biography—An acclaimed biography of Lyndon Johnson that covers his rise to power, his presidency, and the events of the Vietnam War, which ended his presidency; produced in 1991 as part of PBS's *The American Experience* series.

Nixon—An excellent 1995 film exposing the events of Richard Nixon's troubled presidency; Anthony Hopkins plays the embattled but brilliant chief executive.

LOGGING ON

This is a site from which you can obtain extensive information on the White House and the presidency:

http://www.whitehouse.gov/WH/Welcome.html

The Library of Congress White House page is a great source of information and has numerous presidency-related links. The URL is

http://www.loc.gov

The White House archives at Texas A&M are helpful for researching documents and other academic resources. You can reach these archives at

http://www.tamu.edu/whitehouse

USING THE INTERNET FOR POLITICAL ANALYSIS

Take a look at the activities of the president of the United States by clicking on the White House at

http://www.whitehouse.gov

and the Government Documents site, SunSITE, at

http://sunsite.unc.edu/govdocs.html

Try to find the president's schedule for a day or a week, or read at least two speeches he has given within the last few months. After you have read these documents, decide which role the president was playing when he engaged in certain activities or made certain statements: commander in chief, chief legislator, and so on.

You then might want to search a site such as that of the *Congressional Quarterly* at

http://www.cq.com

or AllPolitics at

http://www.allpolitics.com

and look at articles from the same date as the president's speech for an alternative view of what he was proposing.

http:// WWW.

CHAPTER 11

The Bureaucracy

Virtually every modern president, at one time or another, has proclaimed that his administration was going to "fix government." As you can see in Table 11.1, all modern presidents also have put forth plans to end government waste and inefficiency. Their success has been, in a word, underwhelming. Presidents have been generally powerless to affect the structure and operation of the federal bureaucracy significantly.

The bureaucracy has been called the "fourth branch of government," even though you will find no reference to the bureaucracy in the original Constitution or in the twenty-seven amendments that have been passed since 1787. But Article II, Section 2, of the Constitution gives the president the power to appoint "all other Officers of the United States, whose Appointments are not herein otherwise provided for." Article II, Section 3, states that the president "shall take Care that the Laws be faithfully executed, and shall Commission all the Officers of the United States." Constitutional scholars believe that the legal basis for the bureaucracy rests on these two sections in Article II.

THE NATURE OF BUREAUCRACY

A **bureaucracy** is the name given to a large organization that is structured hierarchically to carry out specific functions. Generally, most bureaucracies are characterized by an organization chart. The units of the organization are divided according to the specialization and expertise of the employees.

We should not think of bureaucracy as unique to government. Any large corporation or university can be considered a bureaucratic organization. The fact is that

TABLE 11.1

Selected Presidential Plans to End Government Inefficiency

PRESIDENT	NAME OF PLAN
Lyndon Johnson (1963–1969)	Programming, Planning, and Budgeting Systems
Richard Nixon (1969–1974)	Management by Objectives
Jimmy Carter (1977–1981)	Zero-Based Budgeting
Ronald Reagan (1981–1989)	President's Private Sector Survey on Cost Control (the Grace Commission)
George Bush (1989–1993)	Right-Sizing Government
Bill Clinton (1993–2001)	"From Red Tape to Results: Creating a Government That Works Better and Costs Less"

"Government Civil
Service Reform"

the handling of complex problems requires a division of labor. Individuals must concentrate their skills on specific, well-defined aspects of a problem and depend on others to solve the rest of it.

Public or government bureaucracies differ from private organizations in some important ways, however. A private corporation, such as Microsoft, has a single set of leaders, its board of directors. Public bureaucracies, in contrast, do not have a single set of leaders. Although the president is the chief administrator of the federal system, all bureaucratic agencies are subject to the desires of Congress for their funding, staffing, and, indeed, their continued existence. Furthermore, public bureaucracies supposedly serve the citizen rather than the stockholder.

One other important difference between private corporations and government bureaucracies is that government bureaucracies are not organized to make a profit. Rather, they are supposed to perform their functions as efficiently as possible to conserve the taxpayers' dollars. Perhaps it is this aspect of government organization that makes citizens hostile toward government employees when citizens experience inefficiency and red tape.

These characteristics, together with the prevalence and size of the government bureaucracies, make them an important factor in American life.

THEORIES OF BUREAUCRACY

Several theories have been offered to help us understand better the ways in which bureaucracies function. The classic model, or **Weberian model,** of the modern bureaucracy was proposed by the German sociologist Max Weber.[1] He argued that the increasingly complex nature of modern life, coupled with the steadily growing demands placed on governments by their citizens, made the formation of bureaucracies inevitable. According to Weber, most bureaucracies—whether in the public or private sector—are hierarchically organized and governed by formal procedures. The power in a bureaucracy flows from the top downward. Decision-making processes in bureaucracies are shaped by detailed technical rules that promote similar decisions in similar situations. Bureaucrats are specialists who attempt to resolve problems through logical reasoning and data analysis instead of "gut feelings" and guesswork. Individual advancement in bureaucracies is supposed to be based on merit rather than political connections. Indeed, the modern bureaucracy, according to Weber, should be an apolitical organization.

Other theorists do not view bureaucracies in terms as benign as Weber's. Some believe that bureaucracies are acquisitive in nature. Proponents of the **acquisitive model** argue that top-level bureaucrats will always try to expand, or at least to avoid any reductions in, the size of their budgets. Although government bureaucracies are not-for-profit enterprises, bureaucrats want to maximize the size of their budgets and staffs, because these things are the most visible trappings of power in the public sector. These efforts are also prompted by the desire of bureaucrats to "sell" their prod-

---

[1]Max Weber, *Theory of Social and Economic Organization*, ed. by Talcott Parsons (New York: Oxford University Press, 1974).

ucts—national defense, public housing, agricultural subsidies, and so on—to both Congress and the public.

Because government bureaucracies seldom have competitors, some theorists have suggested that bureaucratic organizations may be explained best by using a **monopolistic model.** The analysis is similar to that used by economists to examine the behavior of monopolistic firms. Monopolistic bureaucracies—like monopolistic firms—are less efficient and more costly to operate because they have no competitors. Because monopolistic bureaucracies usually are not penalized for chronic inefficiency, they have little reason to adopt cost-saving measures or to make more productive uses of their resources. Some economists have argued that such problems can be cured only by privatizing certain bureaucratic functions.

THE SIZE OF THE BUREAUCRACY

In 1789, the new government's bureaucracy was minuscule. There were three departments—State (with nine employees), War (with two employees), and Treasury (with thirty-nine employees)—and the Office of the Attorney General (which later became the Department of Justice). This bureaucracy was still small in 1798. At that time, the secretary of state had seven clerks and spent a total of $500 (about $5,900

The Department of Agriculture inspects meat-packing facilities throughout the United States, certifying the quality and condition of the meat to be sold. Why is it necessary for the U.S. government to have administrative agencies such as the Department of Agriculture?

in 2001 dollars) on stationery and printing. In that same year, the Appropriations Act allocated $1.4 million to the War Department (or $16.4 million in 2001 dollars).[2]

Times have changed. Today, excluding the military, approximately 2.7 million government employees constitute the federal bureaucracy. That number has remained relatively stable for the last several decades. It is somewhat deceiving, however, because there are many others working directly or indirectly for the federal government as subcontractors or consultants and in other capacities.

The figures for federal government employment are only part of the story. Figure 11.1 shows the growth in government employment at the federal, state, and local levels. Since 1970, this growth has been mainly at the state and local levels. If all government employees are counted, then, more than 15 percent of all civilian employment is accounted for by government.

The costs of the bureaucracy are commensurately high and growing. The share of the gross national product taken up by government spending was only 8.5 percent in 1929. Today it exceeds 40 percent.

THE ORGANIZATION OF THE FEDERAL BUREAUCRACY

Within the federal bureaucracy are a number of different types of government agencies and organizations. We have already discussed, in Chapter 10, those agencies that are considered to be part of the Executive Office of the President. Figure 11.2

---

[2]Leonard D. White, *The Federalists: A Study in Administrative History, 1789–1801* (New York: Free Press, 1948).

FIGURE 11.1

Government Employment at Federal, State, and Local Levels

There are more local government employees than federal and state employees combined.

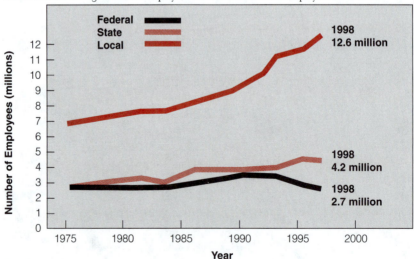

SOURCE: U.S. Department of Labor, Bureau of Labor Statistics, *Monthly Labor Review*, various issues.

FIGURE 11.2

Organization Chart of the Federal Government

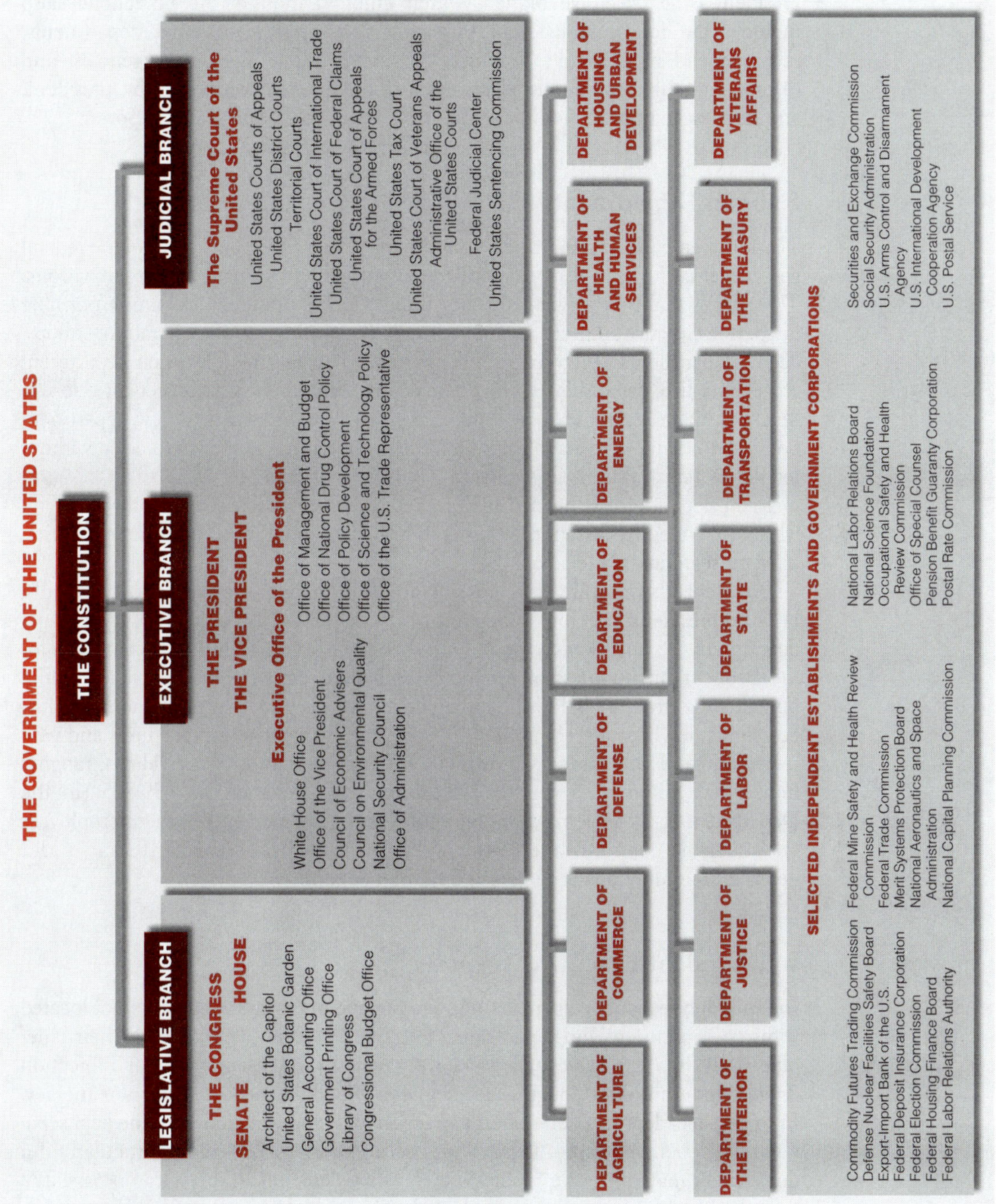

THE GOVERNMENT OF THE UNITED STATES

THE CONSTITUTION

LEGISLATIVE BRANCH

THE CONGRESS
SENATE   HOUSE

Architect of the Capitol
United States Botanic Garden
General Accounting Office
Government Printing Office
Library of Congress
Congressional Budget Office

EXECUTIVE BRANCH

THE PRESIDENT
THE VICE PRESIDENT

Executive Office of the President

White House Office
Office of the Vice President
Council of Economic Advisers
Council on Environmental Quality
National Security Council
Office of Administration

Office of Management and Budget
Office of National Drug Control Policy
Office of Policy Development
Office of Science and Technology Policy
Office of the U.S. Trade Representative

JUDICIAL BRANCH

The Supreme Court of the United States

United States Courts of Appeals
United States District Courts
Territorial Courts
United States Court of International Trade
United States Court of Federal Claims
United States Court of Appeals for the Armed Forces
United States Tax Court
United States Court of Veterans Appeals
Administrative Office of the United States Courts
Federal Judicial Center
United States Sentencing Commission

DEPARTMENT OF AGRICULTURE

DEPARTMENT OF COMMERCE

DEPARTMENT OF DEFENSE

DEPARTMENT OF EDUCATION

DEPARTMENT OF ENERGY

DEPARTMENT OF HEALTH AND HUMAN SERVICES

DEPARTMENT OF HOUSING AND URBAN DEVELOPMENT

DEPARTMENT OF THE INTERIOR

DEPARTMENT OF JUSTICE

DEPARTMENT OF LABOR

DEPARTMENT OF STATE

DEPARTMENT OF TRANSPORTATION

DEPARTMENT OF THE TREASURY

DEPARTMENT OF VETERANS AFFAIRS

SELECTED INDEPENDENT ESTABLISHMENTS AND GOVERNMENT CORPORATIONS

Commodity Futures Trading Commission
Defense Nuclear Facilities Safety Board
Export-Import Bank of the U.S.
Federal Deposit Insurance Corporation
Federal Election Commission
Federal Housing Finance Board
Federal Labor Relations Authority
Federal Mine Safety and Health Review Commission
Federal Trade Commission
Merit Systems Protection Board
National Aeronautics and Space Administration
National Capital Planning Commission
National Labor Relations Board
National Science Foundation
Occupational Safety and Health Review Commission
Office of Special Counsel
Pension Benefit Guaranty Corporation
Postal Rate Commission
Securities and Exchange Commission
Social Security Administration
U.S. Arms Control and Disarmament Agency
U.S. International Development Cooperation Agency
U.S. Postal Service

SOURCE: *United States Government Manual, 1997/98* (Washington, D.C.: U.S. Government Printing Office, 1997), p. 22.

outlines the several bureaucracies within the executive branch, as well as the separate organizations that provide services to Congress, to the courts, and directly to the president. The executive branch, which employs most of the bureaucrats also includes the following types of bureautic structures: (1) cabinet departments, (2) independent executive agencies, (3) independent regulatory agencies, and (4) government corporations. Each has a distinctive relationship to the president, and some have unusual internal structures, overall goals, and grants of power.

Cabinet Departments

The fourteen **cabinet departments** are the major service organizations of the federal government. They can also be described in management terms as **line organizations.** This means that they are directly accountable to the president and are responsible for performing government functions, such as printing money or training troops. These departments were created by Congress when the need for each department arose. The first department to be created was State, and the most recent one was Veterans Affairs, established in 1988. A president might ask that a new department be created or an old one abolished, but the president has no power to do so without legislative approval from Congress.

Each department is headed by a secretary (except for the Justice Department, which is headed by the attorney general) and has several levels of undersecretaries, assistant secretaries, and so on.

Presidents theoretically have considerable control over the cabinet departments, because presidents are able to appoint or fire all of the top officials. Even cabinet departments do not always respond to the president's wishes, though. One reason for the frequent unhappiness of presidents with their departments is that the entire bureaucratic structure below the top political levels is staffed by permanent employees, many of whom are committed to established programs or procedures and who resist change. Each cabinet department employs thousands of individuals, ranging from 4,676 empolyees (in the Department of Education) to 699,865 (in the Department of Defense). Only a handful (less than 1 percent) of these employees are under the control of the president, as you learned in Chapter 10. Table 11.2 describes the functions of each of the cabinet departments.

Independent Executive Agencies

Independent executive agencies are bureaucratic organizations that are not located within a department and report directly to the president, who appoints their chief officials. When a new federal agency is created—the Environmental Protection Agency, for example—Congress decides where it will be located in the bureaucracy. In recent decades, presidents often have asked that a new organization be kept separate or independent rather than added to an existing department, particularly if a department may in fact be hostile to the agency's creation. Table 11.3 on page 272 describes the functions of several selected independent executive agencies.

TABLE 11.2

Executive Departments

DEPARTMENT AND YEAR ESTABLISHED	PRINCIPAL FUNCTIONS
State (1789)	Negotiates treaties; develops foreign policy; protects citizens abroad.
Treasury (1789)	Pays all federal bills; borrows money; collects federal taxes, mints coins and prints paper currency; operates the Secret Service; supervises national banks.
Interior (1849)	Supervises federally owned lands and parks; operates federal hydroelectric power facilities; supervises Native American affairs.
Justice (1870)*	Furnishes legal advice to the president; enforces federal criminal laws; supervises the federal corrections systems (prisons).
Agriculture (1889)	Provides assistance to farmers and ranchers; conducts research to improve agricultural activity and to prevent plant disease; works to protect forests from fires and disease.
Commerce (1913)†	Grants patents and trademarks; conducts a national census; monitors the weather; protects the interests of businesses.
Labor (1913)	Administers federal labor laws; promotes the interests of workers.
Defense (1947)‡	Manages the armed forces (army, navy, air force, and marines); operates military bases; is responsible for civil defense.
Housing and Urban Development (1965)	Deals with the nation's housing needs; develops and rehabilitates urban communities; promotes improvement in city streets and parks.
Transportation (1967)	Finances improvements in mass transit; develops and administers programs for highways, railroads, and aviation; is involved with offshore maritime safety.
Energy (1977)	Is involved in the conservation of energy and resources; analyzes energy data; conducts research and development research.
Health and Human Services (1979)§	Promotes public health; enforces pure food and drug laws; is involved in health-related research.
Education (1979)§	Coordinates federal programs and policies for education; administers aid to education; promotes educational research.
Veterans Affairs (1988)	Promotes the welfare of veterans of the U.S. armed forces.

*Formed from the Office of the Attorney General (created in 1789).
†Formed from the Department of Commerce and Labor (created in 1903).
‡Formed from the Department of War (created in 1789) and the Department of Navy (created in 1798).
§Formed from the Department of Health, Education, and Welfare (created in 1953).

Independent Regulatory Agencies

The **independent regulatory agencies** are typically responsible for a specific type of public policy. Their function is to make and implement rules and regulations in a particular sector of the economy to protect the public interest. The regulatory agencies are administered independently of all three branches of government. They were set up because Congress felt it was unable to handle the complexities and technicalities required to carry out specific laws in the public interest. The regulatory commissions in fact combine some functions of all three branches of government—executive, legislative, and judicial. They are legislative in that they make rules that have the force of law. They are executive in that they provide for the enforcement of those rules. They are judicial in that they decide disputes involving the rules they have made.

Regulatory agency members are appointed by the president with the consent of the Senate, although they do not report to the president. By law, the members of

TABLE 11.3

Selected Independent Executive Agencies

NAME	DATE FORMED	PRINCIPAL FUNCTIONS
Central Intelligence Agency (CIA)	1947	Gathers and analyzes political and military information about foreign countries so that the United States can improve its own political and military status; conducts activities outside the United States, with the goal of countering the work of intelligence services operated by other nations whose political philosophies are inconsistent with our own.
General Services Administration (GSA)	1949	Purchases and manages all property of the federal government; acts as the business arm of the federal government in overseeing federal government spending projects; discovers overcharges in government programs.
National Science Foundation (NSF)	1950	Promotes scientific research; provides grants to all levels of schools for instructional programs in the sciences.
Small Business Administration (SBA)	1953	Protects the interests of small businesses; provides low-cost loans and management information to small businesses.
National Aeronautics and Space Administration (NASA)	1958	Is responsible for the U.S. space program, including the building, testing, and operating of space vehicles.
Environmental Protection Agency (EPA)	1970	Undertakes programs aimed at reducing air and water pollution; works with state and local agencies to help fight environmental hazards.

INFOTRAC®

"CIA Breach Confidence"

regulatory agencies cannot all be from the same political party. Presidents can influence regulatory agency behavior by appointing people of their own parties or people who share their political views when vacancies occur, in particular when the chair is vacant. Members may be removed by the president only for causes specified in the law creating the agency. Table 11.4 describes the functions of selected independent regulatory agencies.

Deregulation and Reregulation. During the presidency of Ronald Reagan in the 1980s, some significant deregulation (the removal of regulatory restraints—the opposite of regulation) occurred, much of which started under President Jimmy Carter. For example, President Carter appointed a chairperson of the Civil Aeronautics Board (CAB) who gradually eliminated regulation of airline fares and routes. Then, under Reagan, the CAB was eliminated on January 1, 1985. During the Bush administration, calls for reregulation of many businesses increased. Indeed, under President Bush, the Americans with Disabilities Act of 1990, the Civil Rights Act of 1991, and the Clean Air Act Amendments of 1991, all of which increased or changed the regulation of many businesses, were passed. Additionally, the Cable Reregulation Act of 1992 was passed. Under President Clinton, the Interstate Commerce Commission was eliminated, and there was deregulation of the banking and telecommunications industries, and many other sectors of the economy. At the same time, there was extensive regulation to protect the environment. Additionally, major attempts to institute general regulatory reform were made in Congress. So far, no significant legislation of that nature has been passed.

TABLE 11.4

Selected Independent Regulatory Agencies

NAME	DATE FORMED	PRINCIPAL FUNCTIONS
Federal Reserve System Board of Governors (Fed)	1913	Determines policy with respect to interest rates, credit availability, and the money supply.
Federal Trade Commission (FTC) Commission (SEC)	1914	Prevents businesses from engaging in unfair trade practices; stops the formation of monopolies in the business sector; protects consumer rights.
Securities and Exchange Commission (SEC)	1934	Regulates the nation's stock exchanges, in which shares of stocks are bought and sold; requires full disclosure of the financial profiles of companies that wish to sell stocks and bonds to the public.
Federal Communications Commission (FCC)	1934	Regulates all communications by telegraph, cable, telephone, radio, and television.
National Labor Relations Board (NLRB)	1935	Protects employees' rights to join unions and bargain collectively with employers; attempts to prevent unfair labor practices by both employers and unions.
Equal Employment Opportunity Commission (EEOC)	1964	Works to eliminate discrimination based on religion, gender, race, color, national origin, age, or disability; examines claims of discrimination.
Federal Election Commission (FEC)	1974	Ensures that candidates and states follow the rules established by the Federal Election Campaign Act.
Nuclear Regulatory Commission (NRC)	1974	Ensures that electricity-generating nuclear reactors in the United States are built and operated safely; regularly inspects the operations of such reactors.

Government Corporations

Another form of bureaucratic organization in the United States is the **government corporation.** Although the concept is borrowed from the world of business, distinct differences exist between public and private corporations.

A private corporation has shareholders (stockholders) who elect a board of directors, who in turn choose the corporate officers, such as president and vice president. When a private corporation makes a profit, it must pay taxes (unless it avoids them through various legal loopholes). It either distributes part or all of the after-tax profits to shareholders as dividends or plows the profits back into the corporation to make new investments.

A government corporation has a board of directors and managers, but it does not have any stockholders. We cannot buy shares of stock in a government corporation. If the government corporation makes a profit, it does not distribute the profit as dividends. Also, if it makes a profit, it does not have to pay taxes; the profits remain in the corporation. Table 11.5 on the next page describes the functions of selected government corporations.

STAFFING THE BUREAUCRACY

There are two categories of bureaucrats: political appointees and civil servants. As noted earlier, the president is able to make political appointments to most of the top

TABLE 11.5

Selected Government Corporations

NAME	DATE FORMED	PRINCIPAL FUNCTIONS
Tennessee Valley Authority (TVA)	1933	Operates a Tennessee River control system and generates power for a seven-state region and for the U.S. aeronautics and space programs; promotes the economic development of the Tennessee Valley region; controls floods and promotes the navigability of the Tennessee River.
Federal Deposit Insurance Corporation (FDIC)	1933	Insures individuals' bank deposits up to $100,000; oversees the business activities of banks.
Export/Import Bank of the United States (Ex/Im Bank)	1933	Promotes the sale of American-made goods abroad; grants loans to foreign purchasers of American products.
National Railroad Passenger Corporation (AMTRAK)	1970	Provides a balanced national and intercity rail passenger service network; controls 23,000 miles of track with 505 stations.
U.S. Postal Service*	1970	Delivers mail throughout the United States and its territories; is the largest government corporation.

*Formed from the Office of the Postmaster General in the Department of the Treasury (created in 1789).

jobs in the federal bureaucracy. The president also can appoint ambassadors to the most important foreign posts. The rest of the individuals who work for the national government belong to the civil service and obtain their jobs through a much more formal process.

Political Appointees

When making political appointments, the president and the president's advisers solicit suggestions from politicians, businesspersons, and other prominent individuals. Appointments to these positions offer the president a way to pay off outstanding political debts. But the president must also take into consideration such things as the candidate's work experience, intelligence, political affiliations, and personal characteristics. Presidents have differed over the importance they attach to appointing women and minorities to top positions. Presidents often use ambassadorships, however, to reward selected individuals for their campaign contributions.

Political appointees are in some sense the aristocracy of the federal government. But their powers, although appearing formidable on paper, are often exaggerated. Like the president, a political appointee will occupy his or her position for a comparatively brief time. Political appointees often leave office before the president's term actually ends. The average term of service for political appointees is less than two years. As a result, most appointees have little background for their positions and may be mere figureheads. Often, they only respond to the paperwork that flows up from below. Additionally, the professional civil servants who make up the permanent civil service but serve under a normally temporary political appointee may not feel compelled to carry out their current boss's directives quickly, because they know that he or she will not be around for very long.

This inertia is compounded by the fact that it is extremely difficult to discharge civil servants. In recent years, less than one-tenth of 1 percent of federal employees have been fired for incompetence. Because discharged employees may appeal their dismissals, many months or even years may pass before the issue is resolved conclusively. This occupational rigidity helps to ensure that most political appointees, no matter how competent or driven, will not be able to exert much meaningful influence over their subordinates, let alone implement dramatic changes in the bureaucracy itself.

History of the Federal Civil Service

When the federal government was formed in 1789, it had no career public servants but rather consisted of amateurs who were almost all Federalists. When Thomas Jefferson took over as president, he found that few in his party were holding federal administrative jobs, so he fired more than one hundred officials and replaced them with his own Jeffersonian (Democratic) Republicans, who were members of the so-called **natural aristocracy**—that is citizens, who, by birth, wealth, and ability, were

U.S. Postal Service employees sort the mail during the night shift at an Austin, Texas, post office. The postal service is the largest single employer in the United States.

thought to be the best suited to rule. For the next twenty-five years, a growing body of federal administrators gained experience and expertise, becoming in the process professional public servants. These administrators stayed in office regardless of who was elected president. The bureaucracy had become a self-maintaining, long-term element within government.

To the Victor Belong the Spoils. When Andrew Jackson took over the White House in 1828, he could not believe how many appointed officials (appointed before he became president, that is) were overtly hostile toward him and his Democratic Party. The bureaucracy—indeed an aristocracy—considered itself the only group fit to rule. But Jackson was a man of the people, and his policies were populist in nature. As the bureaucracy was reluctant to carry out his programs, Jackson did the obvious: he fired federal officials—more than had all his predecessors combined. The **spoils system**—an application of the principle that to the victor belong the spoils—reigned. The aristocrats were out, and the common folk were in. The spoils system was not, of course, a Jacksonian invention. Thomas Jefferson, too, had used this system of patronage in which the boss, or patron, rewards those who worked to get him or her elected.

The Civil Service Reform Act of 1883. Jackson's spoils system survived for a number of years, but it became increasingly corrupt. Also, the size of the bureaucracy increased by 300 percent between 1851 and 1881. Reformers began to look to

On September 19, 1881, President James A. Garfield was assassinated by a disappointed office seeker, Charles J. Guiteau. The long-term effect of this event was to replace the spoils system with a permanent career civil service, with the passage of the Pendleton Act in 1883, which established the Civil Service Commission.

Europe where several countries had established a professional civil service that operated under a **merit system** in which job appointments were based on competitive examinations. The cry for civil service reform became louder.

"Civil Service Commission"

In 1883, the **Pendleton Act**—or **Civil Service Reform Act**—was passed, bringing to a close the period of Jacksonian spoils. The act established the principle of employment on the basis of open, competitive examinations and created the **Civil Service Commission** to administer the personnel service. Only 10 percent of federal employees were covered initially by the merit system. Later laws, amendments, and executive orders, however, increased the coverage to more than 90 percent of the federal civil service. The effects of these reforms were felt at all levels of government, including city governments run by political machines such as New York's Tammany Hall.

The Supreme Court put an even heavier lid on the spoils system in *Elrod v. Burns*[3] in 1976 and *Branti v. Finkel*[4] in 1980. In those two cases, the Court used the First Amendment to forbid government officials from discharging or threatening to discharge public employees solely for not being supporters of the political party in power unless party affiliation is an appropriate requirement for the position. Additional curbs on political patronage were added in *Rutan v. Republican Party of Illinois*[5] in 1990. The Court's ruling effectively prevented the use of partisan political considerations as the basis for hiring, promoting, or transferring most public employees. An exception was permitted, however, for senior policymaking positions, which usually go to officials who will support the programs of the elected leaders.

The Hatch Act of 1939. The growing size of the federal bureaucracy created the potential for political manipulation. In principle, a civil servant is politically neutral. But civil servants certainly know that it is politicians who pay the bills through their appropriations and that it is politicians who decide about the growth of agencies. In 1933, when President Franklin D. Roosevelt set up his New Deal, a virtual army of civil servants was hired to staff the numerous new agencies that were created. Because the individuals who worked in these agencies owed their jobs to the Democratic Party, it seemed natural for them to campaign for Democratic candidates. The Democrats controlling Congress in the mid-1930s did not object. But in 1938, a coalition of conservative Democrats and Republicans took control of Congress and forced through the **Hatch Act**—or the **Political Activities Act**—of 1939.

The main provision of this act is that civil service employees cannot take an active part in the political management of campaigns. It also prohibits the use of federal authority to influence nominations and elections and outlaws the use of bureaucratic rank to pressure federal employees to make political contributions.

In 1972, a federal district court declared the Hatch Act prohibition against political activity to be unconstitutional. The United States Supreme Court, however, reaffirmed the challenged portion of the act in 1973, stating that the government's

---

[3] 427 U.S. 347 (1976).
[4] 445 U.S. 507 (1980).
[5] 497 U.S. 62 (1990).

interest in preserving a nonpartisan civil service was so great that the prohibitions should remain.[6]

The Civil Service Reform Act of 1978. In 1978, the Civil Service Reform Act abolished the Civil Service Commission and created two new federal agencies to perform its duties. To administer the civil service laws, rules, and regulations, the act created the Office of Personnel Management (OPM). The OPM is empowered to recruit, interview, and test potential government workers and determine who should be hired. The OPM makes recommendations to the individual agencies as to which persons meet the standards (typically, the top three applicants for a position), and the agencies generally decide whom to hire. To oversee promotions, employees' rights, and other employment matters, the act created the Merit Systems Protection Board (MSPB). The MSPB evaluates charges of wrongdoing, hears employee appeals from agency decisions, and can order corrective action against agencies and employees.

MODERN ATTEMPTS AT BUREAUCRATIC REFORM

As long as the federal bureaucracy exists, there will continue to be attempts to make it more open, efficient, and responsive to the needs of U.S. citizens. The most important actual and proposed reforms in the last few years include sunshine and sunset laws, contracting out, and providing incentives for efficiency and productivity.

Sunshine Laws

In 1976, Congress enacted the **Government in the Sunshine Act.** It required for the first time that all multiheaded federal agencies—about fifty of them—hold their meetings regularly in public session. The bill defined *meetings* as almost any gathering, formal or informal, of agency members, including conference telephone calls. The only exceptions to this rule of openness are discussions of matters such as court proceedings or personnel problems, and these exceptions are specifically listed in the bill. Sunshine laws now exist at all levels of government.

Contracting Out

One approach to bureaucratic reform is **contracting out.** Contracting out occurs when government services are replaced by services from the private sector. For example, the government might contract with private firms to operate prisons. Supporters of contracting out argue that some services could be provided more efficiently by the private sector. Another scheme is to furnish vouchers to "clients" in lieu of services. For example, it has been proposed that instead of federally supported housing assistance, the government should offer vouchers that recipients could use to "pay" for housing in privately owned buildings.

---

[6]*United States Civil Service Commission v. National Association of Letter Carriers*, 413 U.S. 548 (1973).

The contracting-out strategy has been most successful on the local level. Municipalities, for example, can form contracts with private companies for such things as trash collection. Such an approach is not a cure-all, however, as there are many functions, particularly on the national level, that cannot be contracted out in any meaningful way. For example, the federal government could not contract out all of the Defense Department's functions to a private firm.

Incentives for Efficiency and Productivity

An increasing number of state governments are beginning to experiment with a variety of schemes to run their operations more efficiently and capably. They focus on maximizing the efficiency and productivity of government workers by providing incentives for improved performance.[7]

Today, many governors, mayors, and city administrators are considering ways of making government more entrepreneurial. Some of the more promising tactics have included permitting agencies that do not spend their entire budgets to keep some of the difference and rewarding employees with performance-based bonuses.

At the federal level, the Government Performance and Results Act of 1997 was designed to improve efficiency in the federal work force. The act required that all government agencies (except the Central Intelligence Agency) describe their new goals and establish methods for determining whether those goals are met. Goals may be broadly crafted (for example, reducing the time it takes to test a new drug before allowing it to be marketed) or narrowly crafted (for example, reducing the number of times a telephone rings before it is answered).

BUREAUCRATS AS POLITICIANS AND POLICYMAKERS

Because Congress is unable to oversee the day-to-day administration of its programs, it must delegate certain powers to **administrative agencies.** Congress delegates the power to implement legislation to agencies through what is called **enabling legislation.** For example, the Federal Trade Commission was created by the Federal Trade Commission Act of 1914, the Equal Employment Opportunity Commission was created by the Civil Rights Act of 1964, and the Occupational Safety and Health Commission was created by the Occupational Safety and Health Act of 1970. The enabling legislation generally specifies the name, purpose, functions, and powers of the agency.

In theory, the agencies should put into effect laws passed by Congress. Laws are often drafted in such vague and general terms, however, that they provide little guidance to agency administrators as to how the laws should be put into effect. This means that the agencies themselves must decide how best to carry out the wishes of Congress.

---

[7]See, for example, David Osborne and Ted Gaebler, *Reinventing Government: How the Entrepreneurial Spirit Is Transforming the Public Sector* (Reading, Mass.: Addison-Wesley, 1992); and David Osborne and Peter Plastrik, *Banishing Bureaucracy: The Five Strategies for Reinventing Government* (Reading, Mass.: Addison-Wesley, 1997).

The discretion given to administrative agencies is not accidental. Congress has long realized that it lacks the technical expertise and the resources to monitor the implementation of its laws. Hence, the administrative agency is created to fill the gaps. This gap-filling role requires the agency to formulate administrative rules (regulations) to put flesh on the bones of the law. But it also forces the agency itself to assume the role of an unelected policymaker. (For an example of a recent Environmental Protection Agency policy decision, see this chapter's *At Issue: Who Benefits from "Environmental Justice"?*)

THE RULEMAKING ENVIRONMENT

Rulemaking does not occur in a vacuum. Suppose that Congress passes a new air-pollution law. The Environmental Protection Agency (EPA) might decide to implement the new law by a technical regulation relating to factory emissions. This proposed regulation would be published in the *Federal Register*, a daily government publication, so that interested parties would have an opportunity to comment on it. Individuals and companies that opposed parts or all of the rule might then try to convince the EPA to revise or redraft the regulation. Some parties might try to persuade the agency to withdraw the proposed regulation altogether. In any event, the EPA would consider these comments in drafting the final version of the regulation following the expiration of the comment period.

Once the final regulation has been published in the *Federal Register*, the regulation might be challenged in court by a party having a direct interest in the rule, such as a company that could expect to incur significant costs in complying with it. The company could argue that the rule misinterprets the applicable law or goes beyond the agency's statutory purview. An allegation by the company that the EPA made a mistake in judgment probably would not be enough to convince the court to throw out the rule. The company instead would have to demonstrate that the rule itself was "arbitrary and capricious." To meet this standard, the company would have to show that the rule reflected a serious flaw in the EPA's judgment—such as a steadfast refusal by the agency to consider reasonable alternatives to its rule.

In a budget package signed by the president in 1996, some regulatory relief was obtained. When an agency now issues a new rule, it has to wait sixty days (instead of only thirty days, as was previously required) before enforcing the rule. During that waiting period, businesses, individuals, and state and local governments can ask Congress to overturn the regulation rather than having to sue the agency after the rule takes effect.

Negotiated Rulemaking

Since the end of World War II, companies, environmentalists, and other special interest groups have challenged government regulations in court. In the 1980s and 1990s, however, the sheer wastefulness of attempting to regulate through litigation became more and more apparent. A growing number of federal agencies now encourage businesses and public-interest groups to become involved directly in the

AT ISSUE

Who Benefits from "Environmental Justice"?

About 60 percent of the people who live in Covent, Louisiana, are unemployed and have low incomes. Not surprisingly, when the community learned that the Japanese-owned firm, Shintech, planned to establish a $700 million polyvinyl chloride plant in their area, many residents welcomed the prospect of the new job opportunities that would be created.

The project was approved by Louisiana's Department of Environmental Quality, and it looked as though construction would soon be under way. The Environmental Protection Agency (EPA), however, had other ideas. Concluding that blacks would suffer disproportionately from the alleged cancer-causing emissions from the plant, in 1997 the EPA ordered that construction be delayed.

The EPA's concern with "environmental justice" began in 1993,

when the agency's director, Carol Browner, created the Office of Environmental Justice within the EPA. One of the purposes of the new office was to oversee studies on the effects of alleged industrial pollutants on poorer, mostly black communities. In the following year, the White House supported Browner's initiative by requiring all federal administrative agencies to consider the health and environmental effects of their decisions on minority and low-income communities.

The EPA's decision with respect to the Shintech plant was applauded by a group of white, middle-class residents in Covent. But Louisiana officials, as well as the lower-income residents of Covent, were enraged at the EPA's action.

According to Louisiana's director of economic development, Kevin Reilly, "It is demeaning and despicable for these people to play

the race card," especially when the plant would have provided economic benefits for poor people and blacks. Additionally, a study reported in the *Journal of the Louisiana Medical Society* found that the project would not have created the significant health risk that the EPA claimed it would.* Others criticized the EPA for intruding too extensively into state and local affairs.

FOR CRITICAL ANALYSIS

Should it matter whether those whose health may be jeopardized by an industrial plant's cancer-causing emissions are black or white?

---

*Pranay Gupte and Bonner R. Cohen, "Carol Browner, Master of Mission Creep," *Forbes*, October 20, 1997, p. 175.

---

drafting of regulations. Agencies hope that such participation may help to prevent later courtroom battles over the meaning, applicability, and legal effect of the regulations.

Congress formally approved such a process, which is called *negotiated rulemaking*, in the Negotiated Rulemaking Act of 1990. The act authorizes agencies to allow those who will be affected by a new rule to participate in the rule-drafting process. If an agency chooses to engage in negotiated rulemaking, it must publish in the *Federal Register* the subject and scope of the rule to be developed, the parties that will be affected significantly by the rule, and other information. Representatives of the affected groups and other interested parties then may apply to be members of the negotiating committee. The agency is represented on the committee, but a neutral third party (not the agency) presides over the proceedings. Once the committee

INFOTRAC®

"Green Redlining"

members have reached agreement on the terms of the proposed rule, notice of the proposed rule is published in the *Federal Register*, followed by a period for comments by any person or organization interested in the proposed rule. Negotiated rulemaking often is conducted under the condition that the participants promise not to challenge in court the outcome of any agreement to which they were a party.

Bureaucrats Are Policymakers

Theories of public administration once assumed that bureaucrats do not make policy decisions but only implement the laws and policies promulgated by the president and legislative bodies. Many people continue to make this assumption. A more realistic view, which is now held by most bureaucrats and elected officials, is that the agencies and departments of government play important roles in policymaking. As we have seen, many government rules, regulations, and programs are in fact initiated by the bureaucracy, based on its expertise and scientific studies. How a law passed by Congress eventually is translated into concrete action—from the forms to be filled out to decisions about who gets the benefits—usually is determined within each agency or department. Even the evaluation of whether a policy has achieved its purpose usually is based on studies that are commissioned and interpreted by the agency administering the program.

The bureaucracy's policymaking role often has been depicted by what has been called the "iron triangle." Recently, the concept of an "issue network" has been viewed as a more accurate description of the policymaking process.

Iron Triangles. In the past, scholars often described the bureaucracy's role in the policymaking process by using the concept of an **iron triangle**—a three-way alliance among legislators in Congress, bureaucrats, and interest groups in a given policy area. The presumption was that policy development depended on how a policy affected each component of the iron triangle.

Consider as an example the development of agricultural policy. The Department of Agriculture has nearly 100,000 employees working directly for the federal government and thousands of others who, directly or indirectly, work as contractors, subcontractors, or consultants to the department. Now consider that there are various interest, or client, groups that are concerned with what the federal government does for farmers. These include the American Farm Bureau Federation, the National Cattleman's Association, the National Milk Producers Association, the Corn Growers Association, and the Citrus Growers Association. Finally, go directly to Congress, and you will see that there are two major congressional committees concerned with agriculture—the House Committee on Agriculture and the Senate Committee on Agriculture, Nutrition, and Forestry—each of which has several subcommittees.

Clearly, it is in the Department of Agriculture's interest to support policies that enhance the department's budget and powers. Consider that the secretary of agriculture cannot even buy a desk lamp if Congress does not approve the appropriations for the department's budget. Therefore, the department will lend whatever support it can to those members of Congress who are in charge of deciding which agricultural programs should be cut, maintained, or created and what amount of funds should be allocated to the department.

Various agricultural interest groups will lobby Congress to develop policies that benefit their groups' interests. Members of Congress cannot afford to ignore the wishes of interest groups, because those groups are potential sources of voter support and campaign contributions. Therefore, the legislators involved in the iron triangle will work closely with interest group lobbyists when developing new policy. The legislators also will work closely with the Department of Agriculture, which, in implementing a policy, can develop rules that benefit—or are not adverse to—certain industries or groups.

To be sure, this is a much simplified picture of how the iron triangle works. But you can see how the interests of government agencies, legislators, and interest groups are all involved in the policymaking process. At times, iron triangles have completely thwarted efforts by the president to get the administration's programs enacted.

Issue Networks. With the growth in the complexity of the government, including expansion in the size of the bureaucracy, the increased number of subcommittees in Congress, and the proliferation of interest groups, policymaking also has become more complex. Often, different interest groups concerned about a certain area, such as agriculture, will have conflicting demands, which makes agency decision making difficult. Additionally, government agencies often are controlled by more than one legislative group. Finally, departments may be pressured by the president to take one approach and by legislators to take another. Today, policymaking typically involves a complex attempt to balance many conflicting demands.

Although iron triangles still exist, often they are inadequate as descriptions of how policy is actually made. Many scholars now use the term "issue network" to describe the policymaking process. An **issue network** consists of a group of individuals or organizations that support a particular policy position on the environment, taxation, consumer safety, or some other issue. Typically, an issue network includes legislators and/or their staff members, interest groups, bureaucrats, scholars and other experts, and representatives from the media. Members of a particular issue network work together to influence the president, members of Congress, administrative agencies, and the courts to change public policy on a specific issue. Each policy issue may involve conflicting positions taken by two or more issue networks.

CONGRESSIONAL CONTROL OF THE BUREAUCRACY

Although Congress is the ultimate repository of political power under the Constitution, many political pundits doubt whether Congress can meaningfully control the federal bureaucracy. These commentators forget that Congress, as already mentioned, specifies in an agency's "enabling legislation" the powers of the agency and the parameters within which it can operate. Additionally, Congress has the power of the purse and could, theoretically, refuse to authorize or appropriate funds for a particular agency. Whether Congress would actually take such a drastic measure would depend on the circumstances. It is clear, however, that Congress does have the legal authority to decide whether to fund or not to fund administrative agencies.

Congress also can exercise oversight over agencies through investigations and hearings. Congressional committees conduct investigations and hold hearings to oversee an agency's actions, reviewing them to ensure compliance with congressional intentions. The agency's officers and employees can be ordered to testify before a committee about the details of an action. Through these oversight activities, especially in the questioning and commenting by members of the House or Senate during the hearings, Congress indicates its positions on specific programs and issues. Congress can also ask the General Accounting Office (GAO) to investigate particular agency actions. The Congressional Budget Office (CBO) also conducts oversight studies. The results of a GAO or CBO study may encourage Congress to hold further hearings or make changes in the law. Even if a law is not changed explicitly by Congress, however, the views expressed in any investigations and hearings are taken seriously by agency officials, who often act on those views.

KEY TERMS

acquisitive model 266

administrative agency 279

bureaucracy 265

cabinet department 270

Civil Service Commission 277

contracting out 278

enabling legislation 279

government corporation 273

Government in the Sunshine Act 278

Hatch Act (Political Activities Act) 277

independent executive agency 270

independent regulatory agency 271

iron triangle 282

issue network 283

line organization 270

merit system 277

monopolistic model 267

natural aristocracy 275

Pendleton Act (Civil Service Reform Act) 277

spoils system 276

Weberian model 266

CHAPTER SUMMARY

1 Presidents have long complained about their inability to control the federal bureaucracy. There is no reference to the bureaucracy itself in the Constitution, but Article II gives the president the power to appoint officials to execute the laws of the United States. Most scholars cite Article II as the constitutional basis for the federal bureaucracy.

2 Bureaucracies are rigid hierarchical organizations in which the tasks and powers of lower-level employees are defined clearly. Job specialties and extensive procedural rules set the standards for behavior. Bureaucracies are the primary form of organization of most major corporations and universities.

3 Several theories have been offered to explain bureaucracies. The Weberian model posits that bureaucracies have developed into centralized hierarchical structures in response to the increasing demands placed on governments by their citizens. The acquisitive model views top-level bureaucrats as pressing for ever greater funding, staffs, and privileges to augment their own sense of power and security. The monopolistic model focuses on the environment in which most government bureaucracies operate, stating that bureaucracies are inefficient and excessively costly to operate because they often have no competitors.

4 Since the founding of the United States, the federal bureaucracy has grown from 50 to about 2.7 million employees (excluding the military). Federal, state, and local employees together make up some 15 percent of the nation's civilian labor force. The federal bureaucracy consists of fourteen cabinet departments, as well as numerous independent executive agencies, independent regulatory agencies, and government corporations. These entities enjoy varying degrees of autonomy, visibility, and political support.

5 A self-sustaining federal bureaucracy of career civil servants was formed during Thomas Jefferson's presidency. Andrew Jackson implemented a spoils system through which he appointed his own political supporters. A civil service based on professionalism and merit was the goal of the Civil Service Reform Act of 1883. Concerns that the civil service be freed from the pressures of politics prompted the passage of the

Hatch Act in 1939. Significant changes in the administration of the civil service were made by the Civil Service Reform Act of 1978.

6 There have been many attempts to make the federal bureaucracy more open, efficient, and responsive to the needs of U.S. citizens. The most important reforms have included sunshine laws, contracting out, and strategies to provide incentives for increased productivity and efficiency.

7 Congress delegates much of its authority to federal agencies when it creates new laws. The bureaucrats who run these agencies may become important policymakers, because Congress has neither the time nor the technical expertise to oversee the administration of its laws. In the agency rulemaking process, a proposed regulation is published. A comment period follows, during which interested parties may offer suggestions for changes. Because companies and other organizations have challenged many regulations in court, federal agencies now are allowed to involve parties that will be affected by new regulations in the rule-drafting process.

8 Congress exerts ultimate control over all federal agencies, because it controls the federal government's purse strings. It also establishes the general guidelines by which regulatory agencies must abide.

SELECTED PRINT AND ELECTRONIC RESOURCES

Suggested Readings

Downs, Anthony. *Inside Bureaucracy.* Boston: Little, Brown, 1967. In this classic work on the bureaucracy, Downs provides an economist's explanation of why the bureaucracy is what it is and why bureaucrats and their agencies conduct themselves as they do.

Hill, Michael. *The Policy Process in the Modern State.* Englewood Cliffs, N.J.: Prentice Hall, 1998. This overall view of the policymaking process includes a discussion of the role played by bureaucrats in policymaking.

Osborne, David, and Peter Plastrik. *Banishing Bureaucracy: The Five Strategies for Reinventing Government.* Reading, Mass.: Addison-Wesley, 1997. The author of *Reinventing Government* (1992), David Osborne, joined by Peter Plastrik, goes a step further in promoting an entrepreneurial model of government in which market principles are applied to government administration.

Richardson, William D. *Democracy, Bureaucracy, and Character: Founding Thought.* Lawrence, Kans.: University of Kansas, 1997. The author looks at the founders' views of how government should be administered.

Media Resources

Men in Black—A 1997 science-fiction comedy about an unofficial government agency that regulates the immigration of aliens from outer space who are living on earth.

Missiles of October—A movie retelling the events of October 1962, when the Kennedy administration decided to blockade Cuba to force the Soviet Union to remove its missiles from Cuba. The 1974 film, starring William Devane and Ralph Bellamy, gives an excellent inside view of policymaking involving the State Department, the Defense Department, and the president.

1984—A 1984 adaptation of George Orwell's well-known novel about the bureaucratic world of the future, starring John Hurt and Richard Burton; a superb fable of government versus individual values.

LOGGING ON

The National Partnership for Reinventing Government (NPR), which was started in the early stages of the Clinton administration to "reinvent government," is now online. Go to

http://www.npr.gov

Numerous links to many federal agencies and information on the federal government can be found at the Web site of Federal World. Go to

http://www.fedworld.gov

The Federal Web Locator is an excellent site to access if you want to find information on the bureaucracy. Its URL is

http://www.infoctr.edu/fw

The Federal Register, which is the official publication for executive-branch documents, is online at

http://www.gpo.ucop.edu/search

Another government publication that you might want to examine is the *United States Government Manual*, which describes the origins, purposes, and administrators of every federal department and agency. To access this publication online, go to

http://www.gpo.ucop.edu/catalog/govman.html

If you want to find telephone numbers for government agencies and personnel, you can go to

http://www.info.gov/fed_directory/phone.shtml

"The Plum Book," which lists the bureaucratic positions that can be filled by presidential appointment, is online at

http://www.louisville.edu/library/ekstrom/govpubs/federal/plum.html

USING THE INTERNET FOR POLITICAL ANALYSIS

Be a critical consumer of government information on the World Wide Web. Go to a government locator page, such as FedWorld (cited above), or to the Center for Information Law and Policy at

http://www.law.vill.edu

and compare the Web pages of at least three federal departments or agencies. Answer the following questions for each Web page:

1. Do you get the basic information about the department or agency, including its goals, locations, size, budget, and how citizens can gain access to the agency?

2. Can you tell from the page who the primary clients of the agency are? For example, are the agency's primary clients governments, ordinary citizens, businesses, or labor unions?

3. Is the page well designed, up to date, and easy for the average citizen to use?

4. What is the most valuable information on the page for you?

Chapter 12

The Courts

The judges and justices of the federal court system are not elected but rather are appointed by the president and confirmed by the Senate. This fact does not mean that the federal judiciary is apolitical, however. Indeed, our courts play a larger role in making public policy than courts in any other country in the world today.

As Alexis de Tocqueville, a nineteenth-century French commentator on American society, noted, "scarcely any political question arises in the United States that is not resolved, sooner or later, into a judicial question."[1] Our judiciary forms part of our political process. The instant that judges interpret the law, they become actors in the political arena—policymakers working within a political institution. As such, the most important political force within our judiciary is the United States Supreme Court.

How do courts make policy? Why do the federal courts play such an important role in American government? The answers to these questions lie, in part, in our colonial heritage. Most of American law is based on the English system, particularly the English common law tradition. In that tradition, the decisions made by judges constitute an important source of law.

THE COMMON LAW TRADITION

In 1066, the Normans conquered England, and William the Conqueror and his successors began the process of unifying the country under their rule. One of the ways they did this was to establish the king's courts, or *curiae regis*. Before the conquest, disputes had been settled according to local custom. The king's courts sought to establish a common or uniform set of rules for the whole country. As the number of courts and cases increased, portions of the more important decisions of each year were gathered together and recorded in *Year Books*. Judges settling disputes similar to ones that had been decided before used the *Year Books* as the basis for their decisions. If a case was unique, judges had to create new laws, but they based their decisions on the general principles suggested by earlier cases. The body of judge-made law that developed under this system is still used today and is known as the **common law.**

[1]Alexis de Tocqueville, *Democracy in America* (New York: Harper & Row, 1966), p. 248.

The practice of deciding new cases with reference to former decisions—that is, according to **precedent**—became a cornerstone of the English and American judicial systems and is embodied in the doctrine of *stare decisis* (pronounced *ster*-ay dih-*si-ses*), a Latin phrase that means "to stand on decided cases." The doctrine of *stare decisis* obligates judges to follow the precedents set previously only by their own courts or by higher courts that have authority over them.

INFOTRAC®

"Scalia Contra Common Law Adjudication"

For example, a lower state court in California would be obligated to follow a precedent set by the California Supreme Court. That lower court, however, would not be obligated to follow a precedent set by the supreme court of another state, because each state court system is independent. Of course, when the United States Supreme Court decides an issue, all of the nation's other courts are obligated to abide by the Court's decision—because the Supreme Court is the highest court in the land.

The doctrine of *stare decisis* provides a basis for judicial decision making in all countries that have common law systems. Today, the United States, Britain, and thirteen other countries have common law systems. Generally, those countries that were once colonies of Great Britain, including Australia, Canada, India, and New Zealand, have retained their English common law heritage since they achieved independence.

SOURCES OF AMERICAN LAW

The body of American law includes the federal and state constitutions, statutes passed by legislative bodies, administrative law, and case law—the legal principles expressed in court decisions.

Constitutions

The constitutions of the federal government and the states set forth the general organization, powers, and limits of government. The U.S. Constitution is the supreme law of the land. A law in violation of the Constitution, no matter what its source, may be declared unconstitutional and thereafter cannot be enforced. Similarly, the state constitutions are supreme within their respective borders (unless they conflict with the U.S. Constitution or federal laws and treaties made in accordance with it). The Constitution thus defines the political playing field on which state and federal powers are reconciled. The idea that the Constitution should be supreme in certain matters stemmed from widespread dissatisfaction with the weak federal government that had existed previously under the Articles of Confederation adopted in 1781.

Statutes and Administrative Regulations

Although the English common law provides the basis for both our civil and criminal legal systems, statutes (laws enacted by legislatures) increasingly have become important in defining the rights and obligations of individuals. Federal statutes may relate to any subject that is a concern of the federal government and may cover areas ranging from hazardous waste to federal taxation. State statutes include criminal codes, commercial laws, and laws relating to a variety of other matters. Cities, counties, and other local political bodies also pass statutes, which are called ordinances. These ordinances may deal with such things as zoning schemes and public safety. Rules and regulations issued by administrative agencies are another source of law. Today, much of the work of courts consists of interpreting these laws and regulations and applying them to circumstances in cases before the courts.

Case Law

Because we have a common law tradition, in which the doctrine of *stare decisis* plays an important role, the decisions rendered by the courts also form an important body of law, collectively referred to as **case law.** Case law includes judicial interpretations of common law principles and doctrines as well as interpretations of the types of law just mentioned—constitutional provisions, statutes, and administrative agency regulations. As you learned in previous chapters, it is up to the courts, and particularly the Supreme Court, to decide what a constitutional provision or a statutory phrase means. In doing so, the courts, in effect, establish law. (We will discuss this policy-making function of the courts in more detail later in the chapter.)

THE FEDERAL COURT SYSTEM

The United States has a dual court system. There are state courts and federal courts. Here we focus on the federal courts. Bear in mind, though, that each of the fifty states, as well as the District of Columbia, also has its own fully developed, independent system of courts.

The federal court system derives its power from Article III, Section 1, of the U.S. Constitution. That section limits the **jurisdiction** (the authority to hear and decide cases) of the federal courts to cases that involve either a federal question or diversity of citizenship. A **federal question** arises when a case is based, at least in part, on the U.S. Constitution, a treaty, or a federal law. A person who claims that his or her rights under the Constitution, such as the right to free speech, have been violated could bring a case in a federal court. **Diversity of citizenship** exists when the parties to a lawsuit are from different states or (more rarely) when the suit involves a U.S. citizen and a government or citizen of a foreign country. The amount in controversy must be at least $75,000 before a federal court can take jurisdiction in a diversity case, however.

As you can see in Figure 12.1, the federal court system is basically a three-tiered model consisting of (1) U.S. district courts and various specialized courts of limited jurisdiction (not all of the latter are shown in the figure), (2) intermediate U.S. courts of appeals, and (3) the United States Supreme Court.

U.S. District Courts

The U.S. district courts are trial courts. **Trial courts** are what their name implies—courts in which trials are held and testimony is taken. The U.S. district courts are

FIGURE 12.1

The Federal Court System

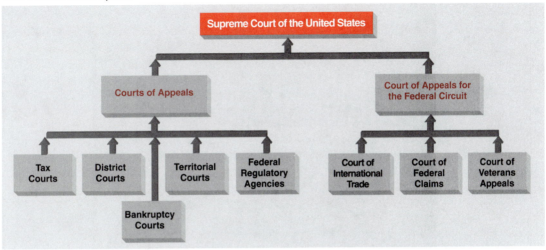

courts of **general jurisdiction,** meaning that they can hear cases involving a broad array of issues. Federal cases involving most matters typically arise in district courts. (The other courts on the lower tier of the model shown in Figure 12.1 are courts of **limited jurisdiction,** meaning that they can try cases involving only certain types of claims, such as tax claims or bankruptcy petitions.)

There is at least one federal district court in every state. The number of judicial districts can vary over time, primarily owing to population changes and corresponding caseloads. Currently, there are ninety-four federal judicial districts. A party who is dissatisfied with the decision of a district court judge can appeal the case to the appropriate U.S. court of appeals, or federal **appellate court.** Figure 12.2 on page 292 shows the jurisdictional boundaries of the district courts (which are state boundaries, unless otherwise indicated by dotted lines within a state), as well as of the U.S. courts of appeals.

U.S. Courts of Appeals

There are thirteen U.S. courts of appeals. Twelve of these courts, including the D.C. Circuit, hear appeals from the federal district courts located within their respective judicial circuits (geographic areas over which they exercise jurisdiction). The Court of Appeals for the Thirteenth Circuit, called the Federal Circuit, has national appellate jurisdiction over certain types of cases, such as cases involving patent law and those in which the U.S. government is a defendant.

Note that when an appellate court reviews a case decided in a district court, the appellate court does not conduct another trial. Rather, a panel of three or more judges reviews the record of the case on appeal, which includes a transcript of the trial proceedings, and determines whether the trial court committed an error.

FIGURE 12.2

Geographic Boundaries of Federal District Courts and Circuit Courts of Appeals

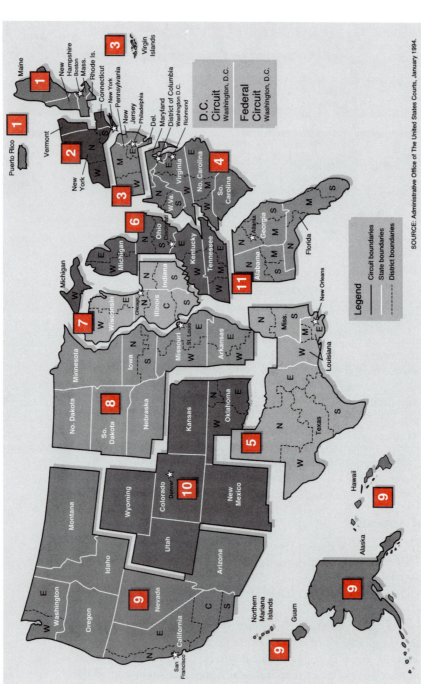

SOURCE: Administrative Office of The United States Courts, January 1994.

Usually, appellate courts do not look at questions of *fact* (such as whether a party did, in fact, commit a certain action, such as burning a flag) but at questions of *law* (such as whether the act of flag burning is a form of speech protected by the First Amendment to the Constitution). An appellate court will challenge a trial court's finding of fact only when the finding is clearly contrary to the evidence presented at trial or when there is no evidence to support the finding.

A party can petition the United States Supreme Court to review an appellate court's decision. The likelihood that the Supreme Court will grant the petition is slim, however, because the Court reviews only a very few of the cases decided by the appellate courts. This means that decisions made by appellate judges usually are final.

The United States Supreme Court

The highest level of the three-tiered model of the federal court system is the United States Supreme Court. When the Supreme Court came into existence in 1789, it had five justices. In the following years, more justices were added, and since 1837 there have been nine justices on the Court.

According to the language of Article III of the U.S. Constitution, there is only one national Supreme Court. All other courts in the federal system are considered "inferior." Congress is empowered to create other inferior courts as it deems necessary. The inferior courts that Congress has created include the federal courts of appeals and the district courts, as well as the federal courts of limited jurisdiction.

Although the Supreme Court can exercise original jurisdiction (that is, act as a trial court) in certain cases, such as those affecting foreign diplomats and those in which a state is a party, most of its work is as an appellate court. The Court hears appeals not

A jury is being sworn in. Most jury trials have between six and twelve jurors. Some trials are held without juries.

only from the federal appellate courts but also from the highest state courts. Note, though, that the United States Supreme Court can review a state supreme court decision only if a federal question is involved. Because of its importance in the federal court system, we will look more closely at the Supreme Court in the next section.

Parties and Procedures

In most lawsuits, the parties are the plaintiff (the person or organization that initiates the lawsuit) and the defendant (the person or organization against whom the lawsuit is brought). There may be numerous plaintiffs and defendants in a single lawsuit. In the last several decades, many lawsuits have been brought by interest groups (see Chapter 7). Interest groups play an important role in our judicial system, because they **litigate**—bring to trial—or assist in litigating most cases of racial or gender-based discrimination, virtually all civil liberties cases, and more than one-third of the cases involving business matters. Interest groups also file *amicus curiae* (pronounced ah-*mee*-kous *kur*-ee-eye) **briefs,** or "friend of the court" briefs, in more than 50 percent of these kinds of cases.

Sometimes, an interest group or other plaintiff will bring a **class-action suit,** in which whatever the court decides will affect all members of a class similarly situated (such as users of a particular product manufactured by the defendant in the lawsuit). The strategy of class-action lawsuits was pioneered by such groups as the National Association for the Advancement of Colored People (NAACP), the Legal Defense Fund, and the Sierra Club, whose members believed that the courts—rather than Congress—would offer the most sympathetic forum for their views.

Both the federal and the state courts have established procedural rules that shape the litigation process. These rules are designed to protect the rights and interests of the parties, to ensure that the litigation proceeds in a fair and orderly manner, and to identify the issues that must be decided by the court—thus saving court time and costs. Generally, these rules are rooted in the adversarial approach to justice followed in American courtrooms and determine what evidence must be disclosed by the parties to each other prior to trial, what evidence will be admissible during the legal contest between the parties, and so on.

The parties must comply with procedural rules and with any orders given by the judge during the course of the litigation. When a party does not follow a court's order, the court can cite her or him for contempt. A party who commits civil contempt (failing to comply with a court's order for the benefit of another party to the proceeding) can be taken into custody, fined, or both, until the party complies with the court's order. A party who commits *criminal* contempt (obstructing the administration of justice or bringing the court into disrepect) also can be taken into custody and fined but cannot avoid punishment by complying with a previous order.

THE SUPREME COURT AT WORK

The Supreme Court, by law, begins its regular annual term on the first Monday in October and usually adjourns in late June or early July of the next year. Special sessions may be held after the regular term is over, but only a few cases are decided in this way. More commonly, cases are carried over until the next regular session.

Of the total number of cases that are decided each year, those reviewed by the Supreme Court represent less than one-half of 1 percent. Included in these, however, are decisions that profoundly affect our lives. In recent years, the United States Supreme Court has decided issues involving capital punishment, affirmative action programs, religious freedom, assisted suicide, abortion, busing, term limits for congresspersons, sexual harassment, pornography, and numerous other matters with significant consequences for the nation. Because the Supreme Court exercises a great deal of discretion over the types of cases it hears, it can influence the nation's policies by issuing decisions in some types of cases and refusing to hear appeals in others, thereby allowing lower court decisions to stand.

Which Cases Reach the Supreme Court?

Many people are surprised to learn that in a typical case, there is no absolute right of appeal to the United States Supreme Court. The Court's appellate jurisdiction is almost entirely discretionary—the Court can choose which cases it will decide. The justices never explain their reasons for hearing certain cases and not others, so it is difficult to predict which case or type of case the Court might select. Chief Justice William Rehnquist, in his description of the selection process in *The Supreme Court: How It Was, How It Is,*[2] said that the decision of whether or not to accept a case "strikes me as a rather subjective decision, made up in part of intuition and in part of legal judgment."

Factors that bear on the decision include whether a legal question has been decided differently by two lower courts and needs resolution by the highest court, whether a lower court's decision conflicts with an existing Supreme Court ruling, and whether the issue could have significance beyond the parties to the dispute. For example, the justices very likely decided to review a case challenging the constitutionality of the Communications Decency Act of 1996 because the case involved the significant issue of the extent to which free speech on the Internet could be regulated.

Another factor is whether the solicitor general is pressuring the Court to take a case. The solicitor general, a high-ranking presidential appointee within the Justice Department, represents the national government in the Supreme Court and promotes presidential policies in the federal courts. He or she decides what cases the government should ask the Supreme Court to review and what position the government should take in cases before the Court. The influence wielded by solicitors general over the Court's decision making has led some to refer to the solicitor general as the "Tenth Justice."

If the Court decides to grant a petition for review, it will issue a writ of *certiorari* (pronounced sur-shee-uh-*rah*-ree). The writ orders a lower court to send the Supreme Court a record of the case for review. More than 90 percent of the petitions for writs of *certiorari* are denied. A denial is not a decision on the merits of a case, nor

---

[2]William H. Rehnquist, *The Supreme Court: How It Was, How It Is* (New York: Morrow, 1987).

does it indicate agreement with the lower court's opinion. (The judgment of the lower court remains in force, however.) Therefore, denial of the writ has no value as a precedent. The Court will not issue a writ unless at least four justices approve of it. This is called the **rule of four.**[3]

Deciding Cases

Once the Supreme Court grants *certiorari* in a particular case, the justices do extensive research on the legal issues and facts involved in the case. (Of course, some preliminary research was necessary before deciding to grant the petition for review.) Each justice is entitled to four law clerks, who undertake much of the research and preliminary drafting necessary for the justice to form an opinion.[4]

---

[3]The "rule of four" is modified when seven or fewer justices participate, which occurs from time to time. When that happens, as few as three justices can grant *certiorari*.

[4]For a former Supreme Court law clerk's account of the role these clerks play in the high court's decision-making process, see Edward Lazarus, *Closed Chambers: The First Eyewitness Account of the Epic Struggles inside the Supreme Court* (New York: Times Books, 1998).

In her chambers, Justice Ruth Bader Ginsburg works on her caseload with one of her law clerks. Each justice has four law clerks, who typically are culled from the "best and the brightest" graduates from U.S. law schools. Some critics of the Supreme Court's practices argue that the clerks have too much power and influence over the Court's decision making.

The Court normally does not hear any evidence, as is true with all appeals courts. The Court's consideration of a case is based on the abstracts, the record, and the briefs. The attorneys are permitted to present **oral arguments.** The Court hears oral arguments on Monday, Tuesday, Wednesday, and sometimes Thursday, usually for seven two-week sessions scattered from the first week in October to the end of April or the first week in May. All statements and the justices' questions are tape-recorded during these sessions. Unlike the practice in most courts, lawyers addressing the Supreme Court can be (and often are) questioned by the justices at any time during oral argument.

The justices meet to discuss and vote on cases in conferences held each Wednesday and Friday throughout the term. In these conferences, in addition to deciding cases currently before the Court, the justices decide which new petitions for *certiorari* to grant. These conferences take place in the oak-paneled chamber and are strictly private—no stenographers, tape recorders, or video cameras are allowed. Two pages used to be in attendance to wait on the justices while they were in conference, but fear of information leaks caused the Court to stop this practice.[5]

Decisions and Opinions

When the Court has reached a decision, its opinion is written. The **opinion** contains the Court's reasons for its decision, the rules of law that apply, and the judgment. In many cases, the decision of the lower court is **affirmed,** resulting in the enforcement of that court's judgment or decree. If the Supreme Court feels that a reversible error was committed during the trial or that the jury was instructed improperly, however, the judgment will be **reversed.** Sometimes the case will be **remanded** (sent back to the court that originally heard the case) for a new trial or other proceeding. For example, a lower court might have held that a party was not entitled to bring a lawsuit under a particular law. If the Supreme Court holds to the contrary, it will remand (send back) the case to the trial court with instructions that the trial go forward.

The Court's written opinion sometimes is unsigned; this is called an opinion *per curiam* ("by the court"). Typically, the Court's opinion will be signed by all the justices who agree with it. Usually, when in the majority, the chief justice will write the opinion. Whenever the chief justice is in the minority, the senior justice on the majority side decides who writes the opinion.

When all justices unanimously agree on an opinion, the opinion is written for the entire Court (all the justices) and can be deemed a **unanimous opinion.** When there is not a unanimous opinion, a **majority opinion** is written, outlining the views of the majority of the justices involved in the particular case. Often, one or more justices who feel strongly about making or emphasizing a particular point that is not made or emphasized in the unanimous or majority written opinion will write a **concurring opinion.** That means the justice writing the concurring opinion agrees (concurs) with the conclusion given in the majority written opinion, but for different reasons. Finally, in other than unanimous opinions, one or more dissenting opinions

---

[5]It turned out that one supposed information leak came from lawyers making educated guesses.

are usually written by those justices who do not agree with the majority. The **dissenting opinion** is important because it often forms the basis of the arguments used years later that cause the Court to reverse the previous decision and establish a new precedent.

Shortly after the opinion is written, the Supreme Court announces its decision from the bench. At that time, the opinion is made available to the public at the office of the clerk of the Court. The clerk also releases the opinion for online publication (see the *Logging on* section at the end of this chapter on pages 310 and 311 for Web sites that publish Supreme Court opinions). Ultimately, the opinion is published in the *United States Reports*, which is the official record of the Court's decisions.

THE SELECTION OF FEDERAL JUDGES

All federal judges are appointed. The Constitution, in Article II, Section 2, states that the president appoints the justices of the Supreme Court with the advice and consent of the Senate. Congress has provided the same procedure for staffing other federal courts. This means that the Senate and the president jointly decide who shall be a federal judge, no matter what the level.

There are over eight hundred federal judgeships in the United States. Once appointed to such a judgeship, a person holds that job for life. Judges serve until they resign, retire voluntarily, or die. Federal judges who engage in blatantly illegal conduct may be removed through impeachment, although such action is extremely rare.

Nominating Judicial Candidates

Judicial candidates for federal judgeships are suggested to the president by the Department of Justice, senators, other judges, the candidates themselves, and bar associations and other interest groups. In selecting a candidate to nominate for a judgeship, the president considers not only the person's competence but also other factors, including the person's political philosophy (as will be discussed shortly), ethnicity, and gender.

The nomination process—no matter how the nominees are obtained—always works the same way. The president makes the actual nomination, transmitting the name to the Senate. The Senate then either confirms or rejects the nomination. To reach a conclusion, the Senate Judiciary Committee (operating through subcommittees) invites testimony, both written and oral, at its various hearings. In the case of federal district court judgeships, a practice used in the Senate, called **senatorial courtesy,** is a constraint on the president's freedom to appoint whomever the administration chooses. Senatorial courtesy allows a senator of the president's political party to veto a judicial appointment in his or her state.

Federal District Court Judgeship Nominations. Although the president nominates federal judges, the nomination of federal district court judges typically originates with a senator or senators of the president's party from the state in which there is a vacancy. If the nominee is deemed unqualified, as a matter of political courtesy the president will discuss with the senator or senators who originated the nomination whether the nomination should be withdrawn. Also, when a nomination is unacceptable politically to the president, the president will consult with the appropriate senator or senators, indicate that the nomination is unacceptable, and work with the senator or senators to seek an alternative candidate.

Federal Courts of Appeals Appointments. There are many fewer federal courts of appeals appointments than federal district court appointments, but they are more important. This is because federal appellate judges handle more important matters, at least from the point of view of the president, and therefore presidents take a keener interest in the nomination process for such judgeships. Also, appointments to the U.S. courts of appeals have become "steppingstones" to the Supreme Court. Typically, the president culls the Circuit Judge Nominating Commission's list of nominees for potential candidates. The president may also use this list to oppose senators' recommendations that may be unacceptable politically to the president.

Supreme Court Appointments. As we have described, the president nominates Supreme Court justices. As you can see in Table 12.1 on page 300, which summarizes the background of all Supreme Court justices to 2000, the most common occupational background of the justices at the time of their appointments has been private legal practice or state or federal judgeships. Those nine justices who were in federal executive posts at the time of their appointments held the high offices of secretary of state, comptroller of the treasury, secretary of the navy, postmaster general, secretary of the interior, chairman of the Securities and Exchange Commission, and secretary of labor. In the "Other" category under "Occupational Position before Appointment" in Table 12.1 are two justices who were professors of law (including William H. Taft, a former president) and one justice who was a North Carolina state employee with responsibility for organizing and revising the state's statutes.

Partisanship and Judicial Appointments

Ideology plays an important role in the president's choices for judicial appointments. As a result, presidential appointments to the federal judiciary have had an extremely partisan distribution. The justices' partisan attachments have been mostly the same as those of the president who appointed them. There have been some exceptions, however. Nine nominal Democrats have been appointed by Republican presidents, three Republicans by Democratic presidents, and one Democrat by Whig president John Tyler.[6]

INFOTRAC®

"Must Joe Robinson Die"

Presidents see their federal judiciary appointments as the one sure way to institutionalize their political views long after they have left office. By 1993, for example, Presidents Reagan and Bush together had appointed nearly three-quarters of all

---

[6]Actually, Tyler was a member of the Democratic Party who ran with William H. Harrison on the Whig ticket. When Harrison died, much to the surprise of the Whigs, Tyler—a Democrat—became president, although they tried to call him "acting president." Thus, some historians would quibble over the statement that Tyler was a Whig.

TABLE 12.1

Background of Supreme Court Justices to 2000

	NUMBER OF JUSTICES (108 = TOTAL)
Occupational Position before Appointment	
Private legal practice	25
State judgeship	21
Federal judgeship	28
U.S. attorney general	7
Deputy or assistant U.S. attorney general	2
U.S. solicitor general	2
U.S. senator	6
U.S. representative	2
State governor	3
Federal executive post	9
Other	3
Religious Background	
Protestant	83
Roman Catholic	11
Jewish	6
Unitarian	7
No religious affiliation	1
Age on Appointment	
Under 40	5
41–50	31
51–60	58
61–70	14
Political Party Affiliation	
Federalist (to 1835)	13
Democratic Republican (to 1828)	7
Whig (to 1861)	1
Democrat	44
Republican	42
Independent	1
Educational Background	
College graduate	92
Not a college graduate	16
Gender	
Male	106
Female	2
Race	
Caucasian	106
Other	2

SOURCE: Congressional Quarterly, *Congressional Quarterly's Guide to the U.S. Supreme Court* (Washington, D.C.: Congressional Quarterly Press, 1996), and authors' update.

federal court judges. This preponderance of Republican-appointed federal judges strengthened the legal moorings of the conservative social agenda on a variety of issues, ranging from abortion to civil rights. Nevertheless, President Bill Clinton had the opportunity to appoint about two hundred federal judges, thereby shifting the ideological make-up of the federal judiciary. Also, Clinton's appointees matched more closely the actual U.S. demographics than did the appointees of his predecessors. By the end of his first term, Clinton had appointed more women and members of minority groups to federal judgeships than any other president.

Ideology also plays a large role in the Senate's confirmation hearings, and presidential nominees to the Supreme Court have not always been confirmed. In fact, almost 20 percent of presidential nominations to the Supreme Court have been either rejected or not acted on by the Senate. Numerous acrimonious battles over both Supreme Court and lower judicial appointments have ensued when the Senate and the president have not seen eye to eye about political matters. In fact, during the late 1990s the duel between the Senate and the president aroused considerable concern about the consequences of the increasingly partisan and ideological tension over federal judicial appointments. As a result of Senate delays in confirming nominations, the number of judicial vacancies mounted, as did the backlog of cases pending in the federal courts.

The Policymaking Function of the Courts

The partisan battles over judicial appointments reflect an important reality in today's American government: the importance of the judiciary in national politics. Because appointments to the federal benches are for life, the ideology of judicial appointees can affect national policy for years to come. Although the primary function of judges in our system of government is to interpret and apply the laws, inevitably judges make policy when carrying out this task. One of the major policymaking tools of the federal courts is their power of judicial review.

Judicial Review

Remember from Chapter 2 that the power of the courts to determine whether a law or action by the other branches of government is constitutional is known as the power of *judicial review*. This power of the judiciary enables the judicial branch to act as a check on the other two branches of government, in line with the checks and balances system established by the U.S. Constitution.

The power of judicial review is not mentioned in the Constitution, however. Rather, it was established by the United States Supreme Court's decision in *Marbury v. Madison*.[7] In that case, in which the Court declared that a law passed by Congress violated the Constitution, the Court claimed such a power for the courts:

> It is emphatically the province and duty of the Judicial Department to say what the law is. Those who apply the rule to a particular case, must of necessity expound and interpret that rule. If two laws conflict with each other, the courts must decide on the operation of each.

If a federal court declares that a federal or state law or policy is unconstitutional, the court's decision affects the application of the law or policy only within that court's

---

[7] 5 U.S. 137 (1803).

jurisdiction. For this reason, the higher the level of the court, the greater the impact of the decision on society. Because of the Supreme Court's national jurisdiction, its decisions can have a significant impact. For example, when the Supreme Court held that an Arkansas state constitutional amendment limiting the terms of congresspersons was unconstitutional, laws establishing term limits in twenty-three other states also were invalidated.[8]

Judicial Activism and Judicial Restraint

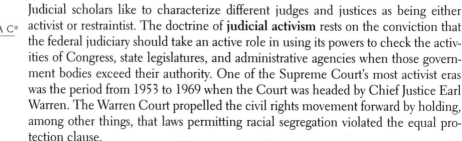

I N F O T R A C®

"Critics Taking Aim
Judicial Activism"

Judicial scholars like to characterize different judges and justices as being either activist or restraintist. The doctrine of **judicial activism** rests on the conviction that the federal judiciary should take an active role in using its powers to check the activities of Congress, state legislatures, and administrative agencies when those government bodies exceed their authority. One of the Supreme Court's most activist eras was the period from 1953 to 1969 when the Court was headed by Chief Justice Earl Warren. The Warren Court propelled the civil rights movement forward by holding, among other things, that laws permitting racial segregation violated the equal protection clause.

In contrast, the doctrine of **judicial restraint** rests on the assumption that the courts should defer to the decisions made by the legislative and executive branches, because members of Congress and the president are elected by the people whereas members of the federal judiciary are not. Because administrative agency personnel normally have more expertise than the courts do in the areas regulated by the agencies, the courts likewise should defer to agency rules and decisions. In other words, under the doctrine of judicial restraint, the courts should not thwart the implementation of legislative acts and agency rules unless they are clearly unconstitutional.

Judicial activism sometimes is linked with liberalism, and judicial restraint with conservatism. In fact, a conservative judge can be activist, just as a liberal judge can be restraintist—and vice versa. In the 1950s and 1960s, the Supreme Court was activist and liberal. Some observers believe that the Rehnquist Court, with its conservative majority, has become increasingly activist in the 1990s.

Ideology and the Rehnquist Court

William H. Rehnquist became the sixteenth chief justice of the Supreme Court in 1986, after fifteen years as an associate justice. He was known as a strong anchor of the Court's conservative wing. With Rehnquist's appointment as chief justice, it seemed to observers that the Court necessarily would become more conservative.

This, in fact, has happened. The Court began to take a rightward shift shortly after Rehnquist became chief justice, and the Court's rightward movement continued as other conservative appointments to the bench were made during the Reagan and Bush administrations. Today, three of the justices (William Rehnquist, Antonin Scalia, and Clarence Thomas) are notably conservative in their views. Four of the justices (John Paul Stevens, David Souter, Ruth Bader Ginsburg, and Stephen

---

[8]*U.S. Term Limits v. Thornton*, 514 U.S. 779 (1995).

The Rehnquist Court
LIBERAL/MODERATE

John Paul Stevens

David Souter

Ruth Bader Ginsburg

Stephen Breyer

SWING VOTES

Sandra Day O'Connor

Anthony Kennedy

CONSERVATIVE

William Rehnquist

Antonin Scalia

Clarence Thomas

Breyer) hold liberal-to-moderate views. The middle of the Court is now occupied by two moderate-to-conservative justices, Sandra Day O'Connor and Anthony Kennedy. O'Connor and Kennedy usually provide the "swing votes" on the Court in

INFOTRAC®

"Rehnquist's Call"

controversial cases. The ideological alignments on the Court vary, however, depending on the issues involved in particular cases.

Certainly, today's Supreme Court has moved far from the liberal positions taken by the Court under Earl Warren (1953–1969) and under Warren Burger (1969–1986). Since the mid-1990s, the Court has issued numerous conservative rulings, many of which you have already read about in this text. Several of these rulings reflect a conservative approach to constitutional law with respect to states' rights and other federalist issues. For example, in 1995 the Court curbed—for the first time in sixty years—the national government's constitutional power under the commerce clause to regulate intrastate activities. The Court held that a federal law regulating the possession of guns in school zones had nothing to do with interstate commerce, and therefore Congress had overreached its powers by attempting to regulate this activity.[9] In 1997, the Court again upheld states' rights when it invalidated portions of the federal gun control law. The Court stated that the federal government lacked constitutional authority to require state officials to perform background checks on prospective gun purchasers.[10] A further decision, rendered by the Court in 2000, concerned the sovereign powers of the states in our federal system. The Court held that Congress exceeded its constitutional authority when it included in the Age Discrmination in Employment Act of 1967 a provision declaring that state employers were to be subject to the act.[11]

In regard to civil rights issues, the Rehnquist Court's generally conservative ("strict") interpretation of the Constitution has had mixed results. In one decision, the Court refused to extend the constitutional right to privacy to include the right of terminally ill persons to end their lives through physician-assisted suicide. Therefore, a state law banning this practice did not violate the Constitution.[12] (Essentially, the Court left it up to the states to decide whether to ban—or to permit—assisted suicide; to date, only one state, Oregon, has passed a law permitting the practice.) In another decision, the Court held that a federal statute expanding religious liberties was an unconstitutional attempt by Congress to rewrite the Constitution.[13]

WHAT CHECKS OUR COURTS?

Our judicial system is probably the most independent in the world. (Some would say that it is too independent—see this chapter's *At Issue: Is the Federal Judiciary Too Powerful?*) But the courts do not have absolute independence, for they are part of the political process. Political checks limit the extent to which courts can exercise judicial review and engage in an activist policy. These checks are exercised by the executive branch, the legislature, the public, and, finally, the judiciary itself.

---

[9]*United States v. Lopez,* 514 U.S. 549 (1995).

[10]*Printz v. United States,* 521 U.S. 898 (1997).

[11]*Kimel v. Florida Board of Regents,* 120 S.Ct. 631 (2000).

[12]*Washington v. Glucksberg,* 521 U.S. 702 (1997).

[13]*City of Boerne v. Flores,* 521 U.S. 507 (1997).

Is the Federal Judiciary Too Powerful?

The extensive influence over national policy wielded by today's federal courts, particularly the Supreme Court, could not possibly have been foreseen by the founders. Indeed, many of the founders had few worries about judicial power. In *Federalist Paper No. 78*, Alexander Hamilton expressed the opinion that the judiciary (meaning the Supreme Court, which was the only court designated in the Constitution) was the "least dangerous branch" of government because it had no enforcement powers. If the Court rendered a decision that was unacceptable to the other branches of government or to the public, there was no way the Court itself could enforce that decision.

In its earliest years, the Court did indeed lack stature and influence. The first Supreme Court chief justice, John Jay, refused to serve a second term because he thought the Court would never play an important role in American society. Jay became governor of New York instead. The next chief justice, Oliver Ellsworth, resigned his position to become an envoy to France. In 1801, when the federal capital was moved to Washington,

no one remembered to include the Supreme Court in the plans. As a result, the Court met in the office of the clerk of the Senate until 1935.

Some of the founders, however, were concerned about the potential danger of giving the judiciary too much power. Madison believed that to combine the powers of the judiciary with those of the legislative and executive branches was the "very definition of tyranny." Jefferson expressed concern over allowing unelected judges to be in charge of interpreting the meaning of the Constitution. In a letter to William Jarvis in 1820, Jefferson wrote, "It is a very dangerous doctrine to consider the judges as the ultimate arbiters of all constitutional questions."

A number of scholars and politicians today claim that the power of the federal courts should be curbed. Proposals for doing this include removing the judiciary's power of judicial review and giving Congress the final say on constitutional interpretation; limiting federal court jurisdiction; and impeaching "activist" federal judges who make policy based on their personal ideological prefer-

ences. Generally, federal judges have been criticized not only by Republicans in Congress but also by the media and other members of the public. Other groups assert that there are enough checks on the judiciary already and that the courts should be left alone.

The problem for judges is that they must weather such criticism in silence. Ethical codes prevent them from explaining to the public — in the media, for example — why it was in the interests of justice to set aside a certain jury verdict or rule a certain way on an issue. The American Bar Association recently has proposed new guidelines that might help to remedy this problem. The guidelines urge state and local bar associations to use press releases, letters to the editor, and other public forums to defend or explain judicial actions in the wake of an "unwarranted" or "unjust" attack regarding a specific case.

FOR CRITICAL ANALYSIS

Why do you suppose the legal profession considers it unethical for judges to defend their rulings publicly?

Executive Checks

President Andrew Jackson was once supposed to have said, after Chief Justice John Marshall made an unpopular decision, that "John Marshall has made his decision; now let him enforce it."[14] This purported remark goes to the heart of **judicial**

---

[14]The decision referred to was *Cherokee Nation v. Georgia*, 30 U.S. 1 (1831).

implementation—the enforcement of judicial decisions in such a way that those decisions are translated into policy. The Supreme Court simply does not have any enforcement powers, and whether a decision will be implemented depends on the cooperation of the other two branches of government. Rarely, though, will a president refuse to enforce a Supreme Court decision, as President Jackson did. To take such an action could mean a significant loss of public support, because of the Supreme Court's stature in the eyes of the nation.

More commonly, presidents exercise influence over the judiciary by appointing new judges and justices as federal judicial seats become vacant. Additionally, as mentioned earlier, the U.S. solicitor general plays a significant role in the federal court system, and the person holding this office is a presidential appointee.

Executives at the state level also may refuse to implement court decisions with which they disagree. A notable example of such a refusal occurred in Arkansas after the Supreme Court ordered schools to desegregate "with all deliberate speed" in 1955.[15] Arkansas governor Orval Faubus refused to cooperate with the decision and used the state's National Guard to block the integration of Central High School in Little Rock. Ultimately, President Dwight Eisenhower had to federalize the Arkansas National Guard and send federal troops to Little Rock to quell the violence that had erupted.

Legislative Checks

Courts may make rulings, but often the legislatures at local, state, and federal levels are required to appropriate funds to carry out the courts' rulings. A court, for example, may decide that prison conditions must be improved, but it is up to the legislature to authorize the funds necessary to carry out such a ruling. When such funds are not appropriated, the court that made the ruling, in effect, has been checked.

Courts' rulings can be overturned by constitutional amendments at both the federal and state levels. Many of the amendments to the U.S. Constitution (such as the Fourteenth Amendment) check the state courts' ability to allow discrimination, for example. Proposed constitutional amendments that were created by a desire to reverse courts' decisions on school prayer and abortion have failed.

Finally, Congress or a state legislature can rewrite (amend) old laws or enact new ones to overturn a court's rulings if the legislature concludes that the court is interpreting laws or legislative intentions erroneously. For example, Congress passed the Civil Rights Act of 1991 in part to overturn a series of conservative rulings in employment-discrimination cases. In 1993, Congress enacted the Religious Freedom Restoration Act (RFRA), which broadened religious liberties, after Congress concluded that a 1990 Supreme Court ruling restricted religious freedom to an unacceptable extent.[16]

According to political scientist Walter Murphy, "A permanent feature of our constitutional landscape is the ongoing tug and pull between elected government and

---

[15]*Brown v. Board of Education*, 349 U.S. 294 (1955)—the second *Brown* decision.
[16]*Employment Division, Department of Human Resources of Oregon v. Smith*, 494 U.S. 872 (1990).

the courts."[17] Certainly, today's Supreme Court and the other two branches of government have been at odds on several occasions in the last decade. Consider the battle over religious rights and the RFRA. On signing the RFRA, President Clinton stated that the act was necessary to reverse the Court's erroneous interpretation of the Constitution in its 1990 decision. According to the president, the elected government's view of religious liberty was "far more consistent with the intent of the founders than [was] the Supreme Court."[18] The Supreme Court responded in kind. In 1997, it invalidated the RFRA, declaring that the act represented an unconstitutional attempt by Congress to add new rights to the Constitution.[19] The Court proclaimed horror at the prospect that "[s]hifting legislative majorities could change the Constitution."

Public Opinion

Public opinion plays a significant role in shaping government policy, and certainly the judiciary is not excepted from this rule. For one thing, persons affected by a Supreme Court decision that is noticeably at odds with their views may simply ignore it. Prayers were banned in public schools in 1962, yet it was widely known that the ban was (and still is) ignored in many southern districts. What can the courts do in this situation? Unless someone complains about the prayers and initiates a lawsuit, the courts can do nothing.

The public also can pressure state and local government officials to refuse to enforce a certain decision. As already mentioned, judicial implementation requires the cooperation of government officials at all levels, and public opinion in various regions of the country will influence whether or not such cooperation is forthcoming.

Additionally, the courts themselves necessarily are influenced by public opinion to some extent. After all, judges are not "islands" in our society; their attitudes are influenced by social trends, just as the attitudes and beliefs of all persons are. Courts generally tend to avoid issuing decisions that they know will be noticeably at odds with public opinion. In part, this is because the judiciary, as a branch of the government, prefers to avoid creating divisiveness among the public. Also, a court—particularly the Supreme Court—may lose stature if it decides a case in a way that markedly diverges from public opinion. Given that it has no enforcement powers, the Court's authority is linked to its stature in the eyes of the public.

Judicial Traditions and Doctrines

Supreme Court justices (and other federal judges) typically exercise self-restraint in fashioning their decisions. In part, this restraint stems from their knowledge that the other two branches of government and the public can exercise checks on the judiciary, as previously discussed. To a large extent, however, this restraint is mandated by

---

[17]As quoted in Neal Devins, "The Last Word Debate: How Social and Political Forces Shape Constitutional Values," *American Bar Association Journal*, October 1997, p. 48.

[18]Devins, "The Last Word Debate."

[19]*City of Boerne v. Flores*, 521 U.S. 507 (1997).

various judicially established traditions and doctrines. For example, in exercising its discretion to hear appeals, the Supreme Court will not hear a meritless appeal just so it can rule on the issue. Also, when reviewing a case, the Supreme Court typically narrows its focus to just one issue or one aspect of an issue involved in the case. The Court rarely makes broad, sweeping decisions on issues. Furthermore, the doctrine of *stare decisis* acts as a restraint because it obligates the courts, including the Supreme Court, to follow established precedents when deciding cases. Only rarely will courts overrule a precedent.

Other judicial doctrines and practices also act as restraints. The courts will hear only what are called **justiciable disputes,** which are disputes that arise out of actual cases and that can be settled by legal methods. In other words, a court will not hear a case that involves a merely hypothetical issue. A party must have some stake in a real controversy before that party can bring a case before a court. Additionally, if a political question is involved, the Supreme Court often will exercise judicial restraint and refuse to rule on the matter. A **political question** is one that the Supreme Court declares should be decided by the elected branches of government—the executive branch, the legislative branch, or those two branches acting together. For example, the Supreme Court has refused to rule on the controversy regarding the rights of gays and lesbians in the military, preferring instead to defer to the executive branch's decisions on the matter. Generally, fewer questions are deemed political questions by the Supreme Court today than in the past.

Higher courts can reverse the decisions of lower courts. Lower courts can act as a check on higher courts, too. Lower courts can ignore—and have ignored—Supreme Court decisions. Usually, this is done indirectly. A lower court might conclude, for example, that the precedent set by the Supreme Court does not apply to the exact circumstances in the case before the court; or the lower court may decide that the Supreme Court's decision was ambiguous with respect to the issue before the lower court. The fact that the Supreme Court rarely makes broad and clear-cut statements on any issue facilitates different interpretations of the Court's decisions by the lower courts.

KEY TERMS

affirm 297	diversity of citizenship 290	limited jurisdiction 291
amicus curiae brief 294	federal question 290	litigate 294
appellate court 291	general jurisdiction 291	majority opinion 297
case law 290	judicial activism 302	opinion 297
class-action suit 294	judicial implementation 305	oral arguments 297
common law 288	judicial restraint 302	political question 308
concurring opinion 297	jurisdiction 290	precedent 289
dissenting opinion 298	justiciable dispute 308	remand 297

reverse 297

rule of four 296

senatorial courtesy 298

stare decisis 289

trial court 290

unanimous opinion 297

writ of *certiorari* 295

CHAPTER SUMMARY

1 American law is rooted in the common law tradition, which was part of our legal heritage from England. The common law doctrine of *stare decisis* (which means "to stand on decided cases") obligates judges to follow precedents established previously by their own courts or by higher courts in their jurisdiction. Precedents established by the United States Supreme Court, the highest court in the land, are binding on all lower courts. Fundamental sources of American law include the U.S. Constitution and state constitutions, statutes enacted by legislative bodies, regulations issued by administrative agencies, and case law.

2 Article III, Section 1, of the U.S. Constitution limits the jurisdiction of the federal courts to cases involving (a) a federal question—which is a question based, at least in part, on the U.S. Constitution, a treaty, or a federal law; and (b) diversity of citizenship—which arises when a lawsuit is between parties of different states or involves a foreign citizen or government. The federal court system is basically a three-tiered model consisting of (a) U.S. district (trial) courts and various lower courts of limited jurisdiction; (b) U.S. courts of appeals; and (c) the United States Supreme Court. Cases may be appealed from the district courts to the appellate courts. In most cases, the decisions of the federal appellate courts are final because the Supreme Court hears only a few cases each year.

3 The Supreme Court begins its annual term on the first Monday in October and usually adjourns in late June or early July of the next year. A special session may be held, but this rarely occurs. The Court's decision to review a case is influenced by many factors, including the significance of the parties and issues involved and whether the solicitor general is pressing the Court to take the case. After a case is accepted, the justices (a) undertake research (with the help of their law clerks) on the issues involved in the case, (b) hear oral arguments from the parties, (c) meet in conference to discuss and vote on the issue, and (d) announce the opinion, which is then released for publication.

4 Federal judges are nominated by the president and confirmed by the Senate. Once appointed, they hold office for life, barring gross misconduct. The nomination and confirmation process, particularly for Supreme Court justices, is often extremely politicized. Democrats and Republicans alike realize that justices may occupy seats on the Court for decades and naturally want to have persons appointed who share their basic views.

5 In interpreting and applying the law, judges inevitably become policymakers. The most important policymaking tool of the federal courts is the power of judicial review. Judges who take an active role in checking the activities of the other branches of government sometimes are characterized as "activist" judges, and judges who defer to such activities sometimes are regarded as "restraintist" judges. The Warren Court of the 1950s and 1960s was activist in a liberal direction, whereas today's Rehnquist Court seems to be activist in a conservative direction. Several politicians and scholars argue that the policymaking powers of the federal courts should be curbed because such extensive powers were not envisioned by the founders, who entrusted Congress, an elected body, with the authority to make policy. Others contend that the courts should be left alone.

6 Checks on the powers of the federal courts include executive checks, legislative checks, public opinion, and judicial traditions and doctrines.

SELECTED PRINT AND ELECTRONIC RESOURCES

Suggested Readings

Braum, Lawrence. *The Supreme Court.* 6th ed. Washington, D.C.: Congressional Quarterly Press, 1998. A noted judicial scholar offers a comprehensive examination of the Supreme Court.

Cheney, Timothy D. *Who Makes the Law: The Supreme Court, Congress, the States and Society.* Englewood Cliffs, N.J.: Prentice Hall, 1998. This is an insightful examination of the Supreme Court's interactions with Congress and with the states and society.

Lazarus, Edward. *Closed Chambers: The First Eyewitness Account of the Epic Struggles inside the Supreme Court.* New York: Times Books, 1998. Lazarus, who served as a clerk to former Supreme Court Justice Harry Blackmun during the Court's 1988–1989 term, gives an eyewitness account of some of the significant ideological struggles waged within the Court, among both law clerks and the justices.

Scalia, Antonin. *A Matter of Interpretation: Federal Courts and the Law.* Ewing, N.J.: Princeton University Press, 1997. Supreme Court Justice Antonin Scalia presents his views on a number of topics, including the distinction between adjudicating and legislating. He contends that the Supreme Court too often engages in making new law rather than interpreting the Constitution.

Media Resources

Court TV—This TV channel covers high-profile trials, including those of O. J. Simpson, the Unabomber, British nanny Louise Woodward, and Timothy McVeigh. (You can learn how to access Court TV from your area at its Web site—see the *Logging on* section below for its URL.)

First Monday in October—A 1981 movie with a light touch that centers on the appointment of the first woman to the U.S. Supreme Court.

Gideon's Trumpet—A 1980 film starring Henry Fonda as the small-time criminal, James Earl Gideon, which makes clear the path that a case takes to the Supreme Court and the importance of cases decided there.

The Magnificent Yankee—A 1950 movie, starring Louis Calhern and Ann Harding, that traces the life and philosophy of Oliver Wendell Holmes, Jr., one of the Supreme Court's most brilliant justices.

Marbury v. Madison—A thirty-minute video on this famous 1803 case that established the principle of judicial review.

LOGGING ON

http:// WWW.

The home page of the federal courts is a good starting point if you are learning about the federal court system in general. At this site, you can even follow the "path" of a case as it moves through the federal court system. Go to

http://www.uscourts.gov

Several Web sites offer searchable databases of Supreme Court decisions. You can access Supreme Court cases since 1970 at FindLaw's site:

http://www.findlaw.com

The following Web site also offers an easily searchable index to Supreme Court opinions, including some important historic decisions:

http://supct.law.cornell.edu/supct

You can find information on the justices of the Supreme Court, as well as their decisions, at

http://oyez.nwu.edu

At the following site, Supreme Court decisions are made available within hours of their release:

http://www.supremecourtus.gov

Court TV's Web site offers information ranging from its program schedule and how you can find Court TV in your area to famous cases and the wills of famous people. For each case it includes on the site, it gives a complete history as well as selected documents filed with the court and court transcripts. You can access this site at

http://www.courttv.com

USING THE INTERNET FOR POLITICAL ANALYSIS

Go to one of the sites on the Web that organizes the Supreme Court's cases, such as the federal courts site or the Cornell site given above. Then look up the list of Supreme Court decisions for a recent time period—say, three months. Select three cases, and read the summary of each case. Try to categorize the federal or constitutional issue that was decided in each case. To whom is the decision important? Does the decision change the relationship between the ordinary citizen and the government? What other kinds of information would make this site more useful to you?

http:// WWW.

PART FOUR

POLICYMAKING

CHAPTER 13

Domestic and Economic Policy

T ypically, whenever a policy decision is made, some groups will be better off and some groups will be hurt. All policymaking generally involves such a dilemma.

Part of the public-policy debate in our nation involves domestic problems. **Domestic policy** can be defined as all of the laws, government planning, and government actions that affect each individual's daily life in the United States. Consequently, the span of such policies is enormous. Domestic policies range from relatively simple issues, such as what the speed limit should be on interstate highways, to more complex issues, such as how best to protect our environment. Many of our domestic policies are formulated and implemented by the federal government, but many others are the result of the combined efforts of federal, state, and local governments.

In this chapter we look at domestic policy issues concerned with poverty and welfare, violence and crime, and the environment. We also examine national economic policies undertaken solely by the federal government. Before we start our analysis, we must look at how public policies are made.

THE POLICYMAKING PROCESS

How does any issue, such as a perceived need for welfare reform, get resolved? First, of course, the issue has to be identified as a problem. With respect to the welfare program, policymakers can learn that it poses a problem by looking at the cost of the federal welfare program, the overlap of the federal program with state welfare programs, the extent to which welfare programs contribute to the elimination of poverty, and nationally published statistics on other aspects of the program.

Often, policymakers simply have to open their local newspapers—or letters from their constituents—to discover that a problem is brewing. Like most Americans, however, policymakers receive much of their information from the national media. Finally, different lobbying groups provide information to members of Congress.

During the 1990s, in those years when there were continuing federal budget deficits, many traditionally protected federal programs were put under the microscope. One of these programs was the welfare program. Congress and the White House gradually accepted that welfare reform was necessary. Indeed, when campaigning for his first presidential term, Bill Clinton promised that he would "change welfare as we know it."

Steps in the Policymaking Process

The passage of the Welfare Reform Act (the popular name for the Personal Responsibility and Work Opportunity Reconciliation Act) in 1996 provides a good example of the steps involved in the policymaking process. No matter how simple or how complex the problem, those who make policy follow a number of steps. Based on observation, we can divide the process of policymaking into at least five steps.

1. **Agenda building:** *The issue must get on the agenda.* This occurs through crisis, technological change, or mass media campaigns, as well as through the efforts of strong political personalities and effective lobbying groups. With respect to the Welfare Reform Act of 1996, members of the 104th Congress, in response to the public's concern over the then-steady federal government deficits and the perceived failure of welfare to reduce poverty rates, included welfare reform as part of their proposed legislative agenda.

2. **Agenda formulation:** *The proposals are discussed among government officials and the public.* Such discussions may take place in the printed media, on television, and in the halls of Congress. Congress holds hearings, the president voices the administration's views, and the topic may even become a campaign issue. For example, Bill Clinton talked about welfare reform throughout his 1992 presidential campaign. The topic was discussed during some of his "town hall meetings." It was on the agenda of the National Governors Conference for several years in a row.

3. **Agenda adoption:** *A specific strategy is chosen from among the proposals discussed.* That is, Congress must enact legislation, executive departments must write new regulations, or the courts must interpret past policies differently. Much of the congressional year prior to the passage of the Welfare Reform Act, for example, was taken up by work on that legislation. After extensive debate, a bill was passed, and the president signed it into law on August 22, 1996. The new legislation was, of course, a compromise. It attempted to meet two objectives—giving more power to the states while at the same time not being "too harsh on poor people."

4. **Agenda implementation:** *Government action must be implemented by bureaucrats, the courts, police, and individual citizens.* Although on the whole the legislation changed the welfare landscape, some states took longer to implement changes than others. Congress also changed some of the restrictions placed on welfare payments during the two years after the act's passage.

5. **Agenda evaluation:** *Increasingly, after a policy is implemented, groups undertake policy evaluation.* Groups both inside and outside government conduct studies to show what actually happens after a policy has been implemented for a given period of time. Based on this "feedback" and the perceived success or failure of the policy, a new round of policymaking initiatives will be undertaken to correct and hopefully improve on the effort. Research groups, for example, have already studied whether the 1996 Welfare Reform Act has increased employment among those who were formerly on welfare.

POVERTY AND WELFARE

Throughout the world, historically poverty has been accepted as inevitable. Even today, little has been done on an international level to eliminate worldwide poverty. The United States and other industrialized nations, however, have sustained enough economic growth in the past several hundred years to eliminate *mass* poverty. In fact, considering the wealth and high standard of living in the United States, the persistence of poverty here appears bizarre and anomalous. How can there still be so much poverty in a nation of so much abundance? And what can be done about it?

A traditional solution has been **income transfers.** These are methods of transferring income from relatively well-to-do to relatively poor groups in society, and as a nation, we have been using such methods for a long time. Today, a vast array of welfare programs exists for the sole purpose of redistributing income. We know, however, that these programs have not been entirely successful. Before we examine the problems posed by the welfare system, let's look at the concept of poverty in more detail and at the characteristics of the poor.

The Low-Income Population

We can see in Figure 13.1 that the number of individuals classified as poor fell rather steadily from 1959 through 1969. Then, for about a decade, the number of poor leveled off, until the recession of 1981 to 1982. The number then fell somewhat until the early 1990s, when it began to increase—until 1995. Since then, it has fallen slightly.

Defining Poverty. The threshold income level, which is used to determine who falls into the poverty category, was originally based on the cost of a nutritionally adequate

FIGURE 13.1

The Official Number of Poor in the United States

The number of individuals classified as poor fell steadily from 1959 through 1969. From 1970 to 1981, the number stayed about the same. It then increased during the 1981–1982 recession. The number of poor then fell somewhat, until the early 1990s. After rising for a few years, the number started to fall in 1995.

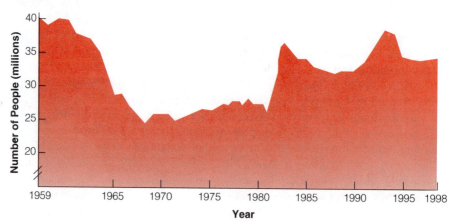

food plan designed by the U.S. Department of Agriculture for emergency or temporary use. The threshold was determined by multiplying the food-plan cost times three, on the assumption that food expenses constitute approximately one-third of a poor family's expenditures. In 1969, a federal interagency committee examined the calculations of the threshold and decided to set new standards. Until then, annual revisions of the threshold level had been based only on price changes in the food budget. After 1969, the adjustments were made on the basis of changes in the consumer price index (CPI). The CPI is based on the average prices of a specified set of goods and services bought by wage earners in urban areas.

The low-income poverty threshold thus represents an absolute measure of income needed to maintain a specified standard of living as of 1963, with the constant-dollar value, or purchasing-power value, increased year by year in relation to the general increase in prices. For 2000, for example, the official poverty level for a family of four was about $17,000. (The poverty level varies with family size and location.)

Transfer Payments as Income. The official poverty level is based on pretax income, including cash but not **in-kind subsidies**—food stamps, housing vouchers, and the like. If we correct poverty levels for such benefits, the percentage of the population that is below the poverty line drops dramatically. Some economists argue that the way in which the official poverty level is calculated makes no sense in a nation that redistributes hundreds of billions of dollars in cash and noncash transfers each year.

These two teenage mothers could be subject to the provisions of the 1996 welfare reform law, which limits their eligibility for federal assistance to two years. States may choose to extend assistance for a longer period of time, however. Although the goal of the law was to get people into employment, it did not provide the child-care benefits usually needed by mothers to allow them to accept jobs.

Major Government-Assistance Programs

Welfare assistance to the poor traditionally has taken a variety of forms. Until 1996, the basic welfare program in the United States was known as Aid to Families with Dependent Children (AFDC). This program provided aid for children who did not receive financial support from the father. With the passage of the Welfare Reform Act of 1996, the states gained more responsibility for establishing welfare rules and managing the welfare program. The AFDC program was abolished, and the U.S. government now turns over to the states, in the form of grants, funds targeted for a program called **Temporary Assistance to Needy Families (TANF).** If a state wishes to increase the amount of payments to individuals for TANF over what the national government gives it, the state has to pay for the additional costs.

The **Supplemental Security Income (SSI)** program was established in 1974 to provide a nationwide minimum income for elderly persons and persons with disabilities who do not qualify for Social Security benefits. The SSI program is one of the fastest-growing programs in the United States. When it started, it cost less than $8 billion annually. Today, that figure is close to $40 billion.

The government also issues **food stamps,** coupons that can be used to purchase food. Food stamps are available for low-income individuals and families. Recipients must prove that they qualify by showing that they do not have very much income (or no income at all). In 1964, about 367,000 Americans were receiving food stamps. By 2000, the number of those receiving food stamps was estimated at more than 28 million. The annual cost of funding food stamps jumped from $860,000 in 1964 to an estimated $25 billion in 2000. Workers on strike, and even some college students, are eligible to receive food stamps. The food-stamp program has become a major part of the welfare system in the United States, although it was started in 1964 mainly to shore up the nation's agricultural sector by distributing surplus food through retail channels.

The **earned-income tax credit (EITC) program** was created in 1975 to help low-income workers by giving back part or all of their Social Security taxes. Currently, more than 20 percent of all taxpayers claim an EITC.

Through these and other programs, hundreds of billions of dollars have been transferred to the poor over the last several decades. Nevertheless, the poverty rate in the United States has not shown any long-run tendency to decline since about 1970.

Poverty's Effect on Children

F. Scott Fitzgerald once wrote that the rich "are different from you and me"; Ernest Hemingway replied, "Yes, they have more money." Are the children of low-income families the same as everyone else, except that they have less money? This has been a major policy question for years. Some have argued that children of very poor families fail in society because their parents are unlike other parents. The policy implications of this debate are crucial, for if children from poor families are just like everyone else, then reducing poverty rates will lead to higher success rates in the economic and social world for such children.

Two relatively recent studies cast doubts on such a possibility.[1] According to researcher Susan Mayer, even if our poverty policies doubled the income of the poorest 20 percent of families, childbearing by teenagers would drop only 2 percent. The high school dropout rate would only decrease from 17.3 percent to about 16 percent. Mayer argues that the parents' skills, honesty, diligence, and health may matter more to children's prospects than whether the family is in poverty. She says that "although children's opportunities are unequal, income inequality is not the primary reason."

Homelessness—Still a Problem

The plight of the homeless remains a problem. Indeed, some observers argue that the Welfare Reform Act of 1996 has increased the numbers of homeless persons. According to the National Alliance to End Homelessness, the number of people without a home on any given night in the United States ranges from 350,000 to as many as 600,000.

It is difficult to estimate how many people are homeless because the number depends on how the homeless are defined. There are *street people*—those who sleep

INFOTRAC®

"Liz's Story"

---

[1]Susan Mayer, *What Money Can't Buy: Family Income and Children's Life Chances* (Cambridge, Mass.: Harvard University Press, 1997); and Greg J. Duncan and Jeanne Brooks-Gunn, eds., *Consequences of Growing up Poor* (New York: Russell Sage Foundation, 1997).

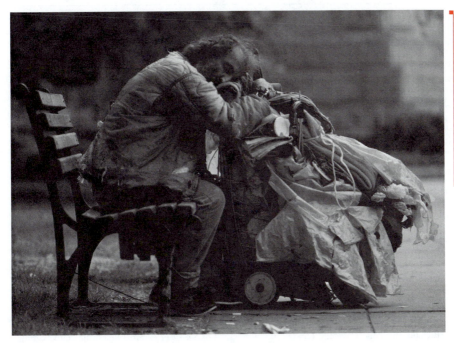

Less than one hundred yards from the White House, a homeless man sleeps, with his head on a cart containing all of his possessions. What should (or can) the government do to help the homeless?

in bus stations, parks, and other areas. Many of these people are youthful runaways. There are the so-called *sheltered homeless*—those who sleep in government-supported or privately funded shelters. Many of these individuals used to live with their families or friends. While street people are almost always single, the sheltered homeless include numerous families with children. Homeless families are the fastest-growing subgroup of the homeless population.

As a policy issue, how to handle the homeless problem pits liberals against conservatives. Conservatives argue that there are not really that many homeless and that most of them are alcoholics, drug users, or mentally ill. Conservatives argue that these individuals should be dealt with either by the mental-health system or the criminal justice system. In contrast, many liberals argue that homelessness is caused by a reduction in welfare benefits and by excessively priced housing. They want more shelters to be built for the homeless.

Recently, cities have been attempting to "criminalize" homelessness. Many municipalities have outlawed sleeping on park benches and sidewalks, as well as panhandling and leaving personal property on public property. In some cities, police sweeps remove the homeless, who then become part of the criminal justice system.

Because there is so much disagreement about the number of homeless persons, the reasons for homelessness, and the possible cures for the problem, there has been no consistent government policy. Whatever policies have been adopted usually have been attacked by one group or another.

CRIME IN THE TWENTY-FIRST CENTURY

The issue of crime has been on the national agenda for years now. Virtually all polls taken in the United States in the last few years show that crime is one of the major concerns of the public. Although there is some evidence that certain crime rates have fallen, on average, the public's concern has not been misplaced.

Crime in American History

In every period in the history of this nation, people have voiced their apprehension about crime. Some criminologists argue that crime was probably as frequent around the time of the American Revolution as it is currently. During the Civil War, mob violence and riots erupted in numerous cities. After the Civil War, people in San Francisco were told that "no decent man is in safety to walk the streets after dark; while at all hours, both night and day, his property is jeopardized by incendiarism and burglary."[2] In 1886, *Leslie's Weekly* reported that "Each day we see ghastly records of crime . . . murder seems to have run riot and each citizen asks . . . 'who is safe?'" From 1860 to 1890, the crime rate rose twice as fast as the population.[3] In

---

[2]President's Commission on Law Enforcement and Administration of Justice, *Challenge of Crime in a Free Society* (Washington, D.C.: Government Printing Office, 1967), p. 19.
[3]Richard Shenkman, *Legends, Lies & Cherished Myths of American History* (New York: HarperCollins, 1988), p. 158.

1910, one author stated that "crime, especially in its more violent forms and among the young, is increasing steadily and is threatening to bankrupt the Nation."[4]

From 1900 to the 1930s, social violence and crime increased dramatically. Labor union battles and racial violence were common. Only during the three-decade period from the mid-1930s to the early 1960s did the United States experience, for the first time in its history, stable or slightly declining overall crime rates.

What most Americans are worried about is violent crime. From the mid-1980s to 1994, its rate rose relentlessly, until 1995. Since then, violent crime rates have declined. Going back even further, the murder rate per 100,000 people in 1964 was 4.9, whereas in 1994 it was estimated at 9.3, an almost 100 percent increase. By 1997, however, the murder rate had declined to 7 per 100,000. These nationwide numbers, however, do not tell the full story. Murder rates are between 50 and 100 per 100,000 people in some major U.S. cities including Washington, D.C.; Detroit; New Orleans; St. Louis; and Birmingham.

A disturbing element with respect to crime is the number of serious crimes committed by juveniles. The number of violent crimes committed by juveniles increased dramatically from the mid-1980s to 1994. Since 1995, however, that number has also declined somewhat.

The Prison Population Bomb

Virtually the instant a new prison is built, it is filled, and complaints arise about overcrowding. The state prison population now exceeds 1.2 million. The federal prison population is currently about 103,000. An estimated 700,000 Americans are in jails.

---

[4]President's Commission, *Challenge of Crime*, p. 19.

To help ease over-crowding, inmates at the New York State Prison at Watertown are incarcerated in barracks-style prison blocks.

"Prisons New Growth
Industry"

As the number of arrests and incarcerations in the United States increases, so does the cost of building and operating prisons. Just since 1990, 215 prisons have had to be built to house the burgeoning prison population, bringing the total number of federal and state prisons in this nation to 1,500. An additional 1,000 new prison beds are needed each week. When operational costs are included and construction costs are amortized over the life of a facility, the cost of sentencing one person to one year in jail or prison averages between $25,000 and $40,000. Thus, the annual nationwide cost of building, maintaining, and operating prisons is about $35 billion today.

When imprisonment keeps truly violent felons behind bars longer, it prevents them from committing more crimes. The average predatory street criminal commits fifteen or more crimes each year when not behind bars. But most prisoners are in for a relatively short time and are released on parole early, often because of prison overcrowding. Then many find themselves back in prison because they have violated parole, typically by using illegal drugs. Indeed, of the more than one million people who are arrested each year, the majority are arrested for drug offenses. Given that from twenty to forty million Americans violate one or more drug laws each year, the potential "supply" of prisoners seems virtually without limit. Consequently, it may not matter how many prisons are built; there will still be overcrowding as long as we maintain the same legislation with respect to psychoactive drugs.

ENVIRONMENTAL POLICY

Human actions may create unwanted side effects—including the destruction of the environment and the ecology (the total pattern of environmental relationships). Every day, humans, through their actions, emit pollutants into the air and the water. Each year, the world atmosphere receives twenty million metric tons of sulfur dioxide, eighteen million metric tons of ozone pollutants, and sixty million metric tons of carbon monoxide.

The Government's Response to Air and Water Pollution

The government has been responding to pollution problems since before the American Revolution, when the Massachusetts Bay Colony issued regulations to try to stop the pollution of Boston Harbor. In the nineteenth century, states passed laws controlling water pollution after scientists and medical researchers convinced most policymakers that dumping sewage into drinking and bathing water caused disease. At the national level, the Federal Water Pollution Control Act of 1948 provided research and assistance to the states for pollution-control efforts, but little was done. In 1952, the first state air-pollution law was passed in Oregon. The federal Air Pollution Control Act of 1955 gave some assistance to states and cities. Table 13.1 describes the major environmental legislation in the United States.

The National Environmental Policy Act. The year 1969 marked the start of the most concerted national government involvement in solving pollution problems. In that year, the conflict between oil exploration interests and environmental interests

TABLE 13.1

Major Federal Environmental Legislation

1899 Refuse Act. Made it unlawful to dump refuse into navigable waters without a permit. A 1966 court decision made all industrial wastes subject to this act.

1948 Federal Water Pollution Control Act. Set standards for the treatment of municipal water waste before discharge. Revisions to this act were passed in 1965 and 1967.

1955 Air Pollution Control Act. Authorized federal research programs for air-pollution control.

1963 Clean Air Act. Assisted local and state governments in establishing control programs and coordinated research.

1965 Clean Air Act Amendments. Authorized the establishment of federal standards for automobile exhaust emissions, beginning with 1968 models.

1965 Solid Waste Disposal Act. Provided assistance to local and state governments for control programs and authorized research in this area.

1965 Water Quality Act. Authorized the setting of standards for discharges into waters.

1967 Air Quality Act. Established air-quality regions, with acceptable regional pollution levels. Required local and state governments to implement approved control programs or be subject to federal controls.

1969 National Environmental Policy Act. Established the Council for Environmental Quality (CEQ) for the purpose of coordinating all federal pollution-control programs. Authorized the establishment of the Environmental Protection Agency (EPA) to implement CEQ policies on a case-by-case basis.

1970 Clean Air Act Amendments. Authorized the Environmental Protection Agency to set national air-pollution standards and restricted the discharge of six major pollutants into the lower atmosphere. Automobile manufacturers were required to reduce nitrogen oxide, hydrocarbon, and carbon monoxide emissions by 90 percent (in addition to the 1965 requirements) during the 1970s.

1972 Federal Water Pollution Control Act Amendments. Set national water-quality goal of restoring polluted waters to swimmable, fishable waters by 1983.

1972 Federal Environmental Pesticide Control Act. Required that all pesticides used in interstate commerce be approved and certified as effective for their stated purpose. Required certification that they were harmless to humans, animal life, animal feed, and crops.

1974 Clean Water Act. Originally called the Safe Drinking Water Act, this law set (for the first time) federal standards for water suppliers serving more than twenty-five people, having more than fifteen service connections, or operating more than sixty days a year.

1976 Resource Conservation and Recovery Act. Encouraged the conservation and recovery of resources. Put hazardous waste under government control. Prohibited the opening of new dumping sites. Required that all existing open dumps be closed or upgraded to sanitary landfills by 1983. Set standards for providing technical, financial, and marketing assistance to encourage solid waste management.

1977 Clean Air Act Amendments. Postponed the deadline for automobile emission requirements.

1980 Comprehensive Environmental Response, Compensation, and Liability Act. Established a "Superfund" to clean up toxic waste dumps.

1990 Clean Air Act Amendments. Provided for precise formulas for new gasoline to be burned in the smoggiest cities, further reduction in carbon monoxide and other exhaust emissions in certain areas that still have dangerous ozone levels in the year 2003, and a cap on total emissions of sulfur dioxide from electricity plants. Placed new restrictions on toxic pollutants.

1990 Oil Pollution Act. Established liability for the clean-up of navigable waters after oil-spill disasters.

literally erupted when a Union Oil Company's oil well six miles off the coast of Santa Barbara, California, exploded, releasing 235,000 gallons of crude oil. The result was an oil slick, covering an area of eight hundred square miles, that washed up on the city's beaches and killed plant life, birds, and fish.

Hearings in Congress revealed that the Interior Department did not know which way to go in the energy-environment trade-off. Congress did know, however, and passed the National Environmental Policy Act in 1969. This landmark legislation

A number of urban areas have a landfill problem. The price of landfill has been going up in many major cities for many years. Nationwide, in contrast, the average per-ton price of landfill has gone down. In other words, people in many regions of the United States pay less today to dump their garbage into landfills than they did ten years ago.

established, among other things, the Council for Environmental Quality. Also, it mandated that an **environmental impact statement (EIS)** be prepared to show the costs and benefits of any major federal action that could significantly affect the quality of the environment. The act gave citizens and public-interest groups concerned with the environment a weapon against the unnecessary and inappropriate use of natural resources by the government.

The Clean Air Act of 1990. The most comprehensive government attempt at cleaning up our environment occurred in 1990. After years of lobbying by environmentalists and counterlobbying by industry, the Clean Air Act of 1990 was passed. This act amended the 1970 Clean Air Act, which, among other things, had required a reduction of 90 percent of the amount of carbon monoxide and other pollutants emitted by automobiles. Even though an automobile purchased in 1990 emitted only 4 percent of the pollutants that a 1970 model did, there was more overall air pollution—because so many more automobiles were being driven. The urban ground-level ozone was also as great as it was before any clean-air legislation. The 1990 Clean Air Act required automobile manufacturers to cut new automobiles' exhaust emissions of nitrogen oxide by 60 percent and the emission of other pollutants by 35 percent. By 1998, all new automobiles had to meet this standard. Regulations that will go into effect beginning with 2004 model cars call for nitrogen oxide tailpipe emissions to be cut by nearly 10 percent by 2007. For the first time, sport utility vehicles and light trucks must meet the same emission standards as automobiles.

Stationary sources of air pollution were also made subject to more regulation under the 1990 act. To reduce **acid rain,** the act required 110 of the oldest coal-burning power plants in the United States to cut their emissions by 40 percent by the year 2001. Controls were placed on other factories and businesses in an attempt to reduce ground-level ozone pollution in ninety-six cities to healthful levels by 2005 (except in Los Angeles, which has until 2010 to meet the standards). The act also required that the production of chlorofluorocarbons (CFCs) be stopped completely by the year 2002. CFCs are thought to deplete the ozone layer and increase global warming. CFCs are used in air-conditioning and other refrigeration units.

ECONOMIC POLICY

Nowhere are the principles of public policymaking more obvious than in the area of economic decisions undertaken by the federal government. The president and Congress (and to a growing extent, the judiciary) are faced constantly with questions concerning economic policy. Consider some of them:

1. Should federal income taxes be lowered, given that the federal government no longer has a budget deficit?
2. Should Social Security and Medicare taxes be raised to cover the inevitable growth in the number of recipients for those two programs?
3. Should the Federal Reserve change interest rates to counteract a possible slowing or overheating of the economy?
4. Should Congress restrict imports to improve our balance of trade?

There are no clear-cut answers to such questions. Each policy action carries with it costs and benefits, known as **policy trade-offs.** The costs are typically borne by one group and the benefits enjoyed by another group.

The Politics of Taxes and Subsidies

Taxes are not just given to us from above. Rather, they are voted on by members of Congress. Members of Congress also vote on *subsidies*, which are a type of negative taxes that benefit certain businesses and individuals.

"Shop Till Your Drop
Tax Moratoria"

We begin our analysis with the premise that in the world of taxes and subsidies, the following is always true: *For every action on the part of the government, there will be a reaction on the part of the public.* Eventually, the government will react with another action, followed by the public's further reaction. The **action-reaction syndrome** is a reality that has plagued government policymakers since the beginning of this nation.

The Tax Code, Tax Rates, and Tax Loopholes. An examination of the Internal Revenue Code, encompassing thousands of pages, thousands of sections, and thousands of subsections, gives some indication that our tax system is not very simple. The 1986 Tax Reform Act was supposed to simplify it somewhat, but once you understand the action-reaction principle of taxation, you can predict that whatever simplification occurred in 1986 will be undone over time.

People are not assessed a lump-sum tax each year; each family does not just pay $1,000 or $10,000 or $20,000. Rather, individuals and businesses pay taxes based on tax rates. The higher the tax rate—the action on the part of the government—the greater the public's reaction to that tax rate. Again, it is all a matter of costs and benefits. If the tax rate on all the income you make is 15 percent, that means that any method you can use to reduce your taxable income by one dollar saves you fifteen cents in tax liabilities that you owe the federal government. Therefore, those individuals paying a 15 percent rate have a relatively small incentive to avoid paying taxes. But consider individuals who were faced with a tax rate of 94 percent in the 1940s. They had a tremendous incentive to find legal ways to reduce their taxable incomes. For every dollar of income that was somehow deemed nontaxable, these taxpayers would reduce tax liabilities by 94 cents.

So, individuals and corporations facing high tax rates will always react by making concerted attempts to get Congress to add **loopholes** (legal methods of reducing tax liability) to the tax law that allow them to reduce their taxable incomes. When the Internal Revenue Code imposed very high tax rates on high incomes, it also provided for more loopholes. Special provisions enabled investors in oil and gas wells to reduce their taxable incomes. Loopholes allowed people to shift income from one year to the next. Other loopholes allowed individuals to form corporations outside the United States in order to avoid some taxes completely.

These same principles apply to other interest groups. As long as one group of taxpayers sees a specific benefit from getting the law changed and that benefit means a lot of money per individual, the interest group will aggressively support lobbying activities and the election and reelection of members of Congress who will push for special tax loopholes. In other words, if there are enough benefits to be derived from influencing tax legislation, such influence will be exerted by the affected parties.

Social Security

Closely related to the question of taxes in the United States is the viability of the Social Security system. Social Security taxes came into existence when the Federal Insurance Contribution Act (FICA) was passed in 1935. When the FICA tax was first levied, it was 1 percent of earnings up to $3,000. By 1963, the percentage rate had increased to 3.625 percent. As of 2000, a 6.2 percent rate was imposed on each employee's wages up to a maximum of $76,200 to pay for Social Security. In addition, employers must pay in ("contribute") an equal percentage. Also, there is a combined employer/employee 2.9 percent tax rate assessed for Medicare on all wage income, with no upper limit.

Social Security Is a Regressive Tax. When people with higher incomes pay lower tax rates than people with lower incomes, we call it a **regressive tax.** Social Security taxes are regressive, because once individuals' incomes exceed the maximum taxable amount, they pay no more Social Security taxes. The Medicare portion of the FICA tax is no longer regressive, because it applies to all wage income, but the Social Security portion remains regressive. A person earning a million dollars in a year pays the same total Social Security taxes as a person earning $76,200.

The Grim Future of the Social Security System. In 1996, Senator Bob Kerrey (D., Neb.) stated that "we are damning our children to a very grim future if we continue to hide our heads in the sand." He was referring to the projected bankruptcy of the Social Security system sometime around the year 2010. After that date, Social Security taxes will have to be raised, Social Security benefits will have to be dramatically curtailed, or spending on other federal programs will have to be reduced. (For more on the future of Social Security, see this chapter's *At Issue: Social Security— How Long Will It Last?* on page 328.) Medicare appears to be in even worse shape. As the number of Americans aged sixty-five and older increases from about thirty-three million today to forty million in the year 2010, and to seventy million in the year 2030, Medicare expenditures as a percentage of total national income are expected to grow dramatically, as can be seen in Figure 13.2.

The Politics of Fiscal and Monetary Policy

Changes in the tax code sometimes form part of an overall fiscal policy change. **Fiscal policy** is defined as the use of changes in government expenditures and taxes to alter national economic variables, such as the rate of inflation, the rate of unemployment, the level of interest rates, and the rate of economic growth. The federal government also controls **monetary policy**, defined as the use of changes in the amount of money in circulation to affect interest rates, credit markets, the rate of inflation, and employment. Fiscal policy is the domain of Congress and the president. Monetary policy, as we shall see, is much less under the control of Congress and the president, because the monetary authority in the United States, the Federal Reserve System, or the Fed, is an independent agency not directly controlled by either Congress or the president.

Fiscal Policy: Theory and Reality. The theory behind fiscal policy changes is relatively straightforward: When the economy is going into a recession (a period of rising unemployment), the federal government should stimulate economic activity by increasing government expenditures, by decreasing taxes, or both. When the economy is becoming overheated with rapid increases in employment and rising prices (a condition of inflation), fiscal policy should become contractionary, reducing

FIGURE 13.2

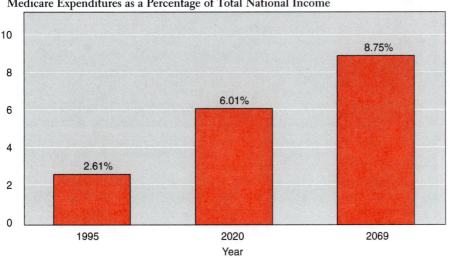

Medicare Expenditures as a Percentage of Total National Income

Social Security— How Long Will It Last?

Although Social Security was never meant as a full and complete retirement program, it has become so over the years for many senior Americans. An increasing percentage of the elderly are relying on Social Security as their main source of income after they reach the age of sixty-five. Given the aging of the American population, it is understandable that many Americans are worried about the future of the Social Security program.

One of the problems with the Social Security system is that people who pay into Social Security think that they are actually paying into a fund, perhaps with their name on it. This is what you do when you pay into a private pension plan. It is not the case, however, with the federal Social Security system. That system is basically a pay-as-you-go transfer system in which those who are working are paying benefits to those who are retired.

Currently, the number of people who are working relative to the number of people who are retiring is declining. Therefore, those who continue to work will have to pay

more of their incomes in Social Security taxes in order to pay for the benefits of those who retire. In the year 2025, when the retirement of the Baby Boomer generation is complete, benefits are projected to cost almost 23 percent of taxable payroll income in the economy. Today this figure is only 14 percent. In today's dollars, that amounts to more than a trillion dollars of additional taxes annually.

As long as Congress continues to increase Social Security benefits while at the same time the labor force grows less rapidly than the number of retirees, financial strain will plague the Social Security system. Social Security also will continue to be a political issue, as well as a focal point of lobbying efforts, particularly by groups that represent older Americans.

Numerous proposals have been made to privatize the Social Security system. One proposal offers a compromise between the current system and full privatization. It would allow individuals to take a portion—2 percentage points—of their Social Security payroll tax and invest it in stocks and bonds to build their own retirement plan.

Politically, the plan for partial privatization has been attacked by a number of groups. Those on the left of the political spectrum argue that many Americans would mismanage their additional after-tax income and not invest wisely. Indeed, several Democrats in the House of Representatives want the opposite: they have argued that the way to keep Social Security working is to increase the Social Security payroll tax. Others contend that after twenty or thirty years of building private Social Security assets, voters would become an investor class less dependent on politicians who write checks and more dependent on policies that create economic growth. Regardless of how the Social Security problem is solved, it must be solved—because there is no way to stop the aging of the population.

FOR CRITICAL ANALYSIS

Future retirement payments under the Social Security system undoubtedly will be less generous than they are today. How will this affect younger Americans' behavior?

government expenditures and increasing taxes. That particular view of fiscal policy was first implemented in the 1930s and again became popular during the 1960s. It was an outgrowth of the economic theories of the British economist John Maynard Keynes. Keynes's ideas, published during the Great Depression of the 1930s, influenced the economic policymakers guiding President Franklin D. Roosevelt's New Deal.

Keynes believed that the forces of supply and demand operated too slowly in a serious recession and that government should step in to stimulate the economy. Such actions thus are guided by **Keynesian economics.** Keynesian (pronounced *kayn*-zeeun) economists believe, for example, that the Great Depression resulted from a serious imbalance in the economy. The public was saving more than usual, and businesses were investing less than usual. According to Keynesian theory, at the beginning of the depression, the government should have filled the gap that was created when businesses began limiting their investments. The government could have done so by increasing government spending or cutting taxes.

Monetary Policy: Politics and Reality. The theory behind monetary policy, like that behind fiscal policy, is relatively straightforward. In periods of recession and high unemployment, we should stimulate the economy by expanding the rate of growth of the money supply. (The money supply is defined loosely as checking account balances and currency.) An easy-money policy is supposed to lower interest rates and induce consumers to spend more and producers to invest more. With rising inflation, we should do the reverse: reduce the rate of growth of the amount of money in circulation. Interest rates should rise, choking off some consumer spending and some business investment. But the world is never so simple as the theory we use to explain it. If the nation experiences stagflation—rising inflation and rising unemployment— expansionary monetary policy (expanding the rate of growth of the money supply) will lead to even more inflation. Ultimately, the more money there is in circulation, the higher prices will be—there will be inflation.

The Monetary Authority—The Federal Reserve System. Congress established our modern central bank, the Federal Reserve System, in 1913. It is governed by a board of governors consisting of seven members, including the very powerful chairperson. All of the governors, including the chairperson, are nominated by the president and approved by the Senate. Their appointments are for fourteen years.

Through the Federal Reserve System, called the Fed, and its **Federal Open Market Committee (FOMC),** decisions about monetary policy are made eight times a year. The Board of Governors of the Federal Reserve System is independent. The

Wall Street during the stock market crash of 1929. Another spectacular drop in the stock market occurred in October 1987. Stock prices tumbled yet again in the fall of 1998.

president can attempt to convince the board, and Congress can threaten to merge the Fed with the Treasury, but as long as the Fed retains its independence, its chairperson and governors can do what they please. Hence, talking about "the president's monetary policy" or "Congress's monetary policy" is inaccurate. To be sure, the Fed has, on occasion, yielded to presidential pressure, and for a while the Fed's chairperson felt constrained to follow a congressional resolution requiring him to report monetary targets over each six-month period. But now, more than ever before, the Fed remains one of the truly independent sources of economic power in the government.

Monetary Policy and Lags. Monetary policy does not suffer from the same lengthy time lags as fiscal policy does, because the Fed can put its policy into effect within a very short period. Nonetheless, researchers have estimated that it takes almost fourteen months for a change in monetary policy to become effective, measured from the time the economy either slows down or speeds up too much to the time the economy feels the policy change.[5] This means that by the time monetary policy goes into effect, a different policy might be appropriate.

In the 1990s, few commentators were able to complain about monetary policy. Inflation had almost disappeared by the end of the decade, which also saw the unemployment rate drop to its lowest level in thirty-five years. The only real question today is the following: How much longer will low unemployment and low inflation coexist?

THE PUBLIC DEBT AND THE DISAPPEARING DEFICIT

"Federal Reserve Holds Theory"

Until the late 1990s, the federal government had run a deficit—spent more than it received—in every year except two since 1960. Every time a budget deficit occurred, the federal government issued debt instruments in the form of **U.S. Treasury bonds.** The sale of these bonds to corporations, private individuals, pension plans, foreign governments, foreign businesses, and foreign individuals adds to the **public debt,** or

[5]Robert Gordon, *Macroeconomics*, 7th ed. (New York: HarperCollins, 1996), p. 431.

Alan Greenspan, the chairman of the Federal Reserve. The Federal Reserve is responsible for our nation's monetary policy. Greenspan is often called to testify before various congressional committees. He finds himself frequently in the "hot seat" if interest rates are rising.

national debt, defined as the total amount owed by the federal government. Thus, the relationship between the annual federal government budget deficit and the public debt is clear: If the public debt is, say, $4 trillion this year and the federal budget deficit is $150 billion during the year, then at the end of the year the public debt will be $4.15 trillion. Table 13.2 shows what has happened to the net public debt over time.

It would seem that the nation increasingly has been mortgaging its future. But this table does not take into account two important variables: inflation and increases in population. In Figure 13.3 on the next page, we correct the net public debt for inflation and increases in population. The per capita net public debt in so-called **constant dollars** (dollars corrected for inflation) reached its peak, as you might expect, during World War II and fell steadily thereafter until the mid-1970s. Since then, except for a slight reduction in 1980, it continued to rise until only very recently.

Is the Public Debt a Burden?

We often hear about the burden of the public debt. Some argue that the government eventually is going to go bankrupt, but that, of course, cannot happen. As long as the government has the ability to pay the interest payments on the public debt through taxation, it will never go bankrupt. What happens is that when Treasury bonds come due, they are simply "rolled over." That is, if a $1 million Treasury bond comes due today, the U.S. Treasury pays it off and sells another $1 million bond.

What about the interest payments? Interest payments are paid by taxes, so what we are really talking about is taxing some people to pay interest to others who loaned money to the government. This cannot really be called a burden to all of society. There is one hitch, however. Not all of the interest payments are paid to Americans. A significant amount is paid to foreigners, because foreigners own over 38 percent of the public debt. This raises the fear of too much foreign control of U.S. assets. So it is no longer the case that we "owe it all to ourselves."

The Problem of "Crowding Out"

Although it may be true that we owe the public debt to ourselves (except for what is owed to foreigners), another issue is involved. A large public debt is made up of a

TABLE 13.2

Net Public Debt of the Federal Government

YEAR	TOTAL (BILLIONS OF CURRENT DOLLARS)	YEAR	TOTAL (BILLIONS OF CURRENT DOLLARS)
1940	$ 42.7	1993	$3,247.5
1945	235.2	1994	3,432.1
1950	219.0	1995	3,603.4
1960	237.2	1996	3,747.1
1970	284.9	1997	3,900.0
1980	709.3	1998	3,870.0
1990	2,410.1	1999	3,840.0
1992	2,998.6	2000	3,747.3*

*Estimate.

SOURCE: U.S. Office of Management and Budget.

FIGURE 13.3

Per Capita Public Debt of the United States in Constant 1992 Dollars

If we correct the public debt for intergovernmental borrowing, the growth in the population, and changes in the price level (inflation), we obtain a graph that shows the per capita net public debt in the United States expressed in constant 1992 dollars. The public debt reached its peak during World War II and then dropped consistently until about 1975. It then grew steadily—until the late 1990s.

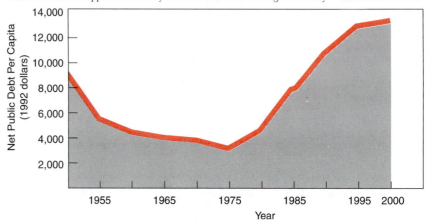

series of annual federal government budget deficits. Each time the federal government runs a deficit, we know that it must go into the financial marketplace to borrow the money. This process, in which the U.S. Treasury sells U.S. Treasury bonds, is called **public debt financing.** Public debt financing, in effect, "crowds out" private borrowing. Consider that to borrow, say, $100 billion, the federal government must bid for loanable funds in the marketplace, just as any business does. It bids for those loanable funds by offering to pay higher interest rates. Consequently, interest rates are increased when the federal government runs large deficits and borrows money to cover them. Higher interest rates can stifle or slow business investment, which reduces the rate of economic growth.

What Happened to the "Permanent" Federal Budget Deficit?

As late as 1997, commentators frequently remarked that the federal budget deficit was a "permanent" part of our economic landscape. They argued that Congress and the president were never able to "spend within their means." Just about every year since the mid-1980s, somebody in Congress introduced a constitutional amendment to balance the federal budget.

A funny thing happened on the way to the forum—the federal budget deficit virtually disappeared by the end of 1998, and the budget actually started to show a surplus. Did this happen because Congress saw evil in its ways and therefore reduced its rate of spending increases? Hardly. Today, federal social spending is at record levels, both in inflation-corrected dollars and as a percentage of gross domestic product (GDP).

In the past ten years, federal domestic expenditures, after taking inflation into account, have increased by 35 percent. In the 1960s, nondefense outlays expressed as a percentage of GDP were 10 percent, rising to 15 percent in the 1970s. Today, these expenditures constitute almost 18 percent of GDP. Certainly, the Republicans did not show themselves to be fiscal conservatives after they took control of Congress in 1995. In their first three budgets (for fiscal years 1996 through 1998), they increased domestic spending by $183 billion, compared to the $155 billion increase in the three years prior to the so-called Republican revolution.

In 1997, the Republicans and Democrats reached a "historic" budget deal with President Clinton's blessing. In inflation-corrected dollars, the $1.7 trillion budget for fiscal year 1999 represented more spending than the federal budgets spent cumulatively from 1800 to 1940.

Obviously, if spending has not decreased, there is only one way to reduce or avoid a federal budget deficit—through increased taxes. That is exactly what has happened. Look at Figure 13.4. There you see that taxpayers, on average, are paying more out of their family budgets to both federal and state and local governments than ever before. Looked at from another point of view, the federal government is now collecting over 20 percent of annual GDP as taxes. This figure was matched only one time before in the history of the United States—at the height of World War II.

FIGURE 13.4

The Budget Is Balanced through Higher Taxes

In the last three decades, the "tax bite" for the typical family budget has increased steadily.

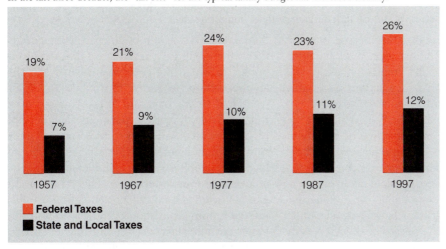

SOURCE: The Tax Foundation, based on a 1997 study using data collected by the Internal Revenue Service, the Department of Commerce, and the U.S. Census Bureau.

KEY TERMS

acid rain 325

action-reaction syndrome 325

constant dollars 331

domestic policy 314

earned-income tax credit (EITC) program 318

environmental impact statement (EIS) 324

Federal Open Market Committee (FOMC) 330

fiscal policy 327

food stamps 318

CHAPTER SUMMARY

1 Domestic policy consists of all of the laws, government planning, and government actions that affect the lives of American citizens. Policies are created in response to public problems or public demand for government action. Major policy problems now facing this nation are poverty and welfare, crime, and the environment.

2 The policymaking process is initiated when policymakers become aware—through the media or from their constituents—of a problem that needs to be addressed by the legislature and the president. The process of policymaking includes five steps: agenda building, agenda formulation, agenda adoption, agenda implementation, and agenda evaluation. All policy actions necessarily result in both costs and benefits for society.

3 In spite of the wealth of the United States, a significant number of Americans live in poverty or are homeless. The low-income poverty threshold represents an absolute measure of income needed to maintain a specified standard of living as of 1963, with the constant-dollar, or purchasing-power, value increased year by year in relation to the general increase in prices. The official poverty level is based on pretax income, including cash, and does not take into consideration in-kind subsidies (food stamps, housing vouchers, and so on).

4 While the overall rate of violent crime has been declining since 1995, crime rates continue to rise in certain areas. Drug dealing and drug abusers have contributed significantly not only to escalating crime rates but also to overcrowded prisons. The prison "population bomb" presents a major challenge to today's policymakers.

5 Pollution problems continue to plague the United States and the world. Since the nineteenth century, a number of significant federal acts have been passed in an attempt to curb the pollution of our environment. The National Environmental Policy Act of 1969 established the Council for Environmental Quality. That act also mandated that environmental impact statements be prepared for all legislation or major federal actions that might significantly affect the quality of the environment.

6 In the area of taxes and subsidies (negative taxes), policymakers have long had to contend with what is known as the action-reaction syndrome. For every action on the part of the government, there will be a reaction on the part of the public, to which the government will react with another action, to which the public will again react, and so on. In regard to taxes, as a general rule, individuals and corporations that pay the highest tax rates will react to those rates by pressuring Congress into creating exceptions and tax loopholes (loopholes allow high-income earners to reduce their taxable incomes). This action on the part of Congress results in a reaction from another interest group—consisting of those who want the rich to pay more taxes. In response, higher tax rates will be imposed on the rich, and so the cycle continues.

7 Closely related to the question of taxes is the viability of the Social Security system. As the number of people who are working relative to the number of people who are retiring declines, those who work will have to pay more Social Security taxes to pay for the benefits of those who retire.

8 Fiscal policy is the use of changes in government expenditures and taxes to alter national economic variables, such as the rate of inflation or unemployment. Monetary policy is the use of changes in the amount of money in circulation so as to affect interest rates, credit markets, the rate of inflation, and unemployment. Fiscal policy was made popular by the British economist John Maynard Keynes, whose ideas influenced Franklin D. Roosevelt's New Deal legislation, as well as the fiscal policies of the government during the 1960s. Keynesian fiscal policy economics usually means increasing government spending during recessionary periods and increasing taxes during inflationary boom periods. The problem with fiscal policy and monetary policy is the lag between the time a problem occurs in the economy and the time when policy changes are actually felt in the economy.

9 Whenever the federal government spends more than it receives, it runs a deficit. The deficit is met by U.S. Treasury borrowing. This adds to the public debt of the federal government. Although the public debt has grown dramatically, when corrected for increases in population and inflation, it fell from the end of World War II to the middle of the 1970s. Since then, it has increased almost to its previous level at the height of World War II. Those who oppose large increases in government spending argue that one effect of the federal deficit is the crowding out of private investment. The federal budget deficit virtually disappeared by the late 1990s, however, and the budget actually has showed a surplus in recent years.

10 As government spending continues to increase, so do taxes—to pay for the increased spending. Federal taxes, as a percentage of gross domestic product, are now as high as they were during World War II. Due to the aging U.S. population, unless the government reduces spending on other programs, increased spending on Medicare and Social Security probably will lead to further budget deficits.

SELECTED PRINT AND ELECTRONIC RESOURCES

Suggested Readings

Friedman, Milton, and Walter Heller. *Monetary versus Fiscal Policy*. New York: Norton, 1969. This is a classic presentation of the pros and cons of monetary and fiscal policy given by a noninterventionist (Friedman) and an advocate of federal government intervention in the economy (Heller).

Miller, Roger LeRoy, et al. *The Economics of Public Issues*. 10th ed. Reading, Mass.: Addison-Wesley, 1999. Chapters 3, 4, 8, 14–18, and 24–27 are especially useful. The authors use short essays of three to seven pages to explain the purely economic aspects of numerous social problems, including the war on drugs, the environment, and poverty.

The President's Council of Economic Advisers. *Economic Report of the President*. Washington, D.C.: U.S. Government Printing Office, published annually. This volume contains a wealth of details concerning current monetary and fiscal policy and what is happening to the economy.

Weaver, Carolyn. *The Frayed Social Contract: Why Social Security Is in Trouble and How It Can Be Fixed*. Washington, D.C.: The American Enterprise Institute, 1998. This book offers a candid look at the future of Social Security and examines some possible alternatives.

Media Resources

America's Promise: Who's Entitled to What?—A four-part series that examines the current state of welfare reform and its impact on immigrant and other populations.

Crimes and Punishments: A History—A controversial documentary that traces the often brutal history of criminal punishment from the medieval era through today.

Rollover—A 1981 film starring Jane Fonda as an ex-film star who inherits a multimillion-dollar empire when her husband is mysteriously murdered and Kris Kristofferson as a financial troubleshooter who helps her try to save the company. The film offers an insider's view of the politics of currency crises.

Young Criminals, Adult Punishment—An ABC program that examines the issue of whether the harsh sentences given out to adult criminals, including capital punishment, should also be applied to young violent offenders.

LOGGING ON

You can find further information on most of the issues discussed in this chapter at Project VoteSmart's Web site. Go to

http://www.
vote-smart.org/issues

For current statistics on poverty in the United States, go to

http://www.census.gov

The National Governors Association offers information on the current status of welfare reform among the various states at

http://www.nga.org

The Federal Bureau of Investigation offers information about crime rates at its Web site:

http://www.fbi.gov

You can also find statistics and other information on crime in the United States at the Web site of the Bureau of Justice Statistics. Go to

http://www.ojp.usdoj.gov/bjs

You can find a large online library of materials relating to drug policy at

http://www.druglibrary.org

To find more information on poverty in the United States and the latest research on this topic, go to the site of the Institute for Research on Poverty at

http://www.ssc.wisc.edu/irp

You can keep up with actions taken by the Federal Reserve by checking the home page of the Federal Reserve Bank of San Francisco at

http://www.frbsf.org

For further information on Social Security, access the Social Security Administration's home page at

http://www.ssa.gov

USING THE INTERNET FOR POLITICAL ANALYSIS

Take your turn at proposing a federal budget, balanced or not. Check out the Web site for the National Budget Simulation at

http://garnet.berkeley.edu:6997

Play the game at this Web site, which allows you to simulate budget cuts by categories of spending. You will decide what should be cut and see what difference it makes in the overall budget. This site provides other budget information through the Economic Democracy Information Network.

If you would like more input into the budget, you might access the Web site for the Concord Coalition at

http://www.
concordcoalition.org

There, you can take part in a poll on what to do with any budget surplus in the coming years.

APPENDIX A

The Declaration of Independence

In Congress, July 4, 1776

A Declaration by the Representatives of the United States of America, in General Congress assembled. When in the Course of human Events, it becomes necessary for one People to dissolve the Political Bands which have connected them with another, and to assume among the Powers of the Earth, the separate and equal Station to which the Laws of Nature and of Nature's God entitle them, a decent Respect to the Opinions of Mankind requires that they should declare the causes which impel them to the Separation.

We hold these Truths to be self-evident, that all Men are created equal, that they are endowed by their Creator with certain unalienable Rights, that among these are Life, Liberty, and the Pursuit of Happiness—That to secure these Rights, Governments are instituted among Men, deriving their just Powers from the Consent of the Governed, that whenever any Form of Government becomes destructive of these Ends, it is the Right of the People to alter or to abolish it, and to institute new Government, laying its Foundation on such Principles, and organizing its Powers in such Forms, as to them shall seem most likely to effect their Safety and Happiness. Prudence, indeed, will dictate that Governments long established should not be changed for light and transient Causes; and accordingly all Experience hath shewn, that Mankind are more disposed to suffer, while Evils are sufferable, than to right themselves by abolishing the Forms to which they are accustomed. But when a long Train of Abuses and Usurpations, pursuing invariably the same Object, evinces a Design to reduce them under absolute Despotism, it is their Right, it is their Duty, to throw off such Government, and to provide new Guards for their future Security. Such has been the patient Sufferance of these Colonies; and such is now the Necessity which constrains them to alter their former Systems of Government. The History of the present King of Great-Britain is a History of repeated Injuries and Usurpations, all having in direct Object the Establishment of an absolute Tyranny over these States. To prove this, let Facts be submitted to a candid World.

He has refused his Assent to Laws, the most wholesome and necessary for the public Good.

He has forbidden his Governors to pass Laws of immediate and pressing Importance, unless suspended in their Operation till his Assent should be obtained; and when so suspended, he has utterly neglected to attend to them.

He has refused to pass other Laws for the Accommodation of large Districts of People, unless those People would relinquish the Right of Representation in the Legislature, a Right inestimable to them, and formidable to Tyrants only.

He has called together Legislative Bodies at Places unusual, uncomfortable, and distant from the Depository of their Public Records, for the sole Purpose of fatiguing them into Compliance with his Measures.

He has dissolved Representative Houses repeatedly, for opposing with manly Firmness his Invasions on the Rights of the People.

He has refused for a long Time, after such Dissolutions, to cause others to be elected; whereby the Legislative Powers, incapable of Annihilation, have returned to the People at large for their exercise; the State remaining in the mean time exposed to all the Dangers of Invasion from without, and Convulsions within.

He has endeavoured to prevent the Population of these States; for that Purpose obstructing the Laws for Naturalization of Foreigners; refusing to pass others to encourage their Migrations hither, and raising the Conditions of new Appropriations of Lands.

He has obstructed the Administration of Justice, by refusing his Assent to Laws for establishing Judiciary Powers.

He has made Judges dependent on his Will alone, for the Tenure of their offices, and the Amount and payment of their Salaries.

He has erected a Multitude of new Offices, and sent hither Swarms of Officers to harrass our People, and eat out their Substance.

He has kept among us, in Times of Peace, Standing Armies, without the consent of our Legislatures.

He has affected to render the Military independent of, and superior to the Civil Power.

He has combined with others to subject us to a Jurisdiction foreign to our Constitution, and unacknowledged by our Laws; giving his Assent to their Acts of pretended Legislation:

For quartering large Bodies of Armed Troops among us:

For protecting them, by a mock Trial, from Punishment for any Murders which they should commit on the Inhabitants of these States:

For cutting off our Trade with all Parts of the World:

For imposing Taxes on us without our Consent:

For depriving us, in many cases, of the Benefits of Trial by Jury:

For transporting us beyond Seas to be tried for pretended Offences:

For abolishing the free System of English Laws in a neighbouring Province, establishing therein an arbitrary Government, and enlarging its Boundaries, so as to render it at once an Example and fit Instrument for introducing the same absolute Rule into these Colonies:

For taking away our Charters, abolishing our most valuable Laws, and altering fundamentally the Forms of our Governments:

For suspending our own Legislatures, and declaring themselves invested with Power to legislate for us in all Cases whatsoever.

He has abdicated Government here, by declaring us out of his Protection and waging War against us.

He has plundered our Seas, ravaged our Coasts, burnt our towns, and destroyed the Lives of our People.

He is, at this Time, transporting large Armies of foreign Mercenaries to compleat the works of Death, Desolation, and Tyranny, already begun with circumstances of Cruelty and Perfidy, scarcely paralleled in the most barbarous Ages, and totally unworthy the Head of a civilized Nation.

He has constrained our fellow Citizens taken Captive on the high Seas to bear Arms against their Country, to become the Executioners of their Friends and Brethren, or to fall themselves by their Hands.

He has excited domestic Insurrections amongst us, and has endeavoured to bring on the Inhabitants of our Frontiers, the merciless Indian Savages, whose known Rule of Warfare, is an undistinguished Destruction, of all Ages, Sexes and Conditions.

In every state of these Oppressions we have Petitioned for Redress in the most humble Terms: Our repeated Petitions have been answered only by repeated Injury. A Prince, whose Character is thus marked by every act which may define a Tyrant, is unfit to be the Ruler of a free People.

Nor have we been wanting in Attentions to our British Brethren. We have warned them from Time to Time of Attempts by their Legislature to extend an unwarrantable Jurisdiction over us. We have reminded them of the Circumstances of our Emigration and Settlement here. We have appealed to their native Justice and Magnanimity, and we have conjured them by the Ties of our common Kindred to disavow these Usurpations, which, would inevitably interrupt our Connections and Correspondence. They too have been deaf to the Voice of Justice and of Consanguinity. We must, therefore, acquiesce in the Necessity, which denounces our Separation, and hold them, as we hold the rest of Mankind, Enemies in War, in Peace, Friends.

We, therefore, the Representatives of the UNITED STATES OF AMERICA, in General Congress Assembled, appealing to the Supreme Judge of the World for the Rectitude of our Intentions, do, in the Name, and by the Authority of the good People of these Colonies, solemnly Publish and Declare, That these United Colonies are, and of Right ought to be, Free and Independent States; that they are absolved from all Allegiance to the British Crown, and that all political Connection between them and the State of Great-Britain, is and ought to be totally dissolved; and that as Free and Independent States, they have full Power to levy War, conclude Peace, contract Alliances, establish Commerce, and to do all other Acts and Things which Independent States may of right do. And for the support of this declaration, with a firm Reliance on the Protection of divine Providence, we mutually pledge to each other our lives, our Fortunes, and our sacred Honor.

The Constitution of the United States of America*

The Preamble

We the People of the United States, in Order to form a more perfect Union, establish Justice, insure domestic Tranquility, provide for the common defence, promote the general Welfare, and secure the Blessings of Liberty to ourselves and our Posterity, do ordain and establish this Constitution for the United States of America.

The Preamble declares that "We the People" are the authority for the Constitution (unlike the Articles of Confederation, which derived their authority from the states). The Preamble also sets out the purposes of the Constitution.

Article I. (Legislative Branch)

The first part of the Constitution is called Article 1; it deals with the organization and powers of the lawmaking branch of the national government, the Congress.

Section 1. Legislative Powers

All legislative Powers herein granted shall be vested in a Congress of the United States, which shall consist of a Senate and House of Representatives.

Section 2. House of Representatives

Clause 1: *Composition and Election of Members.* The House of Representatives shall be composed of Members chosen every second Year by the People of the several States, and the Electors in each State shall have the Qualifications requisite for Electors of the most numerous Branch of the State Legislature.

Each state has the power to decide who may vote for members of Congress. Within each state, those who may vote for state legislators may also vote for members of the House of Representatives (and, under the Seventeenth Amendment, for U.S. senators). When the Constitution was written, nearly all states limited voting rights to white male property owners or taxpayers at least twenty-one years old. Subsequent amendments granted voting power to African American men, all women, and eighteen-year-olds.

Clause 2: *Qualifications.* No Person shall be a Representative who shall not have attained to the Age of twenty five Years, and been seven Years a Citizen of the United States, and who shall not, when elected, be an Inhabitant of that State in which he shall be chosen.

Each member of the House must (1) be at least twenty-five years old, (2) have been a U.S. citizen for at least seven years, and (3) be a resident of the state in which she or he is elected.

Clause 3: *Apportionment of Representatives and Direct Taxes.* Representatives [and direct Taxes][1] shall be apportioned among the several States which may be included within this Union, according to their respective Numbers [which shall be determined by adding to the whole Number of free Persons, including those bound to Service for a Term of Years, and excluding Indians not taxed, three fifths of all other Persons].[2] The actual Enumeration shall be made within three Years after the first Meeting of the Congress of the United States, and within every subsequent Term of ten Years, in such Manner as they shall by Law direct. The Number of Representatives shall not exceed one for every thirty Thousand, but each State shall have at Least one Representative; and until such enumeration shall be made, the State of New Hampshire shall be entitled to chuse three, Massachusetts eight, Rhode Island and Providence Plantations one, Connecticut five, New York six, New Jersey four, Pennsylvania eight, Delaware one, Maryland six, Virginia ten, North Carolina five, South Carolina five, and Georgia three.

A state's representation in the House is based on the size of its population. Population is counted in each decade's census, after which Congress reapportions House seats. Since

---

*The spelling, capitalization, and punctuation of the original have been retained here. Brackets indicate passages that have been altered by amendments to the Constitution.

[1]Modified by the Sixteenth Amendment.
[2]Modified by the Fourteenth Amendment.

early in the twentieth century, the number of seats has been limited to 435.

Clause 4: *Vacancies.*   When vacancies happen in the Representation from any State, the Executive Authority thereof shall issue Writs of Election to fill such Vacancies.

The "Executive Authority" is the state's governor. When a vacancy occurs in the House, the governor calls a special election to fill it.

Clause 5: *Officers and Impeachment.*   The House of Representatives shall chuse their Speaker and other Officers; and shall have the sole Power of Impeachment.

The power to impeach is the power to accuse. In this case, it is the power to accuse members of the executive or judicial branch of wrongdoing or abuse of power. Once a bill of impeachment is issued, the Senate holds the trial.

Section 3. The Senate
Clause 1: *Term and Number of Members.*   The Senate of the United States shall be composed of two Senators from each State [chosen by the Legislature thereof],[3] for six Years; and each Senator shall have one Vote.

Every state has two senators, each of whom serves for six years and has one vote in the upper chamber. Since the Seventeenth Amendment in 1913, all senators are elected directly by voters of the state during the regular election.

Clause 2: *Classification of Senators.*   Immediately after they shall be assembled in Consequence of the first Election, they shall be divided as equally as may be into three Classes. The Seats of the Senators of the first Class shall be vacated at the Expiration of the second Year, of the second Class at the Expiration of the fourth Year, and of the third Class at the Expiration of the sixth Year, so that one third may be chosen every second Year; [and if Vacancies happen by Resignation, or otherwise, during the Recess of the Legislature of any State, the Executive thereof may make temporary Appointments until the next Meeting of the Legislature, which shall then fill such Vacancies].[4]

One-third of the Senate's seats are open to election every two years (unlike the House, all of whose members are elected simultaneously).

Clause 3: *Qualifications.*   No Person shall be a Senator who shall not have attained to the Age of thirty Years, and been nine Years a Citizen of the United States, and who shall not, when elected, be an Inhabitant of that State for

which he shall be chosen.

Every senator must be at least thirty years old, a citizen of the United States for a minimum of nine years, and a resident of the state in which he or she is elected.

Clause 4: *The Role of the Vice President.*   The Vice President of the United States shall be President of the Senate, but shall have no Vote, unless they be equally divided.

The vice president presides over meetings of the Senate but cannot vote unless there is a tie. The Constitution gives no other official duties to the vice president.

Clause 5: *Other Officers.*   The Senate shall chuse their other Officers, and also a President pro tempore, in the Absence of the Vice President, or when he shall exercise the Office of President of the United States.

The Senate votes for one of its members to preside when the vice president is absent. This person is usually called the president pro tempore because of the temporary situation of the position.

Clause 6: *Impeachment Trials.*   The Senate shall have the sole Power to try all Impeachments. When sitting for that Purpose, they shall be on Oath or Affirmation. When the President of the United States is tried, the Chief Justice shall preside: And no Person shall be convicted without the Concurrence of two thirds of the Members present.

The Senate conducts trials of officials that the House impeaches. The Senate sits as a jury, with the vice president presiding if the president is not on trial.

Clause 7: *Penalties for Conviction.*   Judgment in Cases of Impeachment shall not extend further than to removal from Office, and disqualification to hold and enjoy any Office of honor, Trust, or Profit under the United States: but the Party convicted shall nevertheless be liable and subject to Indictment, Trial, Judgment, and Punishment, according to Law.

On conviction of impeachment charges, the Senate can only force an official to leave office and prevent him or her from holding another office in the federal government. The individual, however, can still be tried in a regular court.

Section 4. Congressional Elections: Times, Manner, and Places
Clause 1: *Elections.*   The Times, Places and Manner of holding Elections for Senators and Representatives, shall be prescribed in each State by the Legislature thereof; but the Congress may at any time by Law make or alter such Regulations, except as to the Places of chusing Senators.

---

[3]Repealed by the Seventeenth Amendment.
[4]Modified by the Seventeenth Amendment.

Congress set the Tuesday after the first Monday in November in even-numbered years as the date for congressional elections. In states with more than one seat in the House, Congress requires that representatives be elected from districts within each state. Under the Seventeenth Amendment, senators are elected at the same places as other officials.

Clause 2: Sessions of Congress. [The Congress shall assemble at least once in every Year, and such Meeting shall be on the first Monday in December, unless they shall by Law appoint a different Day.][5]

Congress has to meet every year at least once. The regular session now begins at noon on January 3 of each year, subsequent to the Twentieth Amendment, unless Congress passes a law to fix a different date. Congress stays in session until its members vote to adjourn. Additionally, the president may call a special session.

Section 5. Powers and Duties of the Houses
Clause 1: Admitting Members and Quorum. Each House shall be the Judge of the Elections, Returns, and Qualifications of its own Members, and a Majority of each shall constitute a Quorum to do Business; but a smaller Number may adjourn from day to day, and may be authorized to compel the Attendance of absent Members, in such Manner, and under such Penalties as each House may provide.

Each chamber may exclude or refuse to seat a member-elect.

The quorum rule requires that 218 members of the House and 51 members of the Senate be present in order to conduct business. This rule is normally not enforced in the handling of routine matters.

Clause 2: Rules and Discipline of Members. Each House may determine the Rules of its Proceedings, punish its Members for disorderly Behaviour, and, with the Concurrence of two thirds, expel a Member.

The House and the Senate may adopt their own rules to guide their proceedings. Each may also discipline its members for conduct that is deemed unacceptable. No member may be expelled without a two-thirds majority vote in favor of expulsion.

Clause 3: Keeping a Record. Each House shall keep a Journal of its Proceedings, and from time to time publish the same, excepting such Parts as may in their Judgment require Secrecy; and the Yeas and Nays of the Members of either House on any question shall, at the Desire of one fifth of those Present, be entered on the Journal.

[5]Changed by the Twentieth Amendment.

The journals of the two houses are published at the end of each session of Congress.

Clause 4: Adjournment. Neither House, during the Session of Congress, shall, without the Consent of the other, adjourn for more than three days, nor to any other Place than that in which the two Houses shall be sitting.

Congress has the power to determine when and where to meet, provided, however, that both houses meet in the same city. Neither house may recess in excess of three days without the consent of the other.

Section 6. Rights of Members
Clause 1: Compensation and Privileges. The Senators and Representatives shall receive a Compensation for their services, to be ascertained by Law, and paid out of the Treasury of the United States. They shall in all Cases, except Treason, Felony and Breach of the Peace, be privileged from Arrest during their Attendance at the Session of their respective Houses, and in going to and returning from the same; and for any Speech or Debate in either House, they shall not be questioned in any other Place.

Congressional salaries are to be paid by the U.S. Treasury rather than by the members' respective states. The original salaries were $6 per day; in 1857 they were $3,000 per year. Both representatives and senators currently are paid $136,700 each year.

Treason is defined in Article III, Section 3. A felony is any serious crime. A breach of the peace is any indictable offense less than treason or a felony. Members cannot be arrested for things they say during speeches and debates in Congress. This immunity applies to the Capitol Building itself and not to their private lives.

Clause 2: Restrictions. No Senator or Representative shall, during the Time for which he was elected, be appointed to any civil Office under the Authority of the United States, which shall have been created, or the Emoluments whereof shall have been encreased during such time; and no Person holding any Office under the United States, shall be a Member of either House during his Continuance in Office.

During the term for which a member was elected, he or she cannot concurrently accept another federal government position.

Section 7. Legislative Powers: Bills and Resolutions
Clause 1: Revenue Bills. All Bills for raising Revenue shall originate in the House of Representatives; but the Senate may propose or concur with Amendments as on other Bills.

All tax and appropriation bills for raising money have to originate in the House of Representatives. The Senate, though, often amends such bills and may even substitute an entirely different bill.

Clause 2: The Presidential Veto. Every Bill which shall have passed the House of Representatives and the Senate, shall, before it becomes a Law, be presented to the President of the United States; If he approve he shall sign it, but if not he shall return it, with his Objections to the House in which it shall have originated, who shall enter the Objections at large on their Journal, and proceed to reconsider it. If after such Reconsideration two thirds of that House shall agree to pass the Bill, it shall be sent together with the Objections, to the other House, by which it shall likewise be reconsidered, and if approved by two thirds of that House, it shall become a Law. But in all such Cases the Votes of both Houses shall be determined by Yeas and Nays, and the Names of the Persons voting for and against the Bill shall be entered on the Journal of each House respectively. If any Bill shall not be returned by the President within ten Days (Sundays excepted) after it shall have been presented to him, the Same shall be a Law, in like Manner as if he had signed it, unless the Congress by their Adjournment prevent its Return in which Case it shall not be a Law.

When Congress sends the president a bill, he or she can sign it (in which case it becomes law) or send it back to the house in which it originated. If it is sent back, a two-thirds majority of each house must pass it again for it to become law. If the president neither signs it nor sends it back within ten days, it becomes law anyway, unless Congress adjourns in the meantime.

Clause 3: Actions on Other Matters. Every Order, Resolution, or Vote to which the Concurrence of the Senate and House of Representatives may be necessary (except on a question of Adjournment) shall be presented to the President of the United States; and before the Same shall take Effect, shall be approved by him, or being disapproved by him, shall be repassed by two thirds of the Senate and House of Representatives, according to the Rules and Limitations prescribed in the Case of a Bill.

The president must either sign or veto everything that Congress passes, except votes to adjourn and resolutions not having the force of law.

Section 8. The Powers of Congress
Clause 1: Taxing. The Congress shall have Power To lay and collect Taxes, Duties, Imposts and Excises, to pay the Debts and provide for the common Defence and general Welfare of the United States; but all Duties, Imposts and Excises shall be uniform throughout the United States;

Duties are taxes on imports and exports. Impost is a generic term for tax. Excises are taxes on the manufacture, sale, or use of goods.

Clause 2: Borrowing. To borrow Money on the credit of the United States;

Congress has the power to borrow money, which is normally carried out through the sale of U.S. treasury bonds on which interest is paid. Note that the Constitution places no limit on the amount of government borrowing.

Clause 3: Regulation of Commerce. To regulate Commerce with foreign Nations, and among the several States, and with the Indian Tribes;

This is the commerce clause, which gives to the Congress the power to regulate interstate and foreign trade. Much of the activity of Congress is based on this clause.

Clause 4: Naturalization and Bankruptcy. To establish a uniform Rule of Naturalization, and uniform Laws on the subject of Bankruptcies throughout the United States;

Only Congress may determine how aliens can become citizens of the United States. Congress may make laws with respect to bankruptcy.

Clause 5: Money and Standards. To coin Money, regulate the Value thereof, and of foreign Coin, and fix the Standard of Weights and Measures;

Congress mints coins and prints and circulates paper money. Congress can establish uniform measures of time, distance, weight, and so on. In 1838, Congress adopted the English system of weights and measurements as our national standard.

Clause 6: Punishing Counterfeiters. To provide for the Punishment of counterfeiting the Securities and current Coin of the United States;

Congress has the power to punish those who copy American money and pass it off as real. Currently, the fine is up to $5,000 and/or imprisonment for up to fifteen years.

Clause 7: Roads and Post Offices. To establish Post Offices and post Roads;

Post roads include all routes over which mail is carried—highways, railways, waterways, and airways.

Clause 8: Patents and Copyrights. To promote the Progress of Science and useful Arts, by securing for limited Times to Authors and Inventors the exclusive Right to their respective Writings and Discoveries;

Authors' and composers' works are protected by copyrights established by copyright law, which currently is the 1978

Copyright Act. Copyrights are valid for the life of the author or composer plus fifty years. Inventors' works are protected by patents, which vary in length of protection from three and a half to seventeen years. A patent gives a person the exclusive right to control the manufacture or sale of her or his invention.

Clause 9: Lower Courts. To constitute Tribunals inferior to the supreme Court;

Congress has the authority to set up all federal courts, except the Supreme Court, and to decide what cases those courts will hear.

Clause 10: Punishment for Piracy. To define and punish Piracies and Felonies committed on the high Seas, and Offences against the Law of Nations;

Congress has the authority to prohibit the commission of certain acts outside U.S. territory and to punish certain violations of international law.

Clause 11: Declaration of War. To declare War, grant Letters of Marque and Reprisal, and make Rules concerning Captures on Land and Water;

Only Congress can declare war, although the president, as commander in chief, can make war without Congress's formal declaration. Letters of marque and reprisal authorized private parties to capture and destroy enemy ships in wartime. Since the middle of the nineteenth century, international law has prohibited letters of marque and reprisal, and the United States has honored the ban.

Clause 12: The Army. To raise and support Armies, but no Appropriation of Money to that Use shall be for a longer Term than two Years;

Congress has the power to create an army; the money used to pay for it must be appropriated for no more than two-year intervals. This latter restriction gives ultimate control of the army to civilians.

Clause 13: Creation of a Navy. To provide and maintain a Navy;

This clause allows for the maintenance of a navy. In 1947, Congress created the U.S. Air Force.

Clause 14: Regulation of the Armed Forces. To make Rules for the Government and Regulation of the land and naval Forces;

Congress sets the rules for the military mainly by way of the Uniform Code of Military Justice, which was enacted in 1950 by Congress.

Clause 15: The Militia. To provide for calling forth the Militia to execute the Laws of the Union, suppress Insurrections and repel Invasions;

The militia is known today as the National Guard. Both Congress and the president have the authority to call the National Guard into federal service.

Clause 16: How the Militia Is Organized. To provide for organizing, arming, and disciplining the Militia, and for governing such Part of them as may be employed in the Service of the United States, reserving to the States respectively, the Appointment of the Officers, and the Authority of training the Militia according to the discipline prescribed by Congress;

This clause gives Congress the power to "federalize" state militia (National Guard). When called into such service, the National Guard is subject to the same rules that Congress has set forth for the regular armed services.

Clause 17: Creation of the District of Columbia. To exercise exclusive Legislation in all Cases whatsoever, over such District (not exceeding ten Miles square) as may, by Cession of particular States, and the Acceptance of Congress, become the Seat of the Government of the United States, and to exercise like Authority over all Places purchased by the Consent of the Legislature of the State in which the Same shall be, for the Erection of Forts, Magazines, Arsenals, dock-Yards, and other needful Buildings;—And

Congress established the District of Columbia as the national capital in 1791. Virginia and Maryland had granted land for the District, but Virginia's grant was returned because it was believed it would not be needed. Today, the District covers sixty-nine square miles.

Clause 18: The Elastic Clause. To make all Laws which shall be necessary and proper for carrying into Execution the foregoing Powers, and all other Powers vested by this Constitution in the Government of the United States, or in any Department or Officer thereof.

This clause—the necessary and proper clause, or the elastic clause—grants no specific powers, and thus it can be stretched to fit different circumstances. It has allowed Congress to adapt the government to changing needs and times.

Section 9. The Powers Denied to Congress
Clause 1: Question of Slavery. The Migration or Importation of such Persons as any of the States now existing shall think proper to admit, shall not be prohibited by the Congress prior to the Year one thousand eight hundred and eight, but a Tax or duty may be imposed on such Importation, not exceeding ten dollars for each Person.

"Persons" referred to slaves. Congress outlawed the slave trade in 1808.

Clause 2: Habeas Corpus. The privilege of the Writ of Habeas Corpus shall not be suspended, unless when in Cases of Rebellion or Invasion the public Safety may require it.

A writ of habeas corpus is a court order directing a sheriff or other public officer who is detaining another person to "produce the body" of the detainee so the court can assess the legality of the detention.

Clause 3: Special Bills. No Bill of Attainder or ex post facto Law shall be passed.

A bill of attainder is a law that inflicts punishment without a trial. An ex post facto law is a law that inflicts punishment for an act that was not illegal when it was committed.

Clause 4: Direct Taxes. [No Capitation, or other direct, Tax shall be laid, unless in Proportion to the Census or Enumeration herein before directed to be taken.][6]

A capitation is a tax on a person. A direct tax is a tax paid directly to the government, such as a property tax. This clause was intended to prevent Congress from levying a tax on slaves per person and thereby taxing slavery out of existence.

Clause 5: Export Taxes. No Tax or Duty shall be laid on Articles exported from any State.

Congress may not tax any goods sold from one state to another or from one state to a foreign country. (Congress does have the power to tax goods that are bought from other countries, however.)

Clause 6: Interstate Commerce. No Preference shall be given by any Regulation of Commerce or Revenue to the Ports of one State over those of another: nor shall Vessels bound to, or from, one State, be obliged to enter, clear, or pay Duties in another.

Congress may not treat different ports within the United States differently in terms of taxing and commerce powers. Congress may not tax goods sent from one state to another. Finally, Congress may not give one state's port a legal advantage over those of another state.

Clause 7: Treasury Withdrawals. No Money shall be drawn from the Treasury, but in Consequence of Appropriations made by Law; and a regular Statement and Account of the Receipts and Expenditures of all public Money shall be published from time to time.

Federal funds can be spent only as Congress authorizes. This is a significant check on the president's power.

[6]Modified by the Sixteenth Amendment.

Clause 8: Titles of Nobility. No Title of Nobility shall be granted by the United States: And no Person holding any Office of Profit or Trust under them, shall, without the Consent of the Congress, accept of any present, Emolument, Office, or Title, of any kind whatever, from any King, Prince, or foreign State.

On no person in the United States may be bestowed a title of nobility, such as a duke or duchess. This clause also discourages bribery of American officials by foreign governments.

Section 10. Those Powers Denied to the States
Clause 1: Treaties and Coinage. No State shall enter into any Treaty, Alliance, or Confederation; grant Letters of Marque and Reprisal; coin Money; emit Bills of Credit; make any Thing but gold and silver Coin a Tender in Payment of Debts; pass any Bill of Attainder, ex post facto Law, or Law impairing the Obligation of Contracts, or grant any Title of Nobility.

Prohibiting state laws "impairing the Obligation of Contracts" was intended to protect creditors. (Shays's Rebellion—an attempt to prevent courts from giving effect to creditors' legal actions against debtors—occurred only one year before the Constitution was written.)

Clause 2: Duties and Imposts. No State shall, without the Consent of the Congress, lay any Imports or Duties on Imports or Exports, except what may be absolutely necessary for executing its inspection Laws; and the net Produce of all Duties and Imposts, laid by any State on Imports or Exports, shall be for the Use of the Treasury of the United States; and all such Laws shall be subject to the Revision and Controul of the Congress.

Only Congress can tax imports. Further, the states cannot tax exports.

Clause 3: War. No State shall, without the Consent of Congress, lay any Duty of Tonnage, keep Troops, or Ships of War in time of Peace, enter into any Agreement or Compact with another State, or with a foreign Power or engage in War, unless actually invaded, or in such imminent Danger as will not admit of delay.

A duty of tonnage is a tax on ships according to their cargo capacity. No states may effectively tax ships according to their cargo unless Congress agrees. Additionally, this clause forbids any state to keep troops or warships during peacetime or to make a compact with another state or foreign nation unless Congress so agrees. States can, in contrast, maintain a militia, but its use has to be limited to internal disorders that occur within a state—unless, of course, the militia is called into federal service.

Article II. (Executive Branch)

Section 1. The Nature and Scope of Presidential Power

Clause 1: Four-Year Term. The executive Power shall be vested in a President of the United States of America. He shall hold his Office during the Term of four Years, and, together with the Vice President, chosen for the same Term, be elected, as follows.

The president has the power to carry out laws made by Congress, called the executive power. He or she serves in office for a four-year term after election. The Twenty-second Amendment limits the number of times a person may be elected president.

Clause 2: Choosing Electors from Each State. Each State shall appoint, in such Manner as the Legislature thereof may direct, a Number of Electors, equal to the whole Number of Senators and Representatives to which the State may be entitled in the Congress; but no Senator or Representative, or Person holding an Office of Trust or Profit under the United States, shall be appointed an Elector.

The "Electors" are more commonly known as the "electoral college." The president is elected by electors—that is, representatives chosen by the people—rather than by the people directly.

Clause 3: The Former System of Elections. [The Electors shall meet in their respective States, and vote by Ballot for two Persons, of whom one at least shall not be an Inhabitant of the same State with themselves. And they shall make a List of all the Persons voted for, and of the Number of Votes for each; which List they shall sign and certify, and transmit sealed to the Seat of the Government of the United States, directed to the President of the Senate. The President of the Senate shall, in the Presence of the Senate and House of Representatives, open all the Certificates, and the Votes shall then be counted. The Person having the greatest Number of Votes shall be the President, if such Number be a Majority of the whole Number of Electors appointed; and if there be more than one who have such Majority, and have an equal Number of Votes, then the House of Representatives shall immediately chuse by Ballot one of them for President; and if no Person have a Majority, then from the five highest on the List the said House shall in like Manner chuse the President. But in chusing the President, the Votes shall be taken by States, the Representation from each State having one Vote; A quorum for this Purpose shall consist of a Member or Members from two thirds of the States, and a Majority of all the States shall be necessary to a Choice. In every Case, after the Choice of the President, the Person having the greater Number of Votes of the Electors shall be the Vice President. But if there should remain two or more who have equal Votes, the Senate shall chuse from them by Ballot the Vice President.][7]

The original method of selecting the president and vice president was replaced by the Twelfth Amendment. Apparently, the framers did not anticipate the rise of political parties and the development of primaries and conventions.

Clause 4: The Time of Elections. The Congress may determine the Time of chusing the Electors, and the Day on which they shall give their Votes; which Day shall be the same throughout the United States.

Congress set the Tuesday after the first Monday in November every fourth year as the date for choosing electors. The electors cast their votes on the Monday after the second Wednesday in December of that year.

Clause 5: Qualifications for President. No person except a natural born Citizen, or a Citizen of the United States, at the time of the Adoption of this Constitution, shall be eligible to the Office of President; neither shall any Person be eligible to that Office who shall not have attained to the Age of thirty five Years, and been fourteen Years a Resident within the United States.

The president must be a natural-born citizen, be at least thirty-five years of age when taking office, and have been a resident within the United States for at least fourteen years.

Clause 6: Succession of the Vice President. [In Case of the Removal of the President from Office, or of his Death, Resignation or Inability to discharge the Powers and Duties of the said Office, the same shall devolve on the Vice President, and the Congress may by Law provide for the Case of Removal, Death, Resignation or Inability, both of the President and Vice President, declaring what Officer shall then act as President, and such Officer shall act accordingly, until the Disability be removed, or a President shall be elected.][8]

This former section provided for the method by which the vice president was to succeed to the presidency, but its wording is ambiguous. It was replaced by the Twenty-fifth Amendment.

Clause 7: The President's Salary. The President shall, at stated Times, receive for his Services, a Compensation,

---

[7]Changed by the Twelfth Amendment.
[8]Modified by the Twenty-fifth Amendment.

which shall neither be encreased nor diminished during the Period for which he shall have been elected, and he shall not receive within that Period any other Emolument from the United States, or any of them.

The president maintains the same salary during each four-year term. Moreover, she or he may not receive additional cash payments from the government. Originally set at $25,000 per year, it is currently $200,000 a year plus a $50,000 taxable expense account.

Clause 8: The Oath of Office.   Before he enter on the Execution of his Office, he shall take the following Oath or Affirmation: "I do solemnly swear (or affirm) that I will faithfully execute the Office of President of the United States, and will to the best of my Ability, preserve, protect and defend the Constitution of the United States."

The president is "sworn in" prior to beginning the duties of the office. Currently, the taking of the oath of office occurs on January 20, following the November election. The ceremony is called the inauguration. The oath of office is administered by the chief justice of the United States Supreme Court.

Section 2. Powers of the President
Clause 1: Commander in Chief.   The President shall be Commander in Chief of the Army and Navy of the United States, and of the Militia of the several States, when called into the actual Service of the United States; he may require the Opinion, in writing, of the principal Officer in each of the executive Departments, upon any Subject relating to the Duties of their respective Offices, and he shall have Power to grant Reprieves and Pardons for Offences against the United States, except in Cases of Impeachment.

The armed forces are placed under civilian control because the president is a civilian, but still commander in chief of the military. The president may ask for the help of the heads of each of the executive departments (thereby creating the cabinet). The cabinet members are chosen by the president with the consent of the Senate, but they can be removed without Senate approval.

The president's clemency powers extend only to federal cases. In those cases, he or she may grant a full or conditional pardon, or reduce a prison term or fine.

Clause 2: Treaties and Appointment.   He shall have Power, by and with the Advice and Consent of the Senate, to make Treaties, provided two thirds of the Senators present concur; and he shall nominate, and by and with the Advice and Consent of the Senate, shall appoint Ambassadors, other public Ministers and Consuls, Judges of the supreme Court, and all other Officers of the United

States, whose Appointments are not herein otherwise provided for, and which shall be established by Law; but the Congress may by Law vest the Appointment of such inferior Officers, as they think proper, in the President alone, in the Courts of Law, or in the Heads of Departments.

Many of the major powers of the president are identified in this clause, including the power to make treaties with foreign governments (with the approval of the Senate by a two-thirds vote) and the power to appoint ambassadors, Supreme Court justices, and other government officials. Most such appointments require Senate approval.

Clause 3: Vacancies.   The President shall have Power to fill up all Vacancies that may happen during the Recess of the Senate, by granting Commissions which shall expire at the end of their next Session.

The president has the power to appoint temporary officials to fill vacant federal offices without Senate approval if the Congress is not in session. Such appointments expire automatically at the end of Congress's next term.

Section 3. Duties of the President
He shall from time to time give to the Congress Information of the State of the Union, and recommend to their Consideration such Measures as he shall judge necessary and expedient; he may, on extraordinary Occasions, convene both Houses, or either of them, and in Case of Disagreement between them, with Respect to the Time of Adjournment, he may adjourn them to such Time as he shall think proper; he shall receive Ambassadors and other public Ministers; he shall take Care that the Laws be faithfully executed, and shall Commission all the Officers of the United States.

Annually, the president reports on the state of the union to Congress, recommends legislative measures, and proposes a federal budget. The State of the Union speech is a statement not only to Congress but also to the American people. After it is given, the president proposes a federal budget and presents an economic report. At any time he or she so chooses, the president may send special messages to Congress while it is in session. The president has the power to call special sessions, to adjourn Congress when its two houses do not agree for that purpose, to receive diplomatic representatives of other governments, and to ensure the proper execution of all federal laws. The president further has the ability to empower federal officers to hold their positions and to perform their duties.

Section 4. Impeachment
The President, Vice President and all civil Officers of the United States, shall be removed from Office on Impeachment for, and Conviction of, Treason, Bribery, or other high Crimes and Misdemeanors.

Treason denotes giving aid to the nation's enemies. The definition of high crimes and misdemeanors is usually given as serious abuses of political power. In either case, the president or vice president may be accused by the House (called an impeachment) and then removed from office if convicted by the Senate. (Note that impeachment does not mean removal, but rather the state of being accused of treason or high crimes and misdemeanors.)

Article III. (Judicial Branch)

Section 1. Judicial Powers, Courts, and Judges
The judicial Power of the United States, shall be vested in one supreme Court, and in such inferior Courts as the Congress may from time to time ordain and establish. The Judges, both of the supreme and inferior Courts, shall hold their Offices during good Behaviour, and shall, at stated Times, receive for their Services a Compensation, which shall not be diminished during their Continuance in Office.

The Supreme Court is vested with judicial power, as are the lower federal courts that Congress creates. Federal judges serve in their offices for life unless they are impeached and convicted by Congress. The payment of federal judges may not be reduced during their time in office.

Section 2. Jurisdiction
Clause 1: Cases under Federal Jurisdiction. The judicial Power shall extend to all Cases, in Law and Equity, arising under this Constitution, the Laws of the United States, and Treaties made, or which shall be made, under their Authority;—to all Cases affecting Ambassadors, other public Ministers and Consuls;—to all Cases of admiralty and maritime Jurisdiction;—to Controversies to which the United States shall be a Party;—to Controversies between two or more States; [—between a State and Citizens of another State;—][9] between Citizens of different States;—between Citizens of the same State claiming Lands under Grants of different States, [and between a State, or the Citizens thereof, and foreign States, Citizens or Subjects.][10]

The federal courts take on cases that concern the meaning of the U.S. Constitution, all federal laws, and treaties. They also can take on cases involving citizens of different states and citizens of foreign nations.

Clause 2: Cases for the Supreme Court. In all Cases affecting Ambassadors, other public Ministers and Consuls, and those in which a State shall be a Party, the supreme Court shall have original Jurisdiction. In all the other Cases before mentioned, the supreme Court shall have appellate Jurisdiction, both as to Law and Fact, with such Exceptions, and under such Regulations as the Congress shall make.

In a limited number of situations, the Supreme Court acts as a trial court and has original jurisdiction. These cases involve a representative from another country or involve a state. In all other situations, the cases must first be tried in the lower courts and then can be appealed to the Supreme Court. Congress may, however, make exceptions. Today the Supreme Court acts as a trial court of first instance on rare occasions.

Clause 3: The Conduct of Trials. The Trial of all Crimes, except in Cases of Impeachment, shall be by Jury; and such Trial shall be held in the State where the said Crimes shall have been committed; but when not committed within any State, the Trial shall be at such Place or Places as the Congress may by Law have directed.

Any person accused of a federal crime is granted the right to a trial by jury in a federal court in that state in which the crime was committed. Trials of impeachment are an exception.

Section 3. Treason
Clause 1: The Definition of Treason. Treason against the United States, shall consist only in levying War against them, or, in adhering to their Enemies, giving them Aid and Comfort. No Person shall be convicted of Treason unless on the Testimony of two Witnesses to the same overt Act, or on Confession in open Court.

Treason is the making of war against the United States or giving aid to its enemies.

Clause 2: Punishment. The Congress shall have Power to declare the Punishment of Treason, but no Attainder of Treason shall work Corruption of Blood, or Forfeiture except during the Life of the Person attainted.

Congress has provided that the punishment for treason ranges from a minimum of five years in prison and/or a $10,000 fine to a maximum of death. "No Attainder of Treason shall work Corruption of Blood" prohibits punishment of the traitor's heirs.

Article IV. (Relations among the States)

Section 1. Full Faith and Credit
Full Faith and Credit shall be given in each State to the public Acts, Records, and judicial Proceedings of every other State. And the Congress may by general Laws pre-

---

[9]Modified by the Eleventh Amendment.
[10]Modified by the Eleventh Amendment.

scribe the Manner in which such Acts, Records and Proceedings shall be proved, and the Effect thereof.

All states are required to respect one another's laws, records, and lawful decisions. There are exceptions, however. A state does not have to enforce another state's criminal code. Nor does it have to recognize another state's grant of a divorce if the person obtaining the divorce did not establish legal residence in the state in which it was given.

Section 2. Treatment of Citizens

Clause 1: Privileges and Immunities. The Citizens of each State shall be entitled to all Privileges and Immunities of Citizens in the several States.

A citizen of a state has the same rights and privileges as the citizens of another state in which he or she happens to be.

Clause 2: Extradition. A Person charged in any State with Treason, Felony, or other Crime, who shall flee from Justice, and be found in another State, shall on Demand of the executive Authority of the State from which he fled, be delivered up, to be removed to the State having Jurisdiction of the Crime.

Any person accused of a crime who flees to another state must be returned to the state in which the crime occurred.

Clause 3: Fugitive Slaves. [No Person held to Service or Labour in one State, under the Laws thereof, escaping into another, shall, in Consequence of any Law or Regulation therein, be discharged from such Service or Labour, but shall be delivered up on Claim of the Party to whom such Service or Labour may be due.][11]

This clause was struck down by the Thirteenth Amendment, which abolished slavery in 1865.

Section 3. Admission of States

Clause 1: The Process. New States may be admitted by the Congress into this Union; but no new State shall be formed or erected within the Jurisdiction of any other State; nor any State be formed by the Junction of two or more States, or Parts of States, without the Consent of the Legislatures of the States concerned as well as of the Congress.

Only Congress has the power to admit new states to the union. No state may be created by taking territory from an existing state unless the state's legislature so consents.

Clause 2: Public Land. The Congress shall have Power to dispose of and make all needful Rules and Regulations respecting the Territory or other Property

belonging to the United States; and nothing in this Constitution shall be so construed as to Prejudice any Claims of the United States, or of any particular State.

The federal government has the exclusive right to administer federal government public lands.

Section 4. Republican Form of Government

The United States shall guarantee to every State in this Union a Republican Form of Government, and shall protect each of them against Invasion; and on Application of the Legislature, or of the Executive (when the Legislature cannot be convened) against domestic Violence.

Each state is promised a form of government in which the people elect their representatives, called a republican form. The federal government is bound to protect states against any attack by foreigners or during times of trouble within a state.

Article V. (Methods of Amendment)

The Congress, whenever two thirds of both Houses shall deem it necessary, shall propose Amendments to this Constitution, or on the Application of the Legislatures of two thirds of the several States, shall call a Convention for proposing Amendments, which, in either Case, shall be valid to all Intents and Purposes, as Part of this Constitution, when ratified by the Legislatures of three fourths of the several States, or by Conventions in three fourths thereof, as the one or the other Mode of Ratification may be proposed by the Congress; Provided that no Amendment which may be made prior to the Year One thousand eight hundred and eight shall in any Manner affect the first and fourth Clauses in the Ninth Section of the First Article; and that no State, without its Consent, shall be deprived of its equal Suffrage in the Senate.

Amendments may be proposed in either of two ways: a two-thirds vote of each house (Congress) or at the request of two-thirds of the states. Ratification of amendments may be carried out in two ways: by the legislatures of three-fourths of the states or by the voters in three-fourths of the states. No state may be denied equal representation in the Senate.

Article VI. (National Supremacy)

Clause 1: Existing Obligations. All Debts contracted and Engagements entered into, before the Adoption of this Constitution shall be as valid against the United States under this Constitution, as under the Confederation.

---

[11]Repealed by the Thirteenth Amendment.

During the Revolutionary War and the years of the Confederation, Congress borrowed large sums. This clause pledged that the new federal government would assume those financial obligations.

Clause 2: Supreme Law of the Land. This Constitution, and the Laws of the United States which shall be made in Pursuance thereof; and all Treaties made, or which shall be made, under the Authority of the United States, shall be the supreme Law of the Land; and the Judges in every State shall be bound thereby, any Thing in the Constitution or Laws of any State to the Contrary notwithstanding.

This is typically called the supremacy clause; it declares that federal law takes precedence over all forms of state law. No government, at the local or state level, may make or enforce any law that conflicts with any provision of the Constitution, acts of Congress, treaties, or other rules and regulations issued by the president and his or her subordinates in the executive branch of the federal government.

Clause 3: Oath of Office. The Senators and Representatives before mentioned, and the Members of the several State Legislatures, and all executive and judicial Officers, both of the United States and of the several States, shall be bound by Oath or Affirmation, to support this Constitution; but no religious Test shall ever be required as a Qualification to any Office or public Trust under the United States.

Every federal and state official must take an oath of office promising to support the U.S. Constitution. Religion may not be used as a qualification to serve in any federal office.

Article VII. (Ratification)

The Ratification of the Conventions of nine States shall be sufficient for the Establishment of this Constitution between the States so ratifying the Same.

Nine states were required to ratify the Constitution. Delaware was the first and New Hampshire the ninth.

Done in Convention by the Unanimous Consent of the States present the Seventeenth Day of September in the Year of our Lord one thousand seven hundred and Eighty seven and of the Independence of the United States of America the Twelfth. In witness whereof we have hereunto subscribed our Names,

Go. WASHINGTON
Presid't. and deputy from Virginia

Attest
WILLIAM JACKSON
Secretary

DELAWARE
Geo. Read
Gunning Bedfordjun
John Dickinson
Richard Basset
Jaco. Broom

MASSACHUSETTS
Nathaniel Gorham
Rufus King

CONNECTICUT
Wm. Saml. Johnson
Roger Sherman

NEW YORK
Alexander Hamilton

NEW JERSEY
Wh. Livingston
David Brearley.
Wm. Paterson.
Jona. Dayton

PENNSYLVANIA
B. Franklin
Thomas Mifflin
Robt. Morris
Geo. Clymer
Thos. FitzSimons
Jared Ingersoll
James Wilson.
Gouv. Morris

NEW HAMPSHIRE
John Langdon
Nicholas Gilman

MARYLAND
James McHenry
Dan of St. Thos. Jenifer
Danl. Carroll.

VIRGINIA
John Blair
James Madison Jr.

NORTH CAROLINA
Wm. Blount
Richd. Dobbs Spaight.
Hu. Willaimson

SOUTH CAROLINA
J. Rutledge
Charles Cotesworth
    Pinckney
Charles Pinckney
Pierce Butler

GEORGIA
William Few
Abr. Baldwin

Articles in addition to, and amendment of the Constitution of the United States of America, proposed by Congress and ratified by the Legislatures of the several states, pursuant to the Fifth Article of the original Constitution.

Amendments to the Constitution of the United States
The Bill of Rights[12]
Amendment I.
Religion, Speech, Assembly, and Petition

Congress shall make no law respecting an establishment of religion, or prohibiting the free exercise thereof; or abridging the freedom of speech, or of the press; or the right of the people peaceably to assemble, and to petition the Government for a redress of grievances.

Congress may not create an official church or enact laws limiting the freedom of religion, speech, the press, assembly, and petition. These guarantees, like the others in the Bill of Rights (the first ten amendments), are not absolute—each may be exercised only with regard to the rights of other persons.

Amendment II.
Militia and the Right to Bear Arms

A well regulated Militia, being necessary to the security of a free State, the right of the people to keep and bear Arms, shall not be infringed.

To protect itself, each state has the right to maintain a volunteer armed force. States and the federal government regulate the possession and use of firearms by individuals.

Amendment III.
The Quartering of Soldiers

No Soldier shall, in time of peace be quartered in any house, without the consent of the Owner, nor in time of war, but in a manner to be prescribed by law.

Before the Revolutionary War, it had been common British practice to quarter soldiers in colonists' homes. Military troops do not have the power to take over private houses during peacetime.

Amendment IV.
Searches and Seizures

The right of the people to be secure in their persons, houses, papers, and effects, against unreasonable searches and seizures, shall not be violated, and no Warrants shall issue, but upon probable cause, supported by Oath or affirmation, and particularly describing the place to be searched, and the persons or things to be seized.

[12]On September 25, 1789, Congress transmitted to the state legislatures twelve proposed amendments, two of which, having to do with congressional representation and congressional pay, were not adopted. The remaining ten amendments became the Bill of Rights. In 1992, the amendment concerning congressional pay was adopted as the Twenty-seventh Amendment.

Here the word warrant means "justification" and refers to a document issued by a magistrate or judge indicating the name, address, and possible offense committed. Anyone asking for the warrant, such as a police officer, must be able to convince the magistrate or judge that an offense probably has been committed.

Amendment V.
Grand Juries, Self-incrimination, Double Jeopardy, Due Process, and Eminent Domain

No person shall be held to answer for a capital, or otherwise infamous crime, unless on a presentment or indictment of a Grand Jury, except in cases arising in the land or naval forces, or in the Militia, when in actual service in time of War or public danger; nor shall any person be subject for the same offence to be twice put in jeopardy of life or limb; nor shall be compelled in any criminal case to be a witness against himself, nor be deprived of life, liberty, or property, without due process of law; nor shall private property be taken for public use, without just compensation.

There are two types of juries. A grand jury considers physical evidence and the testimony of witnesses, and decides whether there is sufficient reason to bring a case to trial. A petit jury hears the case at trial and decides it. "For the same offence to be twice put in jeopardy of life or limb" means to be tried twice for the same crime. A person may not be tried for the same crime twice or forced to give evidence against herself or himself. No person's right to life, liberty, or property may be taken away except by lawful means, called the due process of law. Private property taken for use in public purposes must be paid for by the government.

Amendment VI.
Criminal Court Procedures

In all criminal prosecutions, the accused shall enjoy the right to a speedy and public trial, by an impartial jury of the State and district wherein the crime shall have been committed, which district shall have been previously ascertained by law, and to be informed of the nature and cause of the accusation; to be confronted with the witnesses against him; to have compulsory process for obtaining witnesses in his favor, and to have the Assistance of Counsel for his defence.

Any person accused of a crime has the right to a fair and public trial by a jury in the state in which the crime took place. The charges against that person must be so indicated. Any accused person has the right to a lawyer to defend him or her and to question those who testify against him or her, as well as the right to call people to speak in his or her favor at trial.

Amendment VII.
Trial by Jury in Civil Cases

In Suits at common law, where the value in controversy shall exceed twenty dollars, the right of trial by jury shall be preserved, and no fact tried by jury, shall be otherwise re-examined in any Court of the United States, than according to the rules of the common law.

A jury trial may be requested by either party in a dispute in any case involving more than $20. If both parties agree to a trial by a judge without a jury, the right to a jury trial may be put aside.

Amendment VIII.
Bail, Cruel and Unusual Punishment

Excessive bail shall not be required, nor excessive fines imposed, nor cruel and unusual punishments inflicted.

Bail is that amount of money that a person accused of a crime may be required to deposit with the court as a guarantee that she or he will appear in court when requested. The amount of bail required or the fine imposed as punishment for a crime must be reasonable compared with the seriousness of the crime involved. Any punishment judged to be too harsh or too severe for a crime shall be prohibited.

Amendment IX.
The Rights Retained by the People

The enumeration in the Constitution, of certain rights, shall not be construed to deny or disparage others retained by the people.

Many civil rights that are not explicitly enumerated in the Constitution are still held by the people.

Amendment X.
Reserved Powers of the States

The powers not delegated to the United States by the Constitution, nor prohibited by it to the States, are reserved to the States respectively, or to the people.

Those powers not delegated by the Constitution to the federal government or expressly denied to the states belong to the states and to the people. This clause in essence allows the states to pass laws under its "police powers."

Amendment XI
(Ratified on February 7, 1795).
Suits Against States

The Judicial power of the United States shall not be construed to extend to any suit in law or equity, commenced or prosecuted against one of the United States by Citizens of another State, or by Citizens or Subjects of any Foreign State.

This amendment has been interpreted to mean that a state cannot be sued in federal court by one of its citizens, by a citizen of another state, or by a foreign country.

Amendment XII
(Ratified on June 15, 1804).
Election of the President

The Electors shall meet in their respective states, and vote by ballot for President and Vice-President, one of whom, at least, shall not be an inhabitant of the same State with themselves; they shall name in their ballots the person voted for as President, and in distinct ballots the person voted for as Vice-President, and they shall make distinct lists of all persons voted for as President, and of all persons voted for as Vice-President, and of the number of votes for each, which lists they shall sign and certify, and transmit sealed to the seat of the government of the United States, directed to the President of the Senate;—The President of the Senate shall, in the presence of the Senate and House of Representatives, open all the certificates and the votes shall then be counted;—The person having the greatest number of votes for President, shall be the President, if such number be a majority of the whole number of Electors appointed; and if no person have such majority, then from the persons having the highest numbers not exceeding three on the list of those voted for as President, the House of Representatives shall choose immediately, by ballot, the President. But in choosing the President, the votes shall be taken by States, the representation from each State having one vote; a quorum for this purpose shall consist of a member or members from two-thirds of the States, and a majority of all States shall be necessary to a choice. [And if the House of Representatives shall not choose a President whenever the right of choice shall devolve upon them, before the fourth day of March next following, then the Vice-President shall act as President, as in the case of the death or other constitutional disability of the President.][13]—The person having the greatest number of votes as Vice-President, shall be the Vice-President, if such number be a majority of the whole number of Electors appointed, and if no person have a majority, then from the two highest numbers on the list, the Senate shall choose the Vice President; a quorum for the purpose shall consist of two-thirds of the whole number of Senators, and a majority of the whole number shall be necessary to a choice. But no person constitutionally

---

[13]Changed by the Twentieth Amendment.

ineligible to the office of President shall be eligible to that of Vice-President of the United States.

The original procedure set out for the election of president and vice president in Article II, Section 1, resulted in a tie in 1800 between Thomas Jefferson and Aaron Burr. It was not until the next year that the House of Representatives chose Jefferson to be president. This amendment changed the procedure by providing for separate ballots for president and vice president.

Amendment XIII
(Ratified on December 6, 1865). Prohibition of Slavery

Section 1.

Neither slavery nor involuntary servitude, except |as a punishment for crime whereof the party shall have been duly convicted, shall exist within the United States, or any place subject to their jurisdiction.

Some slaves had been freed during the Civil War. This amendment freed the others and abolished slavery.

Section 2.

Congress shall have power to enforce this article by appropriate legislation.

Amendment XIV
(Ratified on July 9, 1868). Citizenship, Due Process, and Equal Protection of the Laws

Section 1.

All persons born or naturalized in the United States, and subject to the jurisdiction thereof, are citizens of the United States and of the State wherein they reside. No State shall make or enforce any law which shall abridge the privileges or immunities of citizens of the United States; nor shall any State deprive any person of life, liberty, or property, without due process of law; nor deny to any person within its jurisdiction the equal protection of the laws.

Under this provision, states cannot make or enforce laws that take away rights given to all citizens by the federal government. States cannot act unfairly or arbitrarily toward, or discriminate against, any person.

Section 2.

Representatives shall be apportioned among the several States according to their respective numbers, counting the whole number of persons in each State, excluding Indians not taxed. But when the right to vote at any election for the choice of electors for President and Vice President of the United States, Representatives in Congress, the Executive and Judicial officers of a State, or the members of the Legislature thereof, is denied to any of the male inhabitants of such State, being [twenty-one][14] years of age, and citizens of the United States, or in any way abridged, except for participation in rebellion, or other crime, the basis of representation therein shall be reduced in the proportion which the number of such male citizens shall bear to the whole number of male citizens twenty-one years of age in such State.

Section 3.

No person shall be a Senator or Representative in Congress, or elector of President and Vice President, or hold any office, civil or military, under the United States, or under any State, who having previously taken an oath, as a member of Congress, or as an officer of the United States, or as a member of any State legislature, or as an executive or judicial officer of any State, to support the Constitution of the United States, shall have engaged in insurrection or rebellion against the same, or given aid or comfort to the enemies thereof. But Congress may by a vote of two-thirds of each House, remove such disability.

This provision forbade former state or federal government officials who had acted in support of the Confederacy during the Civil War to hold office again. It limited the president's power to pardon those persons. Congress removed this "disability" in 1898.

Section 4.

The validity of the public debt of the United States, authorized by law, including debts incurred for payment of pensions and bounties for services in suppressing insurrection or rebellion, shall not be questioned. But neither the United States nor any State shall assume or pay any debt or obligation incurred in aid of insurrection or rebellion against the United States, or any claim for the loss or emancipation of any slave, but all such debts, obligations and claims shall be held illegal and void.

Section 5.

The Congress shall have power to enforce, by appropriate legislation, the provisions of this article.

Amendment XV
(Ratified on February 3, 1870). The Right to Vote

Section 1.

The right of citizens of the United States to vote shall not be denied or abridged by the United States or by any State on account of race, color, or previous condition of servitude.

No citizen can be refused the right to vote simply because of race or color or because that person was once a slave.

---

[14]Changed by the Twenty-sixth Amendment.

Section 2.

The Congress shall have power to enforce this article by appropriate legislation.

Amendment XVI
(Ratified on February 3, 1913).
Income Taxes

The Congress shall have power to lay and collect taxes on incomes, from whatever source derived, without apportionment among the several States, and without regard to any census or enumeration.

This amendment allows Congress to tax income without sharing the revenue so obtained with the states according to their population.

Amendment XVII
(Ratified on April 8, 1913).
The Popular Election of Senators

The Senate of the United States shall be composed of two Senators from each State, elected by the people thereof, for six years; and each Senator shall have one vote. The electors in each State shall have the qualifications requisite for electors of the most numerous branch of the State legislatures.

When vacancies happen in the representation of any State in the Senate, the executive authority of such State shall issue writs of election to fill such vacancies: Provided, That the legislature of any State may empower the executive thereof to make temporary appointments until the people fill the vacancies by election as the legislature may direct.

This amendment shall not be so construed as to affect the election or term of any Senator chosen before it becomes valid as part of the Constitution.

This amendment modified portions of Article I, Section 3, that related to election of senators. Senators are now elected by the voters in each state directly. When a vacancy occurs, either the state may fill the vacancy by a special election, or the governor of the state involved may appoint someone to fill the seat until the next election.

Amendment XVIII
(Ratified on January 16, 1919).
Prohibition.

Section 1.

After one year from the ratification of this article the manufacture, sale, or transportation of intoxicating liquors within, the importation thereof into, or the exportation thereof from the United States and all territory subject to the jurisdiction thereof for beverage purposes is hereby prohibited.

Section 2.

The Congress and the several States shall have concurrent power to enforce this article by appropriate legislation.

Section 3.

This article shall be inoperative unless it shall have been ratified as an amendment to the Constitution by the legislatures of the several States, as provided in the Constitution, within seven years from the date of the submission hereof to the States by the Congress.[15]

This amendment made it illegal to manufacture, sell, and transport alcoholic beverages in the United States. It was repealed by the Twenty-first Amendment.

Amendment XIX
(Ratified on August 18, 1920).
Women's Right to Vote.

The right of citizens of the United States to vote shall not be denied or abridged by the United States or by any State on account of sex.

Congress shall have power to enforce this article by appropriate legislation.

Women were given the right to vote by this amendment, and Congress was given the power to enforce this right.

Amendment XX
(Ratified on January 23, 1933).
The Lame Duck Amendment

Section 1.

The terms of the President and Vice President shall end at noon on the 20th day of January, and the terms of Senators and Representatives at noon on the 3d day of January, of the years in which such terms would have ended if this article had not been ratified; and the terms of their successors shall then begin.

This amendment modified Article I, Section 4, Clause 2, and other provisions relating to the president in the Twelfth Amendment. The taking of the oath of office was moved from March 4 to January 20.

Section 2.

The Congress shall assemble at least once in every year, and such meeting shall begin at noon on the 3d day of January, unless they shall by law appoint a different day.

Congress changed the beginning of its term to January 3. The reason the Twentieth Amendment is called the Lame Duck Amendment is because it shortens the time between when a member of Congress is defeated for reelection and when he or she leaves office.

---

[15]The Eighteenth Amendment was repealed by the Twenty-first Amendment.

Section 3.

If, at the time fixed for the beginning of the term of the President, the President elect shall have died, the Vice President elect shall become President. If a President shall not have been chosen before the time fixed for the beginning of his term, or if the President elect shall have failed to qualify, then the Vice President elect shall act as President until a President shall have qualified; and the Congress may by law provide for the case wherein neither a President elect nor a Vice President elect shall have qualified, declaring who shall then act as President, or the manner in which one who is to act shall be selected, and such person shall act accordingly until a President or Vice President shall have qualified.

This part of the amendment deals with problem areas left ambiguous by Article II and the Twelfth Amendment. If the president dies before January 20 or fails to qualify for office, the presidency is to be filled in the order given in this section.

Section 4.

The Congress may by law provide for the case of the death of any of the persons from whom the House of Representatives may choose a President whenever the rights of choice shall have devolved upon them, and for the case of the death of any of the persons from whom the Senate may choose a Vice President whenever the right of choice shall have devolved upon them.

Congress has never created legislation subsequent to this section.

Section 5.

Sections 1 and 2 shall take effect on the 15th day of October following the ratification of this article.

Section 6.

This article shall be inoperative unless it shall have been ratified as an amendment to the Constitution by the legislatures of three-fourths of the several States within seven years from the date of its submission.

Amendment XXI
(Ratified on December 5, 1933).
The Repeal of Prohibition.

Section 1.

The eighteenth article of amendment to the Constitution of the United States is hereby repealed.

Section 2.

The transportation or importation into any State, Territory, or possession of the United States for delivery or use therein of intoxicating liquors, in violation of the laws thereof, is hereby prohibited.

Section 3.

This article shall be inoperative unless it shall have been ratified as an amendment to the Constitution by conventions in the several States, as provided in the Constitution, within seven years from the date of the submission hereof to the States by the Congress.

The amendment repealed the Eighteenth Amendment but did not make alcoholic beverages legal everywhere. Rather, they remained illegal in any state that so designated them. Many such "dry" states existed for a number of years after 1933. Today, there are still "dry" counties within the United States, in which alcoholic beverages are illegal.

Amendment XXII
(Ratified on February 27, 1951).
Limitation of Presidential Terms.

Section 1.

No person shall be elected to the office of the President more than twice, and no person who has held the office of President, or acted as President, for more than two years of a term to which some other person was elected President shall be elected to the office of President more than once. But this Article shall not apply to any person holding the office of President when this Article was proposed by the Congress, and shall not prevent any person who may be holding the office of President, or acting as President, during the term within which this Article becomes operative from holding the office of President or acting as President during the remainder of such term.

Section 2.

This article shall be inoperative unless it shall have been ratified as an amendment to the Constitution by the legislatures of three-fourths of the several States within seven years from the date of its submission to the States by the Congress.

No president may serve more than two elected terms. If, however, a president has succeeded to the office after the halfway point of a term in which another president was originally elected, then that president may serve for more than eight years, but not to exceed ten years.

Amendment XXIII
(Ratified on March 29, 1961).
Presidential Electors for
the District of Columbia.

Section 1.

The District constituting the seat of Government of the United States shall appoint in such manner as the Congress may direct:

A number of electors of President and Vice President equal to the whole number of Senators and Representatives in Congress to which the District would be entitled if it were a State, but in no event more than the least populous State; they shall be in addition to those appointed by the States, but they shall be considered, for the purposes of the election of President and Vice President, to be electors appointed by a State; and they shall meet in the District and perform such duties as provided by the twelfth article of amendment.

Section 2.
The Congress shall have power to enforce this article by appropriate legislation.

Citizens living in the District of Columbia have the right to vote in elections for president and vice president. The District of Columbia has three presidential electors, whereas before this amendment it had none.

Amendment XXIV
(Ratified on January 23, 1964).
The Anti–Poll Tax Amendment.

Section 1.
The right of citizens of the United States to vote in any primary or other election for President or Vice President, for electors for President or Vice President, or for Senator or Representative in Congress, shall not be denied or abridged by the United States, or any State by reason of failure to pay any poll tax or other tax.

Section 2.
The Congress shall have power to enforce this article by appropriate legislation.

No government shall require a person to pay a poll tax in order to vote in any federal election.

Amendment XXV
(Ratified on February 10, 1967).
Presidential Disability and Vice Presidential Vacancies.

Section 1.
In case of the removal of the President from office or of his death or resignation, the Vice President shall become President.

Whenever a president dies or resigns from office, the vice president becomes president.

Section 2.
Whenever there is a vacancy in the office of the Vice President, the President shall nominate a Vice President who shall take office upon confirmation by a majority vote of both Houses of Congress.

Whenever the office of the vice presidency becomes vacant, the president may appoint someone to fill this office, provided Congress consents.

Section 3.
Whenever the President transmits to the President pro tempore of the Senate and the Speaker of the House of Representatives his written declaration that he is unable to discharge the powers and duties of his office, and until he transmits to them a written declaration to the contrary, such powers and duties shall be discharged by the Vice President as Acting President.

Whenever the president believes she or he is unable to carry out the duties of the office, she or he shall so indicate to Congress in writing. The vice president then acts as president until the president declares that she or he is again able to properly carry out the duties of the office.

Section 4.
Whenever the Vice President and a majority of either the principal officers of the executive departments or of such other body as Congress may by law provide, transmit to the President pro tempore of the Senate and the Speaker of the House of Representatives their written declaration that the President is unable to discharge the powers and duties of his office, the Vice President shall immediately assume the powers and duties of the office as Acting President.

Thereafter, when the President transmits to the President pro tempore of the Senate and the Speaker of the House of Representatives his written declaration that no inability exists, he shall resume the powers and duties of his office unless the Vice President and a majority of either the principal officers of the executive department or of such other body as Congress may by law provide, transmit within four days to the President pro tempore of the Senate and the Speaker of the House of Representatives their written declaration that the President is unable to discharge the powers and duties of his office. Thereupon Congress shall decide the issue, assembling within forty-eight hours for that purpose if not in session. If the Congress, within twenty-one days after receipt of the latter written declaration, or, if Congress is not in session, within twenty-one days after Congress is required to assemble, determines by two-thirds vote of both Houses that the President is unable to discharge the powers and duties of his office, the Vice President shall continue to discharge the same as Acting President; otherwise, the President shall resume the powers and duties of his office.

Whenever the vice president and a majority of the members of the cabinet believe that the president cannot carry out his or her duties, they shall so indicate in writing to Congress. The vice president shall then act as president. When the president believes that she or he is able to carry out her or his duties again, she or he shall so indicate to the Congress. If, though, the vice president and a majority of the Cabinet do not agree, Congress must decide by a two-thirds vote within three weeks who shall act as president.

Amendment XXVI
(Ratified on July 1, 1971).
The Eighteen-Year-Old Vote.

Section 1.
The right of citizens of the United States, who are eighteen years of age or older, to vote shall not be denied or abridged by the United States or by any State on account of age.

No one over eighteen years of age can be denied the right to vote in federal or state elections by virtue of age.

Section 2.
The Congress shall have power to enforce this article by appropriate legislation.

Amendment XXVII
(Ratified on May 7, 1992).
Congressional Pay.

No law varying the compensation for the services of the Senators and Representatives shall take effect, until an election of representatives shall have intervened.

This amendment allows the voters to have some control over increases in salaries for congressional members. Originally submitted to the states for ratification in 1789, it was not ratified until 203 years later, in 1992.

Glossary

A

Acid Rain Rain that has picked up pollutants, usually sulfur dioxides, from industrial areas of the earth that are often hundreds of miles distant from where the rain falls.

Acquisitive Model A model of bureaucracy that views top-level bureaucrats as seeking constantly to expand the size of their budgets and the staffs of their departments or agencies so as to gain greater power and influence in the public sector.

Action-Reaction Syndrome For every action on the part of government, there is a reaction on the part of the affected public. Then the government attempts to counter the reaction with another action, which starts the cycle all over again.

Administrative Agency A federal, state, or local government unit established to perform a specific function. Administrative agencies are created and authorized by legislative bodies to administer and enforce specific laws.

Advice and Consent The power vested in the U.S. Senate by the Constitution (Article II, Section 2) to give its advice and consent to the president on treaties and presidential appointments.

Affirm To declare that a judgment is valid and must stand.

Affirmative Action A policy in job hiring that gives special consideration or compensatory treatment to traditionally disadvantaged groups in an effort to overcome present effects of past discrimination.

Agenda Setting Determining which public policy questions will be debated or considered by Congress.

***Amicus Curiae* Brief** A brief (a document containing a legal argument supporting a desired outcome in a particular case) filed by a third party, or *amicus curiae* (Latin for "friend of the court"), who is not directly involved in the litigation but who has an interest in the outcome of the case.

Anarchy The condition of having no government and no laws. Each member of the society governs himself or herself.

Anti-Federalist An individual who opposed the ratification of the new Constitution in 1787. The Anti-Federalists were opposed to a strong central government.

Appellate Court A court having jurisdiction to review cases and issues that were originally tried in lower courts.

Appointment Power The authority vested in the president to fill a government office or position. Positions filled by presidential appointment include those in the executive branch and the

federal judiciary, commissioned officers in the armed forces, and members of the independent regulatory commissions.

Aristocracy Rule by the best suited, through virtue, talent, or education; in later usage, rule by the upper class.

Australian Ballot A secret ballot prepared, distributed, and tabulated by government officials at public expense. Since 1888, all states have used the Australian ballot rather than an open, public ballot.

B

Bad-Tendency Rule A rule stating that speech or other First Amendment freedoms may be curtailed if there is a possibility that such expression might lead to some "evil."

"Beauty Contest" A presidential primary in which contending candidates compete for popular votes but the results have little or no impact on the selection of delegates to the national convention, which is made by the party elite.

Bicameral Legislature A legislature made up of two chambers, or parts. The U.S. Congress, composed of the House of Representatives and the Senate, is a bicameral legislature.

Bicameralism The division of a legislature into two separate assemblies.

Block Grants Federal programs that provide funds to state and local governments for general functional areas, such as criminal justice or mental-health programs.

Bundling The practice of adding together maximum individual campaign contributions to increase their impact on the candidate.

Bureaucracy A large organization that is structured hierarchically to carry out specific functions.

Busing The transportation of public school students from areas where they live to schools in other areas to eliminate school segregation based on residential patterns.

C

Cabinet An advisory group selected by the president to aid in making decisions. The cabinet presently numbers thirteen department secretaries and the attorney general. Depending on the president, the cabinet may be highly influential or relatively insignificant in its advisory role.

Cabinet Department One of the fourteen departments of the executive branch (State, Treasury, Defense, Justice, Interior,

Agriculture, Commerce, Labor, Health and Human Services, Housing and Urban Development, Education, Energy, Transportation, and Veterans Affairs).

Cadre The nucleus of political party activists carrying out the major functions of American political parties.

Case Law The rules and principles announced in court decisions. Case law includes judicial interpretations of common law principles and doctrines as well as interpretations of constitutional law, statutory law, and administrative law.

Casework Personal work for constituents by members of Congress.

Categorical Grants-in-Aid Federal grants-in-aid to states or local governments that are for very specific programs or projects.

Caucus A closed meeting of party leaders to select party candidates or to decide·on policy; also, a meeting of party members designed to select candidates and propose policies.

Checks and Balances A major principle of the American governmental system whereby each branch of the government exercises a check on the actions of the others.

Chief Diplomat The role of the president in recognizing foreign governments, making treaties, and making executive agreements.

Chief Executive The role of the president as head of the executive branch of the government.

Chief Legislator The role of the president in influencing the making of laws.

Chief of Staff The person who is named to direct the White House Office and advise the president.

Chief of State The role of the president as ceremonial head of the government.

Civil Liberties Those personal freedoms that are protected for all individuals and that generally deal with individual freedom. Civil liberties typically involve restraining the government's actions against individuals.

Civil Rights Generally, all rights rooted in the Fourteenth Amendment's guarantee of equal protection under the law.

Civil Service Commission The initial central personnel agency of the national government; created in 1883.

Class Politics Political preferences based on income level, social status, or both.

Class-Action Suit A lawsuit filed by an individual seeking damages for "all persons similarly situated."

Clear and Present Danger Test The test proposed by Justice Holmes for determining when government may restrict free speech. Restrictions are permissible, he argued, only when speech provokes a "clear and present danger" to the public order.

Cloture A method invoked to close off debate and to bring the matter under consideration to a vote in the Senate.

Coattail Effect The influence of a popular or unpopular candidate on the electoral success or failure of other candidates on the same party ticket. The effect is increased by the party-column ballot, which encourages straight-ticket voting.

Commander in Chief The role of the president as supreme commander of the military forces of the United States and of the state National Guard units when they are called into federal service.

Commerce Clause The section of the Constitution in which Congress is given the power to regulate trade among the states and with foreign countries.

Commercial Speech Advertising statements, which have increasingly been given First Amendment protection.

Common Law Judge-made law that originated in England from decisions shaped according to prevailing customs. Decisions were applied to similar situations and thus gradually became common to the nation.

Compliance The act of accepting and carrying out authorities' decisions.

Concurrent Powers Powers held jointly by the national and state governments.

Concurring Opinion A separate opinion, prepared by a judge who supports the decision of the majority of the court but who wants to make or clarify a particular point or to voice disapproval of the grounds on which the decision was made.

Confederal System A system of government consisting of a league of independent states, each having essentially sovereign powers. The central government created by such a league has only limited powers over the states.

Confederation A political system in which states or regional governments retain ultimate authority except for those powers they expressly delegate to a central government. A voluntary association of independent states, in which the member states agree to limited restraints on their freedom of action.

Conference Committee A special joint committee appointed to reconcile differences when bills pass the two chambers of Congress in different forms.

Consent of the People The idea that governments and laws derive their legitimacy from the consent of the governed.

Conservatism A set of beliefs that includes a limited role for the national government in helping individuals, support for traditional values and lifestyles, and a cautious response to change.

Consolidation The union of two or more governmental units to form a single unit.

Constant Dollars Dollars corrected for inflation; dollars expressed in terms of purchasing power for a given year.

Constituent One of the people represented by a legislator or other elected or appointed official.

Constitutional Power A power vested in the president by Article II of the Constitution.

Continuing Resolution A temporary law that Congress passes when an appropriations bill has not been decided by the beginning of the new fiscal year on October 1.

Contracting Out The replacement of government services with services provided by private firms.

Cooperative Federalism The theory that the states and the national government should cooperate in solving problems.

Corrupt Practices Acts A series of acts passed by Congress in an attempt to limit and regulate the size and sources of contributions and expenditures in political campaigns.

Council of Economic Advisers (CEA) A staff agency in the Executive Office of the President that advises the president on measures to maintain stability in the nation's economy; established in 1946.

Credentials Committee A committee used by political parties at their national conventions to determine which delegates may participate. The committee inspects the claim of each prospective delegate to be seated as a legitimate representative of his or her state.

D

De Facto **Segregation** Racial segregation that occurs because of past social and economic conditions and residential patterns.

Defamation of Character Wrongfully hurting a person's good reputation. The law has imposed a general duty on all persons to refrain from making false, defamatory statements about others.

De Jure **Segregation** Racial segregation that occurs because of laws or administrative decisions by public agencies.

Democracy A system of government in which ultimate political authority is vested in the people. Derived from the Greek words demos ("the people") and kratos ("authority").

Democratic Party One of the two major American political parties evolving out of the Democratic (Jeffersonian) Republican group supporting Thomas Jefferson.

Diplomatic Recognition The president's power, as chief diplomat, to acknowledge a foreign government as legitimate.

Direct Democracy A system of government in which political decisions are made by the people directly, rather than by their elected representatives; probably possible only in small political communities.

Direct Primary An intraparty election in which the voters select the candidates who will run on a party's ticket in the subsequent general election.

Direct Technique An interest group activity that involves interaction with government officials to further the group's goals.

Dissenting Opinion A separate opinion in which a judge dissents from (disagrees with) the conclusion reached by the majority on the court and expounds his or her own views about the case.

Diversity of Citizenship A basis for federal court jurisdiction over a lawsuit between (1) citizens of different states, (2) a foreign country and citizens of a state or of different states, or (3) citizens of a state and citizens or subjects of a foreign country. The amount in controversy must be more than $75,000 before a federal court can take jurisdiction in such cases.

Divided Government A situation in which one major political party controls the presidency and the other controls the chambers of Congress, or in which one party controls a state governorship and the other controls the state legislature.

Divisive Opinion Public opinion that is polarized between two quite different positions.

Domestic Policy Public plans or courses of action that concern issues of national importance, such as poverty, crime, and the environment.

Dominant Culture The values, customs, language, and ideals established by the group or groups in a society that traditionally have controlled politics and government institutions in that society.

Dual Federalism A system of government in which the states and the national government each remain supreme within their own spheres. The doctrine looks on nation and state as coequal sovereign powers. It holds that acts of states within their reserved powers are legitimate limitations on the powers of the national government.

E

Earned-Income Tax Credit (EITC) Program A government program that helps low-income workers by giving back part or all of their Social Security taxes.

Elastic Clause, or Necessary and Proper Clause The clause in Article I, Section 8, that grants Congress the power to do whatever is necessary to execute its specifically delegated powers.

Elector A person on the partisan slate that is selected early in the presidential election year according to state laws and the applicable political party apparatus. Electors cast ballots for president and vice president. The number of electors in each state is equal to that state's number of representatives in both houses of Congress.

Electoral College A group of persons called electors selected by the voters in each state and Washington, D.C.; this group officially elects the president and vice president of the United States. The number of electors in each state is equal to the number of each state's representatives in both houses of Congress. The Twenty-third Amendment to the Constitution permits Washington, D.C., to have as many electors as a state of comparable population.

Elite An upper socioeconomic class that controls political and economic affairs.

Elite Theory A perspective holding that society is ruled by a small number of people who exercise power in their self-interest.

Emergency Power An inherent power exercised by the president during a period of national crisis, particularly in foreign affairs.

Enabling Legislation A statute enacted by Congress that authorizes the creation of an administrative agency and specifies the name, purpose, composition, and powers of the agency being created.

Enumerated Powers Powers specifically granted to the national government by the Constitution. The first seventeen clauses of Article I, Section 8, specify most of the enumerated powers of Congress.

Environmental Impact Statement (EIS) As a requirement mandated by the National Environmental Policy Act, a report that must show the costs and benefits of major federal actions that could significantly affect the quality of the environment.

Equal Employment Opportunity Commission (EEOC) A commission established by the 1964 Civil Rights Act to (1) end discrimination based on race, color, religion, gender, or national origin in conditions of employment and (2) promote voluntary action programs by employers, unions, and community organizations to foster equal job opportunities.

Equal Time Rule A Federal Communications Commission regulation that requires broadcasting stations that give or sell air time to political candidates to make equal amounts of time available to all competing candidates.

Equality A concept that all people are of equal worth.

Equalization A method for adjusting the amount of money that a state must provide to receive federal funds. The formula used takes into account the wealth of the state or its ability to tax its citizens.

Era of Good Feeling The years from 1817 to 1825, when James Monroe was president and there was, in effect, no political opposition.

Era of Personal Politics An era when attention centers on the character of individual candidates rather than on party identification.

Establishment Clause The part of the First Amendment prohibiting the establishment of a church officially supported by the national government. It is applied to questions of state and local government aid to religious organizations and schools, questions of the legality of allowing or requiring school prayers, and questions of the teaching of evolution versus fundamentalist theories of creation.

Exclusionary Rule A policy forbidding the admission at trial of illegally seized evidence.

Executive Agreement A binding international agreement made between chiefs of state that does not require legislative sanction.

Executive Budget The budget prepared and submitted by the president to Congress.

Executive Office of the President (EOP) Established by President Franklin D. Roosevelt by executive order under the Reorganization Act of 1939, the EOP currently consists of nine staff agencies that assist the president in carrying out major duties.

Executive Order A rule or regulation issued by the president that has the effect of law. Executive orders can implement and give administrative effect to provisions in the Constitution, to treaties, and to statutes.

Executive Privilege The right of executive officials to refuse to appear before, or to withhold information from, a legislative committee. Executive privilege is enjoyed by the president and by those executive officials accorded that right by the president.

Expressed Power A constitutional or statutory power of the president, which is expressly written into the Constitution or into statutory law.

F

Faction A group or bloc in a legislature or political party acting together in pursuit of some special interest or position.

Fall Review The time every year when, after receiving formal federal agency requests for funding for the next fiscal year, the Office of Management and Budget reviews the requests, makes changes, and submits its recommendations to the president.

Federal Mandate A requirement in federal legislation that forces states and municipalities to comply with certain rules.

Federal Open Market Committee (FOMC) The most important body within the Federal Reserve System. The FOMC decides how monetary policy should be carried out by the Federal Reserve System.

Federal Question A question that pertains to the U.S. Constitution, acts of Congress, or treaties. A federal question provides a basis for federal jurisdiction.

Federal Register A publication of the executive branch of the U.S. government that prints executive orders, rules, and regulations.

Federal System A system of government in which power is divided by a written constitution between a central government and regional, or subdivisional, governments. Each level must have some domain in which its policies are dominant and some genuine political or constitutional guarantee of its authority.

Federalists The first American political party, led by Alexander Hamilton and John Adams. Many of its members had strongly supported the adoption of the new Constitution and the creation of the federal union.

Fighting Words Words that, when uttered by a public speaker, are so inflammatory that they could provoke the average listener to violence; the words are usually of a racial, religious, or ethnic type.

Filibuster In the Senate, unlimited debate to halt action on a particular bill.

Fireside Chat One of the warm, informal talks by Franklin D. Roosevelt to a few million of his intimate friends—via the radio. Roosevelt's fireside chats were so effective that succeeding presidents have been urged by their advisers to emulate him by giving more radio and television reports to the nation.

First Budget Resolution A resolution passed by Congress in May that sets overall revenue and spending goals for the following fiscal year.

First Continental Congress The first gathering of delegates from twelve of the thirteen colonies, held in 1774.

Fiscal Policy The use of changes in government spending or taxation to alter national economic variables, such as the rate of unemployment.

Fiscal Year (FY) The twelve-month period that is used for bookkeeping, or accounting, purposes. Usually, the fiscal year does not coincide with the calendar year. For example, the federal government's fiscal year runs from October 1 through September 30.

Focus Group A small group of individuals who are led in discussion by a professional consultant to gather opinions and responses to candidates and issues.

Food Stamps Coupons issued by the federal government to low-income individuals to be used for the purchase of food.

Franking A policy that enables members of Congress to send material through the mail by substituting their facsimile signature (frank) for postage.

Free Exercise Clause The provision of the First Amendment guaranteeing the free exercise of religion.

Front-Loading The practice of moving presidential primary elections to the early part of the campaign, to maximize the impact of certain states or regions on the nomination.

Front-Runner The presidential candidate who appears to have the most momentum at a given time in the primary season.

G

Gag Order An order issued by a judge restricting the publication of news about a trial in progress or a pretrial hearing in order to protect the accused's right to a fair trial.

Gender Discrimination Any practice, policy, or procedure that denies equality of treatment to an individual or to a group because of gender.

Gender Gap A term most often used to describe the difference between the percentage of votes a candidate receives from women and the percentage of votes the candidate receives from men. The term came into use after the 1980 presidential election.

General Jurisdiction Exists when a court's authority to hear cases is not significantly restricted. A court of general jurisdiction normally can hear a broad range of cases.

Generational Effect A long-lasting effect of events of a particular time period on the political opinions or preferences of those who came of political age at that time.

Gerrymandering The drawing of legislative district boundary lines for the purpose of obtaining partisan or factional advantage. A district is said to be gerrymandered when its shape is manipulated by the dominant party in the state legislature to maximize electoral strength at the expense of the minority party.

Government A permanent structure (institution) composed of decision makers who make society's rules about conflict resolution and the allocation of resources and who possess the power to enforce those rules.

Government Corporation An agency of government that administers a quasi-business enterprise. These corporations are used when activities are primarily commercial. They produce revenue for their continued existence, and they require greater flexibility than is permitted for departments and agencies.

Government in the Sunshine Act A law that requires all multiheaded federal agencies to conduct their business regularly in public session.

Grandfather Clause A device used by southern states to exempt whites from state taxes and literacy laws originally intended to disfranchise African American voters. It restricted the voting franchise to those who could prove that their grandfathers had voted before 1867.

Great Compromise The compromise between the New Jersey and the Virginia plans that created one chamber of the Congress based on population and one chamber that represented each state equally; also called the Connecticut Compromise.

H

Hatch Act (Political Activities Act) The act that prohibits the use of federal authority to influence nominations and elections or the use of rank to pressure federal employees to make political contributions. It also prohibits civil service employees from active involvement in political campaigns.

Hecklers' Veto Boisterous and generally disruptive behavior by listeners to public speakers that, in effect, vetoes the public speakers' right to speak.

Horizontal Federalism Activities, problems, and policies that require state governments to interact with one another.

Hyperpluralism A situation that arises when interest groups become so powerful that they dominate the political decision-making structures, rendering any consideration of the greater public interest impossible.

I

Ideologue An individual whose political opinions are carefully thought out and relatively consistent with one another. Ideologues are often described as having a comprehensive world view.

Ideology A comprehensive and logically ordered set of beliefs about the nature of people and about the institutions and role of government.

Impeachment As authorized by Article I of the Constitution, an action by the House of Representatives and the Senate to remove the president, vice president, or civil officers of the United States from office for crimes of "Treason, Bribery, or other high Crimes and Misdemeanors."

In-Kind Subsidy A good or service—such as food stamps, housing, or medical care—provided by the government to lower-income groups.

Income Transfer A transfer of income from some individuals in the economy to other individuals. This is generally done by way of the government. It is a transfer in the sense that no current services are rendered by the recipients.

Incorporation Theory The view that most of the protections of the Bill of Rights are applied against state governments through the Fourteenth Amendment's due process clause.

Independent A voter or candidate who does not identify with a political party.

Independent Executive Agency A federal agency that is not part of a cabinet department but reports directly to the president.

Independent Expenditures Nonregulated contributions from PACs, ideological organizations, and individuals. The groups may spend funds on advertising or other campaign activities so long as those expenditures are not coordinated with those of a candidate.

Independent Regulatory Agency An agency outside the major executive departments charged with making and implementing rules and regulations to protect the public interest.

Indirect Technique A strategy employed by interest groups that uses third parties to influence government officials.

Inherent Power A power of the president derived from the loosely worded statement in the Constitution that "the executive Power shall be vested in a President" and that the president should "take Care that the Laws be faithfully executed"; defined through practice rather than through constitutional or statutory law.

Initiative A procedure by which voters can propose a law or a constitutional amendment.

Institution A long-standing, identifiable structure or association that performs certain functions for society.

Instructed Delegate A legislator who is an agent of the voters who elected him or her and who votes according to the views of constituents regardless of personal assessments.

Interest Group An organized group of individuals sharing common objectives who actively attempt to influence policymakers in all three branches of the government and at all levels.

Iron Triangle The three-way alliance among legislators, bureaucrats, and interest groups to make or preserve policies that benefit their respective interests.

Issue Network A group of individuals or organizations—which may consist of legislators or legislative staff members, interest group leaders, bureaucrats, the media, scholars, and other experts—that supports a particular policy position on a given issue, such as one relating to the environment, to taxation, or to consumer safety.

Issue Voting Voting for a candidate based on how he or she stands on a particular issue.

J

Joint Committee A legislative committee composed of members from both chambers of Congress.

Judicial Activism A doctrine holding that the Supreme Court should take an active role in using its powers to check the activities of Congress, state legislatures, and administrative agencies when those government bodies exceed their authority.

Judicial Implementation The way in which court decisions are translated into action.

Judicial Restraint A doctrine holding that the Supreme Court should defer to the decisions made by the elected representatives of the people in the legislative and executive branches.

Judicial Review The power of the Supreme Court or any court to declare unconstitutional federal or state laws and other acts of government.

Jurisdiction The authority of a court to decide certain cases. Not all courts have the authority to decide all cases. Where a case arises and what its subject matter is are two jurisdictional factors.

Justiciable Dispute A dispute that raises questions about the law and that is appropriate for resolution before a court of law.

Justiciable Question A question that may be raised and reviewed in court.

K

Keynesian Economics An economic theory, named after English economist John Maynard Keynes, that gained prominence during the Great Depression of the 1930s. It is typically associated with the use of fiscal policy to alter national economic variables—for example, increased government spending during times of economic downturns.

Kitchen Cabinet The informal advisers to the president.

L

Labor Movement Generally, the full range of economic and political expression of working-class interests; politically, the organization of working-class interests.

Lawmaking The process of deciding the legal rules that govern society. Such laws may regulate minor affairs or establish broad national policies.

Legislative Veto A provision in a bill reserving to Congress or to a congressional committee the power to reject an action or regulation of a national agency by majority vote; declared unconstitutional by the Supreme Court in 1983.

Legislature A government body primarily responsible for the making of laws.

Liberalism A set of beliefs that includes the advocacy of positive government action to improve the welfare of individuals, support for civil rights, and tolerance for political and social change.

Libel A written defamation of a person's character, reputation, business, or property rights. To a limited degree, the First Amendment protects the press from libel actions.

Liberty The greatest freedom of individuals that is consistent with the freedom of other individuals in the society.

Limited Government A form of government based on the principle that the powers of government should be clearly limited either through a written document or through wide public understanding; characterized by institutional checks to ensure that government serves the public rather than private interests.

Limited Jurisdiction Exists when a court's authority to hear cases is restricted to certain types of claims, such as tax claims or bankruptcy petitions.

Line Organization With respect to the federal government, an administrative unit that is directly accountable to the president.

Line-Item Veto The power of an executive to veto individual lines or items within a piece of legislation without vetoing the entire bill.

Literacy Test A test administered as a precondition for voting, often used to prevent African Americans from exercising their right to vote.

Litigate To engage in a legal proceeding or seek relief in a court of law; to carry on a lawsuit.

Lobbying The attempt by organizations or by individuals to influence the passage, defeat, or contents of legislation and the administrative decisions of government.

Logrolling An arrangement in which two or more members of Congress agree in advance to support each other's bills.

Loophole A legal method by which individuals and businesses are allowed to reduce the tax liabilities owed to the government.

M

Madisonian Model A structure of government proposed by James Madison in which the powers of the government are separated into three branches: executive, legislative, and judicial.

Majority More than 50 percent.

Majority Floor Leader The chief spokesperson of the major party in the Senate, who directs the legislative program and party strategy.

Majority Leader of the House A legislative position held by an important party member in the House of Representatives. The majority leader is selected by the majority party in caucus or conference to foster cohesion among party members and to act as spokesperson for the majority party in the House.

Majority Opinion A court opinion reflecting the views of the majority of the judges.

Majority Rule A basic principle of democracy asserting that the greatest number of citizens in any political unit should select officials and determine policies.

Matching Funds For many categorical grant programs, money that the state must provide to "match" the federal funds. Some programs require the state to raise only 10 percent of the funds, whereas others approach an even share.

Media The technical means of communication with mass audiences.

Merit System The selection, retention, and promotion of government employees on the basis of competitive examinations.

Minority Floor Leader The party officer in the Senate who commands the minority party's opposition to the policies of the majority party and directs the legislative program and strategy of his or her party.

Minority Leader of the House The party leader elected by the minority party in the House.

Monetary Policy The use of changes in the amount of money in circulation to alter credit markets, employment, and the rate of inflation.

Monopolistic Model A model of bureaucracy that compares bureaucracies to monopolistic business firms. Lack of competition within a bureaucracy leads to inefficient and costly operations, just as it does within monopolistic firms. Because bureaucracies are not penalized for inefficiency, there is no incentive to reduce costs or use resources more productively.

N

Narrowcasting Broadcasting that is targeted to one small sector of the population.

National Committee A standing committee of a national political party established to direct and coordinate party activities during the four-year period between national party conventions.

National Convention The meeting held every four years by each major party to select presidential and vice presidential candidates, to write a platform, to choose a national committee, and to conduct party business. In theory, the national convention is at the top of a hierarchy of party conventions (the local and state conventions are below it) that consider candidates and issues.

National Politics The pursuit of interests that are of concern to the nation as a whole.

National Security Council (NSC) A staff agency in the Executive Office of the President established by the National Security Act of 1947. The NSC advises the president on domestic and foreign matters involving national security.

Natural Aristocracy A small ruling clique of a society's "best" citizens, whose membership is based on birth, wealth, and ability. The Jeffersonian era emphasized government rule by such a group.

Natural Rights Rights held to be inherent in natural law, not dependent on governments. John Locke stated that natural law, being superior to human law, specifies certain rights of "life, liberty, and property." These rights, altered to become "life, liberty, and the pursuit of happiness," are asserted in the Declaration of Independence.

New Federalism A plan both to limit the national government's power to regulate and to restore power to state governments. Essentially, the new federalism is designed to give the states greater ability to decide for themselves how government revenues should be spent.

Nullification The act of nullifying, or rendering void. Prior to the Civil War, southern supporters of states' rights claimed that a state had the right to declare a national law to be null and void and therefore not binding on its citizens, on the assumption that ultimate sovereign authority rested with the several states.

O

Office-Block, or Massachusetts, Ballot A form of general election ballot in which candidates for elective office are grouped together under the title of each office. It emphasizes voting for the office and the individual, rather than for the party.

Office of Management and Budget (OMB) A division of the Executive Office of the President created by executive order in 1970 to replace the Bureau of the Budget. The OMB's main functions are to assist the president in preparing the annual budget, to clear and coordinate all departmental agency budgets, to help set fiscal policy, and to supervise the administration of the federal budget.

Oligarchy Rule by a few members of the elite, who generally make decisions to benefit their own group.

Ombudsperson A person who hears and investigates complaints by private individuals against public officials or agencies.

Opinion The statement by a judge or a court of the decision reached in a case tried or argued before it. The opinion sets forth the law that applies to the case and details the legal reasoning on which the judgment was based.

Opinion Leader One who is able to influence the opinions of others because of position, expertise, or personality. Such leaders help to shape public opinion.

Opinion Poll A method of systematically questioning a small, selected sample of respondents who are deemed representative of the total population. Opinion polls are widely used by government, business, university scholars, political candidates, and voluntary groups to provide reasonably accurate data on public attitudes, beliefs, expectations, and behavior.

Oral Arguments The verbal arguments presented in person by attorneys to an appellate court. Each attorney presents reasons to the court why the court should rule in his or her client's favor.

Oversight The responsibility Congress has for following up on laws it has enacted to ensure that they are being enforced and administered in the way in which they were intended.

P

Pardon The granting of a release from the punishment or legal consequences of a crime; a pardon can be granted by the president before or after a conviction.

Party Identification Linking oneself to a particular political party.

Party-Column, or Indiana, Ballot A form of general election ballot in which candidates for elective office are arranged in one column under their respective party labels and symbols. It emphasizes voting for the party, rather than for the office or individual.

Party Identifier A person who identifies with a political party.

Party Organization The formal structure and leadership of a political party, including election committees; local, state, and national executives; and paid professional staff.

Party Platform A document drawn up by the platform committee at each national convention, outlining the policies, positions, and principles of the party; it is then submitted to the entire convention for approval.

Patronage Rewarding faithful party workers and followers with government employment and contracts.

Peer Group A group consisting of members sharing common relevant social characteristics. These groups play an important part in the socialization process, helping to shape attitudes and beliefs.

Pendleton Act (Civil Service Reform Act) The law, as amended over the years, that remains the basic statute regulating federal employment personnel policies. It established the principle of employment on the basis of merit and created the Civil Service Commission to administer the personnel service.

Personal Attack Rule A Federal Communications Commission regulation that requires broadcasting stations, if the stations are used to attack the honesty or integrity of persons, to allow the persons attacked the fullest opportunity to respond.

Picket-Fence Federalism A model of federalism in which specific programs and policies (depicted as vertical pickets in a picket fence) involve all levels of government—national, state, and local (depicted by the horizontal boards in a picket fence).

Pluralism A theory that views politics as a conflict among interest groups. Political decision making is characterized by bargaining and compromise.

Plurality The total votes cast for a candidate who receives more votes than any other candidate but not necessarily a majority. Most national, state, and local electoral laws provide for winning elections by a plurality vote.

Pocket Veto A special veto power exercised by the chief executive after a legislative body has adjourned. Bills not signed by the chief executive die after a specified period of time. If Congress wishes to reconsider such a bill, it must be reintroduced in the following session of Congress.

Police Power The authority to legislate for the protection of the health, morals, safety, and welfare of the people. In the United States, most police power is a reserved power of the states.

Policy Trade-Offs The cost to the nation of undertaking any one policy in terms of all of the other policies that could have been undertaken. For example, an increase in the expenditures on one federal program means either a reduction in expenditures on another program or an increase in federal taxes (or the deficit).

Political Action Committee (PAC) A committee set up by and representing a corporation, labor union, or special interest group. PACs raise and give campaign donations on behalf of the organizations or groups they represent.

Political Consultant A paid professional hired to devise a campaign strategy and manage a campaign. Image building is the crucial task of the political consultant.

Political Culture The collection of beliefs and attitudes toward government and the political process held by a community or nation.

Political Party A group of political activists who organize to win elections, to operate the government, and to determine public policy.

Political Question An issue that a court believes should be decided by the executive or legislative branch.

Political Socialization The process through which individuals learn a set of political attitudes and form opinions about social issues. The family and the educational system are two of the most important forces in the political socialization process.

Political Trust The degree to which individuals express trust in the government and political institutions, usually measured through a specific series of survey questions.

Politico The legislative role that combines the instructed-delegate and trustee concepts. The legislator varies the role according to the issue under consideration.

Politics According to David Easton, the "authoritative allocation of values" for a society; according to Harold Lasswell, "who gets what, when, and how" in a society.

Poll Tax A special tax that must be paid as a qualification for voting. The Twenty-fourth Amendment to the Constitution outlawed the poll tax in national elections, and in 1966 the Supreme Court declared it unconstitutional in all elections.

Popular Sovereignty The concept that ultimate political authority rests with the people.

Precedent A court rule bearing on subsequent legal decisions in similar cases. Judges rely on precedents in deciding cases.

President *Pro Tempore* The temporary presiding officer of the Senate in the absence of the vice president.

Presidential Primary A statewide primary election of delegates to a political party's national convention to help a party determine its presidential nominee. Such delegates are either pledged to a particular candidate or unpledged.

Press Secretary The individual responsible for representing the White House before the media. The press secretary writes news releases, provides background information, sets up press conferences, and so on.

Prior Restraint Restraining an action before the activity has actually occurred. It involves censorship, as opposed to subsequent punishment.

Property Anything that is or may be subject to ownership. As conceived by the political philosopher John Locke, the right to property is a natural right superior to human law (laws made by government).

Public Agenda Issues that commonly are perceived by members of the political community as meriting public attention and governmental action. The media play an important role in setting the public agenda by focusing attention on certain topics.

Public Debt Financing The government's spending more than it receives in taxes and paying for the difference by issuing U.S. Treasury bonds, thereby adding to the public debt.

Public Debt, or National Debt The total amount of debt carried by the federal government.

Public Interest The best interests of the collective, overall community; the national good, rather than the narrow interests of a self-serving group.

Public Opinion The aggregate of individual attitudes or beliefs shared by some portion of the adult population. There is no one public opinion, because there are many different "publics."

R

Ratification Formal approval.

Reapportionment The allocation of seats in the House of Representatives to each state after each census.

Recall A procedure allowing the people to vote to dismiss an elected official from state office before his or her term has expired.

Redistricting The redrawing of the boundaries of the congressional districts within each state.

Referendum An electoral device whereby legislative or constitutional measures are referred by the legislature to the voters for approval or disapproval.

Registration The entry of a person's name onto the list of eligible voters for elections. Registration requires meeting certain legal requirements relating to age, citizenship, and residency.

Regressive Tax A tax system in which tax rates go down as income goes up.

Remand To send a case back to the court that originally heard it.

Representation The function of members of Congress as elected officials in representing the views of their constituents.

Representative Assembly A legislature composed of individuals who represent the population.

Representative Democracy A form of government in which representatives elected by the people make and enforce laws and policies.

Reprieve The presidential power to postpone the execution of a sentence imposed by a court of law; usually done for humanitarian reasons or to await new evidence.

Republic The form of government in which sovereignty rests with the people, who elect agents to represent them in lawmaking and other decisions.

Republican Party One of the two major American political parties, which emerged in the 1850s as an antislavery party. It was created to fill the vacuum caused by the disintegration of the Whig Party.

Reverse To annul or make void a judgment on account of some error or irregularity.

Reverse Discrimination The charge that affirmative action programs requiring preferential treatment or quotas discriminate against those who do not have minority status.

Rule of Four A United States Supreme Court procedure requiring four affirmative votes to hear the case before the full Court.

Rules Committee A standing committee of the House of Representatives that provides special rules under which specific bills can be debated, amended, and considered by the House.

S

Sampling Error The difference between a sample's results and the true result if the entire population had been interviewed.

Secession The act of formally withdrawing from membership in an alliance; the withdrawal of a state from the federal Union.

Second Budget Resolution A resolution passed by Congress in September that sets "binding" limits on taxes and spending for the next fiscal year beginning October 1.

Second Continental Congress The 1775 congress of the colonies that established an army.

Sectional Politics The pursuit of interests that are of special concern to a region or section of the country.

Select Committee A temporary legislative committee established for a limited time period and for a special purpose.

Senatorial Courtesy In regard to federal district court judgeship nominations, a Senate tradition allowing a senator of the president's political party to veto a judicial appointment in his or her state simply by indicating that the appointment is personally not acceptable. At that point, the Senate may reject the nomination, or the president may withdraw consideration of the nominee.

Seniority System A custom followed in both chambers of Congress specifying that members with longer terms of continuous service will be given preference when committee chairpersons and holders of other significant posts are selected.

Separate-but-Equal Doctrine The doctrine holding that segregation in schools and public accommodations does not imply that one race is superior to another; and that separate-but-equal facilities do not violate the equal protection clause.

Separation of Powers The principle of dividing governmental powers among the executive, the legislative, and the judicial branches of government.

Service Sector The sector of the economy that provides services—such as food services, insurance, and education—in contrast to the sector of the economy that produces goods.

Sexual Harassment Unwanted physical or verbal conduct or abuse of a sexual nature that interferes with a recipient's job performance, creates a hostile environment, or carries with it an implicit or explicit threat of adverse employment consequences.

Slander The public uttering of a false statement that harms the good reputation of another. The statement must be made to, or within the hearing of, persons other than the defamed party.

Socioeconomic Status A category of people within a society who have similar levels of income and similar types of occupations.

Soft Money Campaign contributions that evade contribution limits by being given to parties and party committees to help fund general party activities.

Sound Bite A brief, memorable comment that easily can be fit into news broadcasts.

Speaker of the House The presiding officer in the House of Representatives. The speaker is always a member of the majority party and is the most powerful and influential member of the House.

Spin An interpretation of campaign events or election results that is most favorable to the candidate's campaign strategy.

Spin Doctor A political campaign adviser who tries to convince journalists of the truth of a particular interpretation of events.

Splinter Party A new party formed by a dissident faction within a major political party. Usually, splinter parties have emerged when a particular personality was at odds with the major party.

Spoils System The awarding of government jobs to political supporters and friends; generally associated with President Andrew Jackson.

Spring Review The time every year when the Office of Management and Budget requires federal agencies to review their programs, activities, and goals and submit their requests for funding for the next fiscal year.

Standing Committee A permanent committee within the House or Senate that considers bills within a certain subject area.

Stare Decisis To stand on decided cases; the judicial policy of following precedents established by past decisions.

State Central Committee The principal organized structure of each political party within each state. This committee is responsible for carrying out policy decisions of the party's state convention.

State of the Union Message An annual message to Congress in which the president proposes a legislative program. The message is addressed not only to Congress but also to the American people and to the world. It offers the opportunity to dramatize policies and objectives and to gain public support.

Statutory Power A power created for the president through laws enacted by Congress.

Super Tuesday The date on which a number of presidential primaries are held, including those of most of the southern states.

Superdelegate A party leader or elected official who is given the right to vote at the party's national convention. Superdelegates are not elected at the state level.

Supplemental Security Income (SSI) A federal program established to provide assistance to elderly persons and disabled persons.

Supremacy Clause The constitutional provision that makes the Constitution and federal laws superior to all conflicting state and local laws.

Supremacy Doctrine A doctrine that asserts the superiority of national law over state or regional laws. This principle is rooted in Article VI of the Constitution, which provides that the Constitution, the laws passed by the national government under its constitutional powers, and all treaties constitute the supreme law of the land.

Symbolic Speech Nonverbal expression of beliefs, which is given substantial protection by the courts.

T

Temporary Assistance to Needy Families (TANF) A state-administered program in which grants from the national government are given to the states, which use the funds to provide assistance to those eligible to receive welfare benefits. The TANF program was created by the Welfare Reform Act of 1996 and replaced the former AFDC program.

Third Party A political party other than the two major political parties (Republican and Democratic). Usually, third parties are composed of dissatisfied groups that have split from the major parties. They act as indicators of political trends and as safety valves for dissident groups.

Totalitarian Regime A form of government that controls all aspects of the political and social life of a nation. All power resides with the government. The citizens have no power to choose the leadership or policies of the country.

Town Meeting The governing authority of a New England town. Qualified voters may participate in the election of officers and in the passage of legislation.

Tracking Poll A poll taken for the candidate on a nearly daily basis as election day approaches.

Trial Court The court in which most cases usually begin and in which questions of fact are examined.

Trustee In regard to a legislator, one who acts according to his or her conscience and the broad interests of the entire society.

Twelfth Amendment An amendment to the Constitution, adopted in 1804, that specifies the separate election of the president and vice president by the electoral college.

Twenty-fifth Amendment An amendment to the Constitution adopted in 1967 that establishes procedures for filling vacancies in the two top executive offices and that makes provisions for situations involving presidential disability.

U

U.S. Treasury Bond Evidence of debt issued by the federal government; similar to corporate bonds but issued by the U.S. Treasury.

Unanimous Opinion A court opinion or determination on which all judges agree.

Unicameral Legislature A legislature with only one legislative body, as compared with a bicameral (two-house) legislature, such as the U.S. Congress. Nebraska is the only state in the union with a unicameral legislature.

Unitary System A centralized governmental system in which local or subdivisional governments exercise only those powers given to them by the central government.

Universal Suffrage The right of all adults to vote for their representatives.

V

Veto Message The president's formal explanation of a veto when legislation is returned to the Congress.

Voter Turnout The percentage of citizens taking part in the election process; the number of eligible voters that actually "turn out" on election day to cast their ballots.

W

War Powers Resolution A law passed in 1973 spelling out the conditions under which the president can commit troops without congressional approval.

Washington Community Individuals regularly involved with politics in Washington, D.C.

Watergate Break-in The 1972 illegal entry into the Democratic National Committee offices by participants in Richard Nixon's reelection campaign.

Weberian Model A model of bureaucracy developed by the German sociologist Max Weber, who viewed bureaucracies as rational, hierarchical organizations in which power flows from the top downward and decisions are based on logical reasoning and data analysis.

Whistleblower Someone who brings to public attention gross governmental inefficiency or an illegal action.

White House Office The personal office of the president, which tends to presidential political needs and manages the media.

White Primary A state primary election that restricts voting to whites only; outlawed by the Supreme Court in 1944.

Writ of *Certiorari* An order issued by a higher court to a lower court to send up the record of a case for review. It is the principal vehicle for United States Supreme Court review.

Writ of *Habeas Corpus* *Habeas corpus* means, literally, "you have the body." A writ of *habeas corpus* is an order that requires jailers to bring a person before a court or judge and explain why the person is being held in prison.

Index

Photo Credits